THE
SIERRA CLU[
GUIDE TO
THE
NATURAL AREAS
OF COLORADO
AND UTAH

D0372817

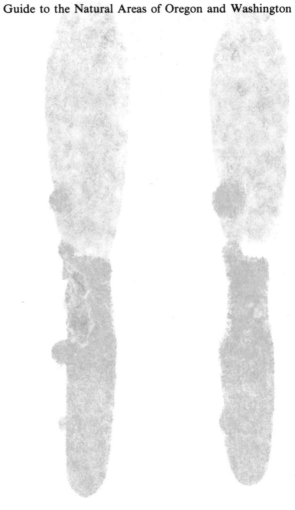

THE
SIERRA CLUB
GUIDE TO
THE
NATURAL AREAS
OF COLORADO
AND UTAH

JOHN PERRY
AND
JANE GREVERUS PERRY

SIERRA CLUB BOOKS · SAN FRANCISCO

The Sierra Club, founded in 1892 by John Muir, has devoted itself to the study and protection of the earth's scenic and ecological resources—mountains, wetlands, woodlands, wild shores and rivers, deserts and plains. The publishing program of the Sierra Club offers books to the public as a nonprofit educational service in the hope that they may enlarge the public's understanding of the Club's basic concerns. The point of view expressed in each book, however, does not necessarily represent that of the Club. The Sierra Club has some fifty chapters coast to coast, in Canada, Hawaii, and Alaska. For information about how you may participate in its programs to preserve wilderness and the quality of life, please address inquiries to Sierra Club, 530 Bush Street, San Francisco, CA 94108.

Library of Congress Cataloging in Publication Data

Perry, John, 1914–
The Sierra Club guide to the natural areas of Colorado
and Utah.

Bibliography
Includes index.
1. Natural areas—Colorado—Guide-books.
2. Natural areas—Utah—Guide-books.   I. Perry, Jane Greverus.
II. Sierra Club.   III. Title.
QH76.5.C6P47   1985   917.88'0433   84–22215
ISBN 0–87156–832–2

Cover design by Gael Towey Dillon

Book design concept by Lilly Langotsky

Illustrations by Nancy Warner

Printed in the United States of America
10 9 8 7 6 5 4 3 2 1

TO THE RANGERS,
FORESTERS, NATURALISTS,
WILDLIFE BIOLOGISTS,
AND OTHER MEN AND WOMEN
WHO CARE FOR OUR FORESTS,
PARKS, AND PRESERVES

CONTENTS

INTRODUCTION

This is a guide to the quiet places, where plants grow, birds sing, and the signs of man are few. Some of these places are within a few steps of parking places; others can be reached only by hours or days of earnest hiking.

Colorado and Utah attract outdoorsmen—not only summer visitors but people who come to stay. In wildernesses and resorts, natives and settlers outnumber visitors. Many campgrounds are full to capacity on summer weekends. Quota systems limit access to some wilderness areas and whitewater streams. Traffic rules govern power boats on popular lakes.

Yet we had no difficulty finding quiet places. Even on a holiday weekend, not far from Salt Lake City, we found a delightful site beside a rushing canyon stream.

People congregate. Most seem to prefer the developed recreation sites, the well-marked trails, the publicized wildernesses. Most come at certain seasons. Those who wish solitude can find it. Near Denver or Salt Lake City on the Fourth of July weekend, this takes ingenuity. Otherwise one simply avoids the small percentage of sites that attract crowds.

Most Coloradans live in the metropolitan strip at the foot of the Front Range. Most Utahns live in the metropolitan strip at the foot of the Wasatch Front. Elsewhere both states are sparsely settled.

CHANGES

We have been conservation activists for many years. Past work in these and other states has given us affection for the public lands and for the men and women responsible for their care and management.

What we see and hear now is frightening. The Reagan Administration's deliberate, systematic ravaging of our public lands proceeds on an immense scale. People who dedicated their lives to caring for these lands are now compelled to facilitate their exploitation and alienation.

We share their feelings of frustration, sorrow, rage, and determination. They showed us roads slashed through wildernesses, dams inundating lovely canyons, coal and oil leases issued hastily, for trifling sums, in once protected areas. People who tried to enforce grazing quotas have been disciplined. Recreation programs have been abolished, public use of public lands discouraged, waterfowl refuges killed by diversion of water to irrigate huge farms.

Could our guidebook tell these stories, too, as well as guide? Such a hybrid would serve neither purpose well. We reserve time and energy for activism.

An incidental effect of Reaganism is our greater difficulty in gathering data. Always, in earlier projects, we have enjoyed warm and generous help from people in federal and state headquarters and field offices. Now people who once were responsible for public information, recreation, wilderness studies, and wildlife management are often unable to assist. Jobs have been abolished; people have been assigned elsewhere; staff cuts have doubled work loads. In some cases, employees have been forbidden to respond to public inquiries.

In writing these guidebooks, we send entries to the appropriate offices, asking that they be checked for accuracy. In the past, the response rate was close to 100%. But this time responses were slow, so we used the telephone. Finally we achieved close to a 100% response, but only because so many men and women, devoted to their lands, did the work after hours, on their own time.

The entries report what was true when we gathered data. But more cuts were in prospect, with effects such as the following:

Campground closed, or open for a shorter season

Trail maintenance discontinued

Snowplowing discontinued on roads once kept open

Publications out of stock or discontinued

Public information office abolished

Recreation staff disbanded

Campfire programs discontinued

The Reagan Administration is cutting the facilities and services available to *you*.

HOW WE SELECT SITES

We use the term *natural area* broadly, generically. We look for places where a visitor can enjoy nature. Many of these areas are roadless, some of them truly pristine, but we do not reject an area that has been logged, grazed, mined, or otherwise disturbed if the healing processes of nature are at work. Nor do we reject a wildlife refuge because its impoundments are man-made and feed crops are planted. When thousands of waterfowl and shorebirds endorse such a refuge, that's good enough for us.

Large National Forests, Parks, and Monuments are automatic selections. We view smaller sites more critically. We don't include a State Park planned for intensive recreation, unless it has a large undeveloped area of interest to hikers and birders. We may note a small State Park briefly because it adjoins a large natural area.

THE PUBLIC DOMAIN

Of the original public domain, 8 million acres remain in Colorado, 22 million in Utah. These public lands, administered by the Bureau of Land Management (BLM), are not subdivided into named units, as are National Forests and Parks. They include some of the most fascinating natural areas of the two states.

Outdoorsmen are just beginning to rediscover this immense natural resource. No previous guidebooks describe these millions of acres. No posted signs identify them. Our task would have been more difficult were it not for the Wilderness Act. This Act required BLM and other land-managing agencies to identify all roadless areas of 5,000 or more acres, then study them to see whether they meet criteria for "wilderness" designation. Their studies helped us identify and describe the best portions of the public domain. The written descriptions weren't enough. We recorded hours of talks with BLM specialists who have hiked and studied these areas. Then we went to see for ourselves.

These BLM entries have been given local names. Visitors will find no welcome signs and—except at a few recreation sites—no facilities. Only by chance will they find a BLM staff member present.

Some of these sites are bordered by good public roads. Some can be reached only on foot or horseback, or by 4-wheel-drive vehicle, a few only by boat. We have omitted sites surrounded by privately owned land, sites with no legal access.

These millions of acres are yours to enjoy. Here you can drive, hike, backpack, ride horseback, camp almost anywhere, and hunt or fish subject to state laws. In most places you're unlikely to meet other visitors.

Much of this land has been leased for grazing, mining, and other purposes. Cattle ranchers have fenced some of it. Such fences don't shut you out. Where public land has been fenced and gated, you have the right to enter, closing the gate behind you.

How do you know you're on public land? In some areas public and private land are intermixed. We've chosen sites with few if any private inholdings, but it's wise to be alert for private boundary postings.

What if a rancher orders you off? It's unlikely to happen, but if it does, go quietly. Some ranchers have used public land for so long they regard it as their own. Tell the BLM office what happened.

OTHER PUBLIC LANDS

We do not include city, county, and regional parks. A few are as large and attractive as sites we do include. However, we have found local authorities reluctant to supply information. Their parks are supported by local taxpayers and are intended for local use.

Military reservations are not included. Some allow limited public use, chiefly by hunters and fishermen. The base near our home has a telephone number one calls to hear whether visitors are permitted today. Permission is unpredictable.

WILDERNESS AREAS

The Forest Service, National Park Service, and other agencies, as well as BLM, were required to identify and study potential wilderness areas. The Administration is supposed to recommend qualifying sites to Congress. If Congress approves a Wilderness Area, it is thereafter preserved.

Timber, mining, and other commercial interests oppose wilderness protection, so the Reagan Administration does also. BLM has been especially reluctant to propose wilderness designations.

When we mention *Wilderness Areas*—thus capitalized—the reference is to sites that have been given this special protection, most of them in previous administrations. Mentions of *wilderness areas,* uncapitalized, refer to areas with wilderness characteristics not yet officially designated at the time we gathered data. Some of them may be, in time.

HOW WE GATHER INFORMATION

Roughly a third of the information assembled here is available somewhere in print: technical reports, species checklists, leaflets, maps, books, pamphlets, reprints, hearing transcripts, etc. The materials we collected for this book occupy 12 feet of shelf space.

Another third is in the files of state and federal agencies, chiefly in local and district offices. When our friends imagined we were hiking in the mountains, we were often combing through dozens of file drawers.

The final third we obtain by questionnaire, interview, and observation. In the past our 9-page questionnaire was completed for more than 80% of the sites. Thanks to Reagan, the yield has dropped below 50%. We rely increasingly on recorded interviews and site visits.

The task would have been impossible if we were strangers here. However, we've visited both states frequently in the past, working on books and films, camping along the Cache la Poudre, hiking in the LaSals. It would have been impossible without the generous aid of dozens of federal and state employees who wanted to help.

HOW TO USE THIS BOOK

We have divided each state into zones. Zone boundaries follow county lines. A map showing these zones precedes each state chapter, together with an alphabetical list of all entries within that state.

At the beginning of each zone section is a map on which sites are spotted with key numbers, together with a list of sites in numerical order. Entries are arranged alphabetically within zones. Once you have a destination in mind, the map will show what other sites are nearby or on your way.

Information in entries is presented in the following standard sequence:

SITE NAME

Parks are for people. Most parks have formal entrances. National Parks are closed to hunting and logging. Parks have more facilities, more supervision, more rules, and more visitors than forests or refuges. National Parks and Monuments were established "to conserve the scenery and the natural and historic objects and the wild life therein and to provide for the enjoyment of same."

National Forests are managed for wood, water, wildlife, and recreation, although critics charge that imbalances exist. Here, campgrounds are less elaborate than in National Parks, and often less congested. Furthermore, one can camp almost anywhere in a National Forest. Fishing and hunting are regulated by state laws. The National Forests of Colorado and Utah have extensive Wilderness Areas.

National Recreation Areas (NRA) give more emphasis to recreation, less to strict preservation. The Arapaho NRA in Colorado and Flaming Gorge NRA in Utah are administered by the U.S. Forest Service. Glen Canyon NRA in Utah is administered by the National Park Service.

Wildlife Areas (Colorado) and *Waterfowl Management Areas* (Utah) were established to provide for public hunting and fishing, and to increase production of game species. In recent years, increasing attention has been given to nongame species. Some of these areas are open to birders, hikers, and other visitors.

National Wildlife Refuges are for birds and beasts. Most have some visitor facilities: auto tour routes, exhibits, visitor centers. Hunting is usually permitted, often in a part of a Refuge and with special rules. A few Refuges permit camping in designated areas.

Public lands administered by BLM have many uses, including grazing, mining, forestry, and geothermal development. Most areas are open to public use.

ADMINISTERING AGENCY

Entries name responsible agencies, not parent departments. Addresses appear in the state prefaces in this book.

ACREAGE

Many National Forests and some other sites have "inholdings," land owned by others, within their boundaries. Entries note this fact when significant.

Acreages for BLM sites do not measure the limits of public ownership. They refer to selected areas, usually Wilderness Study Areas, which are often surrounded by other public land.

HOW TO GET THERE

Directions begin from points easily found on highway maps. For large sites, entries describe main access routes.

Don't rely on these directions. You need the maps described in state prefaces. If the routes leave paved roads, inquire locally; you'll learn about current road conditions, hear something about the area, and meet good people.

OPEN HOURS

Most National Parks are open 24 hours a day. (Some areas, such as the Trail Ridge Road in Rocky Mountain National Park, are closed at night.)

Some State Parks close their gates at night.

National Forests have no gates.

Most National Wildlife Refuges are closed at night.

SYMBOLS

Symbols designate the principal activities available at each site. Most have obvious meanings:

 Without the pack, day hiking. With it, backpacking opportunities.

 Whitewater rafting or kayaking.

 Symbols for ski touring and snowmobiling appear only where a site reported these as significant activities. Parks have special rules. National Forest Travel maps show areas closed to all motor vehicles. Elsewhere in National Forests and on BLM lands, snowmobiles can be used wherever conditions allow.

DESCRIPTION

Each site is briefly characterized: landform, principal physical features, vegetation. Resources for further data varied. For some sites we could obtain month-by-month weather data; others were far from any weather station. Some sites have detailed accounts of their flora and fauna, but many areas have never been studied.

Such blanks can be filled deductively: one can infer the presence of species from studies of similar sites. We chose not to do so, instead inviting readers to do so for themselves (we provide rather full accounts of flora and fauna for the sites that could supply them). For example, if Douglas-fir grows on a north-facing slope at 8,500-ft. elevation in one location, one might expect to find it on a similar slope not far away. The reader who studies the entries will soon recognize common patterns and associations.

Some species lists we received were unreliable. A few listed species, such as wolves, that have long since been exterminated from those places. A few bird species were obvious misidentifications. Some birds listed as "common" aren't common anywhere. And long-obsolete Latin and common names dated a few lists. On the whole, however, patterns were consistent and illuminating. We deleted only the most improbable items.

We have adopted currently accepted common names for birds and mammals. Thus "myrtle warbler" and "Audubon's warbler" are now lumped as "yellow-rumped warbler." The "black-tailed jackrabbit" is now "blacktail jackrabbit." And so on.

FEATURES

Noted first are Wilderness Areas and other large, natural portions of sites, followed by mentions of such outstanding features as canyons, waterfalls, and lakes.

Major recreation centers are noted, chiefly to tell readers where the crowds are.

Because our concern is with natural areas, we give little or no attention to historical sites.

INTERPRETATION

Visitor centers, campfire talks, guided walks, and other naturalist programs for visitors are conspicuously on the decline. Entries report the status in 1984, but further cuts are in prospect.

ACTIVITIES

Camping: Camping in parks is generally limited to campgrounds. One can camp almost anywhere in a National Forest or on the public domain. Entries note campgrounds and the number of sites. For details, see a standard campground guide.

Hiking, backpacking: Before undertaking anything more ambitious than a day hike on marked trails, we strongly recommend visiting the appropriate Forest, Park, or BLM office. Trail conditions can change overnight. Once— not taking our own advice—we hiked for half a day, found a landslide across the route, and had to turn back. Canyon hiking is great sport, but hikers need to understand the flash flood hazard. Colorado and Utah have fabulous wilderness areas, yet to travel them alone, or without map, compass, and emergency supplies, invites disaster.

Horse riding: Many ranches and outfitters offer pack trips, with and without guides. Lists are available from state travel offices, Chambers of Commerce, National Forest headquarters, etc.

Hunting: Prohibited in National Parks. Regulated in wildlife areas. Always subject to state laws.

Fishing: Subject to state laws. Endangered fish species occur in some waters; taking such fish subjects the fisherman to a heavy fine.

Boating: Most "lakes" in these states are reservoirs, often subject to dry-season drawdowns. Lakes in state parks or near metropolitan areas are often crowded in season. Few are large enough to offer quiet cruising. Notable exceptions are Flaming Gorge Reservoir and Lake Powell, both in Utah. Flatwater sections of the Colorado, San Juan, and a few other rivers are very attractive.

Rafting: Float trips through canyons are spectacular experiences. The entries mention some of the best routes. But they don't provide the detailed information you need before launching.

RULES AND REGULATIONS

All sites have them. Parks have the most.

Pets are banned by only a few sites. In National and State Parks, dogs must be leashed; dogs are usually banned from swimming and picnic areas, and often from hiking trails. Wildlife areas require that pets be leashed, except for dogs when used in legal hunting.

Open fires are prohibited altogether in some backcountry areas, and site managers ban them when the fire hazard is high. Outdoorsmen prefer the quick, clean, compact backpacking stoves except when a fire is needed for warmth.

PUBLICATIONS

Entries list leaflets, maps, and other publications issued by sites or their parent agencies. Once you could write for such publications and expect to receive them; fewer sites have the resources to respond today. Your chances are best if you send a stamped, self-addressed envelope (SASE) of suitable size.

National Forest maps and other publications on sale can be obtained by mail.

Federal agencies issue many more publications than the following list shows; we chose the ones relevant to this book. When stocks of a publication are exhausted, it may not be reprinted. And of course, new publications appear. Stop at headquarters, visitor centers, ranger districts, etc., and see what they have.

U.S. Forest Service
11177 West 8th Avenue
P.O. Box 25127
Lakewood, CO 80225

Publications include:
Four Wheeling.
Keeping the Wild in the Wilderness.
National Forests and National Grasslands of the Rocky Mountain Region.

National Park Service
Rocky Mountain Regional Office
655 Parfet Street
P.O. Box 25287
Denver, CO 80225

Publications include:
Camping in the National Park System.
Lesser Known Areas of the National Park System.
National Park Areas of Colorado.
National Park Areas of Utah.
National Park Areas of the Rocky Mountain Region.

REFERENCES

The heading References refers to books and other publications offered by commercial publishers or natural history associations. Site-specific references are listed in entries. References pertaining to a state or region within a state appear in state prefaces. Those pertaining to both states follow here:

General
Frome, Michael. *Rand McNally National Park Guide.* San Francisco: Rand McNally. Annual editions.
Hilts, Len. *Rand McNally National Forest Guide.* San Francisco: Rand McNally, 1976.
Landi, Val. *The Bantam Great Outdoors Guide to the United States and Canada.* New York: Bantam Books, 1978.
Riley, Laura and William. *Guide to the National Wildlife Refuges.* New York: Doubleday, 1979.
Sutton, Ann, and Myron. *Wilderness Areas of North America.* New York: Funk & Wagnalls, 1974.
Tilden, Freeman. *The National Parks.* New York: Knopf, 1976.
Trimble, Stephen. *The Bright Edge: A Guide to the National Parks of the Colorado Plateau.* Flagstaff: Museum of Northern Arizona Press, 1979.

Camping
Rand McNally Campground and Trailer Park Guide. San Francisco: Rand McNally. Annual editions.
Woodall's. Highland Park, IL: Woodall, Annual editions.

Rafting, canoeing, etc.
Anderson, Fletcher, and Ann Hopkinson. *Rivers of the Southwest.* Boulder, CO: Pruett, 1983.

COLORADO

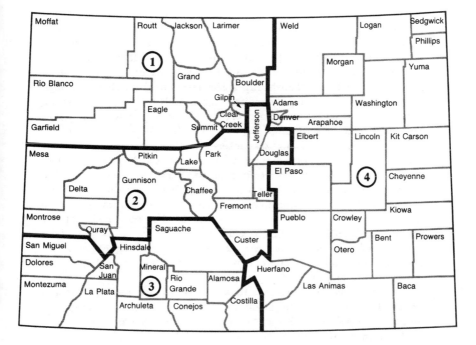

Moffat | Routt | Jackson | Larimer | Weld | Logan | Sedgwick

Phillips

N

COLORADO

Colorado is the highest state in the Union. Three-fourths of the nation's land over 10,000 ft. elevation is here. Colorado has 54 mountains 14,000 ft. or higher ("the Fourteeners"), and about 830 mountains between 11,000 and 14,000 ft. It includes the highest portion of the Rocky Mountains.

Thus it is not surprising that outdoorsmen think of mountains when Colorado is mentioned, and hiking guides mention few trails not in high country. Utah has magnificent mountains too, notably the Uinta and Wasatch Ranges, but canyons are its trademark. Colorado has impressive canyons, but most hikers look upward.

Colorado offers hikers and backpackers everything from quiet streamside trails to remote wilderness adventures. Many hunters and fishermen believe the region was made for them. Rafting has become so popular that trips are rationed on some streams. The 4-wheel-drive vehicle is used here for back-country travel, not for tearing up hillsides. Aspen and Steamboat Springs are only two of the several winter sports centers. By far the most popular outdoor activity is sightseeing, and there is much to see.

The out-of-state visitor soon learns that most people in the parks, forests, and other outdoor sites are Coloradans. The natives are friendly, but don't be surprised to find them occupying most of the campsites.

The state's lowest point is 3,350 ft., where the Arkansas River flows into Kansas. The high plains slope gradually upward for 200 mi. from the eastern border to the base of the Rocky Mountain foothills. Two-fifths of the land area is taken up by these plains.

Then come the mountains, occupying another two-fifths of the state. From the plains, foothills rise to 7,000 to 9,000 ft., towering peaks behind them. Beyond the Front Range are other ranges, generally oriented N–S but with many spurs and extensions in other directions. The Continental Divide follows a wandering course from N to S, roughly dividing the mountainous region in half, rivers on one side flowing to the Pacific, those on the other to the Gulf of Mexico. Among some ranges are "parks," open areas of relatively flat land. In the S central area, between the San Juan Mountains and the Sangre de Cristo Range, is the broad San Luis Valley, crossed by the Rio Grande River.

West of the mountains are high mesas, some above 10,000 ft., which extend to the Utah border. Deep canyons cut into the mesas.

The climate is cool, invigorating. In summer the plains can be hot, but relief often comes in afternoon thundershowers. The mountains are almost always cool, with chilly to cold nights. Humidity is low, and the thin air favors solar radiation; skiers often wear light clothing. Such general conditions are modified by the wide climatic variations that can be experienced within short distances, horizontal or vertical. The difference in annual mean temperatures on Pikes Peak and at Las Animas, 90 mi. away, is about the same as between Iceland and southern Florida.

Winter snow does not halt transmountain motor vehicle travel here as it does in the Sierra Nevada, where many passes are closed for a long winter. Of 36 mountain passes, only 3 are closed in winter, 2 on the Trail Ridge Road in Rocky Mountain National Park, and Independence Pass where SR 82 crosses the Continental Divide. Snow does close much of the high backcountry to hiking and horse riding.

LAND OWNERSHIP

More than one-third of Colorado's land area is federally owned:
National Forests   14,431,240 acres
Public domain, administered by the U.S. Bureau of Land Management
    7,993,935 acres
National Park Service   598,924 acres
U.S. Fish and Wildlife Service   56,857 acres

State landholdings are small, less than 1% of the land area:
    Colorado Division of Wildlife   432,772 acres
    Colorado Division of Parks and Outdoor Recreation   135,617 acres
    (These lands are available for recreation. Federal and state lands used for public buildings, military bases, etc., are not included.)

ZONES

We have divided the state into four zones. Assigning the eastern plains to a zone was obvious and easy. This region, our Zone 4, contains little state or federal land and only a few sites for entries. The mountainous western area is divided roughly into thirds: north, middle, and south.

Zone 1, the N third, is largely federal land. Rocky Mountain National Park is in the E sector. Most of the land in the E and middle sectors is in National Forests. The W is largely semiarid public domain. Dinosaur National Monument is in the NW corner. Zone 1 is crossed W–E by US 40 and I–70.

Zone 2, the middle third, is largely mountainous National Forest land. It also includes the Colorado and Black Canyon of the Gunnison National Monuments and the Curecanti National Recreation Area. BLM-administered lands include a number of candidates for wilderness status. The principal W–E road is US 50.

Zone 3 has the San Luis Valley in its E portion, Ute Indian Reservations in the SW. Much of the remainder is National Forest mountain land, with many tracts of public domain adjoining. Mesa Verde National Park is in the SW. Two National Wildlife Refuges are in the San Luis Valley, as is the Great Sand Dunes National Monument. US 160 is the principal W–E route.

MAPS

After using Utah's splendid Multipurpose Maps, we felt deprived in Colorado. The official Colorado state highway map is an adequate guide to the paved roads, but the mileage of unpaved roads is far greater. After much frustration, we concluded that the National Forest maps are the best available. They show considerable detail in adjoining areas, including federal and state land ownerships. However, keep in mind that some of them were prepared twenty years ago. Once you've settled on an area for backcountry travel, buy the appropriate U.S. Geological Survey quads, and shop for local trail guides.

ROADS

Colorado has over 9,000 mi. of paved state and federal highways. According to one source, there are more than 80,000 mi. of secondary roads, but that's a matter of definition. There are uncounted miles of mine, ranch, and logging roads, used or abandoned, as well as jeep tracks.

Each National Forest has its own road system, including route numbers, so the Forest map is indispensable. Some of these roads are marked "4 W D" (4-wheel drive)—a message not to be ignored. BLM maintains some roads on the land it manages, and there are many more miles of primitive roads or "ways." BLM has no maps for distribution, but usually a staff member can advise.

A pickup truck or other high-clearance vehicle can negotiate many Colorado roads that might hinder an ordinary car. The 4-wheel-drive vehicle has still greater range. Many Coloradans have "secret" campsites accessible only by 4-wheel drive. Its capabilities are not unlimited, however. Don't drive in farther than you're prepared to walk out.

TRAILS

The trail information situation is better. Although most National Forest maps are out of date, more current sources exist, such as the *Recreation Opportunity Guides* (see next section). Rocky Mountain National Park has some trail maps.

Trails Illustrated, Inc. (Box 2374, Littleton, CO 80161), publishes a fine series of trail maps, using the standard topo maps as the base. We found nothing better.

A number of trail guides are listed in the References section on pages 8–10. More are published each year. Some have only local distribution. Look for them in book and outfitter shops and at Forest and Park visitor centers.

Remember that a printed guide can't tell you about the bridge that washed out last week. Consult a Park or Forest Ranger, a BLM staff member, or whoever knows the area, before going far.

RIVERS

Colorado still has some magnificent rivers, although fewer than before the dams were built. Sections of the Colorado and other rivers offer fine whitewater adventures, while other sections can be floated quietly by canoe.

Some of the most popular runs can be made safely only by professional raftsmen. A list of the many outfitters and the rivers they run can be obtained from the Colorado Guides & Outfitters Association, 3944 Sweetwater Rd., Gypsum, CO 81637.

FEDERAL AGENCIES

U.S. Forest Service
Rocky Mountain Region
11177 W. 8th Ave.
Lakewood, CO 80225
(303) 234-4368

The National Forests in Colorado are
Arapaho and Roosevelt
Grand Mesa, Uncompahgre, and Gunnison
Pike and San Isabel
Rio Grande
Routt
San Juan
White River

The combinations shown here were made in recent years, in the name of management efficiency. They still cause confusion. Even Forest Service personnel can't decide whether it is now the "Arapaho and Roosevelt National Forest" or "Arapaho and Roosevelt National Forest*s*." Official usage favors the latter.

While Forests have been combined, their maps haven't been. Arapaho and Roosevelt, for example, each has a National Forest map.

National Forests include 36% of Colorado's land area W of the plains. Each Forest is described in the zone where most of its acreage lies. Only if an important piece of a Forest lies in another zone is it noted there also.

Forest Service budgets have been squeezed. Public information service isn't what it used to be. Publications may be discontinued or out of stock.

Before the cuts took effect, each National Forest in Colorado had produced a massive, looseleaf *Recreation Opportunity Guide (ROG),* containing an immense amount of information about Forest history, resources, and facilities. Included are many pages about camping, hiking, backpacking, and other activities. Popular hiking trails are described in detail, one page each. Choose the page you want and someone will make a photocopy, as long as funds permit. Forest Headquarters, visitor centers, and Ranger District offices have the *ROG*'s, usually for each National Forest in Colorado.

U.S. Bureau of Land Management
Colorado State Office
1037 20th St.
Denver, CO 80202
(303) 837-4481

BLM administers 20% of Colorado's land area W of the plains. The largest concentration of these lands is in the W fifth of the state, but significant areas lie elsewhere, often occupying most of the space between blocks of National Forest lands. Addresses of BLM's District Offices appear in the entries.

Severe budget cuts have depleted BLM's staff, and we observed a marked shift of program emphasis away from encouragement of and service to public recreation. (That's the official policy, not the attitude of staff members, who are always helpful.)

STATE AGENCIES

Colorado has no State Forests. The "Colorado State Forest" in Zone 1 is a unit of the State Parks system.

Colorado Division of Parks and Outdoor Recreation
1313 Sherman St.
Denver, CO 80203
(303) 839-3437

Colorado's system of State Parks compares unfavorably with what we've seen in other states. While these parks serve Colorado residents well, most are of little interest to visitors from elsewhere. Colorado and Alaska were the last two states to initiate State Park systems. Colorado now has 27 units, totaling 135,617 acres, more than half of which is in one site. Many of the parks are planned for intensive water-based recreation ("Ski counterclockwise"). Few have significant natural areas. Operating budgets are conspicuously inadequate.

We have included the few parks with significant natural areas, plus others that may at times have special interest to birders or that serve as convenient campsites near backcountry trailheads.

Note: A campground reservation system is available in some state parks from May 18 to Sept. 16 except as noted in entries. Co residents call toll-free 1-800-421-2435; nonresidents call (303) 778-6691 (toll). Or write Select-A-Seat, 3915 E. Exposition Avenue, Denver, CO 80209.

As in other states, we had to consider what to do about regional, county, and municipal parks. Colorado has some fine ones, chiefly in the Denver area. As before, we decided to omit them. Excellent as some are, these local parks are maintained to serve local residents.

PUBLICATION: Park System Leaflet.
Colorado Division of Wildlife
6060 Broadway
Denver, CO 80216
(303) 825-1192

The Division owns or leases 215 properties totaling almost 450,000 acres. But try to find them! We did—the Division can't offer much help.

When we begin data gathering, we send a request to each land-managing agency. The Division of Wildlife sent us one publication and a letter: "Due to extreme budget cuts . . . we will be unable to provide you with any additional information regarding the various state areas. As a matter of fact, we are being forced to eliminate some of our own publications and there is every possibility that field personnel will be laid off."

The publication was the *Guide to Colorado's State Wildlife Areas.* It lists all 215 properties and provides brief descriptions and simple maps for 21 of them. As for the other 194 sites, "From Steamboat Springs, 7 mi. N" is all the information one can get.

Many states encourage and support their wildlife agencies to promote tourism. Colorado appears to discourage it. Local hunters and fishermen know where the state lands are, but outsiders aren't given guidance.

When HQ couldn't help, we went to look for ourselves. We couldn't visit all 215 sites, but we tried about 80 and found at least the general areas. Some were attractive, and we have entries for them. Some adjoin and enhance State Parks or federal sites.

The Division of Wildlife has a capable professional staff doing the best it can with grossly inadequate support. A notable achievement is Colorado's nongame income tax checkoff. On their income tax returns, citizens can choose to help protect nongame species. Contributions totaled $350,000 in the first year, and more in each year following.

PUBLICATIONS

Guide to Colorado's State Wildlife Areas. $2.00.

Colorado fishing map.

Many publications on hunting and fishing regulations, endangered species, game birds, furbearers, etc.

REFERENCES

GENERAL

Ornes, Robert. *Guide to the Colorado Mountains.* Denver: Colorado Mountain Club, 1970.

Chronic, John, and Halka. *Prairie, Peak, and Plateau.* Bulletin 32, Colorado Geological Survey, 1972. $4.00.

Chronic, Halka. *Roadside Geology of Colorado.* Denver: Mountain Press, 1980.

Grout, William. *Colorado Adventures: 40 Trips in the Rockies.* Denver: Golden Bell Press, 1974.

Young, Robert G., and Joann W. *Colorado West: Land of Geology and Wildflowers.* Grand Junction, CO: Wheelwright Press, 1977.

Agnew, Jeremy. *Exploring the Colorado High Country.* Colorado Springs: Wildwood Press, 1977.

Griffiths, Mel. *Colorado, A Geography.* Boulder, CO: Westview Press, 1983.

PLANTS

Kelly, George W. *A Guide to the Woody Plants of Colorado.* Boulder, CO: Pruett, 1967.

Pesman, M. W. *Meet the Natives: An Easy Way to Recognize Wildflowers, Trees, and Shrubs of the Central Rocky Mountain Region.* Denver: Denver Botanic Garden, 1975.

Nelson, Ruth A. *Handbook of Rocky Mountain Plants.* Estes Park, CO: Rocky Mountain Nature Association, 1980.

Craighead, John, and Frank, Jr., and Roy J. Davis. *Field Guide to Rocky Mountain Wildflowers.* Boston: Houghton Mifflin, 1963.

BIRDS

Bailey, Alfred Marshall. *Pictorial Checklist of Colorado Birds, with Brief Notes on the Status of Each Species in the Neighboring States of Nebraska, Kansas, New Mexico, Utah, and Wyoming.* Denver: Denver Museum of Natural History, 1967.

Bailey, Alfred M., and Robert Niedrach. *Birds of Colorado.* 2 vols. Denver: Denver Museum of Natural History, 1965.

MAMMALS

Lechleitner, R. R. *Wild Mammals of Colorado: Their Appearance, Habits, Distribution, and Abundance.* Boulder, CO: Pruett, 1969.

Armstrong, David M. *Rocky Mountain Mammals.* Estes Park, CO: Rocky Mountain Nature Association, 1975.

REPTILES AND AMPHIBIANS

Hammerson, Geoffrey A. *Amphibians and Reptiles in Colorado.* Denver: Colorado Division of Wildlife, 1982.

HIKING

Lowe, Don, and Roberta. *80 Northern Colorado Hiking Trails.* Beaverton, OR: Touchstone Press, 1973.

DeHaan, Vici. *Hiking Trails of the Boulder Mountain Area.* Boulder, CO: Pruett, 1979.

Brown, Robert Leaman. *Uphill Both Ways: Hiking Colorado's High Country.* Caldwell, ID: Caxton Printers, 1976.

Hagen, Mary. *Hiking Trails of Northern Colorado.* Boulder, CO: Pruett, 1979.

Lowe, Don, and Roberta. *50 West Central Colorado Hiking Trails.* Beaverton, OR: Touchstone Press, 1976.

Martin, Bob. *Hiking Trails of Central Colorado.* Boulder, CO: Pruett, 1980.

Pixler, Paul. *Hiking Trails of Southwestern Colorado.* Boulder, CO: Pruett, 1981.

DeHaan, Vici. *Bike Rides of the Colorado Front Range.* Boulder, CO: Pruett, 1981.

Kenofer, Louis. *Trails of the Front Range.* Boulder, CO: Pruett, 1980.

SKIING

Sudduth, Tom and Sanse. *Colorado Front Range Ski Tours.* Beaverton, OR: Touchstone Press, 1975.

Sudduth, Tom and Sanse. *Central Colorado Ski Tours.* Boulder, CO: Pruett, 1980.

BOATING, RAFTING

Perry, Earl. *Rivers of Colorado: 10 Easy River Trips in the Mountains, Canyons, and Plateaus of Colorado.* Denver: American Canoe Association, 1978.

Anderson, Fletcher, and Ann Hopkinson. *Rivers of the Southwest.* Boulder, CO: Pruett, 1983.

Evans, Laura, and Buzz Belknap. *Dinosaur River Guide.* Boulder City, NV: Westwater Books, 1983.

Hayes, Philip T., and George C. Simmons. *Dinosaur National Monument and Vicinity.* Denver: Powell Society, 1983.

Stohlquist, James. *Colorado Whitewater.* Buena Vista, CO: Colorado Kayak Supply Co., 1982.

ZONE 1

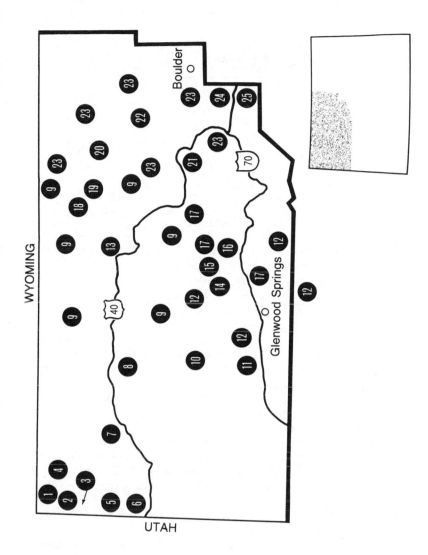

ZONE 1

Includes these counties:

Moffat	Rio Blanco	Eagle
Routt	Garfield	Summit
Jackson	Grand	Clear Creek
Larimer	Boulder	Gilpin

The E portion of Zone 1 includes some of the most heavily used outdoor recreation areas in the United States. In the W portion are miles of roads where passing another car is a major event. Most of the E portion is in National Forests; most of the W is public domain.

Rocky Mountain National Park is in the E, surrounded by the Arapaho and Roosevelt National Forests. The Routt National Forest is in the N central part of the Zone, the White River National in the S central. While all have recreation sites that are sometimes overcrowded, both the Park and the Forests have wilderness areas where hikers and backpackers can enjoy solitude.

Walden, on SR 125, is at the center of North Park, a wide valley ringed by mountains. Here are the Arapaho National Wildlife Refuge and Colorado's North Park Wildlife Areas.

Dinosaur National Monument, in the NW, is largely surrounded by public lands. N of the Monument is some of the state's least-traveled area. If one drives W from Maybell on SR 318, the next gas pump is in Utah, over 100 mi. away. Several interesting sites are in this area, including the Browns Park National Wildlife Refuge and Irish Canyon.

Also in the W are several large and fascinating areas of public lands, roadless and primitive, candidates for wilderness status.

The Colorado River crosses the S part of Zone 1. The entry for Upper Colorado River describes a section attractive to sightseers, hikers, and boaters.

ARAPAHO AND ROOSEVELT NATIONAL FORESTS
U.S. Forest Service
Arapaho: 1,025,142 acres; 1,157,012 acres within boundaries.
Roosevelt: 788,351 acres; 1,082,663 acres within boundaries.

Includes Pawnee National Grassland; see entry in Zone 4. Surrounds Rocky Mountain National Park. The largest blocks are N and S of the

Park. Principal access roads: In the N, SR 14. In the W, SR 125. In the S, US 40 and I-70/US 6.

The *Roosevelt National Forest* is on the N, E, and S of Rocky Mountain National Park, the largest portion in the N. The NW boundary is the Medicine Bow Range, elevations to 13,000 ft. The Rawah Wilderness is on the E side of the range. SR 14 follows the Cache la Poudre River W–E through a steep-walled, forested canyon. The Cache la Poudre Wilderness and the Comanche Peak Wilderness lie between SR 14 and the National Park.

The Forest land E of the Park is fragmented. In the S portion, the dominant feature is the Indian Peaks Wilderness.

The largest portion of the *Arapaho National Forest* is W of Denver, S of Rocky Mountain National Park. It is crossed by I-70 and US 40. The highest mountains in the Forest are here. This portion includes the Mount Evans Wilderness and part of the Indian Peaks Wilderness. Another large block is W of the Park, S of the Rabbit Ears Range, crossed by SR 125. The Arapaho National Recreation Area adjoins the SW corner of the Park.

The Forests have been combined under a single management. They also include the Pawnee National Grassland in Zone 4, E of Fort Collins, N of SR 14 (see entry).

The Dillon Ranger District adjoins and is administered by the White River National Forest. The Middle Park Ranger District adjoins and is administered by the Routt National Forest. Information about these Ranger Districts will be found in those entries.

THE COMBINED FORESTS

The Continental Divide and the Front Range of the Rocky Mountains are the backbone of this spectacular Forest, a region of snowcapped peaks, mountain lakes and streams, tall timber, green valleys with beaver dams, countless wildflowers, and a rich wildlife.

Use of the Forest is heavy: 10 million visits per year. About 1.5 million people live in Denver and other population centers along the Front Range, and growth is rapid. Many of these residents moved here because of outdoor recreation opportunities. Three-fifths of the Forest visitors live nearby.

On a visit in the 1960s, we sought a campsite one Thursday afternoon, assuming we were ahead of the weekend rush—and found only one vacancy. But several nearby tents weren't occupied that night: Denver residents had driven here, pitched tents, and gone home, thus assuring themselves of a weekend space when they arrived Friday evening.

The heaviest use, year-round, is on weekends. Campgrounds usually have some vacancies on weekdays, except at the most popular destinations. Some trails are heavily used. Visits to wilderness and other backcountry areas are increasing more rapidly than visits to developed recreation sites, which are often already at capacity.

About a third of the Forest is open to 4-wheel-drive and other off-road vehicles. Most ORV use is on primitive roads built for logging and other management purposes. Outdoorsmen who know the Forest often have "secret" places, and may tell you all about them except how to get there.

Without 4-wheel drive or another type of high-clearance vehicle, motorized access to quiet places is limited. But the Forest Rangers favor dispersal, which lightens the load on crowded places. Except on the busiest weekends, they can usually suggest pleasant, out-of-the-way destinations.

Slightly more than half of the Forest is roadless. About 443 square miles (two-fifths of the roadless area) is in 7 formally designated Wildernesses, closed to all motor vehicles. In 1982 the Forest reported 300,000 visitor-days in wilderness areas, two-thirds of these days in the Indian Peaks Wilderness. Wilderness use is increasing more rapidly than other forms of recreation. Permits are now (1984) required in the Indian Peaks. However, while some popular campsites have been trampled and otherwise damaged, the impact has not yet been judged serious enough to require rationing by permit in the other six wildernesses. Most wilderness areas have light to moderate use. Planners believe construction of new trails will relieve pressure in the critical areas.

Here, too, the Rangers can be helpful, suggesting routes and destinations that aren't crowded. The peak season for hiking and backpacking is Memorial Day to Labor Day.

Each Ranger District office has a copy of the *Recreation Opportunity Guide (ROG),* a massive looseleaf reference book with an immense amount of well-organized, indexed information about where to go, what to do, and what to see. In the offices we visited, the *ROG*'s were on open reference shelves.

The Forest extends 114 mi. N–S, 65 mi. W–E. It includes several peaks above 14,000 ft. Lowest point is about 5,300 ft. Except for the Pawnee National Grassland, the region is within the Rocky Mountain forest, which includes four zones:

Lower montane forest, 6,000–8,000 ft. Annual precipitation is 14–20 in. Warm summers, cold winters. In the drier E portion, sagebrush and grasses. Ponderosa pine and grasses in the central portion, stands of Douglas-fir and ponderosa pine in the W. Low moisture produces parklike open stands of widely spaced trees. Understory includes chokecherry, mountain-mahogany, bitterbrush, penstemon, wild geranium, golden aster, and wild rye.

Upper montane forest, 8,000–9,000 ft. Broad U-shaped valleys, meandering streams with beaver dams. The climate is cooler, the growing season almost 40 days shorter than in the zone below. Annual precipitation here is 20–25 in. Willows, alder, birch, grasses, and sedges cover the valley floors. Slopes and ridgetops have fairly dense stands of aspen, ponderosa pine, limber pine, lodgepole pine. Understory includes kinnikinnick, common juniper, grouse huckleberry, heartleaf arnica, cinquefoil, and lupine.

Subalpine forest, 9,000–11,000 ft. Steeper ridges, shallow soils, moraine-formed lakes. Cool summers, cold winters; growing season less than 90 days. Annual precipitation is 25–30 in. Willow-birch stands and sedge-grass meadows on valley floors. Limber pine, lodgepole pine, aspen, Engelmann spruce, and subalpine fir on slopes and ridgetops. Understory includes common juniper, woods rose, grouse huckleberry, heartleaf arnica, yarrow, fireweed.

Alpine tundra, above 11,000 ft. Treeline is the boundary. Short, cool summers; long, cold winters. Snowfall is often heavy, and snow remains all year in places. Growing season is 45 days. Vegetation includes hairgrass, buttercup, sedges, grasses, willows, tufted phlox, sandwort, yellow avens, moss campion, alpine bluegrass, sheep fescue.

The *riparian and wetland association* includes willows, cottonwood, mountain alder, shrubby cinquefoil, snowberry, western yarrow, marsh marigold, dandelion, tufted hairgrass, sedge, bluejoint reedgrass.

Birds: 254 species recorded. No general checklist available. The *ROG* lists species typical of various habitats.

General: Mountain chickadee, white-breasted nuthatch, yellow-rumped warbler, pine siskin, broad-tailed hummingbird, northern flicker, violet-green swallow, black-billed magpie, gray-headed junco, house wren, American robin, evening grosbeak, red crossbill, rufous hummingbird, western wood-pewee, tree swallow, Clark's nutcracker, pygmy nuthatch.

Ponderosa pine, Douglas-fir, 7,000–8,000 ft.: Western and mountain bluebirds, western tanager, Cassin's finch, chipping sparrow, dark-eyed junco, black-headed grosbeak, poor-will, Steller's jay, green-tailed towhee, Lewis' woodpecker.

Lodgepole pine, 8,000–10,000 ft.: Gray jay, western goshawk.

Engelmann spruce, subalpine fir, 9,000–11,000 ft.: Ruby-crowned and golden-crowned kinglets, pine grosbeak, white-crowned sparrow, western tanager, Lincoln's sparrow, Steller's jay, hermit thrush, brown creeper, olive-sided flycatcher.

Also recorded: Common loon, western grebe, white-faced ibis, Canada goose, mallard, northern shoveler, common merganser, turkey vulture, goshawk; Cooper's, rough-legged, and ferruginous hawks; blue grouse, white-tailed ptarmigan, mourning dove, Townsend's solitaire, loggerhead shrike, great horned and screech owls, common nighthawk, white-throated swift, hairy woodpecker, Hammond's flycatcher, common raven, common crow; lark, Brewer's, and chipping sparrows; Townsend's, yellow-rumped, and Wilson's warblers.

A checklist is available for the Pawnee National Grassland (see entry in Zone 4).

Mammals: 81 species recorded. Checklist of species "which occur or may occur." Among those recorded: black bear, badger, beaver, muskrat, yellow-belly marmot, coyote, bobcat, mountain lion, porcupine, red and gray foxes, spotted and striped skunks, raccoon, wolverine, Canada lynx, golden-mantled ground squirrel, Abert and red squirrels, pine marten, boreal redback vole, cottontail, snowshoe hare, whitetail jackrabbit, pika, pronghorn, bighorn sheep, elk, mule deer, whitetail deer, many species of voles, shrews, rats, and mice.

Reptiles and amphibians: Eastern fence and short-horned lizards; tiger salamander, boreal and Rocky Mountain toads; boreal chorus, wood, and leopard frogs. Snakes include common water, garter, and smooth green; bull snake, milk snake, and western rattlesnake.

FEATURES

Rawah Wilderness, 73,109 acres, in the NW sector, E side of the Medicine Bow Range. Includes 1,462 acres in the Routt National Forest. Elevations from 8,400 to 13,000 ft. Dense stands of lodgepole pine, spruce, and fir below 11,000 ft., subalpine vegetation, alpine tundra, and barren rock. Rugged alpine scenery. U-shaped valleys with 1,000-ft. walls surround Island and Crater Lakes. Twin Craters, Rawah No. 4, and Iceberg Lakes are in glacial basins. Trout streams. Redfeather Ranger District.

Neota Wilderness, 9,924 acres, near the NW corner of Rocky Mountain National Park. Includes 267 acres in the Routt National Forest. Elevations from 10,000 to 11,800 ft. Large flat-topped ridges with alpine tundra and bare rock faces. Below, spruce-fir forest. West meadow along Neota and Corral Creeks. Trout in streams and Slip Lake. Not a high-use area. Redfeather Ranger District.

Cache la Poudre Wilderness, 9,238 acres, bounded on the N by SR 14. Elevations from 6,100 to 8,300 ft.; dry climate and a long snow-free season. Two major river canyons, open stands of ponderosa pine, rock outcrops. Although campsites along SR 14 are heavily used, this wilderness has few visitors, most of those in deer-hunting season. Poudre Ranger District.

Comanche Peak Wilderness, 66,464 acres, in the Mummy Range, surrounding Crown Point, between SR 14 and Rocky Mountain National Park. Elevations from 7,500 to 12,700 ft. The Cache la Poudre River flows for about 16 mi. through the area. Alpine tundra at higher elevations, spruce and fir forest and lodgepole pine below. Trout in lakes and streams. Poudre Ranger District.

Never Summer Wilderness, 7,043 acres, plus 6,659 acres in the Routt National Forest. W of the Never Summer Mountains, on the W side of Rocky Mountain National Park. Elevations from 8,900 to 12,524 ft. Spruce, fir, and lodgepole pine abundant at lower elevations. Several small lakes. Sulphur Ranger District.

Eagles Nest Wilderness, 82,743 acres, plus 50,945 acres in the White River

NF. In the high, rugged Gore Range, N of I-70, NE of Vail. Peaks over 13,000 ft. Many alpine lakes and ponds, rushing streams. Popular rock-climbing area. From Vail, on I-70, several Forest roads lead N and E to the Wilderness.

Mount Evans Wilderness, 74,401 acres, including 34,127 acres in the Pike National Forest. About 40 mi. SW of Denver. Occupies the slopes of Mt. Evans, except for the highway corridor. Elevations from 8,400 ft. to over 14,000 ft. Four major drainages. Large expanses of alpine tundra. U-shaped and V-shaped valleys. Includes 5,880-acre Abyss Lake. Spruce-fir and lodgepole pine below timberline, with small stands of bristlecone pine near the Mount Goliath Natural Area and the Chicago Creek Basin. Wildflowers noted: American bistort, alpine avens, western yellow paintbrush, alpine primrose, alpine sunflower, sedum rosea, alpine clover, purple fringe, sky pilot, greenleaf mertensia. Clear Creek Ranger District.

Indian Peaks Wilderness, 70,374 acres S of Rocky Mountain National Park. Elevations range from 8,500 to 13,500 ft. Approximately 60% of the Wilderness is above timberline (roughly 10,700 ft.). Dramatic mountain scenery. Vast areas of alpine tundra. Nearly 50 alpine lakes. Cirque basins with remnant glaciers. Chill winds off the snowfields cause a false timberline environment of alpine plants and stunted trees not usually found at this elevation. This area attracts two-thirds of the wilderness visitors. Peak use is July 15–Aug. 31. You are advised to visit in June or Sept. and early Oct. Permits required for overnight camping June 1–Sept. 1. Boulder and Sulphur Ranger Districts.

Vasquez Peak Wilderness Study Area, 12,800 acres of Arapaho-Roosevelt, and Routt National Forest lands. High, rocky terrain, thus far little used by visitors. The drainage contains the headwaters of Vasquez Creek. Mount Nystrom Trail and Vasquez Lake are points of interest.

Arapaho National Recreation Area, 31,456 acres, adjoins the SW corner of Rocky Mountain National Park, on US 34. Two large reservoirs, Lake Granby and Shadow Mountain Lake, are linked to Grand Lake, a natural body of water outside the NRA. The area includes smaller lakes: Willow Creek Reservoir, Meadow Creek Reservoir, and Monarch Lake. The complex includes campgrounds, marinas, and other developments. Much of the shoreline is privately owned and developed. The area is heavily used for water-based recreation. Campground occupancy exceeds design capacity by 50% during the busy season. US 34 becomes the Trail Ridge Road inside the Park and is heavily traveled.

The land area includes 14,000 undeveloped acres, including trailheads for the W side of Indian Peaks Wilderness. Cross-country skiing and snowmobiling are popular.

The Moffat Road, a self-guiding auto tour following the original railroad route over Rollins Pass. From Rollinsville, W of Boulder. Not currently recommended for passenger cars.

Mt. Evans Auto Road is the world's highest passenger car road, ascending to just below the 14,264-ft. summit. From I-70, S on SR 103. 14 mi. from entrance to summit. When we last drove the road, it was in poor repair but presented no difficulties up to Summit Lake Park, maintained by the city and county of Denver. A delightful pair of mountain lakes, snowbanks remaining in August. Drivers of motor homes and cars with travel trailers would do well to stop here. Spectacular views. The mountain slopes are a wilderness area with fine day hiking and backpacking. For short hikes, look for the *Mount Goliath Trail* and *Alpine Garden Loop,* near timberline.

Cache la Poudre Valley offers a fine scenic drive on SR 14 from Fort Collins. This can be part of a loop drive including the Redfeather Lakes. Spectacular scenery, as well as camping, picnicking, and fishing opportunities alongside the road.

INTERPRETATION

Information and publications at Ranger District offices. These offices also have the *Recreation Opportunities Guide,* as do the following:

Clear Creek Visitor Center, Idaho Springs. Exhibits.

Arapaho National Recreation Area Headquarters, at Shadow Mountain Village.

Wilderness Information Station at Monarch Lake, on County Road 6 beyond Lake Granby.

Slide programs, movies, interpretive walks, other naturalist activities at the Greenridge Visitor Center near Shadow Mountain Dam.

Evening campground talks and other naturalist programs have been discontinued because of budget cuts.

ACTIVITIES

Camping: 52 campgrounds, 1,294 sites, including the Arapaho NRA. Earliest opening, May 1; latest closing, Nov. 12. Shorter seasons at higher elevations. Campgrounds often full, especially Memorial Day–Labor Day. No reservations. Informal camping is generally permitted throughout the Forest, in undeveloped areas.

Hiking, backpacking: 932 mi. of managed system trails, plus an unknown mileage of informal trails. Over half of the managed trail mileage is concentrated in one-fifth of the Forest area. Some trails are overused, and trail maintenance budgets are inadequate. Rangers see construction of new trails as one way to relieve pressure on popular routes. Consult Ranger District offices for advice on current trail conditions and little-used routes. The *ROG* has detailed information on a number of trails.

Horse riding: Trails suitable for horse travel can be found throughout the Forest. The *ROG* has information on several trails as well as a list of outfitters for day and pack trips. Natural forage is insufficient, and feed must be carried.

Hunting: A significant but not major activity, chiefly for mule deer, elk, and pronghorn.

Fishing: Chiefly trout. Fishermen outnumber hunters 4 to 1. The ROG has information on fishing waters and stocking.

Boating: The largest lakes are in the Arapaho National Recreation Area. In the Redfeather Ranger District (R.D.), motors up to 10 hp can be used on Chambers and Dowdy Lakes, no motors on other lakes. Dillon Reservoir, 3,200 acres, in the S end of the Arapaho National Forest.

Rafting on the Poudre River: The whitewater stretch is only 3 mi., Class III–IV in June and early July, dangerous during peak runoff, too low in other seasons.

Skiing: Downhill skiing is increasingly popular. Four developed ski areas on Forest land. Season is 155–160 days. Demand exceeds capacity on some peak days.

Ski touring: No data, but cross-country skiing on mid-elevation trails is increasing rapidly.

Snowmobiling is also popular, with occasional conflicts with ski touring. Snowmobiles are excluded, with other motor vehicles, from wildernesses and other restricted areas, but can operate in more than half of the Forest. Many suitable routes.

PUBLICATIONS
  Maps
    Forest map. $1.00.
    Indian Peaks Wilderness.
    Winter Sports Trails, Boulder Ranger District.
  Information pages
    Arapaho National Forest.
    Roosevelt National Forest.
    Rafting.
    Camping in the Arapaho National Recreation Area.
  Leaflets
    Visitor guide, small map.
    Birding Auto Tour.
    Winter Recreation Opportunities, Fraser Experimental Forest.
    Rawah Wilderness, small map.
    Is the Water Safe?
    Mount Evans.
    Snowmobiling on the Sulphur Ranger District.
    Indian Peaks Wilderness.
  Pamphlets
    The Moffat Road. Auto tour guide.

REFERENCES
  Gregory, Lee. *Colorado Scenic Guide, Northern Region.* Boulder, CO: Johnson, 1984.
  Brown, Robert L. *Uphill Both Ways.* Caldwell, ID: Caxton, 1978.

HEADQUARTERS: 301 S. Howes St., Fort Collins, CO 80522; (303) 482-5155.

RANGER DISTRICTS: Boulder R.D., 2995 Baseline Rd., Boulder, CO 80303; (303) 443-5283. Clear Creek R.D. Visitor Center, P.O. Box 730, Idaho Springs, CO 80452; (303) 567-2901. Estes-Poudre R.D., 148 Remington St., Fort Collins, CO 80524; (303) 482-3822. Estes Park Office, 161 Second St., Estes Park, CO 80517; (303) 586-3440. Redfeather R.D., 1600 N. College Ave., Fort Collins, CO 80524; (303) 484-0036. Sulphur R.D., Hot Sulphur Springs, CO 80451; (303) 725-3301. Pawnee National Grassland, 2009 9th St., Greeley, CO 80631; (303) 353-5004.

ARAPAHO NATIONAL WILDLIFE REFUGE
U.S. Fish and Wildlife Service
About 20,000 acres.

3 mi. S of Walden, near intersection of SR 125 and SR 14.

A fine birding area. In mid-August we spent half a day on the Refuge and saw no other visitors but large numbers of waterfowl and other birds, as well as prairie dogs and muskrats.

The Refuge is at 8,200 ft. elevation in North Park, an intermountain glacial basin about 45 mi. N–S, 35 mi. W–E. The Park Range is on the W, Medicine Bow Range on the E and NE, Rabbit Ears Mountains on the S, Never Summer Range on the SE. The Refuge is on both sides of SR 125 for about 10 mi. The Illinois River flows parallel with the highway through the E portion. Meadows on the floodplain are irrigated with river water. Sagebrush grassland on higher rises.

Summers are warm but brief. Waterfowl begin arriving in late Mar. or early Apr. At the peak in May, 5,000 ducks may be present. Canada goose nesting begins in Apr., ducks in early June. The Refuge produces about 5,000 ducklings and 100 to 200 goslings per year. Fall migration peaks in late Sept. or early Oct., with up to 8,000 waterfowl present.

Begin your visit on the 6-mi. auto tour route on the W side, 3 mi. S of Walden. The road skirts a number of small ponds. Such shallow ponds, quick to warm in the spring, are an essential food source. Parking is limited to designated areas, but visitors are free to walk about except where postings forbid.

4 mi. S, County Road 32 leads into the E area. An overlook with a small exhibit offers a view of the area. A bulletin board at the main parking area had only information for fishermen. The river isn't visible from here, but

dense willows mark its bank, and wheeltracks show the way. The cluster of buildings is a subheadquarters; Refuge headquarters was located in town when we visited, but there were plans to move here.

Birds: Wildlife checklist available, includes mammals, fish, amphibians, and reptiles. 155 bird species recorded. Nesting species include great blue heron, black-crowned night-heron, mallard, gadwall, pintail; green-winged, blue-winged, and cinnamon teals; American wigeon, shoveler, Swainson's hawk, golden eagle, northern harrier, prairie falcon, American kestrel, sage grouse, Virginia rail, sora, American coot, killdeer, common snipe, spotted sandpiper, willet, American avocet, Wilson's phalarope, mourning dove, great horned and short-eared owls, common nighthawk, northern flicker, horned lark, barn and cliff swallows, black-billed magpie, American crow, house and marsh wrens, sage thrasher, American robin, western and mountain bluebirds, yellow warbler, house sparrow, western meadowlark; yellow-headed, red-winged, and Brewer's blackbirds; house finch, American goldfinch, lark bunting, vesper and white-crowned sparrows.

Others recorded, seasonally common or abundant, include lesser scaup, rough-legged and ferruginous hawks, violet-green swallow; gray-crowned rosy, black rosy, and brown-capped rosy finches.

Mammals: Common or abundant: whitetail jackrabbit, least chipmunk, Richardson ground squirrel, whitetail prairie dog, beaver, deer mouse, northern grasshopper mouse, mountain vole, muskrat, house mouse, western jumping mouse, coyote, longtail weasel, badger, striped skunk, mule deer, pronghorn. Moose reintroduced nearby.

ACTIVITIES

Hunting: Most of the Refuge is open to hunting sage grouse and pronghorn in state seasons; check HQ for special regulations.

Fishing: River, except where posted; closed to fishing June 1–July 31, the nesting season. Mostly brown trout.

NEARBY: North Park State Wildlife Areas (see entry).

PUBLICATIONS
   Leaflet with map.
   Auto tour guide leaflet.
   Wildlife checklist.

HEADQUARTERS: Box 457, Walden, CO 80480; (303) 723-4717.

BROWNS PARK NATIONAL WILDLIFE REFUGE
U.S. Fish and Wildlife Service
13,654 acres.

From Maybell on US 40, 61 mi. W on SR 318.

Just W of Maybell is a warning sign: "No services next 108 miles." This was the last part of Colorado to be settled; early explorers advised, "Don't." And there isn't much settlement even now. SR 318 is a good, all-weather road. Ahead, in Utah, is a short 14.5% grade; our motor home climbed it; a car towing a large travel trailer might not.

Most of the land on either side is public domain, managed by BLM. High desert, gently rolling, mostly sagebrush with scattered juniper, with a backdrop of red-rock hills. Near the Little Snake River, at Mile Marker 45 (from the UT border), is a green, irrigated valley. Along the way are several BLM roads marked for such places as Douglas Mountain and Lily Park.

Approaching SR 10 at Mile Marker 19, the landscape becomes more colorful, hillsides with bands of green and gray as well as red. Just before SR 10 is a road to the S marked "Gates of Lodore," the portal where the Green River enters Lodore Canyon in Dinosaur National Monument. We turned N on County Road 10 N, a good gravel road, to Irish Canyon (see entry).

Next morning we arrived at the Refuge, turning off SR 318 at County Road 164. The Refuge is on the Green River. Within the boundaries are three land types: steep, rocky mountain slopes, alluvial benchlands, and sedimentary river bottomlands. Highest point is 6,200 ft., lowest 5,355. Annual precipitation is about 8 in.

A bulletin board offers the essential information about the Refuge; leaflets were available in a box. Most visitors take the auto tour route. An exhibit explains that Browns Park lies between Diamond Mountain and Cold Spring Mountain, which protect the park from the full force of the elements. The tour route generally follows the Green River, which is here a placid stream.

The Refuge staff says birding is good "spring, summer, and fall." On a day in August we saw few birds, perhaps because a key marsh had been drained for rehabilitation.

Birds: 199 species recorded. Checklist available. Seasonally common or abundant species include horned, eared, and pied-billed grebes; great blue heron, white-faced ibis, Canada goose, mallard, gadwall, pintail, green-winged and cinnamon teals, American wigeon, shoveler, redhead, ring-necked duck, canvasback, lesser scaup, common goldeneye, ruddy duck, common merganser. Also red-tailed hawk, golden eagle, northern harrier, American kestrel, sage grouse, American coot, killdeer, common snipe, spotted sandpiper, Wilson's and northern phalaropes, common nighthawk, white-throated swift, black-chinned and rufous hummingbirds, northern flicker, western kingbird, Say's phoebe, horned lark; violet-green, tree, rough-winged, barn, and cliff swallows; black-billed magpie, pinyon jay, marsh wren. Also

American robin, loggerhead shrike, European starling, yellow warbler, yellowthroat, yellow-breasted chat, western meadowlark, yellow-headed and red-winged blackbirds, northern oriole, Brewer's blackbird, brown-headed cowbird, western tanager, house finch, pine siskin, American goldfinch, rufous-sided towhee; vesper, lark, sage, white-crowned, and song sparrows.

Mammals: No checklist. Often seen: mule deer, pronghorn, beaver, coyote, prairie dog.

ACTIVITIES

Camping: Primitive camping in designated areas. No water. All year.

Hiking, backpacking: Many opportunities in Refuge and surrounding areas.

Hunting: Waterfowl, deer, cottontail. Special rules; inquire.

Fishing: River, trout. Prohibited Mar. 1–June 15, waterfowl nesting.

Rafting: Rafting and canoeing on Green River. Slack water, shallow, many sandbars. River frozen intermittently, Dec.–Feb. Takeout point for raft trips from upstream in Utah. See entry, Ashley National Forest (Utah Zone 1).

NEARBY

Browns Park Area (see entry, Utah Zone 1).
Dinosaur National Monument (see entry).
Diamond Breaks (see entry).
West Cold Springs Mountain (see entry).
Cross Mountain (see entry).

PUBLICATION: Leaflet with map.

HEADQUARTERS: 1318 Highway 318, Maybell, CO 81640; (303) 365-3613.

BULL GULCH
U.S. Bureau of Land Management
15,000 acres.

On the Colorado River near Burns, N of Dotsero. Land access is blocked by private property. The only public access is by raft from the Colorado River.

More people float past this unit than explore it on foot. State Bridge to Dotsero is one of the popular rafting sections of the Colorado. Some raft parties come ashore here for overnight camping. Some stay to hike the canyons.

The area is irregular in shape, about 10 mi. N–S, 4 mi. at its widest. The NW boundary is on or near the Colorado River for about 7 mi. Steep, rugged topography with stratified cliff, deeply incised gulches and canyons. Bull Gulch, from which the unit takes its name, is in the N sector. Posey Creek is about the middle.

Elevations range from 6,400 ft. along the Colorado River to 9,700 ft. along the E boundary. Some slopes up from the river are relatively steep, but most in the unit are moderate. Travel within the unit is not difficult, although there are no mapped trails.

Riparian vegetation along the river and some canyon bottoms. The pinyon-juniper association predominates on the drier lower slopes; spruce-fir and aspen at higher elevations.

Prairie falcon and bald eagle nest in the area. Winter range for deer and elk.

Bull Gulch is a Wilderness Study Area. Another WSA, 11,940-acre Castle Peak, is less than 2 mi. to the E (see entry), but the intervening land is privately owned.

HEADQUARTERS: BLM, Grand Junction District Office, 764 Horizon Drive, Grand Junction, CO 81501; (303) 243-6552.

BULL CANYON; WILLOW CREEK; SKULL CREEK
U.S. Bureau of Land Management
45,000 acres.

On both sides of the road from Dinosaur to the Harpers Corner part of Dinosaur National Monument; Bull Canyon on the W, Willow Creek on the E, Skull Creek E of Willow.

On the map, these areas look easily accessible. The Bull Canyon and Willow Creek sites adjoin the Monument access road at Plug Hat Rock, where the Monument has an overlook, picnic area, and nature trail, and all three are close to US 40. In fact, access is limited in some places by private land ownership, in some by difficult terrain. The prospective visitor should stop at the BLM office for advice and a look at a detailed map. (East end access via Moffat County Road 123.) It's possible to get in, and well worth it. The view from the overlook is persuasive. BLM evaluators gave these areas the highest rating for scenic values.

Bull Canyon is a 4-mi.-long, heavily eroded sandstone drainage that combines with several creeks and draws. One of these, Buckwater Draw, was a traditional route through the area, and is still a hiker's route. Gradual stream gradients offer good hiking in the canyons of K Creek and Middle Creek. Bull Canyon has spectacular cliffs, one of which cuts off the hiking route. Bull Canyon is habitat for red-tailed hawk, northern harrier, golden eagle, great horned owl. The sandstone cliffs have many caves and hollows. Bull Draw has a 40-ft. waterfall—when water is flowing. Elevations from 6,000 to 8,000 ft.

Willow Creek is dominated by 1,000-ft. sandstone cliffs on the N side. Topography is much the same as the Bull Canyon site. Elevations from 5,860 to 8,115 ft. The unit has several springs and artesian wells. Much of the site is winter range for mule deer. The northern half is used by elk all year.

Skull Creek is characterized by rimrock escarpments—sharp, vertical rock cliffs. Elevations from 6,000 to 8,000 ft. No water except in numerous potholes. The entire area is winter range for mule deer.

Climate: Semiarid. Annual precipitation ranges from 10 to 30 in. Winter snow depth ranges from several inches in the canyons to several feet on mountain and ridgetops. Brief, intense summer thunderstorms. Average temperatures from 20° to 67°F with recorded extremes from −43° to 95°F. Spring and fall are the best hiking seasons.

The dry, often windy climate supports sagebrush, dense pinyon-juniper growth, grasses. Botanists have identified several plant communities. The pinyons, especially in the Skull Creek area, include some of the oldest known specimens, some more than 600 years old. A few ponderosa pine and Douglas-fir.

Birds: 83 species recorded. No checklist. All the species are included in the Dinosaur National Monument checklist; we need not repeat. Stockponds and springs above the rim attract waterfowl, including mallard, green- and blue-winged teals, gadwall, pintail. Sage grouse were also observed above the rim. Cliffs provide nesting for hawks and other birds. Observed: red-tailed hawk, golden eagle, northern harrier, great horned owl. A BLM informant described the birding in the Willow Creek-Skull Creek area as excellent.

Mammals: No checklist. Species reported include mountain lion, bobcat, coyote, badger, yellowbelly marmot, skunk, whitetail prairie dog, gray fox, desert and mountain cottontails, mule deer, pronghorn. The area includes good summer and winter mule deer range.

BLM studies of the area mention several springs, but visitors should assume that no water is available and should carry what they need.

The area has an exceptional concentration of archeological sites: granaries, petroglyphs, remains of structures, lithic scatter, campsites, etc. All are protected by law against disturbance.

HEADQUARTERS: BLM, Craig District Office, 455 Emerson St., Craig, CO 81626; (303) 824-8261.

CASTLE PEAK
U.S. Bureau of Land Management
11,940 acres.

From I-70 at Wolcott, N several mi. on SR 131. Left on dirt road labeled "Milk Creek." Follow signs to Horse Mountain.

An excellent, accessible area with many trails for hiking, backpacking, and horse travel. Topography ranges from gently rolling slopes at lower elevations to the rocky, vertical cliffs of Castle Peak, so named because of the unusual basalt formation at the tip, which resembles a castle. Elevations from 8,000 ft. to Castle Peak's 11,275 ft. Several other peaks are about 10,000 ft. elevation. The area has perennial streams and small lakes and reservoirs, with good fishing.

Dense spruce-fir forest and aspen stands cover most of the area. Occasional meadows provide seasonal wildflower displays. Wildlife is said to be abundant. The site is only about 2 airline mi. from Bull Gulch (see entry), but the intervening land is private and there is no connecting trail.

HEADQUARTERS: BLM, Grand Junction District Office, 764 Horizon Dr., Grand Junction, CO 81501; (303) 243-6552.

COLD SPRINGS MOUNTAIN
See entry, West Cold Springs.

COLORADO STATE FOREST
Colorado Division of Parks and Outdoor Recreation
72,000 acres.

From Fort Collins, 75 mi. W on SR 14.

Colorado has no State Forests. The Colorado State Forest is on land acquired in 1938 from the U.S. Forest Service. On the map it looks like an odd exchange, biting out the midsection of a portion of the Routt National Forest. Recreational use is managed by the Division of Parks and Outdoor Recreation, but the Forest is not precisely a State Park, either. This is trust land, administered for the financial benefit of the public schools, so grazing and logging are among the multiple uses. Also, hunting is permitted.

The Forest is on the W side of the Medicine Bow Range, adjoining the Rawah Wilderness Area of the Arapaho-Roosevelt National Forest at the crest. On the SE it adjoins Rocky Mountain National Park. Along the crest are several peaks above 12,000 ft., including the dramatic Nokhu Crags, which also form the N terminus of the Never Summer Range in the National Park. Several high mountain lakes. Rushing streams drop down the mountainside, flowing into the Canadian and Michigan Rivers. Lowest point is about 8,000 ft.

SR 14 crosses the S end of the Forest, near several camps and trailheads. The entrance is on the W side, with an all-weather road to other campgrounds and trailheads. 4-wheel-drive roads provide access to several sections of the Forest. Hiking trails to several lakes, and hikers can cross into the Rawah Wilderness and a roadless area of Rocky Mountain National Park.

Winter snowfall is heavy at high elevations, summers cool. Fauna and flora similar to those of the adjoining National Forests and National Park.

ACTIVITIES

Camping: 3 campgrounds, 75 sites. Reservations June 15–Sept. 16; see Colorado Preface. Also backcountry camping in designated places.

Hiking, backpacking: About 17 mi. of maintained trails within the Forest. A National Park Service backcountry permit is required for entry to Rocky Mountain National Park.

Horse riding: No local livery, but riders often use the Forest.

Hunting: State regulations. Chiefly big game.

Fishing: Trout in high-country lakes. Flies and lures only.

Boating: North Michigan Reservoir only. No wake.

Ski touring: Marked trail network.

Snowmobiling: Groomed trails.

PUBLICATION: Leaflet with map.

HEADQUARTERS: Division of Parks and Recreation, 1720 West Mulberry, #B-10, Fort Collins, CO 80521; (303) 482-2602. Local telephone: (303) 723-8366.

CROSS MOUNTAIN
U.S. Bureau of Land Management
15,520 acres.

E of Dinosaur National Monument. From US 40 E of Elk Springs, NW on Deerlodge Park Road to parking area at the Yampa River.

The Deerlodge Park Road is access to the E end of Dinosaur NM, ending at a campground and raft-launching site. It skirts the SW corner of the Cross Mountain area, at the Cross Mountain Canyon. Moffat County Road 10 is at the N boundary, Moffat County Road 25 on the W.

The site has wilderness qualities but easy access, offering opportunities for both day hiking and backpacking trips of 2 or 3 days.

Cross Mountain, the E end of the Uinta Range, is oblong, flat-topped, about 9 mi. N–S, 4 mi. W–E. It rises 2,200 ft. above the floodplain of the Yampa River on the E and the Little Snake River on the W. The E side is very steep. Pinyon-juniper covers much of the slopes, colorful rock outcrops appearing as horizontal bands on vertical cliffs. Splendid views across the Yampa River. The W side is more diverse: some gradual slopes, vertical cliffs and overhangs, side drainages and short canyons. Rock outcrops are dark red, tan, yellow, gray, in contrasting bands. Pinyon-juniper association on the upper slopes, sagebrush community below and in openings.

The main ridge is highest at the N end, 7,804 ft. Relatively flat, it has wide, grassy meadows, with pockets of mountain shrubs. Old-growth pinyon-juniper woodlands are at the N and S ends.

The Yampa River has cut through the mountain near the S end, creating a canyon 1,200 ft. deep, with vertical walls of colorful rock. The river is fast flowing, with many roaring rapids. Views into the canyon are limited from the road crossing but excellent from the N and S rims. There are four known springs in the canyon.

Archeological sites have been reported but not systematically explored. Most reports mention campsite debris, rock shelters and caves, petroglyphs. All are legally protected.

Plants: About 2,540 acres of pinyon-juniper woodland on hillsides, valleys, and slopes, forming a canopy 8–20 ft. high. Sagebrush communities cover about 700 acres on rolling hills and open meadows. Grasses on the open ridge, with fine wildflower display during the short summer.

Birds: The canyon provides nesting and roosting areas for golden eagle, red-tailed hawk, American kestrel, and turkey vulture.

Mammals: Bighorn sheep were reintroduced in 1977 and have multiplied sufficiently to permit limited hunting. Mule deer are present in moderate numbers. Elk and pronghorn populations are small. A few wild horses frequent the area.

ACTIVITIES

Hiking, backpacking: No maintained trails. BLM office can recommend routes to the mountain top, where foot travel is not difficult. Hiking the main canyon is possible during dry periods, but is hard going.

Hunting: Chiefly deer. Bighorn permits limited to perhaps 2 per year.

Fishing: Channel catfish is the most common gamefish. The canyon mouth near the parking area is a popular fishing spot.

Kayaking: This section of the Yampa can be run by kayak, but it requires high skill. Class V and VI rapids at high water. *Should not be attempted by raft.*

HEADQUARTERS: BLM, Craig District Office, 455 Emerson St., Craig, CO 81625; (303) 824-8261.

DIAMOND BREAKS
U.S. Bureau of Land Management
36,580 acres.

From CO 318 near UT border, turn S on Moffat County Road 83 across Swinging Bridge over the Green River. Site is on left, between Browns Park National Wildlife Refuge and Dinosaur National Monument. Turn S on rough dirt road to base of the Breaks. (The Swinging Bridge is narrow and has limited load capacity. OK for cars and pickups, not travel trailers and motor homes.) The better gravel road goes to Crouse Canyon in UT. (See entry in UT Zone 1, Diamond Mountain.)

This Wilderness Study Area lies between Browns Park National Wildlife Refuge and Dinosaur National Park. It adjoins the Diamond Mountain Plateau, a scenic area in UT.

The "breaks" are in Diamond Mountain, where Hoy, Davis, Chokecherry, and other creeks have carved their way down to the Green River. The steep green-clad ridges and peaks stand in sharp visual contrast to the dry sagebrush flats of Browns Park. Between the ridges are open draws, exceptionally wide at their bases, narrowing as they ascend. The draws are good hiking routes; Hoy Creek is one of the best.

Elevations from 5,384 ft. to 8,673 ft. From the summits one has splendid views of snowcapped peaks in UT's Uinta Range, the Canyon of Lodore, Cold Springs Mountain, and the Diamond Breaks.

Annual precipitation is 12–20 in., much of this received in spring and summer thunderstorms. Surface water is virtually nonexistent for most of the year; a few springs supply only trickles. Daily temperatures range from −45° to 100°F, but these are the extremes; daily mean temperatures range between 45° and 90°F. Spring and fall are the best hiking times, but summer days are not excessively hot, especially at higher elevations. Average winter snowfall is 40–70 in.

Plants: Sagebrush and pinyon-juniper are the dominant vegetative types. About 60% of the site is covered with pinyon-juniper woodlands forming canopies 8–20 ft. tall. Understory species include big sagebrush, rabbitbrush, prickly pear, western wheatgrass, squirreltail, broom snakeweed, antelope bitterbrush, Indian ricegrass, phlox, and goldenweed. In some areas, especially on the slopes of Offield Mountain, dense stands of curlleaf mountain-mahogany intermix with pinyon-juniper, an obstacle to hiking, but open parks are interspersed. Some of the moister N-facing slopes have stands of Douglas-fir.

Sagebrush communities include both big and black sagebrush. Dominant grass species include Indian ricegrass, western wheatgrass, Sandburg blue-grass, needle-and-thread, and bluebunch wheatgrass. Associates are Idaho fescue, bluegrasses, junegrass, sedges, cheatgrass, arrowleaf balsamroot, rabbitbrush, broom snakeweed. The many wildflowers include fleabane, penstemon, scarlet gilia, lupine, larkspur, hawksbeard, dandelion, phlox, mules-ears.

Birds: Bird lists are available for the two adjacent sites, Dinosaur NM and Browns Park NWR. Many of the upland species presumably occur here.

Mammals: Deer herd is recovering from a low period. About 250–350 elk use this as part of their range. Black bear and mountain lion are presumed present but seldom seen. Common small animals include coyote, ground squirrels, cottontail, jackrabbit, voles, badger, yellowbelly marmot, chipmunk, skunk, raccoon.

Hiking, backpacking: With easy access, this area has wilderness qualities, interesting terrain, fine scenery, and few visitors. Bring water.

HEADQUARTERS: BLM, Craig District Office, 455 Emerson St., Craig, CO 81625; (303) 824-8261.

DINOSAUR NATIONAL MONUMENT
National Park Service
165,351 acres in CO; 38,464 acres in UT.

Dinosaur Quarry: N from US 40 at Jensen, UT. HQ and Harpers Corner: N from US 40 at Dinosaur, CO. Several other roads, some primitive, also enter.

Most visitors spend an hour or two at the Dinosaur Quarry and travel on. Some take the Scenic Drive from Dinosaur, CO, to Harpers Corner. Only a few see the Gates of Lodore, Jones Hole, Rainbow Park, Echo Park, Deer-lodge Park, or other backcountry areas.

The Monument is about 44 mi. W–E (15 mi. in UT, 29 in CO) with a base 4 to 7 mi. N–S. At about the midpoint, an arm extends about 15 mi. N. The shape frames the principal canyons. The Green River flows from the N, is joined by the Yampa from the E, and turns W. The Monument is at the E end of Utah's Uinta Mountains. Erosion has cut deep canyons into high plateaus. Deepest of all is the Canyon of Lodore, walls rising 3,300 ft. above the Green River.

Highest point in the Monument is 9,006-ft. Zenobia Peak, a mountain reached from the E by Douglas Mountain Boulevard—odd name for a primitive fair-weather road! Average elevation is about a mile, the lowest point 4,740 ft., where the Green River exits.

Summers are hot, days occasionally above 100°F, but nights are cool. Days in winter average from 10 to 40°. Most winter nights are below freezing, and occasionally below zero. Average annual precipitation is 8–9 in. in the Quarry area, 12–15 in. in the Harpers Corner area. Most moisture falls as light snow in winter or in summer thunderstorms.

The 80 acres surrounding the dinosaur quarry were proclaimed a National Monument in 1915. In 1938 the boundaries were expanded to include the Green and Yampa River canyons. Much of the land above the canyons is wilderness with difficult access. More people see the canyons from rafts than on foot. Several large tracts of public land on the N and NW Monument boundaries are roadless and candidates for wilderness status.

Plants: Desert terrain, generally open and treeless. Sagebrush and greasewood are the dominant plants on dry rolling land. Riparian species include cottonwood, boxelder, willow, tamarisk. Pinyon pine and juniper on hillsides; at higher elevations, small stands of Douglas-fir and aspen; mountain-mahogany and serviceberry understory. When moisture and temperatures are favorable, displays of spring flowers occur from late April through early June. Prominent: yellow beeplant, desert plume, lupine, locoweed, globemallow, evening primrose, sego lily. Late summer blooms: sunflower, gumweed, rabbitbrush.

Birds: 212 species recorded. Checklist available does not identify habitats. Seasonally common or abundant species include great blue heron, Canada goose, mallard, turkey vulture, red-tailed and rough-legged hawks, golden and bald eagles, northern harrier, kestrel, blue and sage grouse, killdeer, spotted sandpiper, rock and mourning doves, great horned owl, white-throated swift, broad-tailed and black-chinned hummingbirds, northern flicker, western kingbird, ash-throated flycatcher, Say's phoebe, violet-green and cliff swallows, black-billed magpie, pinyon jay, Clark's nutcracker, plain titmouse, dipper; house, canyon, and rock wrens; American robin, mountain bluebird, blue-gray gnatcatcher. Warblers: yellow, yellow-rumped, and black-throated gray. Western meadowlark, northern oriole, Brewer's blackbird, lazuli bunting, house finch, rufous-sided towhee, dark-eyed junco. Sparrows: savannah, lark, chipping, and white-crowned.

There are two known peregrine falcon aeries in Echo Park and Yampa Canyon. Monument staff are working to reintroduce and monitor the birds.

Mammals: 66 species recorded. Checklist available. Common: mountain and desert cottontails, blacktail jackrabbit, deer mouse, bushytail woodrat, least chipmunk, golden-mantled ground squirrel, yellowbelly marmot, whitetail prairie dog, beaver, porcupine, coyote, striped skunk, mule deer.

Reptiles and amphibians: 25 species recorded. Checklist available. Common: northern plateau, northern sagebrush, northern side-blotched, northern tree, and northern whiptail lizards; desert striped whipsnake, Great Basin gopher snake, wandering garter snake. The midget faded rattlesnake, the only venomous species present, is rare.

FEATURES

Quarry Visitor Center. Following discovery of dinosaur fossils here in 1909, enough were removed to assemble 20 skeletons. No more are being removed. Visitors watch paleontologists exposing fossil bones, most of which are left in place. The preparation laboratory is also on view, as well as many exhibits. Frequent Ranger talks. In summer, visitors leave their cars at the lower parking area and travel to the Quarry by shuttle bus.

Split Mountain Gorge is 4 mi. beyond the Quarry. Colorful rock layers. Campground and boat ramp.

Josie Morris Cabin, 11 mi. beyond the Quarry, is remnant of a pioneer woman's homestead in an oasis-like setting created by a spring. Beyond the cabin is a BLM trail into Daniels Canyon, a pleasant day hike. See entry in UT Zone 1.

Harpers Corner has been called the most spectacular viewpoint in CO. From Monument HQ on US 40, Scenic Drive extends 30 mi. to the parking area, passing between BLM areas considered for wilderness status. Fine views and several turnouts along the way.

From the parking lot, a 1-mi. trail follows a knife-edge ridge to the overlook. Railings make it secure. From here one has almost a 360° view. Elevation here is about 7,500 ft. Far below is Echo Park, at the confluence of the Green and Yampa Rivers. White-throated swifts soar, catch the rising air currents and swoop close to visitors' heads.

Echo Park is at the bottom of a steep 13-mi. unpaved road that drops 2,000 ft. through Sand and Pool Creek Canyons, past Indian petroglyphs and Whispering Cave. A primitive campground is near the confluence. 4-wheel drives, some cars, but not travel trailers or motor homes, can make the trip in dry weather. When wet, the road is impassable even for 4-wheel drive. Inquire.

Gates of Lodore is at the N end of the Monument, where the Green River enters Lodore Canyon. Access from SR 318; see entry, Browns Park National Wildlife Refuge. Primitive campground; nature trail; raft ramp.

Deerlodge Park is at the E end of the Monument. Access by local road from US 40. Primitive campground. Launching for Yampa River trips. (See entry, Cross Mountain.)

Yampa Bench Road crosses the Monument from Echo Park Road, extending about 20 mi. E to the Monument boundary, then about 15 mi. SE to US 40 at Elk Springs. Rough, dusty, impassable when wet. Don't try it without consulting a Ranger.

INTERPRETATION

Visitor Center at the Quarry has exhibits, talks, literature.

Headquarters has slide program, literature, information.

Campfire programs at Split Mountain and Green River Campgrounds, from about Memorial Day to mid-Sept. Activities vary; current schedules posted in visitor centers and campgrounds.

Nature trails at Split Mountain, Lodore campground, along Harpers Corner Road; self-guiding tour leaflets.

ACTIVITIES

Camping: 2 campgrounds, 135 sites, E of the Quarry. Primitive campgrounds at Rainbow Park, Echo Park, Deerlodge Park, Lodore. Space is usually available except holiday weekends. Main campgrounds open all year, but water is turned off fall through spring because of freezing; pit toilets are used.

Hiking, backpacking: Mostly day hiking. The only regularly used backpacking area is Jones Hole. In other areas, "backcountry camping" means *on foot,* and at least one-half mile off any established road (paved or unpaved) or trail. Backcountry travel is limited by terrain and climate. Backcountry use permits are required. Backcountry camping is permitted except in designated zones. Open fires are prohibited in some areas. Hiking season May–Sept.

Horse riding: Limited by terrain. Special regulations.

Fishing: Fishing for catfish in rivers is sometimes good. Trout in Jones Creek in Utah, at N boundary near UT–CO line.

Rafting on Green and Yampa Rivers. Commercial outfitters offer trips of one to five days. List of outfitters available. Private trips require permits, and demand exceeds capacity. Day trip through Split Mountain Gorge is popular. Contact River Ranger at HQ for permit information. On the Green River, May–Sept. is most popular. On the Yampa, May–July in most years. High water of late May–early June most popular.

The Harpers Corner road is usually closed by snow Nov.–Apr. Backcountry roads above 6,000 ft. may be closed by winter snow; all backcountry roads are subject to temporary closing by thunderstorms. Such roads are allowed to reopen naturally, with little or no plowing or other work.

July brings the most visitors. Mid-June to Sept. is the busy season, Dec.–Jan. the lightest.

NEARBY (see entries)

Bull Canyon	In UT Zone 1:
Cross Mountain	Browns Park
Diamond Breaks	Daniels Canyon
	Diamond Mountain
	Stewart Lake Waterfowl Management Area

PUBLICATIONS

Leaflet with map.

Information pages on facilities, regulations, natural history, etc., are available on request. May include flora and fauna checklists.

Catalog of sales items available from Dinosaur Nature Association, P.O. Box 127, Jensen, UT 84035. Includes Harpers Corner Trail guide.

REFERENCES

Trimble, Stephen. *The Bright Edge.* Flagstaff: Museum of Northern Arizona Press, 1979.

Hayes, Philip T., and George C. Simmons. *Dinosaur National Monument and Vicinity.* Denver: Powell Society, 1983.

Evans, Laura, and Buzz Belknap. *Dinosaur River Guide.* Boulder City, NV: Westwater Books, 1983.

HEADQUARTERS: P.O. Box 210, Dinosaur, CO 81610; (303) 374-2216.

GOLDEN GATE CANYON STATE PARK
Colorado Division of Parks and Outdoor Recreation
8,787 acres.

From Golden, N 2 mi. on SR 93, then left 14 mi. on Golden Gate Canyon Rd.

Don't expect solitude here, unless perhaps midweek or out of season. Denver and Boulder are minutes away. We include the site because it's large, attractive, and designed for hikers.

In the foothills of the Front Range. From Golden to the entrance, the road climbs more than 3,200 ft. On the W side of the park are many peaks over 9,000 ft., two over 10,000. Panorama Point, in the NW corner, offers a view of nearly 100 mi. of the Continental Divide.

The Park has a network of more than 50 mi. of well-marked, maintained trails. The longest unit is 5.9 mi., but units can be combined.

INTERPRETATION

Visitor center has exhibits, information. Open all year.

Campfire talks at Reverend's Ridge campground in summer.

Camping: 2 campgrounds, 156 sites. Reservations June 1–Sept. 16; see Colorado Preface.

PUBLICATION: Leaflet with map.

HEADQUARTERS: Golden, CO 80403; (303) 592-1502. Camping information (summer): (303) 642-3856.

HACK LAKE
U.S. Bureau of Land Management
3,360 acres.

From Dotsero on I-70, N 7 mi. along the Colorado River, then NW on all-weather road along Sweetwater Creek. In about 9 mi., enter White River NF. A trail from Sweetwater Lake, near the boundary, crosses the unit.

A small site within a much larger area of interest. The White River NF is on the W and N boundaries. The Forest map shows the area and access routes. On the N, the site adjoins the Flat Tops Wilderness Area; the W Mountain Trail into the Wilderness crosses the site. Adjoining on the E is the Dotsero State Wildlife Area, 2,510 acres, maintained for big-game hunting.

Hack Lake is a small pond in a very scenic setting. The site contains rolling hills, cliffs, and steep terrain. Elevations range from 7,600 ft. in the SW corner to 11,034 ft. in the NW corner. Two peaks within the site are about 10,000 ft., several others in the 9,000-ft. range.

The N half of the site has dense spruce-fir forest intermixed with aspen stands. Oak, pinyon-juniper, and sagebrush predominate in the lower and drier S half. Abundant water. Diverse wildlife.

HEADQUARTERS: BLM, Grand Junction District Office, 764 Horizon Drive, Grand Junction, CO 81501; (303) 243-6552.

HOT SULPHUR STATE WILDLIFE AREA
Colorado Division of Wildlife
1,172 acres.

From Hot Sulphur Springs, 2 mi. W on US 40.

For most of the distance from Granby to Kremmling, US 40 runs beside or near the Colorado River. W of Hot Sulphur Springs, it runs through steep-sided Byers Canyon. From the highway, a short dirt road leads to a primitive camping area beside the river. Latrines, trash barrels. About a dozen sites, none marked. We were alone that night except for one man who seemed to be living there in a tiny, ancient travel trailer. A pleasant, quiet overnight stop.

Along the river are numerous pullouts where one can stop to fish or park overnight.

IRISH CANYON
U.S. Bureau of Land Management
14,400 acres.

From Maybell on US 40: 41 mi. W on SR 318; 4 mi. N on County Road 10N.

CR 10N is a good gravel road through rolling grasslands. Ahead we saw rock bluffs, hillsides with scattered pinyon-juniper. At 4.5 mi. from SR 318 the road enters Irish Canyon. We immediately rated it 10 for dramatic scenery. Not more than 50 yards wide, steep walls with layers of red, green, and gray. Colorado's Natural Areas Inventory also called the area "highly scenic."

Near the canyon entrance is an interpretive exhibit, a short walk past Indian petroglyphs. It's easy to miss. We also missed the campground in the canyon but found it on the way back: three simple sites in a grove of mature pinyon pines. Here the canyon was somewhat wider, cream-colored walls forming an amphitheater. Behind us was an inviting side canyon. Driving out from Maybell, we had passed two or three cars. As we cooked dinner in Irish Canyon, two cars passed, heading toward Wyoming. We heard no others that night.

The canyon was cut into Limestone Ridge. Public land on both sides is administered by BLM. 6,600 roadless acres on the E side and 8,740 acres on the W side were inventoried for possible wilderness consideration. Although this site was not recommended, it may be designated an Area of Critical Environmental Concern because of its special botanical, geologic, scenic, and aquatic features. The area includes five different plant communities, a cross section of mid-elevation Uinta Mountain types, with several rare species. The canyon exposes an exceptional array of geological formations. Near the N end of the canyon are the Irish Lakes, two natural intermittent ponds.

Elevations range from 6,100 ft. to 8,636 ft. Annual precipitation is 10–15 in., average winter snowfall 40–60 in. Summers are hot and dry, with cool nights.

An unusual feature is a divide within the canyon. The high point of the canyon floor is near the N end, so drainage is to both N and S.

Some local outdoorsmen sing the praises of Vermillion Creek, a small but picturesque and isolated canyon E of Irish Canyon with interesting petroglyphs. The map indicates access by turning SE just N of Irish Canyon, continuing about 5 mi. to the creek.

Also in the area: the Vermillion Badlands, very colorful, highly eroded soils and formations along Dry Creek and Vermillion Creek E of Irish Canyon.

A wild horse herd frequents Sand Wash Basin.

ACTIVITIES

Camping: 3 primitive sites. No water.

Hunting: Deer, pronghorn, cottontail, chukar, dove.

HEADQUARTERS: BLM, Craig District Office, 455 Emerson St., Craig, CO 81625; (303) 824-8261.

LITTLE YAMPA CANYON
U.S. Bureau of Land Management
17,000 acres.

Principal access is by boat. Land access by 4-wheel drive: US 40 W from Craig to Lay. County Road 17 S to Duffy Mountain access road, signed. Then jeep track.

The Yampa River, originating near Yampa, flows N to Steamboat, then W past Craig and Maybell into Dinosaur National Monument, where it joins the Green River. Until it passes Craig, the river crosses no public lands, federal or state. From Craig to the National Monument, the bordering lands are a mixture of private ownerships and public domain.

This entry concerns a 53-mi. section of the river from just below Craig to County Road 17 S of Lay, on US 40. About 20 mi. of this distance is within Little Yampa Canyon. Here the river follows a sinuous course through an alternation of valleys and canyons. The river flow here is relatively smooth, no great rapids. It has been described as an ideal run for instructing novices, people unfamiliar with rivers, suitable for open canoes as well as rafts and kayaks. This portion of the river is a candidate for inclusion in the Wild and Scenic Rivers system, but no study has begun and supporters doubt that it will ever be made.

Portions of the surrounding area, outside the canyon and public land, are no longer pristine. A description of one section: "This long valley is wholly private. Ranches, auto bodies, hawks, and perhaps an osprey may be seen." More often on view is open, arid, sagebrush country. The canyon is largely untouched, and it may be declared an Outstanding Natural Area unless dam builders prevail. The proposed Juniper-Cross Mountain hydroelectric project would inundate the canyon.

The canyon walls are a pocked buff sandstone. Interesting, sometimes colorful rock outcrops. Stands of cottonwood and boxelder are scattered along the river bottom and on some islands. Along the run are many good primitive campsites.

Nests of raptors and cliff swallows are numerous. Often seen: golden and bald eagles, turkey vulture, osprey, mallard, merganser, Canada goose; mammals include elk, deer, beaver, pronghorn.

Elevations range from 6,050 ft. to 7,000 ft. Annual precipitation is about 12 in., including 50–60 in. of winter snow. June–Sept. is the dry season.

River flow depends on snowmelt. Best floating season is May 1–July 15. In a good year, canoes and kayaks can scrape through as late as Nov. 1.

ACTIVITIES

Hiking: No established trails, but hiking is feasible.

Hunting: Deer, elk, small game.

Fishing: Channel catfish, rainbow and brown trout, mountain whitefish. *Several endangered species inhabit the river, and penalties for taking them are severe.*

Boating: The following reference describes the boating conditions in detail. However, several important changes have been or soon may be made in put-in and take-out sites. Check the BLM office.

Swimming: Some visitors enjoy tubing portions of the river.

REFERENCE: Perry, Earl. *Rivers of Colorado: Ten Easy River Trips in the Mountains, Canyons, and Plains of Colorado.* pp. 11–17. Lorton, VA: American Canoe Association, 1983.

HEADQUARTERS: BLM, Craig District Office, 455 Emerson St., Craig, CO 81625; (303) 824-8261.

MOUNT EVANS STATE WILDLIFE AREA

Colorado Division of Wildlife
4,846 acres.

From El Rancho on I-70, S on SR 74 to Evergreen. Right on Brookvale Rd., N shore of lake, about 8 mi. Look for sign at fork.

Mt. Evans is about 5 mi. W. We don't know why the site carries the name. The Colorado Division of Wildlife has no site map available. The area is well shown on the Arapaho National Forest map. The site adjoins the Forest and trails lead into the Forest. Trails lead to the lower slopes of Mt. Evans, but none is shown leading up.

The site is scenic and hilly; elevation about 8,500 ft. Well forested with ponderosa pine, spruce, Douglas-fir, groves of aspen. Many wildflowers. We noted aster, fireweed, Indian paintbrush, scarlet gilia, Queen Anne's lace, bluebell, monarda, wild rose, thistle, toadflax.

The entrance road leads to a parking area. Visitors told us that most people come here to fish, others to hike or backpack. One hike is a 5-mi. trail to Camp Rock at the edge of the National Forest. In season, big game hunting.

Closed to visitors Jan. 1–June 15, for elk reproduction.
Dogs are prohibited.

HEADQUARTERS: Division of Wildlife, 6060 Broadway, Denver, CO 80216; (303) 297-1192.

NORTH PARK STATE WILDLIFE AREAS
Colorado Division of Wildlife
3,099 acres.

From S of Walden on SR 125 and 14, W on County Road 12.

In North Park, a high mountain valley, the Colorado Division of Wildlife owns and manages several lakes and has easements on 39 mi. of streams and rivers. The 10-mi. drive out to Delaney Butte Lakes is well worth while, especially when combined with a visit to the nearby Arapaho National Wildlife Refuge (see entry). 0.3 mi. from the turnoff, the county road passes the S end of the Walden reservoir. In late August we saw numerous broods of ducklings. Further along were pools of casual water, with avocets and phalaropes.

The three Delaney Butte lakes are in a scenic setting, the buttes rising sharply to the W, mountains with patches of snow on the W and N. We saw a few fishermen, half a dozen RV's, one canoe. No launching ramp, but the shore is such that none is needed. Power boats are permitted. Informal camping almost anywhere. Good birding.

If you're a fisherman, continuing 5 mi. further to Lake John may be worthwhile. According to the Division of Wildlife, the lake is well known for its large rainbows, Snake River cutthroats, and brown trout. Otherwise, don't bother. Much of the shoreline is privately owned, and a trashy trailer camp and marina spoils the view.

Streams in the area are said to provide excellent trout fishing, flies or lures. There is no stocking.

HEADQUARTERS: Division of Wildlife, 6060 Broadway, Denver, CO 80216; (303) 297-1192.

OAK RIDGE STATE WILDLIFE AREA
Colorado Division of Wildlife
8,000 acres.

From Craig, S on SR 13 to Meeker, then 13 mi. SE on SR 132.

The site is on the White River. 260-acre Lake Avery is within the site, close to the highway. Several parcels of BLM land are within or adjacent to the DW land. The White River National Forest is 1 mi. N. A trail follows Big Beaver Creek from the N tip of the lake into the Forest. Elevations range from 6,500 ft. at the river to 8,000 ft. Terrain is gently rolling to hilly. Climate is semiarid. Sparse vegetation, hills dotted with pinyon-juniper.

The area is prime elk and deer range. Other mammals present: black bear, yellowbelly marmot, porcupine, cottontail.

Most visitors are hunters in season, fishermen at any time. Outside of hunting season the area away from the lake and in the nearby Forest offers opportunities for quiet hiking.

ACTIVITIES
Camping: Primitive facilities at Lake Avery. Also at end of a short access road from SR 132 about 2 mi. E of the lake, and from County Road 6 on the N side.

Hunting: Deer, elk, bear, blue grouse, dove, band-tailed pigeon, cottontail.

Fishing: Lake and White River. Rainbow, brook, and cutthroat trout.

HEADQUARTERS: Division of Wildlife, 6060 Broadway, Denver, CO 80216; (303) 297-1192.

RIFLE GAP AND FALLS STATE RECREATION AREA
Colorado Division of Parks and Outdoor Recreation
2,185 land acres; 350 acres of water.

From I-70 at Rifle, N 10 mi. on SR 325.

Standing alone, this park would not be one of our entries, but it is largely surrounded by BLM-administered public domain, and the White River National Forest is nearby. SR 325 along East Rifle Creek leads into a Forest area with numerous foot trails and 4-wheel-drive routes. Hunters often use this SRA as a base camp. Elevation is 6,000 ft.

The SRA has two parts. The reservoir is in the larger portion, with campgrounds, boat ramp, and a captive bison herd. The Rifle Falls area, 3 mi. N on SR 325, has a triple waterfall where the waters of East Rifle Creek drop over a wide travertine dam. The spray creates a lush plant community of mosses, ferns, and wildflowers in an otherwise dry setting. There are several caves, safe enough to explore with a flashlight. Evening programs are offered in summer in the largest cave. The Falls area also has a nature trail.

ACTIVITIES
Camping: 70 sites. Reservations; see Preface.
Hiking, hunting: On adjacent and nearby public lands.
Fishing: Rainbow and German brown trout, walleye, smallmouth bass.

PUBLICATION: Leaflet with map.

HEADQUARTERS: Rifle, CO 81650; (303) 625-1607.

ROCKY MOUNTAIN NATIONAL PARK
National Park Service
266,957 acres.

NW of Boulder. Crossed by US 34.

One of America's most glorious National Parks, on the Front Range of the Rocky Mountains. Lying across the Continental Divide, the Park contains some of America's highest terrain. The valleys are at about 8,000 ft. elevation. 107 named peaks are higher than 12,000 ft. Three miles of the Trail Ridge Road are above 12,000 ft.

Estes Park (which is a town, not a park), the E gateway, is at 7,522 ft. Seen from the E, the Front Range rises steeply, dramatically, to snow-capped peaks. The Park's highest mountain, 14,265-ft. Long's Peak, is near the E boundary. Slopes on the E side of the Park are generally steep, with some sheer drops of up to 3,000 ft. W of the Divide, gradients are gentler.

The Park's magnificence and accessibility have attracted crowds. When the Park was dedicated in 1915, or even when the Trail Ridge Road was opened in 1932, planners could not foresee how many people would come. No major park would be so designed today: a single artery, one of the world's most scenic routes, carrying all traffic across the Park. For the best of reasons, every visitor wants to drive the Trail Ridge Road, most of them in both directions.

On our most recent visit, traffic was heavy. Parking spaces weren't to be had at most overlooks. Campgrounds had been full since early morning. We had no choice but to drive on.

As is true in other National Parks, however, the crowds are concentrated in a relatively small part of the area. Most of the Park is roadless, with splendid foot trails. Nor need one fight traffic to reach a trailhead. More than two dozen trailheads and links with the trail systems of adjoining National Forests are distributed around the perimeter. One can enter and enjoy the Park without ever seeing an automobile.

The Rocky Mountains are considered a young range, the last uplift having ended only 5 to 7 million years ago. Since then, winding V-shaped canyons have been cut by stream action, cirque basins and broad U-shaped valleys by glaciers. Glaciers also scooped the depressions, which became chains of lakes linked by streams, and glaciers deposited the masses of assorted rock debris called *moraines.* The product is a richly varied landscape: cliffs, gorges, waterfalls and cascades, green valleys with meandering streams, tree-clad slopes.

Climate: Variable. Shirtsleeve weather may prevail in E valleys while snow is falling in the high country.

Dec.–Mar.: The lower E slope seldom has deep snow. Arctic conditions prevail above: high winds, sudden blizzards, temperatures sometimes below −35°F.

Apr.–May: A short spring. Flowers bloom at lower elevations late Apr.–early May. Trails are snow-covered through Apr. at mid-elevations, through May in the high country.

Trail Ridge Road opens in late May. It is closed at night.

June–Aug.: Tundra flowers begin blooming late June–early July. Afternoon thunderstorms are common.

Sept.–Nov.: Cool, crisp air; mostly dry weather. Aspen leaves begin changing color mid-Sept. Early snow not uncommon. Trail Ridge Road closes some time in Oct.

Plants: At lower elevations, climate is relatively warm and dry. Here ponderosa pine and juniper are prominent on S-facing slopes, mixing with Douglas-fir on cooler N slopes. Blue spruce, cottonwood, and willow are among the streamside species. Here and there are dense stands of lodgepole pine and groves of aspen, which turn yellow in the fall. Wildflowers such as American pasqueflower, Rocky Mountain iris, wallflower, and penstemon bloom in meadows and glades. Over 9,000 ft., forest species are Engelmann spruce, subalpine fir, and limber pine, with quaking aspen beginning the tree succession in forest openings.

Above the timberline is the tundra community. In few other places can the visitor see as much of this picturesque plant zone without walking far from his car. For 18 mi., the Trail Ridge Road is within this world of miniature plants. About half of the species found here also occur in the Arctic, where the climate is similar. Here the growing season is short: 6 to 12 weeks. The plant community includes grasses, sedges, herbs, dwarfed shrubs. Tundra plants are low, compact, often with showy flowers. Flowering species include alpine avens, alpine forget-me-not, rydbergia, greenleaf mertensia, mountain harebell, Arctic gentian, alpine primrose, western yellow paintbrush, alpine anemone, moss campion, alpine phlox, yellow stonecrop, glacier lily.

Birds: Checklist of 256 species available. Most species are migrants or seasonal residents. 94 are considered rare or accidental. Common or abundant: common loon; eared, western, and pied-billed grebe; great blue heron, white-faced ibis, Canada goose, mallard, gadwall, northern pintail; green-winged, blue-winged, and cinnamon teals; American wigeon, northern shoveler, redhead, canvasback, lesser scaup, common and Barrow's goldeneyes, bufflehead, ruddy duck, common merganser, turkey vulture. Hawks: goshawk, sharp-shinned, Cooper's, red-tailed, Swainson's, rough-legged, ferruginous. Golden and bald eagles, northern harrier, osprey, prairie falcon. Blue grouse, white-tailed ptarmigan, American coot, killdeer, common snipe, spotted sandpiper, willet, greater and lesser yellowlegs, Baird's sandpiper, Wilson's phalarope. Gulls: herring, California, ring-billed, Franklin's; Forster's tern. Band-tailed pigeon, rock and mourning doves, screech and saw-whet owls, poor-will, common nighthawk, white-throated swift, broad-tailed and rufous hummingbirds, belted kingfisher. Woodpeckers: northern flicker, red-headed, Lewis', yellow-bellied and Williamson's sapsuckers, hairy, downy, northern three-toed. Flycatchers: eastern and western kingbirds, Say's phoebe, willow, Hammond's, dusky, western, olive-sided, western wood-pewee. Horned lark. Swallows: violet-green, tree, rough-winged, barn, cliff. Gray, Steller's, and pinyon jays; black-billed magpie, common raven, American crow, Clark's nutcracker. Black-capped and mountain chickadees; white-breasted, red-breasted, and pygmy nuthatches; brown creeper, dipper. House, canyon, and rock wrens; brown thrasher, American robin, hermit and Swainson's thrushes, western and mountain bluebirds, Townsend's solitaire, golden-crowned and ruby-crowned kinglets, water pipit, Bohemian and cedar waxwings, northern and loggerhead shrikes, European starling, solitary and warbling vireos. Warblers: orange-crowned, Virginia's, yellow, yellow-rumped, Townsend's, MacGillivray's, Wilson's. House sparrow, western meadowlark, red-winged and Brewer's blackbirds, northern oriole, brown-headed cowbird. Also black-headed, evening, and pine grosbeaks; lazuli bunting, Cassin's and house finches; gray-crowned, black, and brown-capped rosy finches; common redpoll, pine siskin, American goldfinch, red crossbill, green-tailed towhee. Sparrows: savannah, vesper, lark, tree, chipping, clay-colored, Brewer's, white-crowned, Lincoln's, song; dark-eyed and gray-headed juncos.

Mammals: The checklist covers the Park and Shadow Mountain Recreation Area. The mammals mentioned include numerous species of shrew, vole, and bat; pika, cottontail, snowshoe hare, whitetail jackrabbit, several chipmunks and ground squirrels, yellowbelly marmot, beaver, bushytail woodrat, muskrat, porcupine, coyote, gray wolf, red and gray foxes, black bear, ringtail, raccoon, marten, longtail and shorttail weasels, mink, wolverine, badger, spotted and striped skunks, river otter, mountain lion, lynx, bobcat, elk, mule deer, pronghorn, bighorn sheep, and bison.

FEATURES

Bear Lake is at the end of a paved spur road, at 9,475 ft. elevation. It's a scenic gem that attracts crowds, more cars than can park. From late June through Labor Day, visitors can ride a shuttle bus. A 1/2-mi. nature trail circles the lake. Trail connections for backcountry areas.

Fall River Road, part of the original route across the mountains, is open from Horseshoe Park Junction to Fall River Pass, at the Alpine Visitor Center. Gravel, one-way westbound; pull trailers and motor homes over 25 ft. long prohibited.

Longs Peak attracts many hikers. From SR 7, about 9 mi. S of Estes Park, a short spur road enters the Park, ending at the Longs Peak campground, Ranger Station, and trailhead. A hiking route is feasible without climbing equipment during July, Aug., most of Sept., snow conditions permitting. Otherwise, and on all other routes, winter climbing conditions prevail. Hiking route requires 12–15 hrs. round trip. Hikers should be prepared for sudden, drastic weather changes. Many other destinations can be reached from this trailhead; 2 1/2-mi. hike to tundra.

INTERPRETATION

Visitor centers near the Beaver Meadows entrance on US 36 and at the top of the Trail Ridge Road. Exhibits, films, literature.

Information at entrance stations, Park HQ on US 36 near Estes Park, Ranger Stations.

Campfire programs and *guided hikes* in summer. Printed schedules available at visitor centers, Ranger Stations, campgrounds; posted on bulletin boards.

ACTIVITIES

Camping: In 1984, 4 campgrounds, 580 sites. Moraine Park and Glacier

Basin campgrounds, with 445 sites, require reservations June 30–Aug. 18. Reservations by mail from Ticketron, P.O. Box 2715, San Francisco, CA 94126–2715. These campgrounds open in mid-June. Two others are open all year.

Hiking, backpacking: More than 355 mi. of trails, offering short, easy walks and challenging backcountry treks. Backcountry permit is required for overnight trips. Excellent trail guides are available. Rangers can provide lists of heavily used and lightly used trails. *Handicamp* is a backcountry camping area planned for the disabled, with wheelchair access; call (303) 586-2371 for details.

Horse riding: Because of heavy use, horses are restricted to designated trails. One livery concession offering day rides and pack trips is inside the Park, others nearby.

Fishing: Prohibited in Bear Lake; some other waters may be closed. Many lakes and streams offer trout fishing. State license, regulations.

Boating: Prohibited on Bear Lake. Trail access only to other lakes. Streams are rocky, shallow.

Skiing: Ski area concession at Ski Estes Park at Hidden Valley, 10 mi. W of Estes Park, off the Trail Ridge Road. Snow permitting, from mid-Dec. to mid-Apr.

Ski touring: In the lower valleys, in winter. Snow conditions are poor spring and fall.

Snowmobiling: Prohibited on the E side of the Park. Permitted on Trail Ridge Road to Poudre Lake on W side, snow permitting; registration required. Prohibited elsewhere.

ADJACENT

The Arapaho and Roosevelt National Forests surround the Park. The Routt National Forest adjoins the Park at the NW corner. The Shadow Mountain National Recreation Area, administered by the Arapaho and Roosevelt National Forests, adjoins at the SW corner. Several wilderness areas in these Forests are linked to the Park by trails.

PUBLICATIONS

Park brochure with map. $.50.
Information pages:
General information.
Weather information.
Geology.
Trees.
Seeing Wildlife.
Camping.
Hiking (regulations, trails, etc.).
Hiking in the Longs Peak area.
Longs Peak information.

Off-season information.
Hidden Valley Winter Sports Area.
Bicycling.
Rules about pets.
Bird checklist.
Tundra World. Leaflet.
High Country Stables (concession).
Bear Lake Nature Trail pamphlet.
Publications list.

REFERENCES

Dannen, Kent and Donna. *Rocky Mountain National Park Hiking Trails.* Charlotte, NC: Eastwoods Press, 1982.

Dannen, Kent and Donna. *Walks with Nature in Rocky Mountain National Park.* Charlotte, NC: Eastwoods Press, 1980.

Nilsson, Erik. *Rocky Mountain National Park Trail Guide.* Mountain View, CA: World Publications, 1978.

Collister, Allegra. *Birds of Rocky Mountain Park.* Denver: Denver Museum of Natural History.

Radlauer, Ruth S. *Rocky Mountain National Park.* Chicago: Children's Press, 1977.

Kenofer, Louis. *Rocky Mountain Trails.* Boulder, CO: Pruett, 1980.

HEADQUARTERS: Estes Park, CO 80517; (303) 586-2371.

ROUTT NATIONAL FOREST
U.S. Forest Service
1,127,164 acres; 1,248,187 acres within boundaries.

Three blocks of land. (A) The largest, shaped like an inverted L, extends 68 mi. S from the Wyoming border. It is crossed by US 40 at Rabbit Ears Pass. (B) To the W is a block with no paved road. Access by secondary roads from SR 131 on the E and SR 789 on the W. Together with a portion of the White River National Forest, it forms a large block N of Glenwood Springs. (C) Shaped like a J, the third block extends S from the Wyoming border. The Arapaho and Roosevelt National Forests are on its E and S boundaries. It is crossed by SR 14.

The Routt National Forest straddles the Continental Divide. In the W portion of Block A is the Elkhead Range. Its N–S spine is the Park Range and its S extension, the Gore Range. The Divide runs down the crest of the Park Range to just S of Rabbit Ears Pass, then turns E along the Rabbit Ears Range. The Mt. Zirkel Wilderness is in the N half of this block. On the E side of the S half is the Middle Park Ranger District, part of the Arapaho and Roosevelt National Forests but administered by the Routt.

Block B includes the Flat Tops Wilderness Area, a series of high-elevation plateaus.

The 28-mi. mid-section of Block C is the 71,000-acre Colorado State Forest (see entry). Boundary on the E is the Medicine Bow Range. Boundary of the S portion is the Continental Divide, on the crest of the Rabbit Ears Range. The Arapaho and Roosevelt National Forests are on the other side.

The Forest is within a 3- or 4-hour drive of Denver and other population centers along the Front Range—more than 1.5 million people, with numbers increasing rapidly. A majority of Forest visitors are Colorado residents. Thus the heaviest use is on weekends and holidays; campgrounds at popular locations are at capacity.

Steamboat Springs, where Forest HQ is located, 160 mi. from Denver, is one of several booming resort communities. Here city sales tax revenues leaped by 500% in 10 years, while building construction increased by more than 1700%. Downhill skiing is a major attraction, but visitors come at all seasons.

In responding to our inquiry, the Forest supervisor's office listed Forest visitor activities in this order of popularity: downhill skiing, camping, hunting, fishing, backpacking, snowmobiling, horse riding, ski touring, and rafting.

Perhaps because of weekend crowding, backcountry visits are increasing more rapidly than use of developed campgrounds. Perhaps for the same reason, Forest records show that visits are becoming longer; people spend weekends or vacations in one area rather than traveling about.

We have been in the Routt at several seasons, including the Fourth of July, and were always able to find quiet trails and campgrounds. Forest Rangers encourage dispersal to relieve pressure on crowded sites.

Like other National Forests in Colorado, the Routt has a *Recreation Opportunity Guide (ROG)*. This huge looseleaf book is available in all Visitor Centers and Ranger District offices. Well organized and indexed, it has a tremendous stock of information, from Forest history to detailed descriptions of trails. It tells where the crowds are, and where they aren't. Each of the offices we visited had the *ROG*'s of other National Forests in Colorado.

All three blocks are mountainous, with numerous peaks and ridges over 10,000 ft. Habitats range from sagebrush-grass on the rolling foothills, to dense timber, to alpine tundra. Highly productive watersheds, trout streams, alpine lakes. The North Platte and Yampa Rivers originate in the Forest.

While annual precipitation varies greatly with altitude, average for the Forest is about 15–20 in. Annual snowfall on the mountains is between 275 and 325 in.

Plants: Sagebrush-grass and oakbrush predominate at lowest elevations. Intermediate elevation vegetation types include aspen, lodgepole pine, spruce-fir. Above timberline, alpine tundra.

Extensive fires affected vegetation patterns until fire suppression became effective. Since then, harvesting of lodgepole pine and Engelmann spruce has cleared large blocks. Quaking aspen and lodgepole pine are the first tree species to grow after disturbances. Other common tree species include Douglas-fir, subalpine fir, cottonwood. Despite logging, 70% of the timber stands are classed as old growth.

Common shrubs include mountain maple, alder, serviceberry, bearberry, rhododendron, Oregon grape, thimbleberry, mountain-mahogany, elderberry, chokecherry, raspberry, mountain ash, rabbitbrush, bitterbrush, elder, huckleberry.

Wildflowers include yarrow, pussytoes, heartleaf arnica, columbine, aster, locoweed, sego lily, marsh marigold, bellflower, harebell, Indian paintbrush, fireweed, pipsissewa, aster, clematis, stonecrop, larkspur, fleabane, Coulter's daisy, dogtooth violet, gentian, wild geranium, scarlet gilia, white bog-orchid, sneezeweed, sunflower, Rocky Mountain iris, evening primrose, wild flax, twinflower, lupine, bluebell, monkeyflower, penstemon, phlox, cinquefoil, pasqueflower, coneflower, saxifrage, globemallow, wakerobin, globeflower, false Solomon's-seal, elephanthead, violets, death camas, balsamroot.

Birds: Checklist of 221 species notes seasonality but not abundance. The *ROG* lists bird species by habitats. Those in *coniferous forest* include mountain chickadee, white-breasted nuthatch, yellow-rumped warbler, pine siskin, broad-tailed and rufous hummingbirds, northern flicker, violet-green and tree swallows, black-billed magpie, gray-headed junco, house wren, American robin, evening and pine grosbeaks, red crossbill, western wood-pewee, Clark's nutcracker, pygmy nuthatch, gray and Steller's jays, western goshawk, ruby-crowned kinglet, white-crowned sparrow, western tanager, hermit thrush, olive-sided flycatcher. In *deciduous forest:* western tanager, black-capped chickadee, American robin, mountain bluebird, western wood-pewee, violet-green swallow, black-headed grosbeak, white-breasted nuthatch, hermit thrush, yellow-rumped warbler, western goshawk, yellow-bellied sapsucker. *Mountain meadows:* American robin, yellow-rumped warbler, Lincoln's sparrow, western bluebird, water pipit. *Streams and rivers:* white-crowned, Lincoln's, and chipping sparrows; red-winged blackbird, dipper, dark-eyed junco. *Mountain lakes:* eared grebe, American coot, lesser loon, mallard. *Alpine transition:* Lincoln's and white-crowned sparrows, gray-headed junco, pine grosbeak. *Tundra:* white-tailed ptarmigan, brown-capped rosy finch, Clark's nutcracker, broad-tailed and rufous hummingbirds, water pipit, horned lark. *Soaring:* golden eagle, red-tailed hawk, turkey vulture.

The California Park area has the largest nesting flock of sandhill crane in Colorado. Big Creek Lakes are fishing grounds for osprey, rare in the state.

Mammals: Recorded species list (no indication of habitat or abundance). Includes mule deer, whitetail deer, elk, bighorn sheep, pronghorn, mountain lion, bobcat, black bear; red, gray, and kit foxes; cottontail, snowshoe hare, whitetail jackrabbit, red and fox squirrels; golden-mantled, Richardson's, and thirteen-lined ground squirrels; chipmunk, beaver, pika, porcupine, muskrat, bushytail woodrat, whitetail prairie dog, yellowbelly marmot, mink, pine marten, longtail weasel, spotted and striped skunks, badger, raccoon, ringtail, coyote.

Moose were reintroduced in 1978, and numbers are increasing. One place to look for them is on Snyder Creek Road (Forest Road 755), off SR 125, just N of the Continental Divide, here the boundary with the Arapaho and Roosevelt NF.

FEATURES

Flat Tops Wilderness, 38,870 acres on the Routt NF, 196,360 acres on the White River NF. In Block B, about 30 mi. SW of Steamboat Springs. Flat-topped headlands dominated by the White River Plateau, a flattened dome capped with lava. Wide canyons cut deeply into the plateau forming great amphitheaters ringed by rock escarpments. Above the cliffs is gently rolling grassland with islands of timber. Elevations about 10,000 ft.

In the 1940s, 68,000 acres of spruce were devastated by spruce bark beetle. New trees are growing, but fallen dead trees make some areas nearly impassable. About 1,690 mi. of trails cross the Wilderness, but off-trail hiking is encouraged for the experienced. Abundant wildlife. About 20,000 elk summer in the area. Eighty lakes and about half of the area's 100 mi. of streams offer good trout fishing.

Season: Usually from early July through Oct., occasionally early Nov. Snow persists until late June; many snowbanks remain all summer. Cool temperatures; frost most evenings.

Never Summer Wilderness. 6,659 acres in Routt NF, 7,043 acres in Arapaho and Roosevelt NF. On the Continental Divide W of Rocky Mountain National Park, just S of Cameron Pass. 17 peaks over 12,000 ft.; highest is Howard Mountain, 12,810 ft. Four lakes, several streams with trout.

Usual season: early July through mid-Oct. Weather is unpredictable. Severe summer thunderstorms. Snow any time. Trails include one along the Continental Divide, above timberline, steep and rocky, spectacular views.

Mount Zirkel Wilderness. 140,972 acres. On the Continental Divide in the Park Range. 15 peaks near 12,000 ft. Mt. Zirkel elevation is 12,180 ft. More than 75 lakes, 40 of them named. Many streams flowing to the North Platte and Yampa Rivers. Excellent fishing. Rich wildlife includes elk, mule deer, black bear, fox, coyote, marmot, blue grouse, ptarmigan. Occasional bighorn sheep.

Usual season: early July through mid-Oct. Many snowbanks remain all summer. Temperatures cold; frost most evenings. 200 mi. of trails. This is the most popular wilderness area in the Routt. Wilderness permits are not yet required, but hikers should register at the boundary. Because of ecological damage, camping is now prohibited within 100 to 600 ft. of lake shores and stream banks.

One area to avoid on weekends is the Slavonia Trailhead, N of Steamboat Springs. This is the most popular trailhead for the Mount Zirkel Wilderness for backpackers and day hikers.

Fish Creek Falls, E of Steamboat Springs on Forest Road 320 is just outside the Forest boundary. Over 200 ft. high, dropping into a small canyon. Most spectacular during the runoff in July. Footbridge near the base of the falls. Beyond are several Forest trails.

INTERPRETATION

Exhibits at Forest HQ.

Information, literature at HQ and Ranger District offices.

No campfire programs, guided hikes, other naturalist programs.

ACTIVITIES

Camping: 23 campgrounds, 327 sites. (One other campground has been closed.) Usual season June 15–Nov. 15. Busy season: July 1–Labor Day; water is shut off before and after this period. Closing depends on snow or mud conditions.

Hiking, backpacking: 635 mi. of trails. The ROG has descriptions of many trails: length, elevation, route, terrain, season, description. It also tells which trails are heavily and lightly used.

Horse riding: Day rides and horse packing are both popular. Many trails are suitable. The *ROG* describes a number of recommended trails and lists stables, guides, and outfitters.

Hunting: The Forest has good populations of game birds and mammals. A majority of hunters are Colorado residents who are familiar with Forest roads and trails. Newcomers should consult Rangers or consider using a guide.

Fishing: Excellent trout fishing in numerous mountain lakes and streams. Spring runoff begins in May, continues through June; the *ROG* advises waiting until water is calmer and less dangerous. The *ROG* describes some of the best fishing waters, with access routes.

Boating: No lakes suitable for power boating. Only a few accessible by road are large enough to make a canoe or cartopper worthwhile.

Rafting: In Northgate Canyon of the North Platte River, extending into Wyoming. Average season June 3–July 1, but great year-to-year variation. Hazardous waters; limited access. Daily flow information from North Park Ranger District.

Ski touring: Popular and becoming more so. The ROG has much information and advice on where to go, how to get there, equipment required, waxing techniques, avalanches, and other hazards. ("Always be prepared for an overnight trip.")

Downhill skiing provided the growth impetus for Steamboat Springs and other resorts. The only ski area is partially on Forest land. It accounts for almost one-fourth of all Forest visits. Two-thirds of the skiers are from out of state.

Snowmobiling is increasingly popular. Much of the Forest is open to snowmobiles without restriction. Some areas, such as the Wildernesses, are closed; in some areas snowmobiles are restricted to Forest roads (the Travel Map shows where). The *ROG* describes some of the popular snowmobiling areas. Occasional conflicts with skiers.

PUBLICATIONS

Forest map. $1.00.
Travel map.
Checklists:
Flora: trees, shrubs, grasses, forbs.
Birds.
Mammals.
Fishes.
List of campgrounds.
Flat Tops Wilderness leaflet with map.
Zirkel Wilderness, folder with map.

HEADQUARTERS: 137 10th St., Box 774438, Steamboat Springs, CO 80477; (303) 879-1722.

RANGER DISTRICTS: Bears Ears R.D., 356 Ranney St., Craig, CO 81625; (303) 824-9438. Hahns Peak R.D., 57 10th St., Box 1212, Steamboat Springs, CO 80477; (303) 879-1870. Middle Park R.D., 210 S. 6th St., Box 278, Kremmling, CO 80459; (303) 724-3244. North Park R.D., 612 5th St., Box 158, Walden, CO 80480; (303) 723-4707. Yampa R.D., 300 Roselawn, Box 7, Yampa, CO 80483; (303) 638-4516.

STEAMBOAT LAKE STATE PARK

Colorado Division of Parks and Outdoor Recreation
1,550 acres; 1,053 acres of water.

From Steamboat Springs. 25 mi. N on county 129.

The setting is spectacular: a basin surrounded by mountains just W of the Continental Divide. The lake is attractive. Elevation: 8,069 ft. The Routt National Forest is on three sides a short distance away.

At first we marked it "no entry." The state acquired too little land around the lake, and the park is being hemmed in by resort development. The signs of insufficient budget were conspicuous when we visited. On an August afternoon, our camping permit came from a machine. No posted map or supply of leaflets told us where to find the campground or anything else. Park roads were dusty and in poor repair. We saw an amphitheater but no announcement of any programs.

The park attracts about 300,000 visitors per year, chiefly for water-based recreation. We decided to include a brief entry because of the nearby National Forest trailheads.

Camping: 3 campgrounds, including one at nearby Pearl Lake. 240 sites. Reservations June 15–Sept. 16; see Colorado Preface.

PUBLICATION: Leaflet.

HEADQUARTERS: Box 755, Clark, CO 80428; (303) 879-3922.

UPPER COLORADO RIVER; PUMPHOUSE TO DOTSERO
U.S. Bureau of Land Management
57 river miles.

From Kremmling, about 1 mi. S on SR 9, then SW on Trough Road.

Trough Road begins as a poorly maintained blacktop, changes to graded gravel, then back to potholed blacktop. At first it runs through dry sagebrush hills. Soon patches of conifers appear on hillsides. At 8 mi., the road enters a V-shaped valley. At 9 mi. comes a sudden, sweeping vista of the Colorado River valley. This is Inspiration Point, 500 ft. above the river, overlooking Gore Canyon.

At 11 mi., a BLM sign marks a road to the right, river access. In 1 1/2 mi., it ends at Pumphouse, a popular put-in point for river rafting. For those not embarking, it's a pleasant riverside camping area with latrines and water.

The Gore Canyon Hiking Trail, about 3/4 mi., is mainly used as fishing access along the canyon. Riverside hiking opportunities are intermittent along both sides of the Colorado River in the Pumphouse area.

The first homesteaders arrived in this valley only 100 years ago. The railroad through Upper Gore Canyon was surveyed in 1906. The Dotsero Cutoff, completed in 1934, was one of the last major railroad sections built in the West.

The gravel road, a fine scenic route, follows the river to State Bridge, and beyond it to Dotsero. Most of the land on both sides of the river is public, administered by BLM. Signs identify state-owned land administered by the Division of Wildlife. This appeared to be set aside for big-game hunting. We saw nothing of special interest. We passed few vehicles, most of these carrying or towing rubber rafts.

Rafting is the principal attraction and the best way to see the valley. Rapids are rated Class I and Class II on the International Scale—"very easy" and "easy." Several commercial operators offer raft trips. Pumphouse is the most-used put-in point, and it is sometimes congested on weekend mornings. 80% of the use is 1-day trips from Pumphouse to State Bridge. BLM recommends floating below State Bridge on busy weekends. For trips of longer than a day, several campsites are available, most with river access only.

River water temperature ranges between 34 and 65°F.

NEARBY

Much of the land bordering the river below Pumphouse is public domain. One of the more interesting tracts is Bull Gulch (see entry).

PUBLICATIONS

The Upper Colorado River, Kremmling to Shoshone; River of Changing Landscapes. Folder with map.

Upper Colorado River, Special Recreation Permit Application Map.

Guide to the Upper Colorado River, Kremmling to Dotsero, Colorado. Leaflet.

HEADQUARTERS: BLM, Kremmling Resource Area, P.O. Box 68, Kremmling, CO 80459; (303) 724-3438.

WEST COLD SPRINGS
U.S. Bureau of Land Management
48,800 acres.

N of CO 318, opposite Browns Park National Wildlife Refuge.

On the S face of Cold Springs Mountain, an extension of the Uinta Range in Utah. The rocks of the range are exceptional: resistant pink-to-red quartzite and schists, which form colorful cliffs and talus slopes with streaks of black-and-white schist and gneiss. Horizontal bedding has caused the rock to form short cliffs that fringe the top of the mountain, providing excellent nesting and roosting for birds of prey. The horizontal bedding is presumed responsible for the many springs that give the mountain its name. Water collecting on top of the mountain can escape by only a few streams, notably Beaver Creek, or through joints and faults that cause springs lower down. Below these springs are streaks of lush vegetation.

The springs yield 2–20 gallons per minute in early summer. At least three of the springs are perennial. Beaver Creek, also perennial, is a good fishing stream.

The S slope is generally steep and rugged. Elevations from 5,800 ft. at Browns Park to 8,200 ft. on the highest ridges. On the S boundary are interesting badlands and attractive rolling hills.

Annual precipitation is 12–18 in., with an average snowfall of 40–60 in. The dry season begins in May, but the top of Cold Springs remains moist, usually through June. At the Browns Park weather station, temperatures have ranged between −15° and 94°; the mountaintop is considerably chillier. Fall and spring are ideal for hiking, but the upper slopes aren't excessively hot in summer.

Plants: About 80% of the site is forested, chiefly pinyon-juniper woodland. Some Douglas-fir and limber pine occur on N-facing slopes of Beaver Creek Canyon. Aspen groves and cottonwoods in drainages and around springs. An abundance of wildflowers. Associates, including wildflowers, similar to species found in Diamond Breaks (see entry).

Birds: Upland species presumably similar to those reported by Browns Park NWR, adjacent (see entry).

Mammals: Bighorn sheep were reintroduced in 1983. (Sightings should be reported to the Division of Wildlife.) About 250 elk use the area. Good deer population. Other mammals include coyote, gray fox, bobcat, beaver.

ACTIVITIES

Hiking, backpacking: Easy access. No maintained trails, but satisfactory hiking routes. Availability of water makes this area especially attractive. (Water should be treated.)

Hunting: Chiefly deer.

Fishing: Trout fishing in Beaver Creek said to be excellent.

HEADQUARTERS: BLM, Craig District Office, 455 Emerson St., Craig, CO 81625; (303) 824-8261.

WHITE RIVER NATIONAL FOREST
U.S. Forest Service
1,960,760 acres; 2,089,507 acres within boundaries.

The Forest is in two large, irregular blocks surrounding Glenwood Springs. It is crossed by I-70 and US 24.

Part of a huge area of National Forests, with Routt NF on the N, Arapaho, San Isabel, and Pike NF on the E and SE, Gunnison NF on the S, Grand Mesa NF on the SW. The administrative unit includes the Dillon District of the Arapaho National Forest.

One of the most heavily visited of all National Forests. It has far more downhill skiing than any other National Forest, with 12 major areas. Many areas of the Forest are heavily used, especially those near Aspen, Glenwood Springs, Dillon, and Vail. Recreation use is estimated to be 6 million annual visitor-days. Much of this use occurs on or near roads. Although more than one-third of the Forest is roadless wilderness, heavy recreation use also occurs in much of this area.

The N portion is largely wilderness. One all-weather road follows the North Fork of the White River E from Meeker, providing access to several campgrounds and trailheads. A second all-weather road cuts across the W sector, while a third penetrates from the SE to near campgrounds at Heart Lake and Deep Lake. The central part of this portion is the 400-sq.-mi. White River Plateau and the Flat Tops Wilderness. The Plateau is a lava-capped dome cut by deep canyons forming great amphitheaters ringed by escarpments. Above the cliffs is a gently rolling grassland with islands of trees, many small lakes, miles of streams. Prominent features are the "Chinese Wall" and "Devil's Causeway," a narrow ridge between the drainages of the East Fork of Williams Fork River and North Fork of the White River. Plateau elevation is about 10,000 ft., with peaks rising above 11,000 ft.

The second and larger portion of the Forest also has large wilderness areas, as well as scenic recreation areas accessible by car. This portion is dramatically mountainous, many peaks and ridges over 12,000, the highest 14,259 ft. SR 133, the route from Glenwood Springs to Delta, cuts across the W portion of the Forest, following the Crystal River. SR 82 runs between the E and S portions from Glenwood to Aspen, then crosses the Forest along the Roaring Fork River, just S of the Hunter Fryingpan Wilderness. SR 82 then climbs to Independence Pass, at 12,095 ft. the highest road crossing of the Continental Divide.

From near Aspen, several roads radiate into various parts of the Forest, including the Snowmass ski area and Maroon Lake. Many alpine lakes, rushing streams, waterfalls. Abundant wildlife. This portion of the Forest attracts sightseers, campers, backpackers, horse packers, hunters, fishermen, rock climbers.

Within the Forest are commercial lodges, camps and ski areas, as well as ranches and outfitters offering guide service to hunters and fishermen, packhorse and raft trips.

Plants: Little information was available from the Forest on plant communities and species. The plant zones are alpine, subalpine, upper montane, and lower montane. The principal tree species are Engelmann and blue spruces, Douglas-fir, subalpine fir, quaking aspen, lodgepole pine. Flowering plants and seasons are similar to those on the Routt, Gunnison, and San Isabel

National Forests (see entries). Commenting on habitat for big game, the Forest notes that much of the lodgepole pine, Douglas-fir, spruce-fir, and aspen is classified as mature or overmature, with a general lack of seedlings and saplings. The problems of providing adequate habitat are compounded by decreasing summer and winter range outside the Forest, as a result of human population increases.

Birds: Checklist of 225 species indicates habitat, seasonal abundance, breeding. Seasonally common species include mallard, American wigeon, turkey vulture, red-tailed hawk, American kestrel, killdeer, spotted sandpiper, mourning dove, great horned owl, common nighthawk, broad-tailed hummingbird, northern flicker, yellow-bellied sapsucker, hairy woodpecker, western kingbird, western wood-pewee; violet-green, tree, and barn swallows; gray, Steller's, and scrub jays; black-billed magpie, black-capped and mountain chickadees, dipper, house wren, American robin, hermit and Swainson's thrushes, mountain bluebird, golden-crowned and ruby-crowned kinglets, water pipit, European starling, warbling vireo. Warblers: orange-crowned, yellow, yellow-rumped, MacGillivray's, Wilson's. House sparrow, western meadowlark, red-winged and Brewer's blackbirds, brown-headed cowbird, black-headed grosbeak; purple, Cassin's, and house finches; pine siskin, green-tailed and rufous-sided towhees, gray-headed junco. Sparrows: chipping, Brewer's, white-crowned, Lincoln's, song.

See note on Rock Creek Bird Nesting Area under Features.

Mammals: No checklist available. Species mentioned include mountain lion, bobcat, black bear, weasel, beaver, gray fox, chipmunk, cottontail, mule deer, elk, bighorn sheep. Species reported by adjoining National Forests presumably occur here.

FEATURES

About 8% of Forest visits are in wilderness areas. Wildernesses are fairly heavily used, receiving more than 400,000 visitor-days each year. Heaviest use occurs in the Holy Cross, Eagles Nest, Maroon Bells-Snowmass, and Flat Tops Wildernesses. Most visitors choose the best-known trails and destinations.

Hiking season is from about June 1 to late Oct. Some limited winter hiking occurs along Glenwood Canyon. Ski touring and backcountry winter camping, especially around developed ski areas, are very popular.

Boating is available at three large lakes: Ruedi, Dillon, and Green Mountain.

Flat Tops Wilderness, 196,165 acres, plus 38,870 acres in the Routt NF. About 20 mi. N of Glenwood Springs. A concentration of flat-topped headlands dominated by the White River Plateau. The area is dotted with lakes and ponds, including 30 fishable lakes. Half of the 100 mi. of streams are considered good fishing. About 160 mi. of trails cross the area, but off-trail hiking is recommended to the experienced backcountry traveler. Much of the plateau is gently rolling grassland with patches of timber, bordered by sheer cliffs and wide canyons. Much of the area is at about 10,000 ft. elevation.

Trappers Lake is within the Flat Tops Wilderness, but can be reached by car. Wilderness areas are roadless, but an intrusive road is sometimes "cherry-stemmed"—excluded by drawing the wilderness boundaries around it. The road is well marked from a junction just E of Meeker on SR 13. From here the lake is about 45 mi. At the headwaters of the White River, the lake is one of Colorado's most-photographed scenic gems. Four Forest campgrounds are near the lake, another not far away. Easy trail access to the Wilderness.

Maroon Bells-Snowmass Wilderness, 159,444 acres, plus 19,598 acres in the Grand Mesa, Uncompahgre, and Gunnison National Forests. The Maroon Bells are twin peaks, perhaps the most photographed peaks in Colorado, often seen reflected in Maroon Lake. A "cherry-stem" road from Aspen penetrates the wilderness to the lake. Traffic in summer became so heavy that visitors must now park at Aspen and ride a shuttle bus. Hikers need not use this congested trailhead; others are available around the perimeter. Elevations from 9,000 to over 14,000 ft. Over 100 mi. of trails for foot and horse travel through narrow drainages and sometimes rugged terrain. Alpine lakes, roaring streams. Much of the wilderness is above timberline. Fine displays of spring flowers on the tundra.

Hunter Fryingpan Wilderness, 74,250 acres, NE of Aspen, S of Forest Road 505, N of SR 82. The E boundary is the Continental Divide. A mountainous area, several peaks over 13,000 ft. Some small lakes and streams. This wilderness is the least used in the Forest. Forest trails enter the Wilderness from Lost Man Campground, E of Aspen, and from Forest Roads 105 and 505, at Chapman Campground. (See Forest map.)

Collegiate Peaks Wilderness, 35,525 acres, plus 48,961 acres in the Gunnison NF, 82,152 acres in the San Isabel NF. Identified on the Forest Travel Map. Many peaks over 12,000 ft. Numerous lakes and streams. From Aspen, S on Forest Road 123 (4-wheel-drive), which skirts the Wilderness past McArthur Mountain to Taylor Pass; or SW on SR 82 to Lincoln Gulch Campground, where Forest Road 104 (4-wheel-drive) leading to Grizzly Reservoir, is a cherry-stem road into the Wilderness.

Eagles Nest Wilderness, 50,945 acres, plus 82,743 acres in the Arapaho-Roosevelt NF. In the high, rugged Gore Range, N of I-70, NE of Vail. Peaks over 13,000 ft. Many alpine lakes and ponds, rushing streams. Popular rock-climbing area. From Vail, on I-70, several Forest roads lead N and E to the Wilderness.

Holy Cross Wilderness, 113,642 acres, plus 8,958 acres in the San Isabel NF. (See Forest Travel Map.) From Leadville, N on US 24. At Blodgett campground, about 20 mi. to N of Leadville, Forest Road 703 skirts the Wilderness up to Homestake Reservoir. Several other Forest roads lead from US 24 to the E border of the Wilderness. The Continental Divide forms the S and W boundary. Numerous high peaks include 14,005-ft. Mount of the Holy Cross. About one-third of the area is above timberline. Fishable lakes and streams; wildflower displays; abundant wildlife.

Raggeds Wilderness, 16,578 acres, plus 42,527 acres in the Gunnison NF. (See Forest and Travel Maps.) Forest Road 314, shown on both the Forest Map and the Travel Maps, separates the Raggeds from Maroon Bells-Snowmass Wilderness. It leads S from SR 133, near the town of Placita, to Bogan Flats Campground, on the edge of the Raggeds Wilderness. Scenic peaks. Heavily forested. Wildflower displays.

Rock Creek Bird Nesting Area is a special management unit, preserving a natural area for the benefit of nesting birds. By car via a dirt road (Boss Mine Road) from Blue River Campground, 8 mi. N of Dillon. 2 1/2 mi. SW on this road, then hike 1 1/2 mi. on Rock Creek Trail. Between 9,500 and 10,000 ft. elevation, the unit contains, in a small area, nearly all of the habitat types found in the Gore Range: stream, pond, bog, meadow, willow, aspen, lodgepole pine, spruce-fir, cliff, alpine meadow. Peak numbers of nesting birds in June–July. Visitors are welcome but asked to move quietly. No camping or driving in the meadows.

Deep Creek Canyon is NW of Dotsero. From Glenwood to Dotsero, US 6 is beside the Glenwood Canyon of the Colorado River, crossing a corner of the Forest. At Dotsero, about 1 1/2 mi. N along the river, then left on Forest Road 600, which crosses Deep Creek near the Forest Boundary. Road 600 then climbs steeply to Deep Lake and Hart Lake near the Flat Tops Wilderness.

Deep Creek Canyon is up to 1/4 mi. wide, 1,700 to 2,200 ft. deep. We were told a trail runs for a short distance beside the canyon. The creek bed can be hiked in dry weather, but flash floods are a serious hazard. Good fishing.

The Forest identifies a number of areas as impacted: The Maroon Bells area, Piney Lake, Cataract Creek, Trappers Lake, and Maroon Lakes. Rangers will help to identify attractive less crowded places.

INTERPRETATION

Information and literature at Forest HQ and Ranger District (R.D.) offices.

The Forest has no visitor center, no scheduled campfire talks, guided walks, or other naturalist programs.

ACTIVITIES

Camping: 83 campgrounds, 1,752 sites. Season is generally June–Oct. Some campgrounds open earlier and stay open to about Nov. 10, but without water.

Hiking, backpacking: The Forest has almost 1,500 mi. of trails, for easy day hikes or extended backcountry trips. In many areas, off-trail hiking is feasible. The Forest map was prepared in 1969, partially revised in 1973, so it's advisable to visit an R.D. office before planning a long trek.

Horse riding: Most trails are suitable for horses; some may present problems early in the season. Riders should be familiar with backcountry regulations. Forest HQ could not supply a full list of outfitters, but the area has many ranches, commercial packers, guides, etc.

Hunting: Mostly big game: elk, mule deer, bighorn sheep. Hunters should be aware of private land inholdings in the Forest and of Forest areas closed to motor vehicles.

Fishing: Trout; many fine lakes and streams.

Boating: Motor-propelled boats may be used on Dillon Reservoir, Ruedi Reservoir, Green Mountain Reservoir, Homestake Reservoir, Shoshone Forebay. Swimming and other water-contact sports are prohibited at Dillon. Some smaller lakes are suitable for canoes or cartoppers.

Rafting, kayaking: Several whitewater rivers are nearby—the Colorado, Eagle, and Roaring Fork. Only a few relatively short sections are within the Forest. The Colorado River in Glenwood Canyon is very heavily used by both rafters and kayakers.

Skiing: Skiing is a major Forest activity, accounting for nearly half of all recreation visitor-days. Twelve ski areas, including well-known resorts at Aspen and Vail. Season is generally mid-Nov. to mid-Apr.

Ski touring: Extensive opportunities. Forest *ROG* has details on some recommended trails. Usual season: Nov.–Mar.

Snowmobiling: Wildernesses are closed to all motor vehicles. Most other Forest areas are open to snowmobiles; see Travel Map. Some trails are groomed, but not by the Forest Service.

PUBLICATIONS

Forest map. $1.00.

Travel map.

Leaflets

Flat Tops Wilderness

Maroon Bells-Snowmass Wilderness

Hunter Fryingpan Wilderness

Recreation Opportunities Guide (ROG); available at Forest HQ and R.D. Offices. Pages of interest may be photocopied.

HEADQUARTERS: 9th and Grand Ave., Glenwood Springs, CO 81602; (303) 945-2521.

RANGER DISTRICTS: Aspen R.D., 806 W. Hallam St., Aspen, CO 81611; (303) 925-3445. Blanco R.D., 362 7th St., Meeker, CO 81641; (303) 878-4039. Dillon R.D., 101 West Main, Frisco, CO 80443; (303) 668-3314 (Visitor Center). Eagle R.D., 125 W. Fifth St., Eagle, CO 81631; (303) 328-6398. Holy Cross R.D., 401 Main, Minturn, CO 81645; (303) 827-5715. Rifle R.D., 1400 Access Road, Rifle, CO 81650; (303) 625-2371. Sopris R.D., P.O. Box 248, Carbondale, CO 81623; (303) 963-2266.

ZONE 2

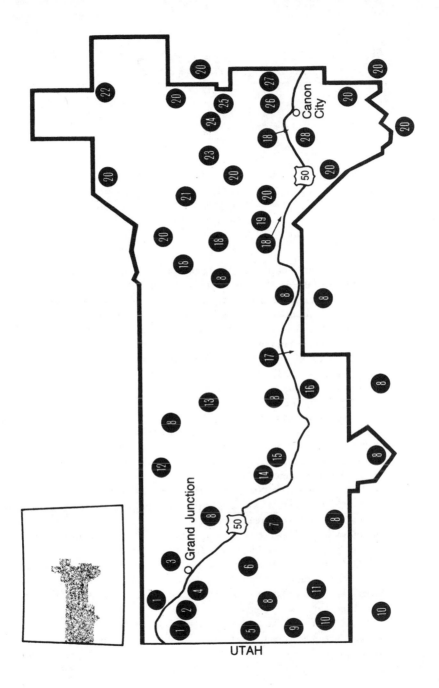

ZONE 2

Includes these counties:

Jefferson	Park	Fremont
Mesa	Gunnison	Custer
Pitkin	Chaffee	Douglas
Lake	Montrose	Teller
Delta	Ouray	

From border to border, most of this zone is occupied by National Forests and blocks of BLM-managed public lands. The Pike and San Isabel National Forests are on the E side of the Continental Divide; the Grand Mesa, Uncompahgre, and Gunnison National Forests are on the W side. Both the Forests and the public domain include spectacular roadless areas and some of the state's highest mountains.

Florissant Fossil Beds National Monument is in the far E of the zone. Just to the S are Cripple Creek and Victor, which are old gold mining towns, and the Dome Rock State Wildlife Area, attractive to hikers. S of Victor, SR 67, built on the old railroad bed, traverses Phantom Canyon, with the Beaver Creek roadless area adjoining on the E.

From Tennessee Pass on the Divide, at the N boundary of the Zone, the Arkansas River flows S, paralleling US 24, then turns E. Browns Canyon is one of the few tracts of public land on the river, which is one of the state's most popular whitewater streams.

On the other side of the Divide, the Gunnison River has not escaped the dam builders. The first barrier is within the National Forest. The Curecanti National Recreation Area includes Blue Mesa Reservoir and two smaller impoundments. The river then escapes into the Black Canyon and Gunnison Gorge, but the dam builders hope to inundate them, too.

The Colorado River enters the NW corner of the zone. Overlooking its valley near Grand Junction is the Colorado National Monument. Downstream is a pleasant area tame enough for canoes; boaters can go ashore to hike the Black Ridge Canyons.

In the W of the zone, a scenic route crosses the high mesa of the Uncompahgre National Forest. In the valley below is the canyon of the Dolores River.

ARKANSAS RIVER

U.S. Bureau of Land Management

Kobe to Parkdale. (Kobe, not shown on highway maps, is on US 24 about 4 mi. N of SR 82.)

US 24 and US 50 parallel the river.

Whitewater rafting has become a major recreation activity here, attracting more than 50,000 people per year. Commercial outfitters offer 1/2-day to 2-day tours. Rafting is generally below Buena Vista. Kayaking is gaining popularity above Buena Vista. Rapids below Buena Vista up to Class IV. (Also see entry, Browns Canyon.)

Land along the river is a mix of BLM, National Forest, and private holdings. A Special Recreation Permit is required for commercial use of BLM land. River running is regulated by the Colorado Division of Parks and Outdoor Recreation.

PUBLICATION: Special Recreation Map.

REFERENCE: Map showing ratings of rapids. Buena Vista, CO: Arkansas River Users Preservation Association.

HEADQUARTERS: BLM, Royal Gorge Resource Area, 831 Royal Gorge Blvd., Canon City, CO 81212; (303) 275-7578.

BEAVER CREEK

U.S. Bureau of Land Management; Colorado Division of Wildlife

26,150 acres; 2,740 acres.

From Canon City, 5 mi. E on US 50. N 1 mi. on SR 67. Right 1/4 mi. to Beaver Creek Road. N 11 mi. to parking area at dead end. Access in the N from Skagway Reservoir: from Victor, S 1/2 mi. on SR 67, then 5 1/2 mi. E on County Road 441.

The SE boundary of the area is Phantom Canyon (see entry). However, chief interest is the canyon of Beaver Creek, which flows S from Skagway Reservoir. The Division of Wildlife calls it "one of the most beautiful wildlife areas you will ever visit—and one of the most rugged. Anyone who plans on making the entire 17-mile hike from the Skagway dam down the Beaver Creek Canyon to the wildlife area parking unit had better be in top physical shape." Hiking down is considerably easier than hiking up.

The BLM area is an irregularly shaped block extending NE from Phantom Canyon. Beaver Creek cuts across the center. A strip of land along the creek is owned by the Division of Wildlife.

Topography varies from rolling hills in the S to 9,000 ft. peaks in the N. Dozens of drainages flow generally S, many joining Beaver Creek. Pinyon-juniper vegetation predominates with conifer forests on higher elevations, riparian species in stream beds.

One man who has known the area for years says its abundant wildlife "runs the gamut from woodticks to mountain lions." Often seen: bobcat, porcupine, rabbit, squirrel, chipmunk, bighorn sheep, many birds. Most visitors come to fish; rainbow, brown, brook, and cutthroat trout all reproduce here.

HEADQUARTERS: BLM, Canon City District Office, 3080 E. Main St., Canon City, CO 81212; (303) 275-0631. Division of Wildlife, 6060 Broadway, Denver, CO 80216; (303) 297-1192.

BLACK RIDGE CANYONS
U.S. Bureau of Land Management
72,440 acres.

On the UT border, on the S side of the Colorado River, W of Grand Junction and the Colorado National Monument. From I-70, take Exit 19, Fruita, S into the Monument. You may have to pay the entrance fee. Drive 11 mi. S from the Monument boundary and turn right at sign for Glade Park Store. Drive 0.2 mi., cross cattleguard, and turn right at sign, "Black Ridge Hunter Access Road." This dirt road, which should only be traveled by high-clearance vehicles, penetrates the area and ends in 12 mi. at the entrance to the arches area in Rattlesnake Canyon. Do not attempt this road in adverse weather. We strongly suggest that users obtain a map of this area before entering. For other access, see map in BLM office. Many people float the river to canyon mouths.

On the sloping NE edge of the Uncompahgre Plateau. Here the plateau is cut by seven major canyon systems draining to the Colorado River. The S edge of the unit is a high ridge. Elevations from about 4,500 ft. at the river to about 6,000 ft. Sloping mesas with rolling, hillock topography between the canyons. The site includes many unusual landforms: more than 20 arches, plus spires, windows, and serrated ridges.

Vegetation within the canyon systems consists of pinyon-juniper woodlands with openings of grasses and sagebrush. Grassy meadows in canyon bottoms, with willow and cottonwood. Mesa tops are generally grassy, open.

This portion of the river is a candidate for designation in the Wild and Scenic Rivers System. Commercial outfitters offer 1- and 2-day float trips from Loma, across the river from the site, to Westwater in Utah.

The terrain offers opportunities for hiking, backpacking, and horse travel. The scenery is delightful, and visitor use is light.

PUBLICATION: Map showing access to arches.

HEADQUARTERS: BLM, Grand Junction District Office, 764 Horizon Dr., Grand Junction, CO 81501; (303) 243-6552.

BLACK CANYON OF THE GUNNISON NATIONAL MONUMENT
National Park Service
13,672 acres.

To South Rim (open all year to Pulpit Rock, the third overlook): from Montrose, 6 mi. E on US 50, then 5 mi. N. To North Rim (closed to traffic in winter): from SR 92 just E of Crawford, 14 mi. on graded road.

The Black Canyon is 53 mi. long. The most spectacular 12-mi. section was chosen for the National Monument. Upstream are the 3 dams of the Curecanti National Recreation Area (see entry). Downstream, a fine section of the canyon is within BLM-managed public land, under consideration for wilderness status (see entry, Gunnison Gorge). Below the Curecanti dams, the river is free, although the dams regulate flow, and proposed downstream dams would inundate a part of the canyon.

The canyon is deep and narrow: 1,730 to 2,700 ft. deep, only 1,100 ft. between rims at The Narrows, as little as 40 ft. wide at the river. It is called "black" because sunlight penetrates the depths for only brief periods.

Most visitors take the South Rim Drive, which ends at High Point. Along the way are overlooks and parking areas with short trails to overlooks. The longest of these trails is about 0.7 mi., from High Point to Warner Point.

South Rim Drive is 8 mi. long. About half of it is kept open in winter, Dec. to late Mar. or early Apr. Proceed beyond Pulpit Rock on skis or snowshoes.

The N rim has fewer visitors, and the views of the canyon and river are at least as impressive. From The Narrows Overlook, one can see where the river is most confined.

It is possible to hike down into the canyon. On our last visit we saw a tiny red tent at the bottom. There are three routes (not trails) from the S rim. The descent is steep, 1,800 ft. in 1 mile. No drinking water on the way down, and river water requires treatment. All trips into the canyon, including day hikes, require permits.

This section of the river is not suitable for rafting; it includes waterfalls up to 40 ft. and sections of wall-to-wall water where no portages are possible.

The Monument boundaries are generally within a mile of the rims. Elevations are about 8,200 to 8,500 ft. Average annual precipitation is 17 in., average snowfall 48 in.

Plants: Checklist available. Most of the area back of the rims has a cover of mountain brush, chiefly Gambel oak and serviceberry. Higher sections have pinyon-juniper woodland, with some trees 460 to 740 years old. Associates are wild rose, mountain-mahogany, rock spirea, snowberry, gooseberry, chokecherry, wax currant. Few plant species grow in the limited sunlight below the rim.

Wildflowers of the Monument include mariposa lily, false Solomon's-seal, death camas, bluebells, pussytoes, arnica, balsamroot, common sunflower, asters, coneflower, goldenrod, salsify, wallflower, wild geranium, lupine, fireweed, evening primrose, gilias, phlox, eriogonum, spring beauty, pasqueflower, Indian paintbrush, penstemon, Canada violet, yellow birdfoot.

Birds: Checklist classifies species by habitat and relative abundance. Common species include mourning dove, turkey vulture, white-throated swift, violet-green swallow, dipper, American robin, mountain bluebird, ruby-crowned kinglet, blue-gray gnatcatcher, yellow warbler, green-tailed towhee, chipping sparrow.

Mammals: Checklist available plus supplementary notes. Common: long-eared, big brown, hoary, and western pipistrel bats; rock squirrel, golden-mantled ground squirrel, least and Colorado chipmunks, pocket gopher, woodrat, porcupine, cottontail, deer.

Reptiles and amphibians: Annotated list available. Common: clouded tiger salamander; Great Basin sagebrush and northern plateau lizards; western smooth green snake, Great Basin gopher snake, wandering garter snake.

Other fauna: Also available are checklists of insects, grasshoppers, and butterflies.

INTERPRETATION
Visitor center near the entrance, S rim.
Guided walks and *campfire programs* in summer.

Camping: 102 sites at South Rim Campground. Opens about May 15; closes when snow begins in late fall. Primitive campground at N rim.

PUBLICATIONS
Folder with map.
Checklists:

Plants.
Birds.
Mammals.
Amphibians and reptiles.
Insects.
Grasshoppers.
Butterflies.
Information pages:
General.
Back country.
Minerals.
Hiking.
Warner Point nature trail guide.

REFERENCE

Trimble, Stephen C. *The Bright Edge.* Flagstaff: Museum of Northern Arizona Press, 1979.

HEADQUARTERS: P.O. Box 1648, Montrose, CO 81402; (303) 249-9661.

BROWNS CANYON
U.S. Bureau of Land Management
6,614 acres.

On the E side of the Arkansas River, S for 7 mi. from opposite Nathrop on US 285. Access over a bridge about 2 mi. N of Nathrop, then S on primitive road.

The valley of the Arkansas River is here a strip of land about 6 mi. wide between two portions of the Pike and San Isabel National Forests. Most of the land W of the river is privately owned. This BLM site, a strip about 2 mi. wide, is on the E side, adjoining Forest land.

Topography is rugged, the land rising steeply from the river, with six major gulches. Elevations from 7,500 ft. to 8,400 ft. Vegetation is sparse, mostly pinyon-juniper with rabbitbrush, prickly pear, yucca, grasses. BLM judged the area to have wilderness qualities.

Birding is said to be good. A 3 1/2 mi. loop trail goes along Middle Cottonwood Gulch, Cottonwood Gulch, and the river. Hiking is said to be feasible along the river and up other gulches. The Forest map shows no connecting trails here, but 4-wheel-drive tracks enter the Forest from adjoining BLM land a couple of miles N. When we inquired locally, we found no one familiar with the BLM land. Better ask at the BLM office.

Nathrop is the put-in point for raft trips on the river through Browns Canyon. Rafting here has had a sudden rise in popularity. Several commercial outfitters offer half-day and full-day trips. Rapids on eastern scale Class II to IV early in the season. Up to Class II in Aug.

See also entry, Arkansas River.

HEADQUARTERS: BLM, Canon City District, 3080 E. Main St., Canon City, CO 81212; (303) 275-0631.

CAMEL BACK
U.S. Bureau of Land Management
10,900 acres.

SW of Delta. The Delta-Nucla Road crosses Roubideau Creek about 5 mi. from Delta. Here a primitive road follows Roubideau Creek for several miles, then enters Potter Canyon. This road is the W boundary of the area.

From the E side of the Uncompahgre Plateau (see entry, Grand Mesa, Uncompahgre, and Gunnison National Forests), numerous streams flow NE to the Gunnison River. Most of the land between the Forests and the river is public domain. We have an entry for the Dominguez Canyons about 12 mi. N. Camel Back is another roadless area, adjoining a 19,770-acre roadless area in the Forests that has been considered for wilderness status.

The chief scenic feature is the canyon of Roubideau Creek, a perennial stream. Like much of the E slope, the area is a series of canyons, mesas, and buttes. Elevations here are relatively low, from about 6,500 ft. at the Forest boundary to 5,000 ft. Cottonwood, willow, and tamarisk dominate the riparian vegetation, pinyon-juniper above.

The canyons and gulches offer relatively easy routes for hiking and horse travel. Nearby are a number of 4-wheel-drive routes to the top of the plateau.

HEADQUARTERS: BLM, Montrose District Office, 2465 S. Townsend, Montrose, CO 81402; (303) 249-7791.

CHATFIELD STATE RECREATION AREA
Colorado Division of Parks and Outdoor Recreation
5,600 acres; 1,150 acres of water.

8 mi. SW of Denver, just off US 85.

Our field notes dismissed this as "no entry, not a natural area." The Army Corps of Engineers built the dam. The reservoir is conspicuously artificial. The area is relatively flat. Two million visitors per year crowd into the site, chiefly for water-based recreation.

But Don and Lee Johnson, writing in *Colorado Outdoors,* report that birding here is unexpectedly rewarding, especially during breeding and migrating seasons. Sightings include species rare in Colorado, such as Caspian tern. Virginia rail are often seen up Plum Creek in a freshwater marsh. The nature trail area has a prairie dog village with burrowing owls. The Corps preserved a heron rookery at the SW end of the lake.

Camping: 153 sites. Reservations; see Colorado Preface.

PUBLICATIONS
Leaflet with map.
Bird checklist, noting seasons.

HEADQUARTERS: 11500 N. Roxborough Park Rd., Littleton, CO 80125; (303) 797-3986.

COLORADO NATIONAL MONUMENT
National Park Service
19,919 acres.

From SR 340 at Grand Junction or Fruita.

The Visitor Center and campground are near the Fruita entrance. From either entrance, the road climbs up canyons to Rim Rock Drive. The Fruita entrance is at 4,674 ft. elevation, the Visitor Center at 5,787 ft. Highest point on the drive is 6,640 ft. Most visitors come for the day, stopping at the many overlooks, perhaps taking a short hike. The scenery is magnificent, looking across the Colorado Valley to the Book Cliffs.

But there's more to the Monument. The Monument is on the N flank of the Uncompahgre Plateau. The land drops abruptly from the rim to the valley 2,000 ft. below. Erosion has carved fascinating shapes into the layers of red, brown, and cream-colored rock: pinnacles, fins, towers, castles, sheer cliffs, caves, windows. Each overlook offers a different set of shapes and patterns that change with the changing angle of sunlight. Within the rocks are fossils of dinosaurs, fish and shellfish, and many other life forms. If it rains, the visitor can witness the continuing process of erosion as rivulets cut new channels in soft rock.

Hiking is the best way to see the Monument. Most of the canyons are accessible. The Monument has 26 mi. of maintained trails. They enter the canyons gently, with switchbacks descending to the canyon floors. Rules do not confine the hiker to these marked routes. One can follow old deer trails or bushwhack. Most of the surrounding land is public domain, so hiking can extend beyond the Monument boundary.

Plants: About 80% of the site is forested, chiefly by the pinyon-juniper association. Understory species include sagebrush, rabbitbrush, mountain-mahogany, cacti, and grasses. A few scattered Douglas-fir and ponderosa pine. Cottonwoods and other riparian species along central drainages. Flowering species include aster, fleabane daisy, desert dandelion, western wallflower, wild geranium, locoweed, sego lily, blue flax, four o'clock, evening primrose, gilia, eriogonum, yellow columbine, wild rose, penstemon.

Birds: Checklist available; we exclude those marked "rare or few records." Hawks: goshawk, Cooper's, red-tailed, prairie falcon, American kestrel. Turkey vulture, golden eagle, Gambel's quail, ring-necked pheasant, chukar, band-tailed pigeon, rock and mourning doves, great horned and pygmy owls, poor-will, common nighthawk, white-throated swift; rufous, black-chinned, and broad-tailed hummingbirds; northern flicker, hairy and downy woodpeckers, yellow-bellied sapsucker. Flycatchers: ash-throated, gray, western, western kingbird, Say's phoebe, western wood-pewee. Horned lark. Swallows: violet-green, barn, cliff. Scrub and pinyon jays, common raven, American crow, Clark's nutcracker, black-billed magpie, black-capped and mountain chickadees, plain titmouse, common bushtit. White-breasted, red-breasted, and pygmy nuthatches. House, Bewick's, canyon, and rock wrens. Catbird, sage thrasher, American robin, western and mountain bluebirds, Townsend's solitaire, blue-gray gnatcatcher, golden-crowned kinglet, loggerhead shrike, European starling; gray, solitary, and warbling vireos. Warblers: yellow, yellow-rumped, black-throated gray, Townsend's, MacGillivray's, yellowthroat, yellow-breasted chat. Western meadowlark, northern oriole, brown-headed cowbird, lazuli bunting; Cassin's, house, and black rosy finches, American and lesser goldfinches, green-tailed and rufous-sided towhees. Sparrows: vesper, black-throated, sage, chipping, Brewer's, white-crowned, Lincoln's, song.

Mammals: Checklist available. Bats: little brown, long-legged, and small-footed myotis; western pipistrel, big brown, western big-eared, pallid. Whitetail and blacktail jackrabbits, desert cottontail, whitetail prairie dog, rock squirrel, whitetail antelope squirrel, least and Colorado chipmunks, plains pocket mouse, Ord's kangaroo rat. Mice: western harvest, canyon, deer, pinyon. Mexican and bushytail woodrat, porcupine, coyote, kit fox, gray fox, black bear, ringtail, badger, spotted and striped skunks, mountain lion, bob-cat, elk, mule deer, bison, desert bighorn.

Reptiles and amphibians: Checklist available. Includes clouded tiger sala-mander; spadefoot, red-spotted, and Woodhouse's toads; canyon treefrog, western leopard frog. Lizards: yellowheaded collared, pale leopard, northern sagebrush, northern plateau, northern tree, northern side-blotched, short-horned, northern whiptail, striped whiptail. Wandering garter snake, desert striped whipsnake, Great Basin gopher snake, Utah milk snake, Mesa Verde night snake, midget faded rattlesnake, Utah blackhead snake.

FEATURES

Rim Rock Drive, 22 mi.

No Thoroughfare Canyon, in the S portion, about 5 mi. long. Several spectacular water or ice-falls over an escarpment after rains or during spring thaw. Good stands of Douglas-fir in some side drainages. Following the central drainage is an 8- to 9-mi. one-day hike. Also overnight trips.

Monument Canyon has a trail ascending from the valley to the Rim Rock Drive, winding along the bases of prominent monoliths. About 5 1/2 mi.

Liberty Cap Trail and *Black Ridge Trail* also ascend from the valley to the Drive.

INTERPRETATION

Visitor Center has exhibits, films, talks, literature. Open 8 A.M.–8 P.M. in summer, otherwise 8 A.M.–4:30 P.M.

Nature trails at Window Rock, Coke Ovens, Otto's Trail, Canyon Rim; 1/2 to 3/4 mi.

Campfire programs and *guided hikes* in summer. *Wayside exhibits.*

ACTIVITIES

Camping: 81 sites. All year. No reservations.

Hiking, backpacking: Overnight hikers should register at visitor center. Long hikes are best planned spring or fall. Water must be carried.

NEARBY

Black Ridge Canyons (see entry). Includes Rattlesnake Canyon, with natu-ral arches.

PUBLICATIONS

Leaflet with map.
Plant list.
Bird checklist.
Mammal checklist.
Reptile and amphibian checklist.

REFERENCE: Trimble, Stephen. *The Bright Edge.* Flagstaff: Museum of Northern Arizona Press, 1979.

HEADQUARTERS: Fruita, CO 81521; (303) 858-3617.

COLORADO RIVER

Below Grand Junction: see entry, Ruby Canyon.

CURECANTI NATIONAL RECREATION AREA

National Park Service
42,114 acres.

Along US 50 W of Gunnison.

Most visitors come here for boating, fishing, and other water-based recreation. While the NRA land around the reservoirs is a narrow strip, it adjoins extensive areas of public domain and National Forest.

Three dams on the Gunnison River have formed a chain of three reservoirs. The largest dam, Blue Mesa, is 342 ft. above the original river channel. It has backed up a pool with 9,180 surface acres—when full, the largest body of water in Colorado— about 20 mi. long, generally less than 1 mi. wide. Several long arms extend up drowned rivers and creeks. US 50 follows the shoreline, sometimes near the water, in places as much as 1/2 mi. back. Blue Mesa Reservoir lies between low, dry mesas with gradual slopes, vegetated with sagebrush and scattered pinyon-juniper.

Morrow Point Lake, downstream to the W, is narrow, only 817 surface acres but about 11 mi. long, in a deep canyon. Boating is limited to small craft hand-carried down Pine Creek Trail.

Still further downstream is the smallest of the reservoirs, Crystal Lake, 301 acres, also set in a deep canyon. A service road leads to the base of the dam (no public access); the land surrounding the lake is roadless.

Several dirt and primitive roads lead from the NRA into the Grand Mesa, Uncompahgre, and Gunnison National Forests, 2–4 mi. N. The Soap Creek Arm of the Blue Mesa Reservoir projects N into the Forests. Forest Road 721 passes the Soap Creek Campground and the N tip of the arm. A trail from near the tip follows Coal Creek N into the West Elk Wilderness Area.

Much of the land between the NRA and the National Forest is public domain managed by the BLM. Included are three tracts identified as Wilderness Study Areas; see Adjacent or Nearby section in this entry.

The Red Creek road leading N from US 50 into the Forests passes through the Sapinero State Wildlife Area, a site of about 15,000 acres of interest chiefly to big-game hunters.

Lowest elevation is 6,547 ft., below Crystal Dam. Lake elevations at full pool are: Crystal, 6,755 ft.; Morrow Point, 7,160 ft.; Blue Mesa, 7,519 ft. Highest point is approximately 9,000 ft. along the rim of the Black Canyon.

Average annual precipitation is 12 in., half of this July–Oct. Average snowfall, 72 in. Average maximum temperatures range from 83°F in July to 25° in Jan., average minimums from 46° in July to −2°F in Jan. Ice fishing Jan.–Mar.

Plants: On dry, S-facing slopes around Blue Mesa Lake: sagebrush, Gambel oak, native grasses. On N-facing slopes and in canyons: Douglas-fir, blue spruce, ponderosa pine, occasional stands of aspen. (The national champion Colorado blue spruce, 15 ft. 8 in. diameter, is in the National Forest nearby.) Understory includes grasses, oakbrush, serviceberry, kinnikinnick, sage. Other plant communities include grassland and sagebrush. Riparian species include dogwood, cottonwood, willow, yellow hawthorn, rushes. Flowering plants include lupine, penstemon, scarlet gilia, Indian paintbrush, cacti.

Birds: Checklist of 224 species available. Reported as most common: common merganser, golden eagle, great horned owl, hairy and downy woodpeckers, gray and Steller's jays, black-billed magpie, common raven, horned lark, black-capped and mountain chickadees, white-breasted nuthatch, dipper, Clark's nutcracker. Seasonally common: mallard, green-winged teal, northern flicker, common crow, red-breasted and pygmy nuthatches, brown creeper, golden-crowned kinglet, European starling, house sparrow, American robin, Townsend's solitaire, red-winged blackbird, dark-eyed junco, red-tailed hawk, bald eagle, sage grouse, killdeer. Other species of interest include sandhill crane, osprey, great blue heron, prairie falcon.

Mammals: 43 species recorded. Included: coyote, prairie dog, beaver, yellowbelly marmot, skunk, weasel, cottontail, whitetail jackrabbit, Colorado chipmunk, deer mouse, mule deer, elk (wintering). Present but seldom seen: mountain lion, badger, black bear, bighorn sheep.

FEATURES

Scenic drives include US 50; SR 92, on the N side of Morrow Point Lake; Forest Road 724, from near the Elk Creek Campground N along East Fork Dry Creek; Soap Creek Road, from near the N side of Blue Mesa Dam; Red Creek Road; Rainbow Lake Road. Dirt roads are passable when dry, treacherous when wet.

SR 92, a paved road, continues W and N into the National Forest. Mesa Creek campground is just inside the boundary. The road twists and turns, ascending to about 9,000 ft. Leaving the Forest after about 6 mi., it becomes straighter and more level. About 11 mi. N is Crawford State Park, on a 397-acre reservoir. 60 campsites.

Morrow Point Boat Tours. Visitors may launch only hand-carried boats on fjordlike Morrow Point Lake. A 30-passenger cruise boat provides 1 1/2-hr. tours with commentary on geology and wildlife.

Cimarron Area, near Morrow Point Dam, has information, historic railroad exhibit, self-guiding tours of underground power plant, campground.

Lake Fork, near Blue Mesa Dam, has information, marina, campground.

Elk Creek, mid-lake, has visitor center, marina, campground, grocery, fish observation pond.

Historic sites in the area include an 1891 trestle of the narrow-gauge Denver and Rio Grande Railroad, the Gunnison Tunnel and Diversion Dam. The significant archeological resources have led to listing the Curecanti as "eligible" on the National Register of Historic Places.

INTERPRETATION

Elk Creek Visitor Center has exhibits, films, talks, literature.

Nature trail.

Campfire programs, Memorial Day–Labor Day.

Guided hikes, Memorial Day–Labor Day.

Other naturalist programs include bald eagle tours, wildlife tours, environmental education, survival education. Inquire.

ACTIVITIES

Camping: 9 campgrounds, 419 sites. Several boat-in sites. Elk Creek Campground open all year, others Memorial Day–Labor Day.

Hiking: 16 mi. of trails on site, easy to difficult. Backpacking access to the National Forest.

Hunting: Elk, mule deer, rabbit, sage and blue grouse.

Fishing: Rainbow, German brown, and mackinaw trout; kokanee salmon. Brook trout in small streams. Ice fishing Jan.–Mar.

Boating: Chiefly on Blue Mesa Lake and its arms. Marina, ramps, rentals. Speed limit for power boats: 40 mph. Boat and canoe camping. The lakes freeze Nov.–Apr.

Swimming: Unsupervised. Mostly July–Aug.

Ski touring: When snow permits. 9 mi. of trail; 1 mi. of maintained track.

Snowmobiling: Only if conditions permit below the high-water line, and along access roads where permitted.

ADJACENT OR NEARBY

Grand Mesa, Uncompahgre, and Gunnison National Forests.

Black Canyon of the Gunnison National Monument.

BLM manages over 500,000 acres of public land in the Gunnison Basin. The following three sites are BLM Wilderness Study Areas. All are between the NRA and the National Forest. The reservoir inundated much prime winter range for deer and elk, making this adjacent land more critical. Park Rangers conducting winter wildlife tours are likely to use this area to spot both big game and bald eagles. Bighorn sheep may be sighted on Dillon Mesa.

Dillon Mesa, 2,520 acres, about 1 mi. N of Blue Mesa Lake. E boundary is Red Creek road. Relatively flat mesa top, steep side slopes on E and W.

The W side has hoodoos, upright fingers of eroded rock with caprocks. Mostly sagebrush grassland with some oakbrush and cottonwood. On the N the site adjoins National Forest land recommended for wilderness status.

Willow Creek, 6,070 acres, is bounded on the N by the National Forest, on the S by the NRA. It lies between the dirt roads up East Fork Dry Creek and Steuben Creek. Rolling topography cut by narrow gulches. Elevation is 7,800 ft. at the S boundary, rising in the N to 9,400 ft. Aspen and spruce occur at higher elevations and on drainage slopes. Thick cover of cottonwood, oakbrush, and willow in drainage bottoms. It adjoins National Forest land recommended for wilderness status.

Steers Gulch, 2,440 acres, is N of the Beaver Creek Campground, adjoining the National Forest. Gently rolling hills and small washes. Terrain becomes more rugged inside the Forest. It adjoins National Forest land recommended for wilderness status.

Sapinero State Wildlife Area, 7,128 acres, is N of Blue Mesa Reservoir. It is crossed by the Red Creek and Elk Creek roads from US 50. It adjoins the National Forest on the N, BLM land on other sides. Elevations from 7,200 ft. near the highway to 9,400 ft. at the Forest boundary. Terrain is flat-topped mesas dropping into deep canyons. Vegetation ranges from big sage-grassland interspersed with oakbrush to spruce-fir with open parks and meadows and stands of aspen. The area is winter range for up to 900 elk, 1,000 deer. Coyote, weasel, and pine marten are common; black bear and bobcat are seen occasionally.

PUBLICATIONS
  Site brochure.
  Leaflets:
    Camping.
    Hiking.
    Ice fishing.
    Snowmobiling.
    Boating.
    Fishing.
    Activity schedule.
    Cimarron history.
    Gunnison Diversion Tunnel.
    Narrow-gauge railroad.
    Morrow Point boat tours.
    Weather information.
    Dam, power plant, and reservoir information.
  Curecanti Storage Unit brochure.
  List of vascular plants.
  Bird checklist.
  Mammals checklist.

REFERENCES

Cook, Kevin J. *Checklist to the Birds of Curecanti NRA*. Globe, AZ: Southwest Parks and Monuments Association, 1977. $0.20.

Hyde, Dr. A. Sidney. *Birds of Colorado's Gunnison Country*. Gunnison, CO: Western State Foundation, 1979.

Prather, Thomas. *Geology of the Gunnison Country*. Gunnison, CO: B & B Printers, 1982.

Vandenbusche, Diana. *The Gunnison Country*. Gunnison, CO: B & B Printers, 1980.

HEADQUARTERS: P.O. Box 1040, Gunnison, CO 81230; (303) 641-2337.

DOLORES RIVER

U.S. Bureau of Land Management; U.S. Forest Service; private holdings. 94 river mi.; indeterminate acreage.

From a point near Cahone on US 666 N to Bedrock on SR 90.

The Dolores River rises in the San Juan National Forest. It flows SW, paralleled by SR 145 to the town of Dolores, where it turns NW. While it then flows within the National Forest boundaries for more than 20 mi., much of the streamside land is privately owned. From the N Forest boundary to Bedrock, the river crosses BLM land, although there are some private holdings.

From Cahone to Bedrock, the Dolores River canyon is scenic and isolated, proposed for inclusion in the Wild and Scenic Rivers System. Rafting has become increasingly popular. We were told more than 40 commercial operators offer trips. When runoff from snowmelt is heavy, the rafting season extends from end of Apr. through mid-June. The season is often shorter, and in some years there's too little spring flow—or that was the situation before McPhee Dam was built upstream. In 1984 the Bureau of Reclamation began filling the pool. Full pool will not be reached before 1986. River flow now depends on management decisions. It will be years more before the effects can be evaluated.

As for Wild and Scenic River status, the outlook is poor. The dam doesn't disqualify this part of the river, but mining and other business interests have persuaded most of Colorado's Representatives and Senators to withhold their support.

Rafting is in two segments: (1) Cahone to Slickrock, 46 river mi., a 2- or 3-day trip; (2) Slickrock to Bedrock, 48 river mi., also 2 or 3 days. From Cahone to Slickrock, the river is in a montane setting: fast whitewater, green forested slopes with red-rock outcrops. Many whitewater enthusiasts float just this segment.

Beyond Slickrock, the river is confined in a twisting, winding canyon with sheer slickrock walls, little vegetation. The river is more placid here, but flash floods can be hazardous.

FEATURE

Dolores River Canyon (25,550 acres). About 30 mi. of this second segment are within a BLM Wilderness Study Area (WSA). Here the deeply incised, meandering canyon is cut through sedimentary layers, exhibiting colorful strata, massive cliffs interspersed with talus slopes. In places the canyon is so narrow that one wall overhangs the stream. Included are tributary canyons and surrounding rimlands. Land access to the perimeter of the roadless area is possible by a network of old mine roads; inquire at BLM office or locally.

The rim and mesa area supports pinyon-juniper woodland with areas of sagebrush. On canyon slopes: sagebrush, Mormon tea, squawbush, buffalo berry, scattered pinyon-juniper. A few isolated ponderosa pine and cotton-wood just under the canyon rim. Riparian growth along stream bottoms.

Hiking, backpacking: A few people, usually among those who have floated the canyon, return in the dry season to hike portions of it. A few hikers enter the WSA from the land side, following tributary canyons. BLM staff members who have hiked the area report seeing numerous Indian petroglyphs and pictographs.

HEADQUARTERS: BLM, Montrose District Office, 2465 S. Townsend, Montrose, CO 81402; (303) 249-7791.

DOME ROCK STATE WILDLIFE AREA
Colorado Division of Wildlife
4,982 acres.

From Divide on US 24, S 5 mi. on SR 67 (toward Cripple Creek). Turn right into Rainbow Valley; the entrance looks private but isn't. 1.8 mi. to site.

The parking area is down a short dirt road. Check before trying it with a trailer or motor home. Just beyond the parking area is an attractive rushing stream, bulletin board, register, and gate. The Division has no available map of the area. Except for Geological Survey quads, the best we've found is the Pike National Forest map. It shows Dome Rock but not the Rainbow Valley road.

Terrain is hilly, moderate slopes. Elevation of Dome Rock is 9,044 ft. We estimate elevation at the stream to be about 8,500. Hillsides are rocky with sparse tree cover of conifers and aspens. Lush riparian vegetation. Many wildflowers.

Visitors are asked to log in and out. Assuming everyone had done so, the average for July–Aug. was about 3 per day. No hunting season was open. 80% of the visitors said they'd come to walk, hike, or backpack; 20%, to fish. The recorded comments were surprising, since this area has no 14,000-ft. peaks or dramatic canyons: "Beautiful!" "Great country!" "Spectacular!"

According to maps, most of the surrounding area is privately owned. The National Forest is on the other side of SR 67. The Florissant Fossil Beds National Monument is a couple of miles to the NW. The National Forest map shows several trails in the area, largely on private land. One visitor had written that his party was hiking to Evergreen Station, which we haven't found on any map; local advice is that it's on the road from US 24 into the National Monument.

We commend this as a worthwhile stop if you're visiting Cripple Creek, Victor, or Phantom Canyon (see entry). SR 67 is a scenic route, especially beyond Cripple Creek.

Prohibited: camping, dogs, open fires.

HEADQUARTERS: Division of Wildlife, 6060 Broadway, Denver, CO 80216; (303) 297-1192.

DOMINGUEZ CANYONS
U.S. Bureau of Land Management
75,800 acres.

From Whitewater, S of Grand Junction, 11 mi. S on US 50 to Deer Creek turn. Turn W and follow dirt road to Bridgeport trailhead. Access is by foot only, via a historic bridge. Access also possible from Escalante Canyon and the Divide Road.

Divide Road is an all-weather road, and leads to two Forest campgrounds. Several primitive roads or jeep trails lead from Divide Road into the Dominguez Canyons site.

The NW site boundary is close to the Gunnison River. Like many of BLM's WSA's, this roadless area is part of a much larger area of public land. The Uncompahgre National Forest adjoins the site on the SW. The Forest map shows access routes as well as foot trails linking this site and the Forest.

Big Dominguez Creek and Little Dominguez Creek form two major winding canyon systems draining off the Uncompahgre Plateau NE to the Gunnison River. Between the canyons are isolated mesas. Elevations at the river are about 4,500 ft. Canyon walls are generally steep to sheer. The mesas rise gradually to the SW, reaching 7,500 ft. at the Forest boundary. Land features include steep-sided isolated buttes, alcoves, hoodoos. Scenic values are highly rated. Dense pinyon-juniper woodland with occasional sage glades cover much of the area. Riparian vegetation and Douglas-fir in the canyons.

The Dominguez Canyons offer easy-to-moderate hiking and horse riding routes. The area is rich in fossilized bones.

Camping: Dominguez Campground is located on the W side of the unit on Big Dominguez Creek. Access off the Divide Road.

NEARBY

Much of the land bordering the river from here downstream to within a few miles of Grand Junction is public domain. BLM's review found no area qualifying as a Wilderness Study Area. Terrain includes gently rolling hills, short red-rock canyons, rocky escarpments. Vegetation is sparse. This section of the river can be floated, but current is slow.

Escalante State Wildlife Area, 7,520 acres, consists of nine scattered parcels. The largest, 3,600 acres, is between Dominguez Canyon and Delta. From Delta, 4 mi. W on 5th St. The Gunnison River crosses the site. Flat to rolling land. River bottom with some cattail marsh, sagebrush flats; pinyon-juniper on slopes rising to the Uncompahgre Plateau. More than 100 bird species reported, including Canada goose, ducks, belted kingfisher, bald and golden eagles, red-tailed hawk, prairie falcon, wild turkey, pheasant, quail, band-tailed pigeon. Mammals include deer, elk, pronghorn.

A BLM staff member called this a "really neat area." Many ducks and geese winter along Roubideau Creek and the Gunnison River, feeding in cultivated fields by day.

A posted sign says the area is closed Apr. 1–July 15, the waterfowl nesting season. However, neither DWL's tiny site map nor boundary postings make clear which land is state property or where a visitor might enter. If you're driving US 50 through Delta, this site offers a pleasant, brief detour. Smaller parcels are along Escalante Creek Road, mentioned earlier. Primitive camping permitted.

HEADQUARTERS: BLM, Grand Junction District Office, 764 Horizon Drive, Grand Junction, CO 81501; (303) 243-6552.

ELEVEN-MILE STATE RECREATION AREA
Colorado Division of Parks and Outdoor Recreation
3,912 acres, plus 3,308 acres of water.

From US 24 at Lake George, 11 mi. SW on Forest Road 245.

The reservoir, about 7 mi. long, is at the edge of the Pike and San Isabel National Forests, which the road from Lake George crosses. A Forest campground is at the SE end of the lake. The park is a popular site for water-based recreation. No trails lead into the Forest.

Elevation is 8,500 ft. Views from the park include Pikes Peak on the E, snowy peaks on the Continental Divide on the W.

ACTIVITIES
Camping: 300 sites. Reservations (see Colorado Preface).
Hunting: In posted areas only, in regular seasons.
Fishing: Brown and rainbow trout, mackinaw, kokanee, northern pike, carp.

PUBLICATION: Leaflet with map.

HEADQUARTERS: Lake George, CO 80827; (303) 748-3401.

ESCALANTE STATE WILDLIFE AREA
See entry, Dominguez Canyons.

FLORISSANT FOSSIL BEDS NATIONAL MONUMENT
National Park Service
5,998 acres.

W of Colorado Springs. From US 24 at Florissant, 2 mi. S on County Road 1.

The Monument is relatively new, authorized in 1969, added to the National Parks system at a time of shrinking budgets. Prior to federal acquisition, the site was operated commercially. The site features fossils of the Oligocene period: standing sequoia stumps, tree foliage, dragonflies, beetles, ants, butterflies, spiders, fishes, some mammals and birds. More than 1,100 insect species have been identified, including almost all the known New World butterfly fossils. Over 140 species of plants were also preserved here. Thousands of specimens have been removed since the site was discovered in 1874.

The site is in a region of grassy hills and ridges, about 50% forested with ponderosa pine, Douglas-fir, Colorado blue spruce, and aspen. Elevation is 8,200 to 8,800 ft. The grassland meadows have many wildflowers, notably Indian paintbrush, locoweed, senecio, scarlet gilia, wild iris, shooting star, columbine. An early settler named this whole valley "Florissant," meaning "blooming."

Summers are short, with warm days and cool nights, sometimes below freezing. Average temperatures drop markedly in Sept. Subzero temperatures are not uncommon in winter. The Jan. average range is from 2° to 36°F. Average annual precipitation is about 14 in., more than three-fourths in Apr.–Aug. Winter snow accumulation is usually 1 1/2 to 2 ft.

Birds: Checklist of 103 species available; does not indicate abundance. Among them: great blue heron, mallard, cinnamon teal, American wigeon, turkey vulture. Hawks: sharp-shinned, Cooper's, red-tailed, Swainson's, rough-legged, ferruginous, northern harrier, American kestrel. Golden and bald eagles, blue grouse, killdeer, common snipe, spotted sandpiper, Wilson's phalarope, mourning dove, great horned owl, broad-tailed and rufous hummingbirds. Woodpeckers: northern flicker, red-headed, hairy, downy; yellow-bellied and Williamson's sapsuckers. Swallows: violet-green, tree, rough-winged, barn, cliff. Black-capped and mountain chickadees; white-breasted, red-breasted, and pygmy nuthatches; brown creeper, rock and house wrens, Bohemian and cedar waxwings. Warblers: Tennessee, yellow, yellow-rumped, MacGillivray's, yellowthroat, Wilson's, American redstart. Sparrows: savannah, vesper, lark, tree, chipping, Brewer's, Harris', white-crowned, Lincoln's, song.

Mammals: Checklist available. Includes least chipmunk; Richardson's, golden-mantled, and thirteen-lined ground squirrels; Abert's squirrel, chickaree, whitetail prairie dog, northern pocket gopher, deer mouse, muskrat, porcupine, cottontail, snowshoe hare, whitetail jackrabbit, coyote, black bear, longtail weasel, badger, mountain lion, bobcat, elk, mule deer, pronghorn.

The Monument is surrounded by privately owned land, but the boundary of Pike and San Isabel National Forests is less than a mile away. The entrance road continues S to Cripple Creek, joining SR 37. (See entry, Phantom Canyon.)

Hiking: 5 mi. of trails. The National Forest map shows a connecting trail.

PUBLICATIONS
    Leaflet with map.
    Weather information.
    Bird checklist.
    Mammal checklist.

HEADQUARTERS: P.O. Box 185, Florissant, CO 80816; (303) 748-3253.

GRAND MESA, UNCOMPAHGRE, AND GUNNISON NATIONAL FORESTS

U.S. Forest Service

2,953,191 acres; 3,163,408 acres within boundaries.

Forest land forms an irregular ring around Delta and Montrose, S of I-70. US 50 crosses the center of the area, W–E; US 550 S from Montrose. Various secondary roads penetrate or cross the Forest.

Three National Forests were combined in 1976, forming the second largest Forest in the Lower 48: Grand Mesa: 346,141 acres E of Grand Junction, N of Delta. Uncompahgre: 944,237 acres; two large blocks and one small one, W and S of Montrose. Gunnison: 1,662,813 acres, on the N, E, and S of Gunnison.

The W and N boundaries are formed by the Uncompahgre Plateau and Battlement Mesa. The W half of the Forest is within the Colorado Plateau Province, a region characterized by high, flat-topped mesas and rolling plateaus. The E boundary follows the Continental Divide and Elk Mountains. The S boundary includes the N slopes of the San Juan Mountains and the crest of the Wilson Mountains. The E half of the Forest is characterized by rugged mountains. Elevations range from about 6,000 ft. to peaks over 14,000 ft. Castle Peak, in West Elk Wilderness, is the highest point (14,259 ft.), and San Luis Peak, in La Garita Wilderness, is second highest (14,014 ft.).

Detailed information on climate was not available, but the various habitats are indicative. Precipitation ranges from 15 in. or less at lower elevations and in rain shadow to 55 in. on upper slopes. Snowfall is heavy in the high country; some peaks remain snow-covered through the summer. Heavy summer thunderstorms are common.

Grand Mesa. The Grand Mesa is America's largest table mountain, an island in the sky with more than 300 lakes. The most popular lakes are clustered around the mesa rims at about 10,000 ft. elevation, most of them on good gravel roads. SR 65 passes through the heart of the lakes region. Rim Drive Road is a scenic route to Lands End, above a 500-ft. vertical drop, a spectacular viewpoint. Many other lakes can be reached only by 4-wheel drive or on foot or horseback. Vegetation on the mesa is grassy meadows with large patches of forest, chiefly spruce and aspen.

Uncompahgre. The N portion lies on the crest and slopes of the high, mesalike Uncompahgre Plateau, a long, almost level tableland broken by sharp, rugged canyons extending into pinyon-juniper hills below. The S portion is on the N slopes of the San Juan Mountains. High, jagged peaks; deep, narrow canyons; open alpine grasslands. Principal peaks include Uncompahgre, 14,306 ft.; Mt. Sneffels, 14,143 ft.; Wetterhorn, 14,020 ft.

Gunnison. Mountainous; in the Rockies; 27 peaks over 12,000 ft. Many high mountain lakes, rushing trout streams.

All three areas have splendid scenery, fine forests, abundant wildlife, extensive trails, good fishing.

Delta is 261 mi. from Denver. Because of this distance from population centers, the Forest is less heavily used for recreation than are closer areas. In relation to size, this Forest has one-fourth as many visitors as the Arapaho-Roosevelt. That is still well over 2 million visitor-days per year, but campsites in campgrounds or undeveloped areas and solitude are easier to find. The Forest has almost 500,000 acres of proclaimed wilderness, where only a few places show signs of man's use.

Major use areas are Taylor River Canyon and SR 65 across Grand Mesa.

Plants: The Forest includes four major climatic and vegetation zones: alpine, subalpine forest, upper montane forest, and lower montane forest. About three-fourths of the land is forested.

Alpine vegetation grows above timberline. It includes grasses, grasslike forbs, low shrubs, and stunted trees. Spring flowers appear as the snow melts.

Subalpine forest features Engelmann spruce and subalpine fir. Below are lodgepole pine, Douglas-fir, quaking aspen. On the lower slopes are ponderosa pine, pinyon pine, juniper, Gambel oak. Unforested areas include mountain meadow, mountain bunchgrass, aspen-forb associations. The aspen association occurs typically in forest openings and at the edges of conifer stands. Aspens supply browse to deer and elk. Aspen leaves become brightly colored in the fall.

Riparian vegetation occurs in moist areas around springs, streams, lakes, and bogs. Here other common forest species are joined by willows, cottonwoods, and alders.

Wildflowers include cliffrose, virgin's bower, bush cinquefoil, black common chokecherry, pussytoes, columbine, Gunnison mariposa, heartleaf arnica, aster, arrowleaf balsamroot, Indian paintbrush, Rocky Mountain beeplant, larkspur, shooting star, eriogonum, ballhead gilia, sunflower, lupine, common monkeyflower, mountain bluebell, penstemon, phacelia, polemonium, cinquefoil, pasqueflower, pyrola, globemallow, white desert plume, mountain thermopsis, salsify.

Birds: Checklist is available for the Gunnison only; 207 species recorded. The *Recreation Opportunities Guide (ROG)* lists birds typical of various habitats: *Coniferous forests (general):* mountain chickadee, white-breasted and pygmy nuthatches, yellow-rumped warbler, pine siskin, broad-tailed and rufous hummingbirds, northern flicker, violet-green and tree swallows, black-billed magpie, gray-headed junco, house wren, American robin, evening grosbeak, red crossbill, western wood-pewee, Clark's nutcracker. *Ponderosa pine (7,000–8,000 ft.):* western bluebird, western tanager, Cassin's finch, chipping sparrow, mountain bluebird, black-headed grosbeak, poor-will. *Douglas-fir (7,000–8,000 ft.):* Steller's jay, green-tailed towhee, mountain chickadee, Lewis' woodpecker, pygmy nuthatch. *Engelmann spruce-subalpine fir (9,000–11,000 ft.):* gray and Steller's jays, ruby-crowned and golden-crowned kinglets, pine grosbeak, white-crowned and Lincoln's sparrows, western tanager, hermit thrush, olive-sided flycatcher. *Aspen (8,000–9,000 ft.):* western tanager, black-capped chickadee, American robin, mountain bluebird, western wood-pewee, violet-green swallow, black-headed grosbeak, white-breasted nuthatch, hermit thrush, yellow-rumped warbler, yellow-bellied sapsucker. *Mountain meadows:* American robin, yellow-rumped warbler, Lincoln's sparrow, western bluebird, water pipit. *Streams and rivers:* white-crowned, chipping, and Lincoln's sparrows; dipper, red-winged blackbird. *Mountain lakes:* mallard. *Soaring above:* golden eagle, red-tailed hawk, turkey vulture.

Mammals: No printed checklist, but Forest HQ supplied lists for Uncompahgre and Gunnison; no indication of habitat or abundance. Included: water, dwarf, vagrant, and masked shrews. Bats: Townsend big-eared, big brown, pallid, silver-haired, western pipistrel; long-legged, small-footed, long-eared, and little brown myotis. Pika, snowshoe hare, whitetail and blacktail jackrabbits, mountain cottontail, yellowbelly marmot, whitetail prairie dog, Richardson and golden-mantled ground squirrels; rock, red, and Abert squirrels; whitetail antelope squirrel; Colorado, least, and Uinta chipmunks; chickaree, Botta and northern pocket gophers, Ord kangaroo rat, beaver, muskrat, porcupine. Mice: silky pocket, western harvest, house, western jumping, canyon, deer, brush, pinyon, northern grasshopper. Heather, meadow, redback, mountain, and longtail voles. Also coyote; red, gray, and kit foxes; raccoon, badger, spotted and striped skunks, elk, mule deer, pronghorn, bighorn sheep.

WILDERNESS AREAS

West Elk, 176,092 acres NW of Gunnison. Elevations from 8,000 up to 14,259 ft. (at Castle Peak). The Area includes portions of the West Elk Range, Anthracite Range, and Beckwith Mountains. Striking geological formations such as The Castles, with high, sheer walls. Numerous lakes and streams. Opportunities for both day hikes and extended trips, on foot or horse.

Maroon Bells-Snowmass Wilderness Area, 19,598 acres, plus 159,444 acres in the White River NF. The Maroon Bells, twin peaks, are perhaps the most-photographed mountains in Colorado. A paved road leads to Maroon Lake, but summer visitation is so heavy that cars must be parked some distance away, shuttle buses providing transport from there. Foot trails enable the most indolent visitor to set foot in a proclaimed wilderness. More energetic hikers can, with some planning and effort, escape from crowds. More than 100 mi. of trails. Many alpine lakes and streams. Much of the Wilderness Area is above timberline.

The following 5 areas were included in the Colorado Wilderness Act of 1980. Forest HQ told us they have no descriptions or other printed information available to visitors. These notes from other sources and maps:

Big Blue Wilderness Area, 98,235 acres, NE of Ouray, NW of Lake City. The S portion is mountainous. Uncompahgre Peak is 14,309 ft., Wetterhorn Peak 14,015. Streams drain from these mountains N to the Gunnison River. One access is from US 50 E of Cimarron, S on road along Cimarron Creek to Big Cimarron and Beaver Lake campgrounds. Trails from here into the NW corner of the Wilderness, where trails generally follow creeks.

La Garita Wilderness Area, 79,822 acres, plus 24,164 acres in the Rio Grande NF. This Wilderness Area contains San Luis Peak (14,014 ft.), the highest point in the S portion of the Gunnison NF, and straddles the Continental Divide. Access isn't easy. Approaching from the N, the nearest paved road is SR 114; a primitive road leads S about 17 mi. to the Stone Cellar Campground, then about 5 mi. S to a trailhead at the Wilderness boundary. From Creede on SR 149, a primitive road runs N about 9 mi. to a trailhead; the last few miles require 4-wheel drive. Three peaks tower above 14,000 ft. Many others exceed 12,000. Alpine meadows, rushing streams, beaver dams, talus slopes, forests of tall conifers, abundant wildlife. Excellent fishing in streams and Machin Lake. Many miles of mapped trails, especially in the Rio Grande sector.

Collegiate Peaks Wilderness Area, 48,961 acres, plus 82,152 acres in the San Isabel NF, 35,525 acres in the White River NF. W of US 24 between Aspen and Buena Vista. 8 peaks over 14,000 ft., some attracting technical climbers. Timberline lakes, high mountain streams, conifer forests. Principal trailheads in the San Isabel NF; Forest map shows trailhead along Forest Road 209 between Taylor Park reservoir and Cottonwood Pass.

Raggeds Wilderness Area, 42,527 acres, plus 16,578 acres in the White River NF. On the Colorado highway map, follow SR 133 E from Delta, beyond Paonia. The blue road S of Paonia Reservoir leads to Erickson Springs campground. The Wilderness Area is between here and Marble, to the N. Ragged Mountain, 12,094 ft., is midway. Forest Road 314 in the White River NF separates the Raggeds from Maroon Bells-Snowmass Wilderness Area. Scenic peaks. Heavily forested. Numerous small lakes. Wildflower displays.

Lizard Head, 20,342 acres, plus 20,816 acres in the San Juan NF, W of Telluride. The Sunshine and Matterhorn campgrounds on SR 145 are near the E boundary. The area straddles the San Miguel Mountains. Wilson Peak is 14,017 ft., Lizard Head 13,113. Several over-14,000-ft. peaks are in the San Juan portion. Massive rock outcrops, cirque lakes, fishing in swift mountain streams. Large areas of alpine vegetation and spruce-fir forest. Light visitor use.

Mount Sneffels, 16,200 acres. Mt. Sneffels, 14,150 ft., is in the extreme E of the Area, W of Ouray. The Forest map shows Blue Lakes Trail originating at Camp Bird, SW of Ouray on SR 361. The trail crosses Blue Lake Pass, S of Mt. Sneffels, passes the Blue Lakes, and continues N.

SCENIC DRIVES

SR 65, from I-70/US 6 E of Grand Junction, S across Grand Mesa to SR 92 E of Delta. Access to numerous lakes, campgrounds, trailheads.

SR 135 from Gunnison to Almont and Forest Highway up Taylor Canyon to Taylor Park Reservoir. Scenic, river and rock canyon walls.

US 550, from Ouray S to Silverton, over Red Mountain Pass, 11,018 ft.

Kebler Pass Road, CR 12 from Crested Butte to SR 133 at Paonia Reservoir. Especially beautiful during the fall aspen color change.

Divide Road, Forest Road 402, runs along the crest of the Uncompahgre Plateau, SE from SR 141 S of Grand Junction. Unpaved, scenic. Some guidebooks say this is a fair-weather road for ordinary autos. Forest HQ says not: "Last year, 4-wheel-drive and some high-clearance pickups were able to use the road after Aug. 1. It is not suitable for passenger cars." This drive is a fine adventure, to be taken slowly. Take along the book *Uncompahgre,* listed in References for this entry.

ACTIVITIES

Camping: 68 campgrounds, 1,057 sites. Season for most: May 31–Sept. 6. Campgrounds are open before and after these dates but without water. Informal camping is permitted in most of the Forest, with special rules protecting the environment.

Hiking, backpacking: No data on total trail mileage, but the Forest has an extensive network of trails suitable for short hikes or outings of several days. The Forest has three National Recreation Trails: Crag Crest, 11 mi. long, following the Grand Mesa Ridge; Bear Creek, 6 mi. long, in the mountains near Ouray; and a third designed for ski touring. The *ROG* has pages for many of these trails with sketch maps, mileages, descriptions, elevations, hiking season, etc. When we visited, Ranger District offices would supply a photocopy of the trail map selected by a visitor. A number of the trails are described in *Uphill Both Ways;* see References for this entry.

Horse riding: Most trails are suitable for horses; a few are unsuitable or closed to horses. Some damage has been caused by off-trail riding, cutting across switchbacks, trampling around campsites, and overgrazing; riders are asked to minimize impact. The *ROG* has details on trails recommended for horse travel. List of outfitters available.

Hunting: Deer, elk, turkey, grouse.

Fishing: The *ROG* has details on numerous streams and lakes with good trout fishing. Spring runoff usually begins late May and continues through much of June; fishing is better when the water is calmer.

Boating: Only 9 of the many lakes are as much as 3/4 mi. long. Trout Lake and Silver Jack Reservoir are on the Uncompahgre. Overland and Taylor Park Reservoirs are on the Gunnison NF. Island, Eggleston, and Leon Lakes and Park and Bonham Reservoirs are on Grand Mesa NF. The *ROG* lists lakes where motors are permitted; some are restricted to protect public water supply. Many small lakes are suitable for canoes and cartoppers. Ranger District offices have information.

Rafting: Canoes, kayaks, and rafts are used on sections of the East, Taylor, Gunnison, San Miguel, and Uncompahgre Rivers. The *ROG* has information on two sections of the Taylor River, one of 18 mi., the other 27. Here, rapids are rated up to III. Some commercial river-rafting companies operate, but public use is medium to light.

Skiing: Ski resorts at Telluride, Crested Butte, and Powderhorn; helicopter skiing at Lake City. Downhill skiing represents about 10% of all public recreation on the Forest. Season: Dec. 1–Apr. 1.

Ski touring: Many excellent opportunities throughout the Forest. Usual season: Nov.–May. Maintained trails on the Grand Mesa and at Lake City.

Snowmobiling: Forest-wide except in wildernesses and other closed areas, shown on the Travel Maps. The *ROG* has recommended corridors. Groomed trails on the Grand Mesa and at Lake City.

PUBLICATIONS

Forest maps, Grand Mesa and Uncompahgre. $1.00 each.

Combined forest map, travel map, and interagency map, Gunnison NF, $1.00.

Leaflets:

Maroon Bells-Snowmass Wilderness.

West Elk Wilderness.

Crag Crest National Recreation Trail (includes ski-touring trails).

Grand Mesa Recreation Trails.

Information pages:

Descriptions of 32 trails; 5 pages.

Camping, general information.

Bird checklist, Gunnison.

REFERENCES

Marshall, Muriel. *Uncompahgre.* Caldwell, ID: Caxton Printers, 1981.

Brown, Robert L. *Uphill Both Ways.* Caldwell, ID: Caxton Printers, 1978.

Barrell, Joseph. *Flora of the Gunnison Basin.* Rockford, IL: Natural Land Institute, 1969.

Young, Robert C., and Joann. *Geology and Wildflowers of the Grand Mesa, Colorado.* Grand Junction, CO: Authors, 1968.

HEADQUARTERS: 2250 Highway 50 S, Delta, CO 81416; (303) 874-7691.

RANGER DISTRICTS: Cebolla R.D., 216 N. Colorado, Gunnison, CO 81230; (303) 641-0471. Taylor River R.D., 216 N. Colorado, Gunnison, CO 81230; (303) 641-0471. Collbran R.D., P. O. Box 338, Collbran, CO 81624; (303) 487-3249. Grand Junction R.D., Federal Building, 4th and Rood, Grand Junction, CO 81502; (303) 242-8211. Norwood R.D., P.O. Box 388, Norwood, CO 81423; (303) 327-4261. Ouray R.D., 101 N. Uncompahgre,

Montrose, CO 81401; (303) 249-3711. Paonia R.D., N. Rio Grande St., Paonia, CO 81428; (303) 527-4131.

GUNNISON GORGE
U.S. Bureau of Land Management
19,560 acres.

Adjoins the Black Canyon of the Gunnison National Monument on the downstream side. Access by local roads from US 50 at and N of Olathe.

Canyons attract dam builders. This one is no exception. The Gunnison River is formed by joining of the East and Taylor Rivers NE of the city of Gunnison. One dam is on the Taylor River. Just below Gunnison is the chain of reservoirs formed by three dams in the Curecanti National Recreation Area (see entry). The river is then released into the Black Canyon (see entry, Black Canyon of the Gunnison National Monument).

The Monument is a place for passive viewing. Visitors drive along the rim, pause for short walks to overlooks. The canyon has almost vertical walls, and there is no developed trail down to the river.

Downstream, this BLM site includes 13 mi. of river canyon. The area is roadless; visitors must approach the canyon on foot. Four developed trails lead to the bottom. The steep, narrow inner canyon is carved into dark Precambrian rock. Above this the walls flare out, become less steep; here the river cut through softer, light-colored sedimentary layers.

The river is swift, clear, and cold, one of the best trout fisheries in Colorado. The rapids attract a select group of boaters: those willing to carry their rafts or kayaks down a steep trail. ("You have to be crazy to try it," said one who had.)

The canyon has many wintering bald eagle and is prime habitat for peregrine falcon. River otters have been reintroduced, with apparent success.

This section of the river has been proposed for inclusion in the Wild and Scenic Rivers System. The BLM site was recommended for wilderness status. Construction of a dam would defeat both proposals. The dam builders and their allies have successfully stalled congressional action that would protect the canyon.

ACTIVITIES

Hiking, backpacking: No trail maps are available. Large maps can be seen at the BLM office. Chukar Trail is the most popular. Trailhead is at the end of a dirt road in Chukar Canyon, near the S end of the site. One steep mi. down. Ute Trail is the most developed and easiest, with 8–11% grades. Trailhead is near the N end of the site, reached by Peach Valley Road. 4 1/2 mi. to the bottom.

Rafting: Boaters use the Chukar Trail. Take-out is at the confluence with the North Fork, 13 mi. downstream.

HEADQUARTERS: BLM, Montrose District Office, 2465 S. Townsend, Montrose, CO 81302; (303) 249-7791.

LITTLE BOOK CLIFFS WILD HORSE RANGE
U.S. Bureau of Land Management
27,722 acres.

From Grand Junction, NE on I-70 and SR 789 to DeBeque. W on Winter Flats road, SW on 27 1/4 Road.

The S end of the area is close to I-70 at Palisade, but the only access shown is a 4-wheel-drive road up a wash from Cameo. The route from DeBeque passes through colorful sculptured badlands along the S side of South Shale Ridge and leads to the N portion of the unit.

The Wild Horse Act of 1971 requires management of all unbranded horses and burros on public lands. This area was dedicated in 1980. It currently maintains a herd of about 65 wild horses. A count is made yearly. If there are too many horses for the range to support, the surplus is rounded up and offered for adoption. Wild horses are often sighted in sagebrush parks in the NW sector. During the winter, Coal Canyon and Main Canyon are good viewing areas.

The SW boundary of the unit is the 2,000-ft. high face of the Book Cliffs. N of the cliffs is a gradual upward slope, a plateau highly dissected by four major canyon systems. The canyons have steep cliff walls up to 1,000 ft. high. Rock formations include small natural bridges and hoodoos. The site is highly rated for scenic beauty.

Vegetation in the canyons is chiefly big sagebrush, rabbitbrush, and fourwing saltbush. Pinyon-juniper woodlands dominate the uplands, with scattered sagebrush parks.

The cliffs and canyon walls are formidable barriers to travel, but the system of canyon bottoms offers practical routes for both hikers and horse riders. Motor vehicles are restricted to established roadways.

Heat and gnats may deter summer visitors.

NEARBY

The highway map shows a huge, apparently roadless area extending N from Grand Junction about 80 mi. to SR 64. Most of the N half is drained by Piceance Creek, the S half by Roan Creek. Most of the land in this area is public domain, managed by BLM, although there are many private landholdings, especially along the creeks.

Four roadless areas totaling over 72,000 acres, in addition to Little Book-cliffs, were identified as possible Wilderness Study Areas, then dropped from consideration. When we reviewed these with a BLM specialist, he described one of the four as "outstanding," another as "excellent hiking." Private landholdings make access difficult, however.

If you visit BLM's Grand Junction office, ask about this area.

PUBLICATION: Leaflet with map.

HEADQUARTERS: BLM, Grand Junction District Office, 764 Horizon Dr., Grand Junction, CO, 81501; (301) 243-6552.

MCINTYRE HILLS AND GRAPE CREEK
U.S. Bureau of Land Management
38,700 acres.

Access through Webster Park and the Copper Gulch Road. (Webster Park, about 2 mi. W of Canon City, is not shown on the state highway map. Inquire locally.) McIntyre Hills is N and W, along the Arkansas River. Grape Creek is S of Copper Gulch. Hiking access from the S via SR 169 and DeWeese Reservoir, on an abandoned railroad grade.

BLM staff members call this splendid hiking country. Crossing the area N–S is a 2-day trip. Public use is light, about 200 to 300 visitor-days per year. There are no roads except the dirt roads separating the area into three parts.

The McIntyre Hills portion is a mixture of rolling hills and steep, rugged mountains. Meandering streams have cut the area into a maze of interconnecting valleys and gullies, drainages flowing generally S to N. Many of these are the courses of intermittent streams with sand and gravel beds, natural footpaths.

Pinyon-juniper vegetation predominates, with some pine and fir at higher elevations, cottonwoods in the larger streambeds. Many raptors frequent the cliffs.

Grape Creek flows from the Deweese Reservoir, S of the site, NE to the Arkansas River. The middle portion of the unit lies between the Copper Gulch road and Grape Creek. Elevations from about 6,400 ft. to 8,300 ft. Topography is steep and rugged. Several gulches cross the area, SW to NE. Vegetation here is sparse: pinyon-juniper, some ponderosa pine along Grape Creek, grasses, rabbitbrush, prickly pear, yucca.

The Lower Grape Creek area is hilly on the W side, steep and mountainous on the E, where the creek flows. Similar vegetation.

BLM designated all three portions as Wilderness Study Areas.

HEADQUARTERS: BLM, Canon City District Office, 3080 E. Main St., Canon City, CO 81212; (303) 275-0631.

PAONIA STATE RECREATION AREA
Colorado Division of Parks and Outdoor Recreation
1,507 acres; 309-acre reservoir.

16 mi. NE of Paonia on SR 133.

Paonia Reservoir and the surrounding area are best shown on the Gunnison National Forest map. The Forest boundary is 1/4 mi. to 3 mi. away on the W, S, and E. Nearby trailheads for such areas as the West Elk Mountains and Dark Canyon. Elevation 6,900 ft.

Camping: Primitive, 23 sites.

PHANTOM CANYON
U.S. Bureau of Land Management and private ownerships.
Indeterminate acreage.

From Canon City, E 5 mi. on US 50, then N on County Road 67.

The road N to Victor, along Eightmile Creek, through Phantom Canyon, is scenic, with historical interest, worth taking. Signs warn that it's a bad road. Autos can make it with some bouncing. Motor homes and large travel trailers not advised. 18-wheelers can't get through the tunnel.

This region was gold-mining country. Today's road follows the old railroad, which ran from Florence through Victor to Cripple Creek, connecting with main lines. At Victor, a town kept marginally alive by tourism, exhibits in a fascinating museum include the railroad schedule, showing 58 passenger trains per day arriving from Florence. What's left is a 4-mi., 45-min. trip on the Cripple Creek and Victor Railroad.

Adjoining on the E is BLM's Beaver Creek Wilderness Study Area. Near the road N from Cripple Creek is the Dome Rock State Wildlife Area. See entries.

PIKE AND SAN ISABEL NATIONAL FORESTS

U.S. Forest Service
2,217,446 acres; 2,524,784 acres within boundaries.

Irregular in shape, extending from the Rampart Range near Colorado Springs to the Continental Divide. Crossed by US 24. A narrow portion extends SE from Salida almost to US 160. A separate block extending for about 45 mi. S of Canon City is crossed by SR 96 and SR 165. A much smaller, isolated block is S of US 160, crossed by SR 12.

The Forest also administers the Comanche National Grasslands, 418,887 acres, on the E plain (see entry in Zone 4).

The Forest is part of a huge area of National Forest land. It adjoins the Arapaho and Roosevelt National Forests on the N; the White River NF on the NW; the Grand Mesa, Uncompahgre, and Gunnison NF on the W; the Rio Grande NF on the SW.

The scenic E portion of the Forest is heavily used because of its proximity to Denver and Colorado Springs. Its most spectacular feature is 14,110-ft. Pikes Peak. Most other peaks in this portion are less than 10,000 ft. high. The Rampart Range is impressive because it rises abruptly from the E plain.

The W side is breathtaking, peak after peak higher than 14,000 ft., 25 of them, with many more between 12,000 and 14,000 ft. Mt. Elbert, at 14,433 ft. the highest point in CO, is SW of Leadville. Mt. Massive (14,421 ft.) is a short distance to the N, La Plata Peak (14,335 ft.) a short distance S. Many of these peaks are in the Sawatch Range. Between these lofty pinnacles, streams and glaciers have carved deep canyons, and several roads cross at passes. Streams on the E side of the Continental Divide run to the Arkansas River, which has its headwaters in the N sector. The river flows S at the foot of the range, paralleled by US 24 to just S of Buena Vista, then by US 285 and SR 291 to Salida, where it turns E and is paralleled by US 50.

The narrow strip of Forest land extending SE from Salida is on the Sangre de Cristo Range, which has several peaks over 14,000 ft., including three just S of the Forest boundary.

Principal lakes of the Forest are Turquoise, 1,600 acres, W of Leadville; Twin Lakes, 1,700 acres, near the intersection of US 24 and SR 82; and 500-acre Rampart Reservoir NW of Colorado Springs. The Sawatch Range on the W side of the Forest is dotted with high mountain lakes, above 10,000 ft., offering fine fishing to anyone who hikes in. The Forest has about 700 mi. of fishable streams.

SR 12, Walsenburg to Trinidad, crosses the disjunct block of Forest land that contains the Spanish Peak Wilderness Area. This block is on the E slope of the Sangre de Cristo Range. Except for a mile or two NW of Cuchara Pass, the road is lined with private inholdings. A ski area near Cuchara has caused a small boom in construction of weekend hillside chalets. The Wilderness Area is on the E side of SR 12. On the W side, Forest Road 413 leads to campgrounds at Blue Lake and Bear Lake. Hiking trails.

Plants: Forest HQ supplied no information on the climatic and vegetation zones of the region. We found much similarity to the adjoining National Forests: the same four major zones: alpine, subalpine, upper montane, and lower montane. For general description, see entry for the Arapaho and Roosevelt National Forests.

Birds: Checklist of 261 species available. Most are migrants or seasonal residents. Omitting those marked *occasional* or *rare,* the list includes the following: horned, eared, western, and pied-billed grebes; American white pelican, great blue heron, snowy egret, black-crowned night-heron, Canada goose, mallard, gadwall, pintail; blue-winged, green-winged, and cinnamon teals; American wigeon, shoveler, redhead, ring-necked duck, canvasback, lesser scaup, common goldeneye, bufflehead, ruddy duck, common merganser, turkey vulture. Hawks: sharp-shinned, Cooper's, red-tailed, Swainson's, rough-legged, ferruginous. Golden eagle, northern harrier, prairie falcon, American kestrel, scaled quail, ring-necked pheasant, wild turkey, sora, American coot, semipalmated and mountain plovers, killdeer, common snipe, long-billed curlew; spotted, solitary, Baird's, least, semipalmated, and western sandpipers; willet, lesser yellowlegs, American avocet, Wilson's phalarope. Gulls: herring, ring-billed, Franklin's, Bonaparte's. Forster's and black terns. Band-tailed pigeon, rock and mourning doves. Owls: barn, screech, great horned, burrowing, long-eared, short-eared. Common nighthawk, white-throated swift, broad-tailed and rufous hummingbirds, belted kingfisher. Woodpeckers: northern flicker, red-headed, Lewis', hairy, downy, yellow-bellied and Williamson's sapsuckers. Eastern, western, and Cassin's kingbirds; Say's phoebe. Flycatchers: willow, least, Hammond's, dusky, western, olive-sided; western wood-pewee. Horned lark. Swallows: violet-green, tree, bank, rough-winged, barn, cliff. Jays: gray, blue, Steller's, scrub, pinyon. Black-billed magpie, common raven, American crow, Clark's nutcracker, black-capped and mountain chickadees, plain titmouse, common bushtit, brown creeper, dipper. Also house, canyon, and rock wrens; catbird, brown and sage thrashers, American robin, hermit and Swainson's thrushes, western and mountain bluebirds, Townsend's solitaire, blue-gray gnatcatcher, golden-crowned and ruby-crowned kinglets, Bohemian and cedar waxwings, northern and loggerhead shrikes, European starling; solitary, red-eyed, and warbling vireos. Warblers: orange-crowned, yellow, yellow-rumped, blackpoll, ovenbird, northern waterthrush, MacGillivray's, yellowthroat, yellow-breasted chat, Wilson's, American redstart. Western meadowlark; yellow-headed, red-winged, and Brewer's blackbirds; northern oriole, common grackle, brown-headed cowbird. Grosbeaks: black-headed, blue, evening, pine. Indigo and lazuli buntings, Cassin's and house finches; gray-crowned, black, and brown-capped rosy finches; common redpoll, pine siskin, American and lesser goldfinches, red and white-winged crossbills, green-tailed and rufous-sided towhees, lark bunting. Sparrows: vesper, lark, tree, chipping, Harris', white-crowned, fox, Lincoln's, song. Slate-colored, Oregon, and gray-headed juncos; McCown's, Lapland, and chestnut-collared longspurs.

Mammals: List notes species present; no indication of abundance. Included —Bats: big brown, Brazilian freetail, hoary, pallid, silver-haired, Townsend's big-eared; fringed, little brown, long-eared, long-legged, small-footed, and Yuma myotis. Badger, beaver, pine marten, mink, raccoon, muskrat, yellow-belly marmot, river otter, red and gray foxes, whitetail prairie dog, longtail and shorttail weasels; spotted, striped, and hog-nosed skunks; wolverine, coyote, bobcat, mountain lion, ringtail, black bear, porcupine. Numerous species of shrews, voles, mice, squirrels, woodrats. Snowshoe hare, blacktail and whitetail jackrabbits, cottontail. Mule deer, elk, mountain bighorn, mountain goat, pronghorn.

FEATURES

Sangre de Cristo Wilderness Study Area, 87,300 acres, plus 133,700 acres in the Rio Grande NF. A high, rugged, mountainous area between the San Luis Valley on the W, Wet Mountain Valley on the E. The S end is on the side of 14,363-ft. Mt. Blanca, highest in the Sangre de Cristo range. Two primitive roads cross the range, at Hayden Pass and Medano Pass. Several peaks are higher than 14,000 ft., many more above 13,000. Average annual precipitation: 25 in. at lower elevations, over 30 in. on high slopes, most of the latter falling as snow. Lower slopes have pinyon-juniper association. Higher: oak, aspen, spruce. Above timberline, alpine species, wildflowers as snow melts.

A primitive road from Villa Grove to Coaldale crosses the ridge at Hayden Pass, passing the Hayden Creek campground. From Westcliffe on SR 69, the Hermit Lake Road runs W, passing through the Middle Creek State Wildlife Area and ascending to a region of high mountain lakes. Near the ridge, and at Hermit Pass, the map shows this as a 4-wheel-drive route. Several 4-wheel-drive tracks ascend to and cross the ridge.

The Forest map shows numerous trails ascending from E and W sides. Terrain is too steep and rugged for a ridgeline trail. Forest HQ has information on climbing the "Fourteeners." Difficulty ranges from a 4-mi. hike ascending 2,600 ft. to technical climbs.

Spanish Peaks Wilderness Study Area, 19,600 acres in a separated portion of the Forest crossed by SR 12 between Walsenburg and Trinidad. The wilderness area is E of SR 12. The Peaks are twin mountains formed by volcanic rock intrusions into sedimentary layers. Filling of vertical cracks created numerous dikes, some of them forming vertical free-standing walls from one to 100 ft. thick, up to 100 ft. high, extending as much as 14 miles.

East Spanish Peak is 12,683 ft., West Spanish Peak 13,626 ft. Lowest point in the area is 8,400 ft. Pinyon-juniper association with large patches of oakbrush on the lower slopes. On intermediate slopes, ponderosa pine, Douglas-fir, white fir. In the subalpine zone, bristlecone pine, Engelmann spruce, subalpine fir. Above timberline, alpine flora. Average annual precipitation from 19 in. on lower slopes to over 28 in., 40 to 50 percent of the latter falling as snow.

Access from SR 12 is by a dirt road at Cucharas Pass, a scenic drive that crosses Cordova Pass at 11,246 ft. (Before 1980, Cordova was called "Apishapa Pass.") Cordova Pass is the trailhead for West Spanish Peak. Primitive camping along the road. The John B. Farley Memorial Wildflower identification trail is a 1/4-mi. loop; printed trail guide.

On the W side of SR 12 are four Forest Service campgrounds. Fishing in streams and small lakes.

Buffalo Peaks Wilderness Study Area, 57,000 acres, SE of Leadville. Access is by Weston Pass road (shown on highway maps), which leaves US 24 S of Malta, following Big Union Creek and the South Fork of the South Platte River. Elevations from 9,200 ft. to 13,326 ft. at West Buffalo Peak. The Forest map shows several trails in the area N of the Peaks, a region of rolling alpine hills with large, wet meadows. Below this alpine zone are large stands of Engelmann spruce on N-facing slopes. Patches of bristlecone pine. Lower: Douglas-fir, lodgepole and limber pines, aspen. A few minor streams have brook trout. Wildlife includes blue grouse, ptarmigan, elk, mule deer, bighorn sheep.

Average annual precipitation 18–26 in. at lower elevations, 30–40 in. on high slopes, over 70% of the latter falling as snow.

Mount Evans Wilderness Area, 34,127 acres, plus 40,274 acres in the Arapaho and Roosevelt NF. About 40 mi. SW of Denver. From I-70, S on SR 103. Occupies the slopes of Mt. Evans, except for a highway corridor to the top. Elevations from 8,400 ft. to over 14,000 ft. Large expanses of alpine tundra. U-shaped and V-shaped valleys. Includes the 5,880-acre Abyss Lake Scenic Area, featuring a lake at 12,550 ft. elevation in a rock-rimmed gorge. Spruce, fir, and lodgepole pine below timberline, with small stands of bristlecone pine near the Mount Goliath Natural Area and the Chicago Creek Basin. Trails for easy, attractive day hikes and longer treks. *Mount Evans Auto Road* is the world's highest passenger car road, ascending to just below the 14,264-ft. summit. When we last drove the road, it was in poor repair but presented no difficulties up to Summit Lake. Drivers of motor homes and cars with travel trailers would do well to stop there. Spectacular views. Trout streams.

Lost Creek Wilderness Area, 105,090 acres, NW of Colorado Springs, between US 285 and US 24. The area is largely surrounded by Forest roads, with several National Forest campgrounds on or near the perimeter. The 15,120-acre Lost Creek Scenic Area is the core, established before the Wilderness Area. Here, within an hour's drive of both Denver and Colorado Springs, is the most rugged and spectacular part of the Pike NF. Picturesque stone formations—domes, half-domes, spires, pinnacles, balanced rocks, huge boulders, a natural arch—are interspersed with aspen groves and stands of spruce and fir. Bristlecone pine is at high elevations. A dozen peaks over 10,000 ft., two over 12,000.

Lost Creek disappears into granite slides nine times before becoming Goose Creek. Wildlife includes elk, deer, Rocky Mountain bighorn sheep, mountain lion, black bear.

The rugged terrain makes off-trail hiking difficult, but a network of trails is available for foot and horse travel. Designation of the far larger Wilderness Area has diverted some of the visitors, but the Scenic Area remains popular. The Wilderness Area also has numerous high peaks in the Platte River, Kenosha, and Tarryall Mountains, and a network of trails. Several trout streams. Ask a Ranger to recommend routes and destinations.

Collegiate Peaks Wilderness covers 159,000 acres, about half in the Pike and San Isabel NF. Eight peaks over 14,000 ft., timberline lakes, high mountain streams, splendid scenery. Technical climbing areas. Between Aspen and Buena Vista.

Holy Cross Wilderness, only 8,958 acres here, plus 113,642 acres in the White River NF. From Leadville, N on US 24. Principal access routes in the White River NF. At Blodgett campground, about 20 mi. to N of Leadville, Forest Road 703 skirts the Wilderness up to Homestake Reservoir. Several other Forest roads lead from US 24 to the E border of the Wilderness. The Continental Divide forms the S and W boundary. Numerous high peaks include 14,005-ft. Mount of the Holy Cross. About one-third of the area is above timberline. Fishable lakes and streams; wildflower displays; abundant wildlife.

Greenhorn Mountain Wilderness Study Area, 22,330 acres, SW of Pueblo, W of Rye. Central feature is Greenhorn Mountain, rising from 7,600 ft. on the S end to 12,367 ft. E slopes, facing the Colorado plains, are steep and rocky, others less so. Numerous small canyons and sharp ridges. About two-thirds of the area is forested, from pinyon-juniper at low elevations to spruce-fir just below timberline. Average annual precipitation ranges from 12–23 in. at low elevations to 35–45 in. on high slopes, 60% of the latter falling as snow. Hiking and backpacking are the principal activities, but they make up only about 3,600 visitor-days per year.

Pikes Peak is Colorado's most famous mountain. While not the highest, 14,110 ft., it has the greatest vertical rise from its base. Certainly it has been ascended by more visitors than any other of the "Fourteeners." Some 300,000 of them drive the 18-mi. toll road to the top, while others ride the Manitou Incline, a cog railway. The views from the mountain are spectacular. Near the top, even the alpine tundra gives way to bare rock and, in summer, patches of old snow.

Some hardy souls make the ascent on foot, 13 mi. each way, more of a round trip than most hikers can manage in one day, especially with such thin air near the top. Lodgings are available 7 mi. from the top, and at the top. An open shelter is just below timberline.

Rampart Recreation Area is a popular boating, picnicking, and hiking area NW of Colorado Springs, on 500-acre Rampart Reservoir. Boat speed is limited, swimming and other water contact sports prohibited. Two campgrounds. A 13-mi. trail circles the lake.

Turquoise Lake Recreation Area has 6 campgrounds, 2 boat ramps.

Twin Lakes Recreation Area is popular for fishing and boating. Natural lakes have been enlarged and developed for hydroelectric power. The Colorado Trail can be hiked N for 30 mi. from here to Tennessee Pass and S for 25 mi. to Cottonwood Creek, W of Buena Vista. The area around the lakes was closed to camping in 1984, perhaps temporarily.

INTERPRETATION

The Forest has no visitor center and maintains no program of campfire talks or other naturalist activities.

ACTIVITIES

Camping: 88 campgrounds, 1,830 sites. General camping season: Memorial Day–Labor Day. Some high elevation sites have shorter seasons. Most campgrounds are open for use at other times but without water or trash collection; snow may make some inaccessible. Informal camping is permitted elsewhere in the Forest, unless posted.

Hiking, backpacking: 1,288 mi. of trails. Hiking season in the high country is usually June 15–Oct. 1.

Horse riding: Most trails are open to horse travel. Forest HQ can supply a list of outfitters and guides.

Hunting: Some of the state's best hunting for elk, deer, mountain bighorn, pronghorn, bear.

Fishing: Many lakes, including alpine lakes. 700 mi. of fishable streams.

Skiing: Six ski areas partly or entirely on NF land.

Ski touring: Increasingly popular. See Publications.

PUBLICATIONS

Forest maps (Pike, San Isabel). $1.00 each.

Travel maps (showing areas closed to motorized vehicles).

San Isabel NF, small leaflet.

Bird checklist.

Recreation site directory.

Flower Identification Guide to the John B. Farley Memorial Trail.

Lost Creek Scenic Area leaflet.

Pikes Peak leaflet.

Pikes Peak Auto Highway folder.

Rampart Recreation Area leaflet.

Ski touring folders for:

Black Forest Park

Rampart Reservoir
Pikes Peak Region
Leadville Ranger District

REFERENCE
Gregory, Lee. *Colorado Scenic Guide, Northern Region.* Boulder, CO: Johnson Books, 1983.

HEADQUARTERS: 1920 Valley Drive, Pueblo, CO 81008; (303) 545-8737.

RANGER DISTRICTS: Leadville R.D., 130 W. 5th St., Leadville, CO 80461; (303) 486-0752. Salida R.D., 230 W. 16th, Salida, CO 81201; (303) 539-3591. San Carlos R.D., 248 Dozier St., Canon City, CO 81212; (303) 275-1626. Pikes Peak R.D., 320 W. Fillmore St., Colorado Springs, CO 80907; (303) 636-1603. South Park R.D., Fairplay, CO 80440; (303) 836-2404. South Platte R.D., 393 S. Harlan, Lakewood, CO 80226; (303) 234-5707.

POWDERHORN
U.S. Bureau of Land Management
50,140 acres.

SW of Gunnison. On the highway map, the area is within the triangle formed by SR 149 SW of Powderhorn, the blue road SE from Powderhorn, and the Gunnison National Forest. Access is by jeep trails from the N to trailheads at Indian Creek and 10 Mile Springs. Inquire at BLM office or obtain BLM's site map.

The larger portion of this site is in Zone 3, but the trailheads are in Zone 2. Because of the outstanding natural and scenic qualities of the area, 40,480 acres were designated as the Powderhorn Primitive Area in 1973. Study required by the Wilderness Act added additional acreage. Mountain landscapes, dense forests, plentiful water, and abundant wildlife makes this an exceptionally attractive wilderness. In part because of the 4-wheel-drive access roads, it has few visitors, about 500 per year, two-thirds of them from Colorado.

Elevations range from 8,800 ft. to 12,644 ft., the higher terrain in the S, where the Cannibal and Calf Creek Plateaus extend into the National Forest. Drainage is generally to the N, toward the Gunnison River at Blue Mesa Reservoir. The three Powderhorn Canyons—West, Middle, and East Forks —run N toward the community of Powderhorn. Plateaus and steep-sided ridges characterize the high elevations, steep-sided drainages below. The landscape includes cirque basins, glacial tarns, morainal deposits and lakes, and U-shaped valleys.

The area includes 67 mi. of streams, almost all perennial, and several mountain lakes: Upper and Lower Powderhorn (33 acres), Devils Lake (43 acres) and Hidden Lake (2 acres). The Powderhorn Lakes are at 11,859 ft. elevation.

Climate at higher elevations is severe. Temperatures range from −50° to 95°F. Frost may occur in any month. Annual precipitation is about 14 in. in the N, about 32 in. at higher elevations to the S, most of the latter as snow. Daily thunderstorms can be expected in summer. Strong winds are common above timberline.

Plants: Timberline is at 11,000 ft. Above are twisted, stunted Engelmann spruce and subalpine fir, cushion and low-tufted plants, areas of kobresia (a sedgelike plant), boulder fields, and talus slopes. Rather dense spruce-fir stands occur at 8,500 ft. up to timberline, with a belt of aspen forest just below. Ponderosa pine grows at 7,000–9,000 ft. on dry mesas and S-facing slopes; Douglas-fir is at similar altitudes on moister, N-facing slopes. Meadows are common in the woodlands of the lower mountains and subalpine areas. Big sagebrush parks interspersed with ponderosa pine occur at the lower elevations, often with rabbitbrush and antelope bitterbrush as associates. Along watercourses are willow, alder, birch, with cattails, sedges, rushes, bulrushes, spikerushes.

Birds: No checklist. The area is said to have a diverse bird population, including some waterfowl and shorebirds.

Mammals: No checklist, but partial list of species, including chipmunk, ground squirrels, red squirrel, snowshoe hare, cottontail, pocket gopher, pika, marmot, porcupine, bobcat, coyote, mountain lion, black bear. Beaver said to be numerous. Estimated 360 head of elk, 220 mule deer, 5 bighorn sheep.

ACTIVITIES

Hiking, backpacking: Access makes this an area for backpacking rather than day hiking. Visitors stay for an average of 2 1/2 days. Registers are at the principal trailheads. Most trails follow streams.

Horse riding: Unloading ramps at the principal trailheads.

Fishing: A major visitor activity. Trout in streams and lakes.

PUBLICATION: Powderhorn Wilderness Study Area map.

HEADQUARTERS: BLM, Montrose District Office, 2465 S. Townsend, Montrose, CO 81402; (303) 249-7791.

RUBY CANYON OF THE COLORADO RIVER
U.S. Bureau of Land Management
26 river miles.

From Loma, on I-70, to Westwater Ranger Station in Utah.

This section of the Colorado River can usually be floated all year. Spring runoff begins in April, with peak flows in May and June. There are no rapids requiring technical skill, but strong eddies in some sections, especially Black Rocks, require caution. Rafts, kayaks, and canoes are all suitable. At very high water with no wind, the trip can be made in 6–8 hours; at low water with no wind, in 15 hours. However, strong upstream winds are common in the afternoons, especially in spring, and they can virtually halt downstream progress. Boaters should be prepared for an unexpected night in the canyon.

About 8,000 people per year make this run. Take-out is at Westwater Ranger Station. See entry, Colorado River, Utah Zone 2. Major rapids are below Westwater. Permits are required beyond this point, and the number issued is limited.

The land on the S side of the river is largely public domain, much of it included in Wilderness Study Areas. (See entry, Black Ridge Canyons.) Many of the canyons are most easily reached by boat, and there are numerous good campsites. Hiking side trips can be planned for an hour or for several days.

The canyon was named for the common color of the sandstone walls. It is composed of steeply stair-stepping layers of different formations. Some cliffs exceed 500 ft. in height. Natural arches are in Rattlesnake Canyon (see Black Ridge Canyons entry), massive pinnacles in Mee, Moore, and Knowles Canyons. The arches are not readily viewed from the canyon bottom.

Wildlife: Commonly seen are mule deer, beaver, bats, ducks, Canada goose, great blue heron, cliff swallow, songbirds. Raptors include golden and bald eagles, vultures, great horned owl.

Two endangered fish species occur in the canyon: the Colorado squawfish and the humpback chub. If caught, they should be returned to the water. If the dorsal fin carries a tag, report the number promptly to the Grand Junction or Moab BLM office.

This section of the Colorado has been proposed for inclusion in the Wild and Scenic Rivers system. Opposition of commercial interests has thus far deterred congressional action.

Flash floods are a hazard in side canyons.

PUBLICATION: Folder with map. (Free when we obtained it, but a $0.50 charge was under consideration.)

HEADQUARTERS: BLM, Grand Junction District Office, 764 Horizon Drive, Grand Junction, CO 81501; (303) 243-6552.

SEWEMUP MESA
U.S. Bureau of Land Management
19,140 acres.

S of Gateway on SR 141, beyond Salt Creek Canyon road, a primitive road that forms the NW boundary of the site. Access to the site is only from canyons along SR 141.

Scenic, roadless, very rough topography. Identified as a Wilderness Study Area. SR 141 runs between the Dolores River and the foot of the cliffs on the E boundary of the site. On the W and SW the site adjoins LaSal Division of the Manti-LaSal National Forest (see entry, Utah Zone 3). The National Forest map is useful.

Sewemup Mesa is a mesa top isolated by sheer cliff faces 500–700 ft. high on the NW and E. The rolling mesa top is dissected by many shallow canyons. Elevation at the river is about 4,600 ft. From the cliff tops, the mesa slopes upward. Highest point in the site is 7,276 ft. On the W side the land slopes down into Sinbad Valley, a collapsed salt dome.

Dense pinyon-juniper woodland covers most of the mesa. Extensive outcroppings of slickrock. Entrada Knolls in the NW corner add visual interest.

BLM's site review concluded that this is "one of the last areas in this region which represents a high pinyon-juniper mesa ecosystem undisturbed by the works of man."

SR 141 S from Gateway is a scenic drive. Gateway, at the junction of the Dolores River and West Creek, was named for pillars at the entrance to the valley.

HEADQUARTERS: BLM, Grand Junction District Office, 764 Horizon Drive, Grand Junction, CO 81501; (303) 243-6552.

TABEGUACHE CREEK
U.S. Bureau of Land Management
7,270 acres.

The creek appears on the official highway map just S of Uravan on SR 141. The Meadows Trail, a primitive road, is the N boundary. The site adjoins the National Forest.

Within the adjoining Grand Mesa, Uncompahgre, and Gunnison National Forests, the creek flows through a roadless area being considered for wilderness status. The creek flows W to the Dolores River.

The creek, a perennial stream, has cut a narrow, deep, winding canyon. Surrounding are benchlands, ridges, and mesas divided by tributary canyons. The land slopes gradually to the SW. Elevations between 6,000 and 7,000 ft.

Predominant vegetation is relatively thick pinyon-juniper, with cottonwood, willow, and other riparian species beside the stream.

The National Forest map shows several trails in the area, including one continuing into the Forest along Tabeguache Creek.

HEADQUARTERS: BLM, Montrose District Office, 2465 S. Townsend, Montrose, CO 81402; (303) 249-7791.

THE PALISADE
U.S. Bureau of Land Management
26,050 acres.

Near the UT border, SW of Grand Junction. The SE boundary follows SR 141 and West Creek for about 10 mi. NE from Gateway. The W boundary is near but not on the Dolores River.

The Palisade is a rocky ridge dividing the rough triangle between the Dolores River and West Creek, which join at Gateway. Elevation at the river is about 4,600 ft., slopes rising to about 7,500 ft. The ridge is narrow and steeply rising at the S end. To the N it becomes higher with more gradual slopes. Topography includes vertical cliffs; deep, rugged canyons; and rolling to flat desert valley bottoms dissected by gulches. The area is about 22 mi. E of Arches National Park. It has hoodoos but no arches.

Higher elevations have open, sloping to flat grasslands and meadows with moderate to heavy stands of intermixed pinyon-juniper and oak brush. Some aspen and ponderosa pine in upper drainages. Some riparian vegetation along North Fork.

Good views from high points include the LaSal Mountains in UT. BLM's review rated the area's scenic qualities "outstanding." The area is roadless and was recommended for wilderness study.

Although there are no established trails, the terrain offers natural hiking routes. Both streams are perennial, with good fishing. Winter habitat for deer, elk, golden eagle. This area is one of two critical habitats in CO for the Nokomis Fritillary, a rare butterfly.

HEADQUARTERS: BLM, Grand Junction District Office, 764 Horizon Drive, Grand Junction, CO 81501; (303) 243-6552.

TOMAHAWK STATE WILDLIFE AREA
Colorado Division of Wildlife
1,680 acres.

From US 24 near Hartsel, NW 6 mi. on SR 9. Look for sign on E side.

Don't bother with Antero Reservoir, shown on the highway map near here, unless your interests are in boating, fishing, or camping overnight. The 4,000-acre reservoir is popular and lacks attractive natural qualities. Swimming and other water contact is prohibited.

Tomahawk offers a pleasant short walk if you're passing this way. The entrance road rises to a narrow, forested ridge. Park here and walk, looking down about 200 ft. to a lush green meadow with a meandering stream. The site contains 6 mi. of the Middle Fork of the South Platte River, a favorite with fly fishermen.

VEGA STATE RECREATION AREA
Colorado Division of Parks and Outdoor Recreation
1,830 acres; 900-acre reservoir.

E of Grand Junction. From I-70, E on SR 330 12 mi. beyond Collbran.

The area is best shown on the Grand Mesa National Forest map. The park is near the Forest boundary. From here a 4-wheel-drive route leads into the lakes region of the Forest. An auto road into the area leads S from Collbran.

Damming Plateau Creek formed the reservoir in a setting of mountain meadow. Elevation is 8,000 ft. The park is popular for water-based recreation, including scuba diving, and for winter sports: ice skating, ice fishing, and ski touring.

Nature trail features aspen forest, subalpine vegetation.

ACTIVITIES
Camping: Primitive, 110 sites. Reservations; see Colorado Preface.
Fishing: Trout. Said to be excellent.
Boating: Ramp.

HEADQUARTERS: Box 186, Collbran, CO 81624; (303) 487-3407.

ZONE 3

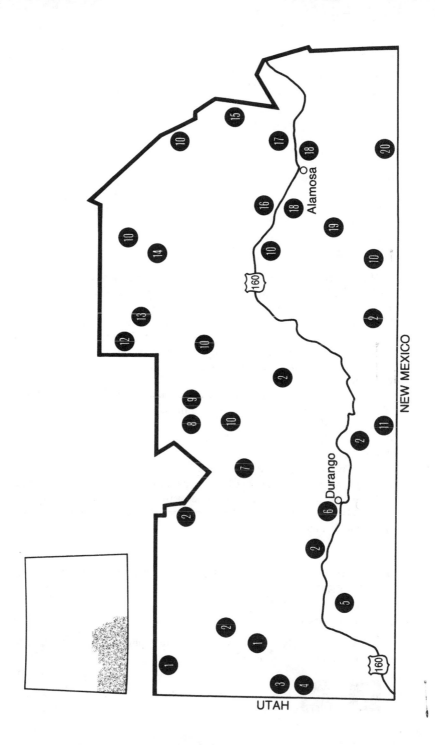

ZONE 3

Includes these counties:

San Miguel	Mineral	Archuleta
Hinsdale	Rio Grande	Conejos
Saguache	Alamosa	Costilla
Dolores	Montezuma	
San Juan	La Plata	

Of the three mountainous zones, this one is furthest from population centers, especially in travel time. Its mountains, forests, canyons, and rivers are no less splendid, and fewer areas are crowded.

Its NE boundary is the Sangre de Cristo Range, its NW the Continental Divide on the crest of the San Juan Mountains. Within the zone are two National Forests, the San Juan and Rio Grande. They share Colorado's largest, grandest, and least accessible Wilderness Area, the 460,000-acre Weminuche.

The San Luis Valley is the state's largest. Framed by National Forests, most of the valley land is privately owned, although some large tracts of BLM-managed land are in the W and S. Also within the valley are the Great Sand Dunes National Monument, the Alamosa and Monte Vista National Wildlife Refuges, and several State Wildlife Areas.

US 160 is the route to the W portion of the San Juan National Forest. From this highway, a number of paved and unpaved roads follow the Las Animas and lesser streams uphill into Forest areas with many trails and campgrounds. This is also the route to Mesa Verde National Park, at the edge of the Ute Mountain Indian Reservation.

ALAMOSA AND MONTE VISTA NATIONAL WILDLIFE REFUGES
U.S. Fish and Wildlife Service
10,352 and 14,189 acres.

> Alamosa is 4 mi. E of Alamosa, on US 160. Monte Vista is 6 mi. S of the town of Monte Vista, on SR 15.

These two refuges—12 airline mi. and 30 road mi. apart—were established to preserve waterfowl habitat and protect some of the remaining wetlands along the Rio Grande River. Both should be seen. Although they are ecologically similar, each offers the visitor a different set of viewpoints.

In the San Luis Valley at about 7,600 ft. elevation. The region is dry, only about 7 in. of precipitation per year. Snowmelt from the Sangre de Cristo and San Juan Mountains supplies the river, and canals irrigate the valley. The river follows a meandering course through the Alamosa unit, with numerous sloughs and oxbows. Old river channels form several large ponds below the E bluffs. Wetlands in the desert attract large numbers of birds and other wildlife.

The Monte Vista unit is not on the river but is partially watered by it. Most of the wetlands here are man-made, created by careful water management, using dikes, pumps, ditches, and artificial ponds. The birds do not discriminate.

Begin your visit at the Alamosa Visitor Center, near the entrance. Take the River Road walk and Rio Grande Birding Trail. Then it's an 11-mi. drive to the Bluff Overlook, a splendid vantage point for birding.

At Monte Vista, drive the 6-mi. Avocet Trail. Near the end of the Trail are farm fields where you might see sandhill cranes during their migration and, with rare good luck, a whooping crane.

In the Monte Vista Refuge, 12 mi. of county road provide good wildlife viewing. Parking areas and restrooms, intended for hunter use during the hunting season, are available for others in other seasons. Automobiles are restricted to the tour route and the county roads.

Plants: Cottonwood, willow, and other riparian species on bottomlands. Stands of bulrush and cattail. Grass and rush meadows. Desert greasewood-rabbitbrush community. About 350 acres are planted in feed crops each year.

Birds: Checklist available. 189 species recorded. Good all-year birding. Fewer species are present in winter, but these include bald and golden eagles and other raptors. Seasonally common or abundant: snowy egret, black-crowned night-heron, Canada goose, mallard, gadwall, pintail; green-winged, blue-winged, and cinnamon teals; northern shoveler, redhead, common merganser, ring-necked pheasant, sora, American coot, killdeer, common snipe, spotted sandpiper, American avocet, Wilson's phalarope, mourning dove, great horned and short-eared owls, common nighthawk. Also northern flicker, horned lark; violet-green, tree, barn, and cliff swallows; black-billed magpie, black-capped chickadee, marsh wren, sage thrasher, European starling, yellow-rumped warbler, common yellowthroat, house sparrow, western meadowlark; yellow-headed, red-winged, and Brewer's blackbirds; brown-headed cowbird, house finch, pine siskin, American goldfinch; savannah, vesper, tree, white-crowned, and song sparrows.

In 1941, the total whooping crane population had declined to 21, and numbers fluctuated uncertainly thereafter. Since 1975, biologists have been removing eggs from whooping crane nests in Canada and placing them in sandhill crane nests in Idaho. A number of the whooping crane chicks raised by sandhills now migrate between the Idaho refuge and the Bosque del Apache National Wildlife Refuge in New Mexico, with a stopover at Monte Vista. Large concentrations of sandhills visit Monte Vista mid-Feb. through Apr. and early Oct. through mid-Nov.

Hunting: In designated areas. Special rules. Ducks, geese, pheasant, snipe, dove, cottontail, jackrabbit.

NEARBY
Hot Creek State Wildlife Area; Rio Grande State Wildlife Area. (See entries).
Smith Reservoir State Wildlife Area, 900 acres of land, 700 of water. From Alamosa, 21 mi. E on US 160 to Blanca, then 4 mi. S. Chiefly a fishing site, but birders may wish to look in here before or after visiting the federal refuge. Informal camping.

PUBLICATIONS
Refuge leaflet.
Bird checklist.
Hunting maps.
Hunting regulations.
The Way of the Whooping Crane. Leaflet.

HEADQUARTERS: Alamosa-Monte Vista National Wildlife Refuge, P.O. Box 1148, Alamosa, CO 81101; (303) 589-4021.

ANIMAS RIVER CANYON
San Juan National Forest; U.S. Forest Service
15,620 acres.

5 mi. S of Silverton on US 550.

When we gathered data and visited this area, it was public domain administered by BLM. We were told it might be transferred to the San Juan National Forest, which abuts it on both sides. By the time we sent the entry for checking, the transfer had been made, but we thought it best to keep the area as a separate entry.

The strip is about 13 mi. long, about 3 mi. wide in the N half, only 1 mi. wide in the S. The narrow-gauge Durango and Silverton Railroad runs through the scenic, high-walled river gorge. There are no roads.

Elevation at the river is about 8,500 ft. The gorge is densely forested, with narrow, steep, side drainages. An E extension of West Needles Mountains lies within the unit, including the flank of 13,077-ft. Snowdon Peak. Rugged mountain terrain. Above the gorge in the N part of the unit are meadows, gently rolling to flat. Vegetation includes alpine tundra, spruce and aspen forests, and riparian communities.

On the E side of the gorge is the enormous Weminuche Wilderness Area, some of the most splendid and inaccessible backcountry of Colorado. In summer, two of the daily trains stop in the canyon for backpackers who hike from there up into the Wilderness Area. Another hiking route is from Molas Lake, just outside the N end of the area, down Molas Creek into the canyon, across, and up into the Wilderness. See entry for San Juan NF.

About 6 mi. from the S end of the strip, the river leaves it, flowing SW. This end is high and rugged, with six distinct peaks, several above 13,000 ft. Almost all this area is in alpine tundra. Below the peaks are several cirque basins with cold, cascading creeks. Of the several trails in this area, the most popular is Highland Mary Lakes, leading into the adjoining Weminuche Wilderness. Use of this trail is estimated to be 86 visits per day for a 120-day season.

This strip and some adjoining National Forest land is under consideration for wilderness status.

Here is one of a very few places in the United States where one can ride a train through a spectacular canyon with wilderness on both sides.

HEADQUARTERS: San Juan National Forest, 701 Camino del Rio, Federal Building, Durango, CO 81301; (303) 247-4874.

BLANCA WILDLIFE HABITAT AREA
U.S. Bureau of Land Management
5,390 acres.

From Alamosa on US 285, N 5 mi. on SR 17; E 7 mi. on Twomile Road. We were told about this site too late to go there. It's an unusual undertaking for BLM, managing a part of its land as a National Wildlife Refuge. BLM has not published an invitation to visitors, but we were told they are welcome. We suggest inquiring at the District Office first. The site is closed Mar. 15–June 30 for waterfowl nesting.

The area is midway between Alamosa and the Great Sand Dunes National Monument, on the W side of the Sangre de Cristo Range. Elevation is about 7,500 ft. Although the surrounding area is arid, artesian wells supply a small chain of wetlands.

The highway map shows San Luis Lakes, just off the Sand Dunes Monument Road. The San Luis Lakes are a Division of Wildlife site. We stopped there and saw little of interest, although the birding may be good at times and we were told the Division planned improvements.

The BLM site has greater diversity: a few large, permanent ponds; many smaller ponds; tall, dense wet meadows with greasewood near water and islands in the marsh. Wetlands have been created, and the water is managed to provide optimum habitat for migrating and nesting waterfowl.

The site is experimental, and attention is given to nongame as well as game species. No swallows were known to nest here previously, but habitat improvements have attracted nesting tree and violet-green swallows. Other nesting species include Canada goose, mallard, teals, pintail, gadwall, and a variety of nongame waterfowl and shorebirds.

HEADQUARTERS: BLM, Canon City District Office, 3080 E. Main St., Canon City, CO 81212: (303) 275-0631.

CROSS CANYON; CAHONE CANYON; SQUAW-PAPOOSE CANYON
U.S. Bureau of Land Management
29,085 acres.

On the UT border. N from Pleasant Valley Road, the route to Hovenweep National Monument, or by local road W from US 666 at Cahone.

An area of deep, winding canyons draining SW toward the San Juan River in Utah. Stream-cut in uplifted sedimentary layers, the canyons range in depth to 850 ft. Many rock outcrops, ledges, talus slopes. Desolate, dry, more typical of Utah than Colorado. Cross Canyon has water (not potable) most of the year.

Pinyon-juniper is the predominant vegetation type, with understory of sagebrush, Mormon tea, mountain-mahogany, rabbitbrush, cliffrose, bitterbrush. Canyon bottoms have a riparian zone with cottonwood, willow, tamarisk, boxelder, saltbrush, sedges, rushes, cattails.

The canyon bottoms provide natural routes for hiking and horse riding. The Morrison Formation, one of the sedimentary layers, contains plant and animal fossils. The area includes many archeological sites, including numerous Anasazi ruin sites.

HEADQUARTERS: BLM, Montrose District Office, 2465 S. Townsend, Montrose, CO 81402; (303) 249-7791.

DOLORES RIVER
See entry in Zone 2.

DOME LAKES STATE WILDLIFE AREA
Colorado Division of Wildlife
419 acres of water.

From Gunnison, 8 mi. E on US 50. S 20 mi. on SR 114. S 8 mi. on Road NN14.

Within the valley of Cochetopa Creek; elevation 9,129 ft. On the W side of the Continental Divide, which runs here along the crest of the Cochetopa Hills. The Grand Mesa, Uncompahgre, and Gunnison National Forests surround the valley on three sides, enclosing a mixture of private, state, and BLM land.

The valley is drained by Cochetopa Creek, which flows N to a tributary of the Gunnison River. The two lakes, together about 2 mi. long, are said to have some of the best brook trout fishing in the Gunnison area. Fishing is also good in Cochetopa Creek.

SR 114 and Road NN14 both continue into the National Forest and across the Divide. Backcountry access by several primitive and 4-wheel-drive roads.

Camping: Two areas. No fixed sites. Latrines, drinking water.

GREAT SAND DUNES NATIONAL MONUMENT
National Park Service
38,659 acres.

From Alamosa, 14 mi. E on US 160, then 16 mi. N on SR 150.

At the E edge of the San Luis Valley. The Monument is at the base of the forested, snowcapped Sangre de Cristo Mountains. Prevailing SW winds have shaped desert sands into an area of picturesque, unstabilized dunes—among the world's highest, some about 700 ft. from base to top. Medano Creek forms the E boundary of the dunes for several miles before it disappears into the sand. The movement of the dunes is dramatized at their downwind edge, where a forest is slowly being buried in sand that has crossed the creek boundary. Base elevation is about 8,000 ft.

Summer daytime temperatures rarely exceed 90°F. Nights are cool, in the high 40s. Afternoon thunderstorms are common July–Aug. Winter temperatures can drop as low as −25°, with high winds.

Adults and children alike delight in climbing to the tops of the dunes, following their crests, often descending in great leaps. Morning and evening are the best times for this, especially in summer, because the sand becomes hot at midday. Much of the visual excitement of the dunes is in their shifting patterns of colors and shadows as the day progresses. One should see them at different hours from dawn until after sunset, and—if possible—by moonlight.

The Monument adjoins the Rio Grande National Forest; the Pike and San Isabel Forests are nearby. The Mosca Pass Trail offers a pleasant short hike up into the forested hills. A 4-wheel-drive road also enters the Forests.

Few animals are seen on the dunes by day. Among those that may be seen at night is the giant sand treader camel cricket, a species unique to this area. Many more animals are seen in the adjoining Forests.

INTERPRETATION

Visitor center has exhibits, films, talks, literature, guided walks. Open 8 A.M.–8 P.M. Memorial Day–Labor Day, otherwise 8 A.M.–5 P.M. daily.

Nature trail, 1/2 mi.

Campfire programs, Memorial Day–Labor Day.

ACTIVITY

Camping: 88 sites, all year. No reservations, and no overflow space is provided when the campground is full. Backcountry camping permitted at designated sites in the Medano Corridor Zone (see Park map), and in the Wilderness Zone. Both are reachable only by 4-wheel-drive vehicles.

In the Wilderness Zone, be prepared for strong winds, shifting sands, and no water. No fires and no pets in either backcountry area.

PUBLICATIONS

Leaflet with map.
Great Sand Dunes. Folder.
Vascular plant checklist.
Mammals checklist.
Information pages:
General: camping, fees, weather, rules.
Weather history.
Nearby camping facilities.
Bibliography.
Publications for sale.

REFERENCE: *Great Sand Dunes: The Shape of the Wind.* Globe, AZ: Southwest Parks and Monuments Association, 1978.

HEADQUARTERS: Mosca, CO 81146; (303) 378-2312.

HOT CREEK STATE WILDLIFE AREA
Colorado Division of Wildlife
3,494 acres.

From Monte Vista on US 160/285, S 20 mi. on SR 15. Where SR 15 turns E, look for right turn, gravel road, marked for Hot Creek and La Jara Reservoir. About 3 mi.

We were delighted to find this site, a lush green canyon amidst desert hills. The access road from SR 15 begins as graded gravel. It then turns S toward La Jara Reservoir, and a dirt track continues W to Hot Creek. Our motor home made it to the canyon's edge without difficulty. A car might make the descent to the canyon floor. We walked down. The road follows the creek for about 3 mi.

Hot Creek, a tributary of the Rio Grande, is fed by a warm spring. Dense riparian vegetation on the canyon floor: cottonwoods, willows, rushes, cattails, many wildflowers. Many birds, including a black-crowned night-heron rookery. As we turned back, we spotted a small herd of desert bighorn sheep above us. Colored tags identified them as transplants. The Division of Wildlife asks that such sightings be reported.

Here is solitude. We may have been the only visitors since the last hunting season, 8 months before.

Adjoining this site on the S are 9,000 acres of public land managed by BLM under a cooperative wildlife management agreement with the state agency. Access to the BLM land is by a primitive road that leaves the La Jara Reservoir road about 2 1/2 mi. from the Hot Creek turnoff. The primitive road follows Poso Creek.

La Jara Reservoir is 10 mi. from SR 15 on a wide, graded gravel road that, when we visited, was mostly corduroy. The lake is over 2 mi. long, shallow, surrounded by low hills, some of them forested. We didn't see the advertised boat ramp, but a cartopper could be launched almost anywhere, and nothing larger would be appropriate.

The lake is surrounded by grassy flats, much trampled by cattle. We considered it unattractive.

ACTIVITIES
Camping: Where you wish. A few latrines at La Jara.
Hunting: Big game; small game; waterfowl.
Fishing: Rainbow trout at Hot Creek.

HEADQUARTERS: Division of Wildlife, 6060 Broadway, Denver, CO 80216;
(303) 297-1192.

HOVENWEEP NATIONAL MONUMENT
National Park Service
345 acres in CO, 440 in UT.

From Pleasant View on US 666, 20 mi. NW of Cortez, follow signs W for
25 mi. on pavement, gravel, and dirt.

"Our resources are primarily archeological," the Area Manager wrote. "This
certainly does not mean that there is nothing here for the nature-loving
populace. The lack of asphalt and its related amenities assure a high desert
experience."

You're not likely to see this part of Colorado and Utah unless you visit
Hovenweep. The Colorado area is characterized by canyons draining SW to
the San Juan River. Highest point in Hovenweep is 6,600 ft. Annual precipitation is about 9 in.

The Monument preserves the ruins of structures built by the Pueblos, who
abandoned the area before the year 1300, after a long drought. While they
lived here, draws draining into the canyons were terraced to hold soil and
provide irrigation water.

Plants: Some pinyon-juniper woodland, with big sagebrush, rabbitbrush,
buckwheat, snakeweed, wavyleaf oak, Utah serviceberry. Flowering species
of the area include prince's plume, golden currant, jimson weed, prickly pear,
mallow, penstemon, scarlet gilia, virgin's bower, datil yucca, four o'clock,
sunflower, tansy mustard, cliffrose, thistle.

Birds: Checklist available, noting habitats and seasons. 71 species recorded.
Seasonally common species include turkey vulture, red-tailed hawk, northern
harrier, Cooper's hawk, American kestrel, mourning dove, long-eared and
great horned owls, poor-will, common nighthawk, northern flicker, ash-
throated flycatcher, horned lark, scrub and pinyon jays, common raven,
mountain chickadee, plain titmouse, rock wren, loggerhead shrike, western
meadowlark, Brewer's blackbird, house finch, rufous-sided towhee, black-
throated and white-crowned sparrows, Oregon and gray-headed juncos.

Mammals: Checklist available. Species include California and small-footed myotis, coyote, rock squirrel, whitetail antelope squirrel, Colorado chipmunk, silky pocket mouse, Ord kangaroo rat, deer and pinyon mice, whitethroat and Mexican woodrats, blacktail jackrabbit, desert cottontail.

Reptiles and amphibians: Checklist available. Species include Utah tiger salamander, western spadefoot and red-spotted toads. Lizards: yellow-headed collared, long-nosed leopard, northern plateau, sagebrush, tree, northern whiptail. Snakes: striped whipsnake, Great Basin gopher, prairie rattlesnake.

Camping: 31 campsites. All year. Water supplied mid-Apr. to mid-Nov.

NEARBY: Cross Canyon (see entry).

PUBLICATIONS
Monument leaflet with map.
Bird, mammal, reptile and amphibian checklists. $.05 ea.
Trail guide. $.50.

HEADQUARTERS: McElmo Route, Cortez, CO 81321. No telephone.

MESA VERDE NATIONAL PARK
National Park Service
51,894 acres.

From Cortez, 10 mi. E on US 160 to entrance road.

Mesa Verde is not to be missed. The access road climbs to the mesa, at 8,000 ft. high above the surrounding country. Here prehistoric Indians built hundreds of dwellings on mesa tops and in alcoves along cliff ledges. The Park includes 9 major canyons.

It is a natural area, of course, permanently preserved, portraying how an aboriginal people lived with nature. The museum is devoted in part to natural history. The Rangers we talked with were keenly interested in the local vegetation and wildlife.

However, protection of the ruins on display and others not yet studied requires that visitors be confined to developed areas. Hiking is strictly limited to 5 trails. The backcountry is off limits.

Summer daytime temperatures range from 85° to 100°F., nights as cool as 55°. Winter lows between 15° and −25°F. The Park is open all year, weather permitting.

The Park has a bird checklist. Because visitors can't visit all the Park's habitats, we do not summarize the list. The leaflet notes that deer, eagles, and mountain lion make their home here.

INTERPRETATION
Amphitheater for evening programs.
Visitor center.
Museum.
Guided walks.

Camping: 477 sites. Open May 1–mid-Nov. No reservations.

PUBLICATIONS
Leaflet with map.
General information pages.
Flowers of Mesa Verde National Park.
Bird checklist.
Trail information.
Publications list.
Various publications on Indian culture.

REFERENCE
Trimble, Stephen. *The Bright Edge.* Flagstaff: Museum of Northern Arizona Press, 1979.

HEADQUARTERS: Mesa Verde National Park, CO 81330; (303) 529-4475.

MONTE VISTA NATIONAL WILDLIFE REFUGE
See entry, Alamosa and Monte Vista National Wildlife Refuges.

NAVAJO STATE RECREATION AREA
Colorado Division of Parks and Outdoor Recreation
2,672 acres of land. 3,273 acres of water in CO, 12,400 in NM.

From Durango, 45 mi. SE on SR 172 to Arboles, then S off SR 151 1 mi. to site.

Navajo Dam, on the San Juan River in New Mexico, has backed up a pool 35 mi. long, extending into Colorado. The shoreline is irregular. In Colorado, an arm of the reservoir extends up the Piedra River. Adjoining the SRA is the Navajo Reservoir State Wildlife Area, 1,500 acres managed by the Division of Wildlife. The surrounding area is within the Southern Ute Indian Reservation.

The SRA's visitor facilities are concentrated in less than a mile of lake front. New Mexico has a campground and other facilities at the S end. Most of the shoreline is undeveloped, and even on busy weekends one can find quiet areas to explore on foot or by boat. In places the reservoir is narrow, and it extends up many side canyons.

Elevations range from about 6,085 ft. at normal pool to 6,500 ft. on surrounding hills. Highest point nearby, outside the state area, is 8,551-ft. Piedra Peak.

Boating, fishing, and other water-based activities attract most of the visitors, but there are opportunities for hiking, including an old stagecoach road and an abandoned railroad bed.

Wildlife: No checklists available. Waterfowl, shorebirds, raptors, and songbirds are plentiful, as well as game birds: dove, grouse, and turkey. Mammals noted: beaver, mink, fox, deer, elk, rabbit, bobcat, mountain lion.

INTERPRETATION

Visitor center features Anasazi exhibits.

Interpretive programs; ask about topics and schedules.

ACTIVITIES

Camping: 90 sites.

Fishing: Bluegill, catfish, largemouth bass, trout, kokanee salmon. CO license good only in CO waters; NM license required across the border.

Boating: NM honors CO registration, but NM regulations apply across the border.

PUBLICATION: Leaflet with map.

HEADQUARTERS: P.O. Box 1697, Arboles, CO 81121; (303) 883-2208.

PERINS PEAK STATE WILDLIFE AREA
Colorado Division of Wildlife
3,821 acres, plus 1,600 acres of BLM land.

From Durango, about 3 1/2 mi. W on US 160. N about 1 mi. on Lightner Creek road, then continue N on unpaved Dry Fork road.

No great excitement here, but if you're spending some time in Durango, this site offers a quiet walk. The site was purchased in 1969 to provide winter range for an elk herd that was being squeezed by residential development N of Durango. Elevation ranges from 6,800 ft. at the E boundary to 8,723 ft. on Barnroof Point. Most of the terrain is rolling. Big sagebrush and scrub oak are the chief natural vegetation, with some stands of ponderosa pine and Douglas-fir. DW cleared about 350 acres of oakbrush and planted grasses. About 500 elk and 450 mule deer now use this as winter range and some elk calve here in the spring. Black bear, bobcat, and mountain lion are frequent visitors. Other mammals include porcupine, beaver, pine marten, and weasel. Golden and bald eagles are sometimes seen in winter.

Park and walk up the Dry Fork road. In about 2 mi., take the left fork. This becomes a 4-wheel-drive track, entering the San Juan National Forest in about 1/2 mi. One may camp in the National Forest.

Snowmobiles are banned. The Dry Fork road may be closed to vehicles in winter.

POWDERHORN
See entry in Zone 2.

REDCLOUD PEAK; HANDIES PEAK
U.S. Bureau of Land Management
48,900 acres.

The NE corner of the site is close to Lake City. N boundary is Henson Creek Road. Lake Fork Road, along the Lake Fork of the Gunnison River, crosses the area.

The area between Silverton and Lake City saw much gold and silver mining in the late 1800s. Many visitors are attracted by the network of old mine roads that gives 4-wheel-drive vehicles access to the backcountry. These two contiguous areas are roadless, a factor in qualifying them for wilderness status. (Two dirt roads that penetrate the SW area were "cherry-stemmed"—excluded from the proposed wilderness.)

The area was described to us as "classic Colorado high country." Redcloud Peak is 14,034 ft. Nearby Sunshine Peak is 14,001 ft. Several nearby peaks are over 13,000 ft. Much of the area is tundra, above timberline. The high country appeals to both hikers and climbers. Splendid vistas.

Foot access to the two principal peaks in the NE sector is along Silver Creek. Cooper Lake, a small alpine reservoir, drains into Cooper Creek, another perennial stream. Silver and Cooper Creeks flow S into Lake Fork. Several other creeks drain to the N. Timberline is at about 11,500 ft. Below this level are subalpine fir and spruce. Aspen occurs on lower S-facing slopes.

On the S side of the Lake Fork, Handies Peak is 14,048 ft., and others nearby top 13,000. A rugged area of high mountains, cirque basins enclosing alpine lakes, steep drainages, many waterfalls during spring runoff. Vast meadows of alpine tundra at high elevations. Forested areas extend from 8,600 ft. elevation to about 12,200 ft. Engelmann spruce-subalpine fir in drainage bottoms and on lower slopes. Above 11,000 ft. are pure, stunted spruce stands. Douglas-fir on steep, rocky slopes between 8,600 and 10,000 ft. Extensive stands of aspen where conifers were removed by fire or avalanche.

The site is summer range for elk, bighorn sheep, and mule deer.

From the Lake Fork road, a dirt road branches off to the W along Cottonwood Creek, giving access to the central part of the area. A popular trail begins at Cottonwood Creek and runs S of Cataract Gulch to Cataract Lake in the National Forest, near the Continental Divide and the Weminuche Wilderness. Trails leading to the top of Handies Peak are also popular, one of them entering from Lake Fork road along Grizzly Gulch.

Snowfall is heavy in the high country, accumulating to 20–25 feet in areas sheltered from wind, drifts persisting through July. We were told the economy of the area is so dependent on tourism that great efforts are made to clear snow from the public roads, including the high passes, early in the spring.

Camping: BLM has a 22-unit campground at the confluence of Mill Gulch and Lake Fork.

HEADQUARTERS: BLM, Montrose District Office, 2465 S. Townsend, Montrose, CO 81402; (303) 249-7791.

RIO GRANDE NATIONAL FOREST
U.S. Forest Service
1,851,792 acres; 1,961,084 acres within boundaries.

In SW CO, on the NM border. The major portion is within a triangle: Salida, Silverton, Conejos. This portion is crossed by US 160 and SR 149. A separate strip extends SE from Salida. No paved roads cross this strip.

A rugged, mountainous, scenic area surrounding the fertile San Luis Valley. Its NW and SW boundaries are the Continental Divide, on the crest of the impressive San Juan Mountains, with numerous peaks over 13,000 ft. Headwaters of the Rio Grande River are in the far W of the area. The river follows a sinuous course E across the center of the area. It is paralleled by SR 149, a convenient corridor along which are campgrounds, picnic areas, trailheads, and 4-wheel-drive routes to the high country.

Another corridor is US 160, SW from the town of South Fork, along the South Fork of the Rio Grande, with access to a number of campgrounds, trailheads, and backcountry routes.

The strip of Forest extending SE from Salida is on the W slope of the towering Sangre de Cristo Mountain Range. It meets the Pike and San Isabel NF at the crest.

Elevations range from about 7,800 ft. in the foothills to over 13,000 ft. in the San Juans along the Continental Divide and over 14,000 ft. in the Sangre de Cristos. Most of the Forest is between 9,000 and 11,000 ft.

Summers are cool, with afternoon showers common in July and August. Winters are severe, with considerable snow. The San Juans cause a rain shadow, so the San Luis Valley is very dry, and the Sangre de Cristo range is drier than the San Juans. Summer temperatures rarely exceed 80°F. Winter temperatures of −20°F are common, with extremes as low as −50°F.

Annual precipitation ranges from 10 in. in foothills to 50 in. on high slopes; about two-thirds of this falls as winter snow. High-country trails are usually closed by snow from late fall to late spring.

The Forest adjoins the San Juan NF on the W, the Grand Mesa, Uncompahgre, and Gunnison NF on the N, the Pike and San Isabel NF on the E. While its center is within a half-day's drive of the cities of the Front Range, other attractive Forests are closer, and the Rio Grande is not as heavily impacted by recreationists. Annual recreation visitor-days total about 2 million, more than half of this away from developed sites.

The Forest has more than 2,100 miles of roads, most unpaved, many primitive. More than one-fourth of the nonwilderness area is open to off-road vehicle use. High-clearance and 4-wheel-drive vehicles give campers, hunters, and others access to many remote, scenic areas.

Almost one-fourth of the Forest is in proclaimed or proposed Wilderness Areas. Wilderness use is still less than about 150,000 visitor-days per year, but is increasing.

The Forest has 1,350 mi. of trails, about one-third of them in wilderness areas, two-thirds elsewhere. Trail maintenance is best on the more popular routes.

Visitors should stop at Forest HQ or any Ranger District to consult the *Recreation Opportunities Guide (ROG)*, a massive looseleaf volume. It has a wealth of information about camping, hunting, fishing, horse riding, and other activities. It includes pages for many trails, each with sketch map, description, access, season of use, and difficulty rating.

Plants: 66% of the area is forested. Spruce-fir and aspen are the principal forest types, each accounting for about one-fourth of the total area. The many aspen stands, a result of past fires, are gradually giving way to conifers. Of the unforested area, montane grass constitutes almost a third, alpine vegetation slightly less. Soils, terrain, and other factors have combined to produce great habitat diversity and intermixing of plant communities: timber stands, parks, meadows, and grasslands.

Life zones are similar to those described in the entry for adjoining San Juan National Forest. Below the highest peaks of largely bare rock, often snow-covered, is tundra, where the growing season is short and spring flowers appear as snow melts. Flowering begins early on the lower slopes, extending upward as snow recedes, reaching a peak in late June and July. Flowering species include subalpine buttercup, columbine, purple loco, shooting star, milkweed, scarlet gilia, Indian paintbrush, penstemon, rabbitbrush, alpine sunflower, wild rose, marsh marigold, wild iris, harebell, coneflower, kinnikinnick, alpine forget-me-not, aster, fairy slipper, lupine, star gentian, twinflower.

Birds: Forest HQ reports that over 200 bird species occur in the Forest and San Luis Valley. Partial checklist available. Reported as seasonally common or abundant: blue grouse, mourning dove, great horned owl, green-tailed towhee, gray-headed junco, hairy woodpecker, pine grosbeak, horned lark, mountain bluebird, Steller's and gray jays, goshawk, kestrel, red-tailed hawk, bald and golden eagles, ptarmigan, common raven, American robin, black-billed magpie, American crow, broad-tailed hummingbird, pygmy nuthatch. Noted as of special interest to birders: peregrine falcon, sandhill crane, rosy finch, western tanager, pygmy nuthatch.

Mammals: Forest HQ reports that 63 mammal species occur in the Forest. Partial checklist available. Reported: yellowbelly marmot, longtail weasel, red and Abert squirrels, porcupine, beaver, muskrat, black bear, coyote, striped skunk, marten, pika, snowshoe hare, cottontail, pronghorn, mule deer, elk. Present but seldom seen: mountain lion, bobcat, bighorn sheep.

FEATURES

Sangre de Cristo Wilderness Study Area, 130,672 acres, plus 87,160 acres in the Pike and San Isabel NF. A high, rugged, mountainous area between the San Luis Valley on the W, Wet Mountain Valley on the E. The S end is on the side of 14,363-ft. Mt. Blanca, highest in the Sangre de Cristo range. Two primitive roads cross the range, at Hayden Pass and Medano Pass. Several peaks are higher than 14,000 ft., many more above 13,000. Average annual precipitation: 15 in. at lower elevations, over 30 in. on high slopes, most of the latter falling as snow. Lower slopes have pinyon-juniper association. Higher: oak, aspen, spruce. Mammals include black bear, mountain lion, mule deer, elk, bighorn sheep.

The Forest map shows numerous trails ascending from E and W sides. Difficulty ranges from a 4-mi. hike ascending 2,600 ft. to technical climbs.

South San Juan Wilderness, 88,463 acres, plus 39,783 acres in the San Juan NF. The area is W of Antonito. Access from SR 17 via Forest Roads 250, 114, and 118. Alternatively, traveling from Pagosa Springs on US 84, access is by Forest Roads 665 and 657. Alpine plateau bordered by the Continental Divide on the W, dissected by tributaries of the Conejos River. Numerous lakes, many with trout. Part of the area is above timberline; elevations to over 13,000 ft. The Conejos, San Juan, and Blanco Rivers have their headwaters here. Vegetation includes alpine plants, spruce, fir, aspen, shrubs, grasses. Abundant wildlife. Trails are chiefly in the drainages, and there are almost unlimited opportunities for off-trail hiking. Opportunities for camping, backpacking, horse riding, hunting, fishing, ski touring. Present visitor use is relatively light, 30,000 visitor-days in 1981, increasing.

The Forest Service and the State of Colorado recommended that 25.6 mi. of the Conejos River within the South San Juan Wilderness be added to the National Wild and Scenic River System as a Wild River. Recommended for Recreation designation was the 13.2 mi. from Platoro Reservoir to the confluence with South Fork. Congress has yet to act.

Weminuche Wilderness, 168,940 acres, plus 294,457 acres in the San Juan NF. This huge area straddles the Continental Divide from the Animas River near Silverton on the W to Wolf Creek Pass, where US 160 crosses the Divide. It is the largest wilderness area in CO, one of the best known and most popular. The few convenient access routes have relatively heavy use, but the interior is vast, pristine, inaccessible to day and weekend hikers. Noting that some high peaks have numbers rather than names, one informant said, "There haven't been enough people back in there to name them."

Average elevation is over 10,000 ft., with snowy peaks over 14,000. Much of the area is above timberline. Numerous clear mountain lakes, swift cold streams. Alpine meadows and high stands of spruce; large areas of bare rock and rock slides.

Annual precipitation from 27 in. at lower elevations to 45 in. on high slopes, much of this falling as snow. Temperatures range from 80°F to −30° and lower. Frost can occur at any time; a few semipermanent snowpacks. The hiking season in the high country begins about July 1. Abundant wildlife. Good trout fishing.

The large primeval areas have no established trails. Many backpackers take the narrow-gauge railroad from Durango to Needleton and hike up Needle Creek to Chicago Basin. Another popular route is the Los Pinos River Trail from Vallecito Reservoir to Emerald Lake. In general, the Rio Grande portion of the Weminuche is less intensively used. The most popular route is from Thirty Mile Campground up Weminuche Creek.

The Needle Mountains attract many mountain climbers.

La Garita Wilderness Area: 24,164 acres, plus 79,822 acres in the Grand

Mesa, Uncompahgre, and Gunnison NF. The Area straddles the Continental Divide, including part of the San Juan range. Access isn't easy, and recreation use was about 20,000 visitor-days in 1981. Approaching from the N, the nearest paved road is SR 114; a primitive road leads S about 17 mi. to the Stone Cellar Campground and Guard Station, then about 5 mi. S to a trailhead at the Wilderness boundary. From Creede on SR 149 an allweather road runs N about 10 mi. to a trailhead. From the trailhead, Wheeler Geologic Area is 7 mi. by trail and 14 mi. by jeep. The La Garita boundary is an additional 2-mi. hike. Three peaks in the Area tower above 14,000 ft. Many others exceed 12,000. Alpine meadows, rushing streams, beaver dams, talus slopes, forests of tall conifers, abundant wildlife. Excellent fishing in streams and Machin Lake. Machin Lake and the trail through Half Moon Pass to Wheeler Geologic Natural Area are the most popular.

Wheeler Wilderness Study Area, 11,390 acres, S of La Garita Wilderness. Access by 4-wheel-drive from SR 149. Now known as the Wheeler Geologic Natural Area. This was one of the first National Monuments, designated by President Theodore Roosevelt in 1908. No discovery record predates that year, though the site may have been seen by sheepherders or prospectors. Frank C. Spencer, Supervisor of the Rio Grande NF, made his way there in 1908: "It was a truly remarkable sight, well worth all our discomforts and labors. There before us, enhanced by the rays of the setting sun, lay the vista of what seemed to us an enchanted city. Spires and domes, castles and cathedrals, mosques and temples, with their fluted columns and wonderfully carved friezes, were arrayed in a confusing panorama of form and color."

Auto tours: A number of drives along rivers and over high passes offer splendid sightseeing. A pamphlet describing them is no longer available. Information is available in the Ranger District offices.

The Cumbres and Toltec Scenic Railroad operates a steam engine on narrow-gauge tracks on the original 64-mi. route between Antonito, CO, and Chama, NM, through parts of the Forest inaccessible by auto.

INTERPRETATION

Visitor Center at Del Norte has displays, literature, and information. Open 8 A.M.–5 P.M. daily in summer, otherwise Mon.–Fri. Information and publications at all Ranger District offices.

The Forest has no campfire talks, guided walks, or other naturalist programs.

ACTIVITIES

Camping: 38 campgrounds, 621 units. Generally open Memorial Day–Labor Day. Campgrounds are open at other times, weather permitting, but without water or trash collection. Informal camping is permitted throughout the Forest except where posted.

Hiking, backpacking: 1,350 mi. of trails. Some trails are signed and maintained, others not. The Forest map was compiled in 1974. Inquire at a Ranger

District office about trail conditions. High-country trails are generally snowed in from late fall to late spring.

Horse riding: Most trails are suitable for horse travel, but rangers warn that some are steep, narrow, boggy, rocky, hazardous. Check with the nearest Ranger District. Numerous outfitters offer day and pack trips. District Offices in LaJara, Saguache, Del Norte, and Creede have information.

Hunting: Big game: elk, deer, bighorn sheep, pronghorn, black bear, mountain lion. List of outfitters and guides available. Small game: cottontail, snowshoe hare, blue grouse, white-tailed ptarmigan, dove, band-tailed pigeon, squirrel, turkey, pheasant.

Fishing: Many lakes, miles of trout streams.

Boating: Most lakes are small, high, cold, remote. Most boating is by fishermen with cartoppers or other light craft.

Rafting: On the Rio Grande. Because it's shallow and rocky, rafts are better than canoes or kayaks, though all are used, chiefly in spring runoff, from Thirty Mile Campground to State Bridge. Commercial trips and rentals are available.

Skiing: Wolf Creek Ski Area, on US 160 between Pagosa Springs and Del Norte. Season from Nov. to Apr. Average annual snowfall: 435 in.

Ski touring: Good opportunities. No groomed trails. Information about marked trails is available at Ranger District offices.

Snowmobiling: Opportunities for snowmobiling abound. Contact Ranger District offices for information. The Forest Travel Map shows areas where snowmobile use is restricted.

PUBLICATIONS
Forest map. $1.00.
Travel map. Free.
Weminuche Wilderness. Folder with map.

HEADQUARTERS: 1803 West Highway 160, Monte Vista, CO 81144; (303) 852-5941.

RANGER DISTRICTS: Alamosa/Conejos R.D., Highway 285 North, La Jara, CO 81140; (303) 274-5193. Creede R.D., Creede, CO 81130; (303) 658-2556. Del Norte R.D., Del Norte, CO 81132; (303) 657-3321. Saguache R.D., Saguache, CO 81149; (303) 655-2547.

SAN JUAN NATIONAL FOREST
U.S. Forest Service
1,860,931 acres; 2,101,461 acres within boundaries.

In SW Colorado, near Durango. Crossed by US 550 and US 160.

Spectacular scenery, swift-flowing rivers, heavy winter snows, dense forests, vast areas of wilderness, miles of hiking trails.

330 mi. from Denver, the San Juan is not as heavily impacted by weekend visitors as Forests closer to the Front Range. The E and N boundaries generally follow the Continental Divide and the crest of the Wilson Mountains on the E and N. This is a region of high, rugged mountains, dozens over 10,000 ft. elevation, many over 12,000 ft., several over 14,000. The San Juan Mountains dominate the E portion of the Forest.

The Forest is at the junction of two physiographic provinces: the Southern Rocky Mountain, and the Colorado Plateau. Elevations decline along the watersheds of the several rivers: the Dolores, and the San Juan and its tributaries: the Mancos, Animas, Los Pinos, and Piedra. To the S and W are foothills, mesas, and deep canyons. Lowest point is about 6,000 ft.

The Forest has about 125 natural lakes, 10 reservoirs, 1,210 mi. of perennial streams.

2,220 mi. of Forest roads, some requiring high-clearance or 4-wheel-drive vehicles. ORV's are permitted in about two-thirds of the Forest, and they have worn miles of unplanned tracks.

Plants: About 72% forested, chiefly spruce-fir, aspen, ponderosa pine, Douglas-fir/white fir. *Alpine tundra* is above 11,000 ft. This area is rugged, large areas of exposed rock. Depressions and bowls contain poorly drained soil, often standing water. Cool summers; frost can occur any night. Long winters; snow cover usually lasts from Sept. to July. Vegetation on moist sites: tufted hairgrass, sedges, and willows; in dry areas: fescues, sedges, bluegrasses, many forbs, scattered patches of stunted spruce or fir.

Annual precipitation is 45–60 in. per year, snowfall 200–300 in. per year. Snowpack depth averages 70–90 in. by Apr. 1. Snow on peaks is usually melted by late Aug., with only a few perennial snowfields remaining. No glaciers.

Subalpine forest is found from 8,500 to 11,500 ft. on mountain slopes and canyon sideslopes. Vegetation: sedge-grass meadows, forested areas of Engelmann spruce, subalpine fir, aspen. Average annual precipitation is 25–45 in. Cool summers, cold winters. The hiking season varies by elevation, usually May–Nov. at 8,500 ft., late Jun.–Oct. at 11,500 ft.

Upper montane forest occurs from 8,000 to 9,500 ft.: upper foothills, lower mountain slopes, canyon sideslopes. A drier area, annual precipitation 23–30 in. Major tree species: Douglas-fir, white fir, subalpine fir, Engelmann spruce, blue spruce, aspen. Ponderosa pine and Gambel oak at the lower elevations. Winter snow cover usually lasts from late Nov. to early May. The ski touring season is Dec.–early Apr.

Lower montane forests are at 6,000–8,500 ft.: lower to mid-foothills and canyon sides. Annual precipitation 15–25 in. Vegetation: ponderosa pine, Gambel oak, and Douglas-fir in the upper portions, pinyon-juniper with grasses and shrubs below.

Birds: No published checklist. 238 species recorded, of which 66 were judged occasional or rare. Others, resident or migrant, include eared, western, and pied-billed grebes; great blue heron, snowy egret, black-crowned night-heron, American bittern, Canada goose, mallard, gadwall, American wigeon, pintail; green-winged, blue-winged, and cinnamon teals; shoveler, redhead, lesser scaup, common goldeneye, ruddy duck, common merganser, turkey vulture, goshawk; sharp-shinned, Cooper's, red-tailed, Swainson's, rough-legged, and ferruginous hawks; golden and bald eagles, northern harrier, prairie and peregrine falcons, American kestrel. Also wild turkey, blue grouse, white-tailed ptarmigan, chukar, ring-necked pheasant, sandhill crane, American coot, snowy and mountain plovers, killdeer, common snipe; spotted, solitary, least, and western sandpipers; greater and lesser yellowlegs, long-billed dowitcher, American avocet, Wilson's phalarope, ring-billed and Franklin's gulls, Forster's and black terns. Also band-tailed pigeon, rock and mourning doves; great horned, burrowing, long-eared, and short-eared owls; poor-will, common nighthawk, broad-tailed and rufous hummingbirds, belted kingfisher, northern flicker; Lewis', hairy, downy, and northern three-toed woodpeckers; yellow-bellied and Williamson's sapsuckers. Also eastern and western kingbirds, Say's phoebe; alder, Hammond's, western, and olive-sided flycatchers; western wood-pewee. Swallows: violet-green, tree, bank, rough-winged, barn, and cliff. Jays: gray, Steller's, scrub, and pinyon. Black-billed magpie, common raven, American crow, black-capped and mountain chickadees, white-breasted and pygmy nuthatches, brown creeper, dipper; house, marsh, and rock wrens; catbird, sage thrasher, American robin, hermit and Swainson's thrushes, veery, western and mountain bluebirds, Townsend's solitaire, blue-gray gnatcatcher, ruby-crowned kinglet, water pipit, Bohemian and cedar waxwings, northern and loggerhead shrikes, starling, warbling vireo. Warblers: Virginia's, yellow, yellow-rumped, MacGillivray's, common yellowthroat, Wilson's. House sparrow, bobolink, western meadowlark; yellow-headed, red-winged, and Brewer's blackbirds; northern oriole, brown-headed cowbird, western tanager, black-headed and evening grosbeaks; house, gray-crowned rosy, and brown-capped rosy finches; pine siskin, American goldfinch, red crossbill, green-tailed and rufous-sided towhees, lark bunting. Sparrows: savannah, vesper, lark, tree, chipping, Brewer's, white-crowned, Lincoln's, and song. White-winged, slate-colored, Oregon, and gray-headed juncos.

Mammals: No published checklist. Recorded: unspecified shrews, mice, rats, voles, moles, bats, weasels, skunk, ground squirrels. Black bear, raccoon, ringtail, yellowbelly marmot, pika, blacktail and whitetail jackrabbits, snowshoe hare, cottontail, whitetail prairie dog, least and Colorado chipmunks, Abert's and red squirrels, marten, mink, badger, coyote, red and gray foxes, bobcat, mountain lion, mule deer, elk, bighorn sheep, mountain goat.

FEATURES

Weminuche Wilderness, 294,457 acres in the San Juan NF, 164,715 acres in the Rio Grande NF. This huge area straddles the Continental Divide from the Animas River near Silverton on the W to Wolf Creek Pass, where US 160 crosses the Divide.

Average elevation is over 10,000 ft., with snowy peaks over 14,000. Much of the area is above timberline. Numerous clear mountain lakes, swift cold streams. Alpine meadows and high stands of spruce; large areas of bare rock and rock slides.

Annual precipitation from 25 in. at lower elevations to 50 in. on high slopes, much of this falling as snow. Temperatures range from 90°F to −30° and lower. Frost can occur at any time; limited semipermanent snowpacks. The hiking season in the high country begins about July 1. Abundant wildlife. Good trout fishing.

240 mi. of trails. Large primeval areas have no established trails. Many backpackers take the narrow-gauge railroad from Durango to Needleton and hike up Needle Creek to Chicago Basin. Another popular route is the Los Pinos River Trail from Vallecito Reservoir to Emerald Lake.

The Needle Mountains attract many mountain climbers.

Animas River Canyon. See entry. This strip of land was public domain, administered by BLM, when we visited and gathered data. It has since been made part of the San Juan NF, which borders it on both sides. We decided to keep it as a separate entry. The Durango and Silverton narrow-gauge railroad makes daily runs between Durango and Silverton, early May to mid-Oct., through this scenic canyon. It also offers winter trips from Durango to Cascade Creek and return. Make reservations a month or more in advance.

Piedra Wilderness Study Area, 41,500 acres. From US 160 between Bayfield and Pagosa Springs, N on Forest Road 620–622. Moderately broad slopes and valleys covered by ponderosa pine, spruce-fir, and aspen. The Piedra River is the primary drainage. The Piedra River Canyon has rapids, pools, small waterfalls. Elevations from 6,820 to 10,520 ft. Cool summers, cold winters with heavy snows. About 55 mi. of established trails. Abundant wildlife. River otter was reintroduced in 1978. Fishing considered good.

Opportunities for camping, backpacking, horse travel, hunting, fishing, rafting, ski touring. Visitor use is still relatively light.

South San Juan Wilderness, 39,783 acres, plus 87,811 acres in the Rio
Grande NF. The area is E of Pagosa Springs. Access from US 84 by Forest
Roads 665 and 657. Bottomlands, canyons, glaciated uplands, uneven mountains, high hills. Part of the area is above timberline; elevations to over 13,000
ft. The Conejos, San Juan, and Blanco Rivers have their headwaters here.
Vegetation includes alpine plants, spruce, fir, aspen, shrubs, grasses. Abundant wildlife. 164 mi. of trails. Opportunities for camping, backpacking, horse
travel, hunting, fishing, ski touring. Present visitor use is relatively light but
increasing.

Lizard Head Wilderness, 20,816 acres in the San Juan National Forest,
20,342 acres in the Uncompahgre NF. Access from SR 145 at Trout Lake, S
of Telluride. High mountain terrain; several peaks over 14,000 ft. Massive
rock outcrops, cirque lakes, swift mountain streams; fishing. Large areas of
alpine and spruce-fir vegetation. Only 19 mi. of established trail, but links with
other Forest trails. Light visitor use.

Vallecito Reservoir is a popular camping, fishing, boating, and water skiing
area, with hiking trails nearby. 22 mi. shoreline.

Scenic Drives. Most roads inside the Forest are scenic, often spectacular.
Two main highways merit special note: US 550, Montrose to Durango, and
US 160, Durango to Del Norte. Both cross high passes with expanses of
tundra, follow and cross splendid mountain streams, provide fine views.
Campgrounds, points of interest, and tempting side roads along the way.
Sections of US 550 are hazardous during heavy storms.

Dolores River Canyon, from 2,000 to 2,600 ft. deep, has colorful strata like
the Grand Canyon. One viewpoint can be reached by Forest Road 502 from
Dove Creek on US 666. A Forest Service Campground is at the overlook. See
entry, Dolores River, in Zone 2.

Treasure Falls, 110 ft. high, is off US 160 near the Wolf Creek Campground.
Windy Pass Trail and Treasure Mountain Trail nearby.

INTERPRETATION
The Forest provides little in the way of interpretive programs.

ACTIVITIES
Camping: 42 campgrounds, 890 sites. Camping season is Memorial Day to
mid-Nov. No reservation system; campgrounds are most likely to be full on
holiday weekends. Advice may be obtained from Ranger District offices.

Hiking, backpacking: 1,155 mi. of established trails, with many opportunities for off-trail hiking. Water is generally available. Some trails are overused.
Rangers can direct you to the less-traveled trails. For spring and fall hiking,
trails at lower elevations are recommended.

Horse travel: All trails are open to horse travel. Horse packing is a significant activity; it's best to carry feed. The Forest has no list of stables or
outfitters.

Hunting: 85% of the hunting is for big game: mule deer, elk, black bear, bighorn sheep. 650,000 acres of big game winter range. Many hunters from out of the area.

Fishing: 94 natural lakes, 10 reservoirs, 281 perennial fishing streams. Most stream habitat is poor quality because of steep gradients and seasonal variations. Well-known fishing waters include the Animas River, Vallecito Reservoir, Lemon Reservoir.

Boating: Power boating at Vallecito. No hp limit stated. Ramps. Marinas. Canoes and cartoppers are permitted on all reachable waters.

Dolores River is a popular rafting and kayaking stream (see entry in Zone 2). From Cahone, downstream from Dolores, to Bedrock on SR 90, is 105 river mi., a 5-day trip. Canyon is deep, with sheer walls that sometimes overhang the stream. Most of the whitewater is between Cahone and Slickrock on SR 141, the first 2 days of the trip. This section of the river is within or near the Forest boundary. The second and drier section is through land managed by BLM. Season is May to mid-June when runoff is good; some years have short season or none. Commercial operators.

Some rafting on the Animas River, but this is "not real whitewater."

Skiing: The Forest has one major ski area: Purgatory. 60 to 70% of the skiers are from out of state. Demand exceeds capacity, and additional ski areas will doubtless be developed.

Ski touring: Very popular; principal areas at Molas Pass and La Plata Canyon. Groomed trails only on private land and at Purgatory. Overnighting facilities are limited to camping.

Swimming: at Vallecito Reservoir. Season Memorial Day to mid-Sept., but the water is cold.

PUBLICATIONS

Forest map. $1.00.

Information pages:

Welcome to the San Juan National Forest.
Hiking Trails (Durango Area).
Fishing Opportunities (Durango Area).
Off Highway Vehicle Opportunities (Durango Area).
Camping Opportunities (Durango Area).
Weminuche Wilderness. Map, information.

REFERENCES

Gebhardt, Dennis. *A Backpacking Guide to the Weminuche Wilderness in the San Juan Mountains of Colorado.* Durango, CO: Basin Reproduction and Printing, 1976.

Pixler, Paul. *Hiking Trails of the San Juans.* Boulder, CO: Pruett, 1983.

HEADQUARTERS: 701 Camino del Rio, Durango, CO 81301; (303) 247-4874.

RANGER DISTRICTS: Dolores R.D., 501 Railroad Ave., Dolores, CO 81323; (303) 882-7296. Mancos R.D., U. S. Highway 160, Mancos, CO 81328; (303) 533-7716. Animas R.D., 701 Camino Del Rio, Durango, CO 81301; (303) 259-0195. Pine R.D., 419 Pearl St., Bayfield, CO 81122; (303) 884-2512. Pagosa R.D., U. S. Highway 160, Pagosa Springs, CO 81147; (303) 264-2268.

SLUMGULLION SLIDE
U.S. Bureau of Land Management
1,640 acres.

On SR 149 about 3 mi. SE of Lake City.
About 700 years ago an earth flow from the W edge of Cannibal Plateau moved 4 1/2 mi. into the valley, blocking the Lake Fork of the Gunnison River and creating Lake San Cristobal. A smaller earth flow beginning about 350 years ago still continues at about 1/2 in. per day. SR 149 circles the tip of the slide.

The site adjoins a 31,990-acre roadless area in the Grand Mesa, Uncompahgre, and Gunnison National Forests. Most of the land is steep, rising from 9,600 ft. to 10,700 ft. within a mile. Most of the area is forested with spruce, aspen, and Douglas-fir. Trees growing on the active slide are leaning; those on stable soil are straight. BLM has fixed stakes across the slide to show the progressive movement.

SR 149 continues E past Windy Point Overlook. At Slumgullion Pass is a Forest Service campground and Forest Road 788 NE to Deer Lakes and several backcountry campgrounds.

HEADQUARTERS: BLM, Montrose District Office, 2465 S. Townsend, Montrose, CO 81402; (303) 249-7791.

TRICKLE MOUNTAIN WILDLIFE HABITAT AREA
U.S. Bureau of Land Management
52,565 acres.

From Saguache on US 285, 15 mi. W on SR 114. The area is mostly N of the highway.

The area crossed by SR 114 is surrounded on three sides by the Rio Grande National Forest. Most of the area is public land administered by BLM. Two sections are state land. Private holdings are along the highway and creek bottoms.

In 1977, BLM developed a Habitat Management Plan for an area of 147,230 acres, including 84,215 acres of National Forest land. The area is of special interest to visitors because of its wildlife and the data gathered in support of the plan. It is one of a very few places where bighorn sheep, elk, mule deer, and pronghorn use the same area. The bighorn herd is one of the largest and healthiest in Colorado.

In the NW corner of the San Luis Valley, the WHA is bounded on the N and W by the Continental Divide on the crest of the Cochetopa Hills. Saguache Creek and Rabbit Canyon are on the S. E boundary is the ridge between Findley Gulch and Dry Gulch. Elevations in the WHA range from 7,840 ft. at Saguache Creek to 13,266 ft. on Antero Peak. Within the BLM land, the range is from about 8,000 ft. to 10,400 ft. Here the topography is typified by mesas topped by rolling hills, cut by steep-sided drainages. Creek bottoms are mostly narrow, talus slopes ascending steeply to rimrock. Open grassy slopes are common on mesa tops, hilltops, and lower hillsides.

Climate is mild and dry. Temperatures range from a high mean of 65°F to a low mean of about 19°F. Average annual precipitation varies from 8 to 16 in. on the BLM land, up to 35 in. on Antero Peak. Snow falls in winter, but the greatest precipitation occurs July–Sept.

Plants: The most extensive habitat type is mountain and intermountain grassland. BLM has inventoried the subtypes and principal plant species. Vegetation along gullies and drainages is often dominated by rabbitbrush, with fourwing saltbush and pingue. The mountain shrub habitat includes such species as currant, bush rockspires, mountain-mahogany. Forest subtypes include pinyon-juniper, Douglas-fir, and ponderosa pine. Spruce, fir, limber pine, and bristlecone pine occur in scattered areas, sometimes locally abundant.

Habitats and Wildlife: Riparian woodlands and wet meadows attract the greatest variety of wildlife. Mammals include raccoon, beaver, longtail vole, cottontail, northern pocket gopher. Birds include mallard, red-winged blackbird, yellow warbler, northern flicker, black-billed magpie, cliff swallow, warbling vireo, mourning dove, blue grouse.

Whitetail jackrabbit and horned lark are common in *mixed grassland-brushland.* Porcupine and mountain bluebird are typical of *coniferous woodlands.* Common in *pine-fir forests* are Colorado chipmunk, snowshoe hare, Abert squirrel, Steller's jay, dark-eyed junco, mountain chickadee, western tanager. Bushytail woodrat and rock wren occur on *rocky slopes.* Some species, including deer mouse, coyote, turkey vulture, common raven, common nighthawk, are found throughout the area.

Mammals: Black bear and mountain lion are sighted occasionally. Bobcat are trapped. Introduced to the area in 1951, the bighorn herd has increased to about 300 animals. Elk use of the BLM lands is mostly in winter; elk population has increased to about 500. Pronghorn population is about 150.

Other common species include golden-mantled ground squirrel, least chipmunk, northern pocket gopher, Ord's kangaroo rat, little brown myotis, big brown bat, blacktail jackrabbit, Gunnison prairie dog, northern grasshopper mouse. Voles: boreal redback, meadow, montane, longtail.

Birds: BLM's bird list also includes as seasonally common or abundant: mallard, green-winged teal, rough-legged hawk, golden eagle, American kestrel, killdeer, rock dove, great horned owl, broad-tailed and rufous hummingbirds, northern flicker, yellow-bellied sapsucker, downy woodpecker, Say's phoebe; barn, cliff, violet-green, and tree swallows; pinyon and gray jays, Clark's nutcracker, sage thrasher, American robin, Townsend's solitaire, loggerhead shrike, yellow-rumped warbler, common yellowthroat, western meadowlark; yellow-headed, red-winged, and Brewer's blackbirds; house finch, green-tailed and rufous-sided towhees; savannah, vesper, sage, Brewer's, white-crowned, and song sparrows; dark-eyed and gray-headed juncos.

ACTIVITIES

Camping: No established sites.

Hiking: The Rio Grande National Forest map shows numerous trails and primitive roads within the BLM area and extending into the Forest.

All motor vehicles must remain on established roads.

HEADQUARTERS: BLM, Canon City District Office, 3080 E. Main St., Canon City, CO 81212; (303) 275-0631.

TWIN PEAKS

U.S. Bureau of Land Management
3,300 acres, plus 9,600 acres in New Mexico.

From Antonito on US 285, E on local road to the Rio Grande River, then S.

The land area is of no great interest: low hills on the W, rolling lands to the E and S. Vegetation is low-growing bitterbrush and rabbitbrush, with scattered pinyon and juniper trees.

What gives the site special interest is the canyon of the Rio Grande River. Across the New Mexico border, this canyon is included in the national system of Wild and Scenic Rivers. The last 8 river-miles in CO are no less scenic, but local opposition has thus far blocked Wild and Scenic designation.

Private rafting parties often put in at Lobatos Bridge, E of Antonito. Few commercial outfitters offer trips on this section. Consult the BLM office.

HEADQUARTERS: BLM, Canon City District Office, 3080 E. Main St., Canon City, CO 81212; (303) 275-0631.

ZONE 4

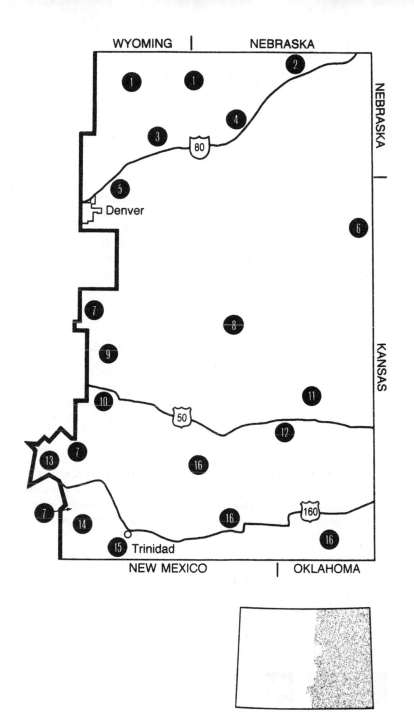

ZONE 4

Includes these counties:

Weld	Kiowa	Arapahoe
Sedgwick	Bent	Lincoln
Phillips	Huerfano	El Paso
Yuma	Baca	Crowley
Denver	Logan	Otero
Elbert	Morgan	Prowers
Kit Carson	Washington	Las Animas
Pueblo	Adams	

This is by far the largest of our four zones, yet it has the fewest sites. Zone 4 is the eastern plain. Most of the land is privately owned. The principal land uses are farming and ranching. Large areas are irrigated.

Of the 16 sites described in this zone, about half would not have been included were they further west. In the long drive from Kansas, however, any oasis has appeal. The Queens State Wildlife Area is an example. No one could call it outstandingly scenic or natural, but we enjoyed our overnight stop there. Our black Labrador enjoyed it even more, romping in the lake with two small boys until all three were exhausted.

The zone does have some excellent mountain scenery, at Spanish Peaks. Its other principal features are the South Platte River, crossing the N half of the zone, and the Arkansas, crossing the S. Along these two rivers are numerous large and small impoundments and wetlands, including some reservoirs heavily used for boating. Many of these sites are of interest to birders, as are the two National Grasslands.

BARR LAKE STATE PARK
Colorado Division of Parks and Outdoor Recreation
691 acres; 1,900 acres of water.

From Denver, NE on I-76. Just beyond Mile Marker 22, turn right. This turn and the next two are marked for the Park, though not conspicuously.

A hot spot for birds. Like Chatfield State Recreation Area (see entry in Zone 2), this lake is artificial, near Denver, surrounded by relatively flat land. It doesn't attract huge crowds. There is no campground; only sailboats, hand-propelled craft, and boats with electric trolling motors are permitted, and only at the N end. Swimming is prohibited. On a fine Saturday morning in August we found only 3 cars in the refuge area.

This area, at the S end, is planned for bird watching, with boardwalks, viewing platforms, observation blinds, and shore trails. However, when the reservoir is drawn down, as we found it, birding requires a 30-power scope; binoculars won't suffice—the water's edge is too far away. Better vantage points may be found along the 9-mi. trail circling the lake.

The reservoir is relatively young. Public use began in 1977. Parts of the shoreline have naturalized, with tall cottonwoods and dense shoreline vegetation. The bird list, prepared in early days, is inadequate, naming only 55 species. It does not include white pelican, for example, which were numerous when we visited.

Channel catfish, small- and largemouth bass, perch, trout, crappie, and bluegill are stocked.

PUBLICATIONS
Leaflet with map.
Bird checklist.

HEADQUARTERS: Division of Parks and Outdoor Recreation, 1313 Sherman, Denver, CO 80203; (303) 866-3437. Park manager: (303) 659-6005.

BONNY STATE RECREATION AREA
Colorado Division of Parks and Outdoor Recreation
5,000 acres; 1,940 acres of water.

From Burlington on I-70, 22 mi. N on US 385.

The park is popular for water-based recreation. It adjoins 11,000 acres owned or leased by the Division of Wildlife. Rolling hills. Elevation about 3,700 ft. Areas of forest. Hiking along the South Fork of the Republican River.

Camping: 203 sites. Reservations; see Preface.

HEADQUARTERS: Idalia, CO 80735; (303) 354-7306.

COLORADO SPRINGS STATE WILDLIFE AREA
Colorado Division of Wildlife
5,000 acres.

From Colorado Springs, 20 mi. S on I-25. Exit 125.

Most of the site is on the W side of the highway. A smaller portion on the E side can be reached from Exit 123. Both sites are planned chiefly for the "nonconsuming user": the hiker, birder, student of nature. They offer an opportunity to walk for a couple of hours in natural surroundings.

The larger portion is basically shortgrass prairie with yucca and cholla cactus. Fountain Creek provides riparian habitat. Part of the E portion is planted in feed crops. Over 200 bird species have been observed. Mammals include prairie dog, beaver, muskrat, raccoon, squirrel, coyote, mule deer.

Nature trail, 1 1/2 mi., is on the E side, near the parking area.

Hunting: Waterfowl, quail, dove. No rifles or handguns.

Access is limited by parking space; when parking lots are full no cars are admitted.
No camping.

COMANCHE NATIONAL GRASSLAND; PIKE AND SAN ISABEL NATIONAL FOREST
U.S. Forest Service
418,887 acres.

Two blocks, both SE of Pueblo. The Timpas Unit is S of La Junta, crossed by US 350 and SR 109. The Carrizo Unit is S of Springfield, on the Oklahoma boundary, crossed by US 160 and US 287/385. Both areas are a mixture of public and private lands.

On Colorado's E plain, the area seems almost level and featureless from a passing car. A closer look discloses surprising variety of habitats: canyon-mesa; yucca-sand sagebrush; shortgrass prairie; intermediate grass prairie; irrigated and nonirrigated cropland; ponds; marshes. The Grassland is of special interest to birders.

Birds: 235 species recorded. Checklist available. Birders may blink at several of the listings: species far outside the ranges given in guidebooks, and not marked *occasional* or *accidental.* However, the list is said to have been prepared by experts. Most species are migrants or seasonal residents.

Omitting those marked *rare* or *accidental,* the list includes pied-billed and horned grebes, white pelican, double-crested cormorant, great blue and green herons, snowy egret, black-crowned night heron, American bittern, white-faced ibis; Canada, Ross', snow, and white-fronted geese; mallard, gadwall, pintail; green-winged, blue-winged, and cinnamon teals; shoveler, American wigeon, redhead, ring-necked duck, canvasback, lesser scaup, bufflehead, ruddy duck, common and hooded mergansers. Also turkey vulture, bald and golden eagles. Hawks: sharp-shinned, goshawk, Cooper's, red-shouldered, red-tailed, Harlan's, Swainson's, rough-legged, ferruginous. Northern harrier, prairie falcon, merlin, American kestrel, Mississippi kite.

Also lesser prairie chicken, bobwhite, scaled quail, ring-necked pheasant, Merriam's turkey, chukar. Sandhill crane, Virginia rail, sora, American coot. Semipalmated, mountain, black-bellied, and upland plovers; killdeer, common snipe, long-billed curlew. Sandpipers: stilt, pectoral, semipalmated, least, western, spotted, solitary. Long-billed dowitcher, willet, lesser and greater yellowlegs, sanderling, American avocet, Wilson's phalarope, ring-billed and Franklin's gulls, black and Forster's terns.

Yellow-billed cuckoo, roadrunner. Owls: barn, screech, great horned, burrowing, long-eared, short-eared, saw-whet. Common nighthawk, chimney and white-throated swifts, ruby-throated hummingbird, belted kingfisher, northern flicker. Woodpeckers: red-bellied, red-headed, hairy, downy, ladder-backed, Lewis'. Eastern, western, and Cassin's kingbirds; great crested, ash-throated, least, olivaceous, and olive-sided flycatchers; eastern and Say's phoebe, western wood-pewee.

Horned lark. Swallows: tree, bank, rough-winged, barn, and cliff. Common and white-necked ravens, common crow; pinyon, scrub, and blue jays; black-billed magpie, black-capped chickadee, plain titmouse, brown creeper. Wrens: rock, canyon, house, Bewick's, marsh, cactus. Mockingbird, catbird, brown and curve-billed thrashers, American robin, Swainson's and gray-cheeked thrushes, veery, Townsend's solitaire; mountain, western, and eastern bluebirds. Blue-gray gnatcatcher, water pipit, cedar waxwing, northern and loggerhead shrikes, European starling; gray, Bell's, and warbling vireos. Warblers: yellow-rumped, yellow-throated, orange-crowned, yellow, ovenbird, northern water thrush, MacGillivray's, yellowthroat, yellow-breasted chat, Virginia's, blackpoll, American redstart.

House sparrow, western meadowlark; red-winged, yellow-headed, and Brewer's blackbirds; brown-headed cowbird, common grackle, northern oriole, rose-breasted, black-headed, and blue grosbeaks; indigo and lazuli buntings, pine siskin, dickcissel, American and lesser goldfinches, purple finch;

brown, rufous-sided, and green-tailed towhees; lark bunting, Oregon and gray-headed juncos. Sparrows: Cassin's, savannah, grasshopper, Baird's, vesper, lark, rufous-crowned, tree, chipping, clay-colored, Brewer's, field, Harris', white-crowned, white-throated, fox, Lincoln's. Longspurs: chestnut-collared, McCown's, Lapland, Smith's.

Mammals: Checklist available; no indication of abundance. Includes black bear, raccoon, opossum, longtail weasel, blackfooted ferret, spotted and striped skunks, badger; red, swift, and gray foxes; coyote, mountain lion, bobcat, mule deer, whitetail deer, pronghorn, blacktail prairie dog, spotted and thirteen-lined ground squirrels, rock squirrel, plains and Mexican pocket gophers, Ord kangaroo rat, muskrat, beaver. Plains and western harvest mice. Mice: deer, house, white-footed, pinyon, brush. Silky and hispid pocket mice, northern grasshopper mouse; Mexican, eastern, and whitethroat woodrats; hispid cotton rat, porcupine, desert and eastern cottontails, blacktail jackrabbit, eastern mole, desert shrew, Colorado chipmunk. Bats: silver-haired, big brown, hoary, big freetail, western big-eared, pallid; little brown and small-footed myotis.

Reptiles and Amphibians: Turtles: common snapping, ornate box, yellow mud, painted, western spiny softshell. Lizards: yellow collared, lesser earless, eastern fence, northern prairie, horned, eastern and Texas short-horned; Great Plains, northern and southern many-lined skinks; checkered whiptail, six-lined racerunner. Snakes: plains hognose, western coachwhip, bull, king, prairie rattlesnake, massasauga, pygmy rattlesnake, blue racer, plains blackheaded, prairie ringneck, Kansas glossy, corn, Central Plains milk, Texas long-nosed, common water, red-sided and plains garter, western ribbon, northern lined, Texas night, worm. Amphibians: plains and western spadefoot; Rocky Mountain, Great Plains, and green toads; bullfrog, leopard and cricket frogs, barred tiger salamander.

NEARBY

Cimarron National Grassland, 108,337 acres, is in the SW corner of Kansas, a few miles E of the Comanche NG. It is also managed by the Pike and San Isabel NF. The species checklists apply to both. Cimarron offers a 50-mi., 3-hr. self-guided tour, with leaflet and markers. The tour begins at Elkhart, Kansas, on US 56. Drive N 2 mi. on SR 27, turn left, drive 5 mi. W to the first marker.

PUBLICATIONS
   Bird checklist.
   Checklist of mammals, reptiles and amphibians, fishes.
   Cimarron Auto Tour leaflet.

HEADQUARTERS: Pike and San Isabel National Forests, 1920 Valley Drive, Pueblo, CO 81008; (303) 545-8737.

RANGER DISTRICTS: Timpas Unit, East Highway 50, La Junta, CO 81050; (303) 384-2181. Carrizo Unit, 212 E. 10th St., Springfield, CO 81073; (303) 523-6591. Cimarron NG, 737 Villymaca St., Elkhart, KS 67950; (316) 697-4621.

HUERFANO STATE WILDLIFE AREA
Colorado Division of Wildlife
544 acres.

Access is best seen on the San Isabel National Forest map. From Walsenburg NW to Gardner on SR 69, then SW on county road beyond Red Wing to Singing River Ranch.

The acreage is small, but it includes 2 1/2 mi. of good trout water on the Huerfano River. Much of the surrounding land is BLM, and the San Isabel National Forest boundary is nearby. The site is on the E side of the Sangre de Cristo Range. From here one can hike or backpack up Huerfano Gorge, through dense conifer forests to timberline and high-altitude lakes. A pleasant, scenic, out-of-the-way campsite.

HEADQUARTERS: Division of Wildlife, 6060 Broadway, Denver, CO 80216; (303) 297-1192.

HUGO STATE WILDLIFE AREA
Colorado Division of Wildlife
3,600 acres; 26 acres of water.

From Hugo on US 40/287, 13 mi. S, then 2 mi. E.

A natural area? No. But if you pass nearby, stop to see what management can do to enhance a habitat. The site is described as a "geological outcropping" in the expanse of E prairie. The unique factor, a series of live springs, prompted the Division of Wildlife to acquire the site in 1970. Then began the development of ponds, now 19 of them. Plantings included trees, shrubs, and plots of feed crops. This development has attracted waterfowl, dove, quail, rabbits, antelope, and mule deer, as well as many songbirds. Prairie dogs (introduced) promptly constructed a town.

JOHN MARTIN RESERVOIR
Colorado Division of Wildlife; U.S. Army Corps of Engineers
20,625 land acres; 1,700 water.

From Hasty on US 50, 3 mi. S.

The reservoir, about 5 mi. long, was formed by damming the Arkansas River.
Below the dam is a 75-acre impoundment called "Lake Hasty" and a campground. The Reservoir is subject to drawdowns. The summers of 1982, 1983,
and 1984 have seen high water, resulting in excellent boating. The water level
of Lake Hasty is maintained for recreation.

The Corps manages the dam and campground. The 16,802 acres upstream
are leased to the Division of Wildlife. The reservoir has an irregular 45-mi.
shoreline at elevation 3,850. Uplands are rolling prairie with sandstone canyons. Along the lake shore, we saw gently sloping beaches, bluffs 30 or more
ft. high.

The Corps recreation area is well signed. The Wildlife Area is not, and the
campground attendant could tell us nothing about it. However, access is not
difficult. We saw many dirt tracks leading down to the shore on both sides
of the reservoir, with several tents and RV's.

Plants: Prairie has prickly pear, cholla cactus, tumbleweed, fireweed, wild
mustard, sunflower, yucca. Unusually large patches of prickly pear and yucca
on the N side. River bottomland has cottonwoods, elms, willows, salt cedars,
patches of thick brush.

Birds: No checklist. Area is on the Central Flyway, with good year-round
birding. Reported: white pelican, Canada and snow geese, mallard, canvasback, American wigeon, blue-winged teal, bobwhite, scaled quail, Swainson's
and red-tailed hawks; bald and golden eagles; great horned, barn, and screech
owls; lark bunting, western kingbird.

Mammals: Bobcat, prairie dog, beaver, raccoon, opossum, rock squirrel,
spotted ground squirrel, cottontail, coyote, fox, pronghorn, deer.

ACTIVITIES
Camping: 65 sites in the Corps's attractive campground. Primitive camping
is permitted on the Reservoir side.

Hunting: Waterfowl, pheasant, grouse, dove.

Fishing: Reservoir, river, and Lake Hasty. Catfish, smallmouth bass, trout,
walleye, crappie, bluegill.

Boating: Ramps. Power boating on reservoir.

Rafting: On Arkansas River below the dam; limited by release of water.

Swimming: Reservoir and Lake Hasty.

PUBLICATION: Folder with map (from the Corps).

HEADQUARTERS: Corps: John Martin Reservoir, Star Route, Hasty, CO 81044; (303) 336-3476. Division of Wildlife: 6060 Broadway, Denver, CO 80216; (303) 297-1192.

PAWNEE NATIONAL GRASSLAND; ARAPAHO AND ROOSEVELT NATIONAL FORESTS
U.S. Forest Service
193,060 acres.

30 mi. E of Ft. Collins; N of SR 14.

The Grasslands are attractive to birders because of the extraordinary number of species that can be seen. Auto birding tours are popular at all seasons. May–June is favored because of the many migrant species present and the wildflowers.

The total Grassland area is 775,000 acres. The federal land is in two large blocks. Terrain is relatively flat, at about 5,000 ft. elevation. Most of it is shortgrass prairie, with some cultivated fields. Much of the area is open to hunting and ORV's.

FEATURES
A few miles to the W, the *Pawnee Buttes* would be inconspicuous foothills. They stand only 250 ft. high. In this flatland, they are dramatic landmarks, visible for miles. The buttes are an important nesting site for raptors. They were formed at a time when fast-melting glaciers sent tremendous torrents of water over the plains, stripping away layers of earlier deposition. The area is rich in fossils. The buttes appear on the state highway map NE of Keota. Dirt roads approach to within a mile. The trail to the buttes is a popular hike.

Plants: Wildflower displays are an attraction, peaking in May–June. Typical species: prickly pear, scarlet globemallow, Colorado loco, sand lily, milkvetch.

Birds: Checklist of 229 species available, noting seasonality and abundance. Common or abundant species include mallard, common merganser, Swainson's and ferruginous hawks, golden eagle, northern harrier, American kestrel, killdeer, mountain plover, ring-billed gull, mourning dove, common nighthawk, northern flicker, eastern and western kingbirds, Say's phoebe, western wood-pewee, horned lark, barn swallow, black-billed magpie, black-capped chickadee, house and rock wrens, American robin, loggerhead shrike,

European starling. Warblers: yellow, yellow-rumped, Wilson's. House sparrow, western meadowlark, red-winged and Brewer's blackbirds, northern oriole, brown-headed cowbird, house finch, American goldfinch, lark bunting. Sparrows: vesper, lark, tree, Brewer's, white-crowned. Dark-eyed junco.

Mammals: No checklist. Mentioned: prairie dog, jackrabbit, coyote, badger, swift fox, mule deer, pronghorn.

Auto tour routes. Self-guiding tours of 34 to 170 mi.

Camping: Campground is 1/2 mi. N of SR 14 at Briggsdale.

PUBLICATIONS
Bird checklist.
Birding auto tour.
Auto Winter Birding Tours.

HEADQUARTERS: 2009 9th St., Greeley, CO 80631; (303) 353-5004.

PIKE AND SAN ISABEL NATIONAL FORESTS
See entry in Zone 2. The county lines that serve as zone boundaries cut across three portions of the Forests. The disjunct portion that contains the Spanish Peaks Wilderness Area is almost entirely within Zone 4.

PREWITT RESERVOIR STATE WILDLIFE AREA
Colorado Division of Wildlife
493 land acres; 2,431 water.

From Merino, 13 mi. SW of Sterling on US 6: 3 mi. S on County Road 25.

The highway sign announces this as a state fishing area. At the gate is an alarming array of posted regulations prohibiting off-road vehicles, whitewater wakes, keg beer, fishing in waterfowl season, fireworks, and other sins. The gravel entrance road crosses gently rolling fields, ablaze with sunflowers when we visited.

It's an attractive place for quiet camping, walking, and birding. The lake appears to be more than 3 mi. long, about 1 mi. wide. The water level was down, exposing a wide sandy beach. Scattered cottonwoods around the perimeter, some of them large. On an Aug. Monday, one RV was parked at a campsite, a young woman was sunbathing on the beach near her car, and a car with two fishermen was just leaving. A few sand castles and minor picnic debris said there had been more visitors on the weekend.

Birding seemed good. We saw about 200 white pelicans and more than 35 great blue herons at one end of the lake, along with coots and a few ducks. Shorebirds were too distant for recognition. In the cottonwoods, we spotted western kingbirds, northern flickers, and red-headed woodpeckers.

ACTIVITIES

Camping: Primitive, no fixed sites, latrines. Weekends may be busier, but only one party was camping when we were there.

Hiking: Mostly for birding along the beach.

Fishing: The only fishermen we saw said they hadn't been there before, and couldn't provide information.

Hunting: Waterfowl, upland game.

Swimming: The water is shallow. We threw a stick as far as we could, and our Labrador was still leaping when he retrieved it.

HEADQUARTERS: Division of Wildlife, 6060 Broadway, Denver, CO 80216; (303) 297-1192.

PUEBLO STATE RECREATION AREA
Colorado Division of Parks and Outdoor Recreation
15,755 acres; 1,245 acres of water.

PUEBLO STATE WILDLIFE AREA
Colorado Division of Wildlife
1,600 acres.

6 mi. W of Pueblo, between US 50 and SR 96.

Close to Pueblo, the SRA attracts large numbers of visitors for water-based recreation. We note it because of the large acreage and the adjoining Pueblo State Wildlife Area.

The reservoir was formed by damming the Arkansas River. The SRA surrounds the reservoir. The Wildlife Area is on both sides of the river for more than 8 mi. upstream. Management changes have included blasting about 50 potholes for waterfowl, planting feed crops, introducing wild turkeys, placing nest boxes for prairie falcons on the river cliffs, and building guzzlers for wildlife water supply.

Elevations range from 4,900 ft. to 5,000 ft. Annual precipitation is about 12 in.

The Wildlife Area has about 22 mi. of roads and trails in rolling and hilly terrain.

Camping: 214 sites. Reservations; see Colorado Preface.

HEADQUARTERS: Division of Parks and Outdoor Recreation, 1313 Sherman St., Denver, CO 80203; (303) 866-3437. Site telephone: (303) 561-9320. Division of Wildlife, 6060 Broadway, Denver, CO 80216; (303) 297-1192.

QUEENS STATE WILDLIFE AREA
Colorado Division of Wildlife
1,276 land acres; reservoirs of 1,930, 1,607, and 3,696 acres.

SE Colorado. From Lamar, 5 mi. W on US 50; N 16 mi. on US 287; right on county road.

The landscape is typical of E Colorado: flat, open, treeless except for cotton-woods along streams and beside ponds. Many wildflowers in uplands. The reservoirs are not picturesque. There is only scanty shoreline vegetation. However, we found it a pleasant, quiet place to spend the night. On the afternoon of a fine day in early Aug., three boats were on the lake. They had left by dinner time. One other RV was parked for the night.

No facilities, other than a boat ramp. Camp where you please. Swim at your own risk. Moderately good birding. Coyotes called during the night.

RIVERSIDE RESERVOIR
U.S. Bureau of Land Management
3,150 acres.

NW of Denver. From Masters on US 34, N on county road. Shown on state highway map.

You probably can't find this site on your own. We couldn't. We include it because a visiting birder will almost surely hear about it. Among other things, it has an island where 200 to 250 pairs of white pelicans nest.

The problem is access. Of the 3,150 acres, 2,780 are submerged at full pool. The 370 acres of dry land are in an odd sawtooth pattern along the lake shore. The only legal public access is a small parcel on the county road at the SE corner.

While federal ownership of the reservoir seems clear, controversy arose over a 1903 grant to the Riverside Reservoir and Land Co. and its subsequent lease of hunting and fishing rights to a private club. Currently, the site is open for day use, and BLM is seeking improved public access. Restrooms are the only visitor facility.

Probably best to check with one of the following BLM offices.

HEADQUARTERS: BLM, Canon City District Office, 3080 East Main, Canon City, CO 81212; (303) 275-0631. Northeast Resource Area Office, Denver Federal Center, Denver, CO 80225; (303) 234-4988.

SOUTH PLATTE RIVER
Colorado Division of Wildlife
17,017 acres; 200 acres of water.

From I-76, Crook exit. The site includes about 14 mi. along the South Platte River E and W of the Crook road, between I-76 and US 138. The Duck Creek block is N of Crook. The Red Lion block is N of US 138 about 8 mi. E of Crook.

The site along the river is maintained chiefly for waterfowl hunting. The Red Lion block includes Jumbo Reservoir, 200 acres, and a number of shallow ponds with associated wetlands developed for waterfowl breeding. Elevation is about 4,000 ft. Shortgrass prairie and riparian vegetation. The Division reports that more than 100 species of birds have been recorded. The breeding area is closed Apr. 1–June 30.

HEADQUARTERS: Division of Wildlife, 6060 Broadway, Denver, CO 80216; (303) 297-1192.

SPANISH PEAKS STATE WILDLIFE AREA
Colorado Division of Wildlife
13,700 acres

From Aguilar, between Walsenburg and Trinidad on US 85/87, 17 mi. SW on county road. (The county road continues to SR 12.)

The site is S of the Spanish Peaks (see Spanish Peaks Wilderness Area in entry for Pike and San Isabel National Forests, Zone 2). The county road has a connection to Cordova Pass.

This site is lower, elevations from 7,000 to 8,000 ft. Gently rolling. Sparse vegetation: pinyon-juniper and grasses, some ponderosa.

ACTIVITIES
Camping: Primitive, in designated areas.
Hunting: Good wild turkey population. Also dove, band-tailed pigeon, rabbit, deer, elk.
Fishing: Trout and catfish in several ponds.

TRINIDAD STATE RECREATION AREA
Colorado Division of Parks and Outdoor Recreation
About 2,300 acres of land, 800 of water, depending on pool level.

From Trinidad on I-25, 3 mi. W on SR 12.

The lake, about 1 1/2 mi. long, was formed by damming the Purgatoire River. The U.S. Army Corps of Engineers built the dam, leased the recreation area to the state.

The site leaflet admonishes, "Ski counterclockwise." It's a popular recreation area, where the state collects a fee at the gate.

The setting, in the Rocky Mountain foothills, is attractive. The Spanish Peaks area of the Pike and San Isabel National Forests is a few miles W. The hills around the lake are about 500 ft. high, with a thick pinyon-juniper cover. The site has well-prepared checklists of plants and animals and two nature trails.

However, it is not within our definition of a natural area. It is included because it makes a pleasant overnight stop on the way to the Rockies.

ACTIVITIES
Camping: 62 sites. Reservations (see Colorado Preface).
Hunting: Dove, quail, squirrel, rabbit only.
Fishing: Trout, bass, catfish, walleye.
Boating: Ramp. No hp limit.
Swimming: Not permitted.

PUBLICATIONS
Leaflet.
Plant checklist.

Wildlife checklist.
Information for campers.

HEADQUARTERS: Route 1, Box 360, Trinidad, CO 81082; (303) 846-6951.

UTAH

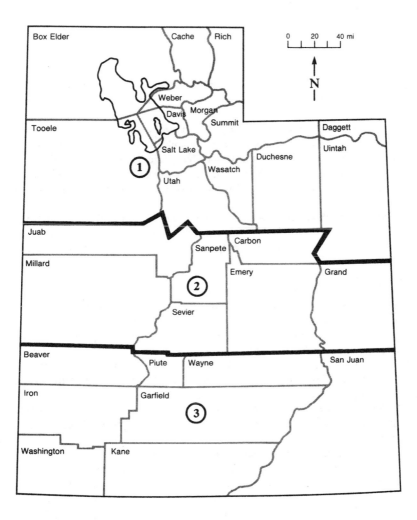

UTAH

Much of Utah is still pristine. The opportunities to visit and explore natural areas are almost unlimited. The scenery is spectacular. Few places are ever crowded.

Of Utah's 54.4 million acres, 33.5 million are owned by the federal government. More than 22 million acres are public domain, undivided lands managed by the U.S. Bureau of Land Management. Eight million acres are within National Forests, almost 2 million acres in National Parks, Monuments, Recreation Areas, and Historic Sites. Only Alaska has as many National Parks.

Most of Utah is mountainous. Principal ranges are the Wasatch, running N–S through the middle of the state, and the Uintas, a W–E range in the NE. Crests of these ranges are generally higher than 10,000 ft. Highest point is Kings Peak in the Uinta Range, rising to 13,498 ft. Lowest area is the Virgin River Valley in the SW, with elevations of 2,500 to 3,500 ft.

Western Utah is almost entirely within the Great Basin, which has no outlet to the sea. The Great Salt Lake Desert is flat and barren, except for a few mountain ranges. Further S is typical basin-and-range topography, the higher ranges trapping considerable moisture. The rivers of western Utah flow to the Great Salt Lake or vanish in the dry desert.

Across the Wasatch Range, eastern Utah is drained by the Colorado and Green Rivers. Tributaries flow through canyons or narrow mountain valleys, finally into desert canyons.

Southern Utah is a region of colorful canyons and high plateaus. Relatively little land is suitable for farming or grazing, and few people live here. The spectacular scenery attracts many visitors.

Utah is the second driest state. Air from the Pacific has crossed the Sierras or the Cascades before reaching Utah, losing much of its moisture. Only the high ridges extract much precipitation from passing air masses. Annual precipitation averages less than 5 in. in the Great Salt Lake Desert, up to 40 in. and more on parts of the Wasatch Range. Areas below 4,000 ft. generally receive less than 10 in. of moisture per year.

Mean annual temperature declines about 3°F for each 1,000 ft. increase in altitude and 1.5 to 2°F for each degree increase in latitude. Thus the high northern parts of the state are 6 to 8 degrees F colder than lower regions to the S. Summer temperatures above 100°F occur throughout the state; in some regions, maximums exceed 110°. Below-zero temperatures are uncommon, except at high altitudes.

While Utah is generally arid, snowfall is moderately heavy in the mountains. Winter sports are popular. Runoff from melting snow sometimes causes flooding on the W side of the Wasatch Range. When floods occur, as they did in 1983, high-water conditions may persist for some time because there is no outlet.

The 1983 floods occurred just after we completed field work. By telephone and mail we sought to learn how our sites had been affected. Great damage was reported on the W side of the Wasatch Range, especially around Great Salt Lake. More flooding was forecast for the spring of 1984, and the forecast was fulfilled. Record snows fell in the winter of 1984–85, threatening another spring of damaging runoff. Entries note where flood damage occurred. Before planning a visit to any of these sites, inquire.

When to visit? In the high mountains, late spring or summer—after snow has melted and trails have had a chance to dry. The outdoor season is longer on the lower slopes. Spring and fall are ideal for the deserts and most canyons, but summers are not intolerable, and nights are cool. Winter weather is seldom bitter. Sunny skies prevail most of the year.

How to go? Utah's highways are wonderfully scenic, outside the parks as well as inside, but the best natural areas are away from paved roads. Drive if you must; 4-wheel-drive vehicles can be rented, and motorized backcountry tours are available. Horses and horsepacking tours are also available, chiefly for the mountains. Outfitters offer raft trips of a half-day up to several days through splendid whitewater canyons. Other canyons have placid streams, suitable for canoes, small rafts, and outboards; cruise boats operate on some waters. Houseboats can be rented on Lake Powell.

Best of all, go on foot. Utah is a hiker's delight, from high mountains to deep canyons, from short strolls to one- or two-week wilderness treks.

For information about outfitters and rentals, begin with the

Utah Travel Council
Council Hall
Salt Lake City, UT 84114
(801) 533-5681

Also write to the Chamber of Commerce in the city nearest the area you plan to visit.

ZONES

We have divided the state into 3 zones.

Zone 1, the upper third, is divided by the Wasatch Range. W of the Range are the Great Salt Lake Desert, Great Salt Lake, Utah Lake, the principal waterfowl wetlands, and most of the state's population. E of the Range are the Uinta Mountains, Utah's portions of the Flaming Gorge National Recreation Area and Dinosaur National Monument, and sections of the Green

River. Most of the high country is within three National Forests: the Wasatch-Cache, Ashley, and Uinta.

Zone 2, the middle third, is also divided by the Wasatch Range. The Fishlake, Wasatch-Cache, Uinta, and Manti-La Sal National Forests occupy most of the high country. To the W is basin-and-range topography, with some interesting mountain country. To the E are the drainages of the Green and Colorado Rivers and such features as the San Rafael Swell, Goblin Valley, Arches National Park, and the Moab area, including the N entrance to Canyonlands National Park.

Zone 3 is the land of canyons, plateaus, National Parks, and National Forests. The Dixie and Fishlake National Forests are in the W, with Bryce Canyon and Zion National Parks. Capitol Reef National Park is in the central area, Canyonlands to the E with two portions of the Manti-La Sal National Forest. While the Glen Canyon Dam is in Arizona, most of Lake Powell is in Utah. In Zone 1, backpackers go to the mountains. In Zone 3 most of them choose the canyons, for a day's hike or adventurous treks of a week or two.

MAPS

Utah's official highway map is adequate for travel on federal and state highways. Unless the printing has improved, it's difficult to tell whether a blue road is paved, improved, or graded. For travel off the main roads, you need something better.

The Utah Travel Council has produced a superb set of eight Multipurpose Maps, covering the entire state. Every state should have such splendid maps. Beautifully printed, they show every public park, forest, wildlife area, historic site, marina, ski area, and other points of interest, as well as many backcountry roads and trails. The reverse sides provide campground guides, descriptions of the National Parks and other major sites, and a list of points of interest, plus the addresses and telephone numbers of agencies providing tourist information. These maps were free when we acquired ours.

We consider these maps invaluable for travel in Utah. Each entry carries a notation: (MP #3.), for example, means the site appears on Multipurpose Map No. 3. Multipurpose Maps are available from the Utah Travel Council; address given earlier.

Each National Forest has its own system of Forest Roads. Only the principal roads appear on general maps. Maps for each Forest are available at Forest Headquarters.

For backcountry hiking and horse travel, the U.S. Geological Survey topographic maps are indispensable. They're available from local outfitters. However, note the date on each map. Some are quite old. In any case, the maps won't tell you about current trail conditions.

ROADS

In addition to paved roads, the Multipurpose Maps show improved gravel, graded, and dirt roads, and jeep trails. Most improved gravel roads are suitable for all-weather travel by ordinary cars. Graded roads are more variable; many are fair-weather routes. Some dirt roads may be negotiable by ordinary cars in dry weather, but low-clearance vehicles may have difficulties.

Motorized travel in Utah's backcountry, including large sections of the National Forests, some National Parks, and much BLM-managed land, often requires 4-wheel drive. Such vehicles can be rented in Moab and other centers. Our References include guides to ORV trails not shown on general maps.

According to the land managers we interviewed, ORV's have become a destructive nuisance in only a few areas. Most people use them for transportation, not racing or hill climbing. Wilderness areas, of course, are closed to all motorized travel. Each National Forest issues a Travel Plan, showing the areas closed to motor vehicles.

TRAILS

Some trails are nicely maintained footpaths, although trail maintenance budgets have been cut almost everywhere. Others are unmarked routes for foot travel, along canyon bottoms, long-abandoned mine roads, or cattle tracks. Some offer short, easy hikes; other require several days with periods of scrambling, wading, even swimming. To see the most and best of Utah, go on foot.

National Parks and National Forests usually have trail maps. Many trail guides are available. We list those we found and those recommended by site managers. Doubtless there are others, privately published and locally sold.

Two trail guides proved especially useful. Entries note the hikes described, with page numbers:

Barnes, F. A. *Canyon Country Hiking and Natural History.* Salt Lake City: Wasatch, 1977.

Hall, Dave. *The Hiker's Guide to Utah.* Billings, MT: Falcon Press, 1982.

FEDERAL AGENCIES

U.S. Bureau of Land Management
Utah State Office
University Club Building
136 East South Temple
Salt Lake City, UT 84111
(801) 524-5311

BLM manages nearly half the land area of Utah. The largest areas are in Zones 2 and 3. Addresses of BLM's District Offices appear in entries.

U.S. Forest Service
Public Information
125 South State St.
Salt Lake City, UT 84111
(801) 524-5030

National Forests in Utah include the Ashley, Dixie, Fishlake, Manti-La Sal, Uinta, and Wasatch-Cache. Flaming Gorge National Recreation Area is within the Ashley. We have an entry in Zone 1 for a small piece of the Sawtooth, most of which is in Idaho.

National Park Service
Public Information
125 South State St.
Salt Lake City, UT 84111
(801) 524-4165

National Parks in Utah are Arches, Bryce Canyon, Canyonlands, Capitol Reef, and Zion. National Monuments: Cedar Breaks, Dinosaur (part), Hovenweep (part), Natural Bridges, Rainbow Bridge, and Timpanogos Cave. National Recreation Area: Glen Canyon.

U.S. Fish and Wildlife Service
Region VI
Federal Building
125 South State St.
Salt Lake City, UT 84111
(801) 524-5630

National Wildlife Refuges are Bear River, Fish Springs, and Ouray.

STATE AGENCIES

Utah State Lands and Forestry
3100 State Office Building
Salt Lake City, UT 84114
(801) 533-5381

When Utah became a state, it received title to 4 noncontiguous mile-square sections in each 36-section township—more than 3 1/2 million acres. Perhaps this grant seemed great wisdom at the time, but the mad checkerboard has confounded state and federal land managers ever since. Efforts have been made to consolidate holdings, thus far with little success. Recently Utah legislators have proposed "Project Bold," which would exchange 2 1/2 million acres of state land for solid blocks of federal land.

Maps show seven State Forests, but they are not officially designated as such; they are areas where state holdings form relatively solid blocks. All the state trust lands are managed to produce revenue for schools. Recreation and wildlife management have low priority.

We were advised to omit these Forests, but we saw signs of change. The land managers responded readily to our questionnaire. We were told of plans for latrines and primitive campgrounds. Hunters use the Forests, and some areas are popular with local hikers. Since no biological studies have been made, we can't provide full descriptions.

Utah State Division of Parks and Recreation
1636 West North Temple
Salt Lake City, UT 84116
(801) 533-6012.

The Division maintains 43 parks, beaches, reserves, historical monuments, and parkways. These areas comprise 63,000 land acres and give access to the Great Salt Lake, Utah Lake, and other waters. The largest park has almost 22,000 acres. (Another has over 25,000, but most of it is not yet open to visitors.)

We found the parks attractive but with few significant natural areas. They are intended for such recreation uses as picnicking, boating, swimming, and camping. Our entries include the parks with natural areas and others that are convenient bases for visiting nearby natural areas.

PUBLICATIONS
Utah's Part of the Earth Campground Directory.
The State Parks of Utah.
Utah Snowmobiling (in cooperation with the Utah Travel Council).
Your Snowmobile Guide—Monte Cristo, Hardware Ranch, Northern Utah Complex.

Utah State Division of Wildlife Resources
1596 West North Temple
Salt Lake City, UT 84116
(801) 533-9333

Acquisition of wetlands for public shooting and management began in 1911. The Public Shooting Grounds Waterfowl Management Area may have been the first man-made development for public waterfowl hunting in the United States. The Division now has 18 waterfowl management areas (WMA's) totaling 80,000 acres and manages what was, in 1982, an additional 150,000 acres between the surveyed meander line of Great Salt Lake and the then existing water level. These and a number of upland wildlife areas are shown on the Multipurpose Maps.

When we first asked the Division for information, the director replied that the WMA's "are for intensive wildlife management programs and are not designed for formal public visits." He recommended that we direct visitors to the federal Bear River Migratory Bird Refuge.

However, there seemed to be policy disagreements within the Division. We visited most of the WMA's and were puzzled. A few had locked gates and "No Trespassing" signs. A few were wide open, others posted with signs that stopped short of saying "Keep out." We met local managers who told us they welcome birders and other visitors, and we found their sites interesting.

Then came the flood of 1983. We received this communication from the Division in 1984:

> More flooding is in store for marshes along the east side of the Great Salt Lake . . . the damage has been not only to the elaborate diking and canal systems on the management areas (many of which have been completely destroyed or heavily silted), but also to emergent vegetation in the areas which has been killed by salt water incursion . . . waterfowl depend heavily on such vegetation for food and cover . . .
>
> Farmington Bay has been about half destroyed and we expect the other half to go this year. . . . Almost one half of Ogden Bay was wiped out last spring, with much of the remaining marsh expected to be destroyed by July of 1984 . . .

And so on.

Waterfowl areas in central and southern Utah have benefited at least temporarily from the additional water. The Clear Lake WMA was of minor interest when we visited; now it has hundreds of acres of new marsh.

We have scrapped our entries for the marshes around the Great Salt Lake. It may be several years before the water subsides and years more before dikes are rebuilt, salt flushed away, and vegetation restored.

We have entries for Clear Lake and Desert Lake in Zone 2.

PUBLICATION:
Utah Hunting and Fishing Guide. Free.

REFERENCES

GENERAL

Barnes, F. A. *Canyon Country Exploring.* Salt Lake City: Wasatch, 1978.

Barnes, F. A. *Canyon Country Scenic Roads.* Salt Lake City: Wasatch, 1980.

Barnes, F. A. *Canyon Country Geology for the Layman and Rockhound.* Salt Lake City: Wasatch, 1978.

Geerling, Paul F. *Down the Grand Staircase.* Boulder City, NV: Westwater Books, 1981.

Roylance, Ward J. *Utah, a Guide to the State.* Salt Lake City: Utah, A Guide to the State Foundation, 1982.

CAMPING

Barnes, F. A. *Canyon Country Camping.* Salt Lake City: Wasatch, 1978.

HIKING

Barnes, F. A. *Canyon Country Hiking and Natural History.* Salt Lake City: Wasatch, 1977.

Hall, Dave. *The Hiker's Guide to Utah.* Billings, MT: Falcon Press, 1982.

BOATING

Nichols, Gary C. *River Runners' Guide to Utah.* Boulder City, NV: Westwater Books, 1982.

PLANTS

Johnson, Carl H. *Common Native Trees of Utah.* Logan, UT: Agricultural Experiment Station, 1970.

Patrow, Pauline M. *Flowers of the Southwest Mesa.* Globe, AZ: Southwest Parks and Monuments Association, 1982.

BIRDS

Hayward, C. Lynn, Clarence Cottam, A. M. Woodbury, and Herbert H. Frost. *Birds of Utah.* Provo, UT: Brigham Young University Press, 1976.

ZONE 1

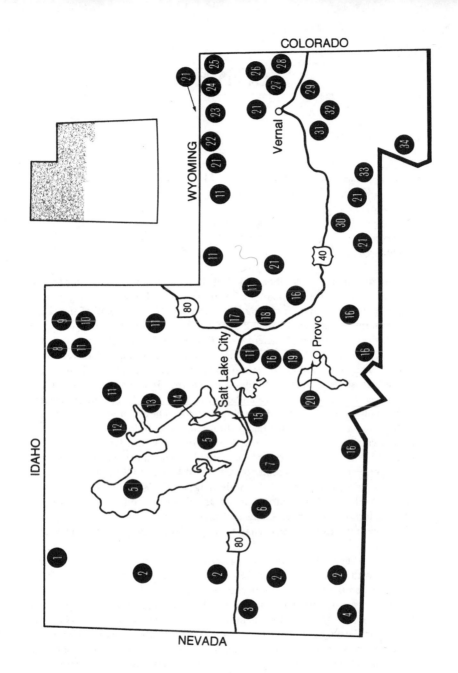

ZONE 1

Includes these counties (Multipurpose Maps Nos. 2, 3, 4, 7, and 8):

Box Elder	Morgan	Uinta
Cache	Rich	Utah
Daggett	Salt Lake	Wasatch
Davis	Summit	Weber
Duchesne	Tooele	

This zone includes the upper third of the state, from the N border to just S of Utah Lake. It is divided N–S by the Wasatch Range.

Except for the mountains along the Idaho border, the area W of the range is within the Great Basin, which has no outlet to the sea. This area was once part of the vast lakebed of ancient Lake Bonneville. Most of it is now flat, dry desert, almost featureless except for isolated mountain ranges that were once islands. The W section of Interstate 80 is the least interesting ride in Utah.

The largest wet remnant of the old lake is the Great Salt Lake, a shallow inland sea second only to the Dead Sea in saltiness. The lake is fed by streams that supply extensive wetlands on the N and E. These wetlands are feeding, resting, and nesting areas for many thousands of waterfowl. The largest and most accessible wetland is the Bear River Migratory Bird Refuge of the U.S. Fish and Wildlife Service, one of the nation's great waterfowl sites. The state has eight waterfowl management areas (WMA's) around the lake.

We have entries for several mountain ranges in the W half of the zone. They are relatively small, the largest about 40 mi. long, 5 mi. wide, too dry to support forests. The upper slopes are cooler than the desert floor, and they offer opportunities for pleasant day hiking or riding, away from vehicles and crowds.

The crestline of the Wasatch Range is generally over 10,000 ft. Most of the range is within the Wasatch-Cache and Uinta National Forests. Roads from the valley, on the W side, lead up canyons into the mountains, to resorts and to a network of Forest roads and trails. More than half of Utah's population lives along the Wasatch Front, and the accessible parts of the National Forests are heavily used, winter and summer. Our entries report which areas are often crowded and where one can find quiet places. Even on Labor Day weekend, we had no difficulty finding a quiet campsite beside a mountain stream.

Serious floods are common on the W side of the Range. The U.S. Geological Survey reports that during the past century more than 300 flash floods have been caused by heavy rains, and 135 floods by snowmelt. The area is so flat that a modest change in the water level of the Great Salt Lake makes a great change in its shoreline. At the highest recorded level, the lake covered 2,200 square miles; at the lowest, only 900 square miles.

In the winter of 1982–1983, snowfall on the range was heavy and the spring thaw rapid. Flood damage along the Wasatch Front was extensive. In early 1984 the Great Salt Lake was still 5 ft. above the preflood level, inundating bordering areas.

Our entries are based on preflood conditions. Entries were sent to site managers for review, and we report what they had to say about present and future flood conditions. Entries for the eight WMA's around Great Salt Lake have been deleted, since their future is uncertain.

The highest mountains in UT are the Uintas, in the NE part of the zone, the only major range running W–E. With many peaks over 13,000 ft., numerous mountain lakes and streams, fine forests, and a vast wilderness area, the Uintas attract hikers and horsepackers from far away.

From Salt Lake City, the principal route to the northern Uintas is SR 150 from Kamas, a scenic route through a region with many mountain lakes. This area, within the Wasatch-Cache National Forest, has many campgrounds and resorts. It is the most heavily impacted part of the Uintas. To the E, from the crest of the Uintas N to the Wyoming border, the Forest is largely roadless. Here are the highest peaks. The High Uintas Primitive Area, a large roadless wilderness on both sides of the ridge, is considered by many outdoorsmen the most splendid part of the state. Many are attracted by the "wilderness" label, and some trails are busy at times. Still, anyone who wants isolation can find it.

The more accessible S slopes of the Uintas are in the Ashley National Forest. From N of US 40, many spur roads lead into the Forest, many of them terminating at campgrounds and trailheads.

US 40 is also the main route to the Flaming Gorge National Recreation Area, N of Vernal. This NRA is also part of the Ashley National Forest. The dam across the Red Canyon of the Green River is in UT. Most of the 91-mi.-long reservoir is in Wyoming. The drowning of a spectacular canyon is regrettable, but this reservoir seems less offensively artificial than most. Above the dam, canyon walls still rise from the water. N of the canyon, natural slopes drop steeply to the water's edge. Below the dam, Red Canyon is little changed except for the regulated stream flow. A trail follows the canyon and rafting the river here is popular.

The Green River flows E from the canyon into an area called Browns Park, which extends into Colorado. Most of the land between Browns Park and Dinosaur National Monument is public. There is much of interest here, especially for the motorist who enjoys exploring little-traveled backcountry roads.

Most visitors to Dinosaur National Monument park at the visitor center, take the bus to the quarry, look around, and leave. There's much more to see and do, including hiking and backpacking in roadless areas of the Monument and adjoining lands. (Our entry for Dinosaur National Monument is in Colorado, Zone 1.)

From Browns Park, the Green River flows through spectacular canyons in the Colorado portion of the National Monument, turns back into UT and flows SW through arid country. Stewart Lake Waterfowl Management Area and Ouray National Wildlife Refuge are along the river. This section of the river can be rafted but is considered of minor interest. At the Sand Wash Raft Ramp, however, begins the float trip through Desolation Canyon; see Green River entry, Zone 2.

The State Parks in Zone 1 are popular recreation sites but not, in our terms, natural areas. We have included several of them because they are attractive and convenient bases for exploring nearby natural areas.

Zone 1 has two large freshwater lakes. In the N, Bear Lake is shared with Idaho. Utah Lake is S of Salt Lake City. Each has a busy State Park popular with boaters and fishermen. Except for these parks, the shorelines are privately owned.

ARGYLE AND NINE MILE CANYONS
U.S. Bureau of Land Management
About 100,000 acres.

> From US 40, 2 mi. W of Myton, S on road marked "Sand Wash." In 2 mi. take right fork, not the Sand Wash road. 28 mi. to Nine Mile Canyon. Left road is 10 mi. to dead end. Right is 31 mi. through Nine Mile and Argyle Canyons to SR 33; the junction is 13 mi. N of US 50 and 6. (MP #3.)

This is a pleasant backcountry drive where one seldom meets another car. The graded road is passable for automobiles in dry weather. After driving the 61 mi. from Myton to SR 33, one can return to Myton on 47 mi. of paved road via SR 33 and US 40.

The route from Myton was an old wagon road, the main route between the Uinta Basin and the railroad at Price. The first 24 mi. S of Myton cross the open badlands of the Uinta Basin. The road then descends through Gate Canyon into Nine Mile Canyon. The red sandstone canyon walls are steep, picturesque. On the walls are Indian petroglyphs as well as more recent petroglyphs made by wagoners with axle grease. Old ranch buildings are on the bottomland. Nine Mile Canyon is on the State Register of Historic Places. Canyon vegetation is pinyon pine, Utah juniper, sagebrush, and greasewood. Wildlife includes chukar, coyote, cottontail, deer, elk.

If one hiked the Nine Mile Creek drainage about 12 mi. beyond the road's end, one would come to the Green River near the Sand Wash Raft Ramp.

ASHLEY NATIONAL FOREST
(Includes Flaming Gorge National Recreation Area.)
U.S. Forest Service
In UT: 1,288,422 acres; 1,300,908 acres within boundaries. In WY: 96,277 acres; 104,701 acres within boundaries.

> NE Utah, extending into Wyoming. SR 44, N from Vernal, crosses the E side to Flaming Gorge. Several roads from US 40 penetrate from the S. A disjunct portion is S of Duchesne, crossed by SR 33. (MP #3.)

The Uintas are the only large range in the conterminous United States with a W–E ridgeline. The Ashley occupies the E half of the range and much of the S slopes of the W half. Kings Peak, 13,528 ft., is the highest point in UT; 26 summits and subordinate peaks are above 13,000 ft. Lowest elevation is at the Green River: 5,475 ft. The rugged terrain and severe climate have preserved the wilderness quality of a large portion of the Forest. Only SR 44 crosses the main body of the Forest, and much of the area is roadless.

The main W–E ridgeline is narrow and sinuous. Subordinate ridges extend S, separating drainage basins. Nine of the highest peaks are on the ridge dividing the Uinta and Yellowstone River drainages. Before glaciation, this area was a broad upland cut by V-shaped canyons. Glaciers cut broad, open cirque basins with high, steep walls. The canyons were widened and deepened into U-shaped troughs, often dammed by glacial moraine to form lakes and ponds.

On the E side of the Forest, Flaming Gorge Dam, in the canyon of the Green River, created a 66-sq.-mi. reservoir extending N into Wyoming. Below the dam, the river turns E through Red Canyon and Browns Park into Colorado.

The upper slopes receive up to 40 in. of precipitation annually, most of it as winter snow. Annual precipitation at the lower elevations is about 12 in. The Forest has more than 500 mountain lakes and 400 mi. of fishing streams.

May through Sept. is the visitor season at lower elevations, July–Aug. in the high country. The Forest attracts over a million visitors a year, although many never venture beyond the car-accessible campgrounds. Some backcountry destinations have been damaged by overuse, but it has not yet been judged necessary to limit access. Rangers encourage backpackers and trail riders to choose less traveled routes.

Plants: More than 850 plant species have been identified in the Forest. Checklists available at Forest HQ. Life zones include the *alpine,* generally above 11,000 ft., characterized by tundra cushion plants, sedge, alpine grasses and shrubs; *subalpine,* with spruce, fir, alpine willow, wet meadow and bog; *montane,* with spruce, fir, lodgepole pine, aspen, and Douglas-fir; and *transition,* with ponderosa pine, sagebrush, Utah juniper, shrubs. Many habitat types are produced by differences of altitude, soil type, moisture, and orientation.

Forests cover 50–70% of the area. Lodgepole pine, Engelmann spruce, Douglas-fir, and subalpine fir occur in large stands on lower slopes. Quaking aspen grows in scattered patches. Meadows and willow fields in forest openings.

Birds: 209 species recorded. Waterfowl include common loon; horned, eared, western, and pied-billed grebes; whistling swan, Canada and snow geese, mallard, gadwall, pintail, green-winged teal, American wigeon, lesser scaup, common and Barrow's goldeneyes, bufflehead, ruddy duck, hooded and common merganser. Many wading birds and shorebirds.

Raptors include turkey vulture, goshawk; sharp-shinned, Cooper's, red-tailed, Swainson's, and rough-legged hawks; northern harrier, golden and bald eagles, osprey, prairie and peregrine falcons, American kestrel. Blue, ruffed, and sage grouse; white-tailed ptarmigan, ring-necked pheasant. Owls: great horned, screech, pygmy, long-eared, and short-eared. Black-chinned and broad-tailed hummingbirds. Woodpeckers: hairy, downy, northern three-toed; northern flicker; yellow-bellied and Williamson's sapsuckers. Bohemian and cedar waxwings. Warblers include orange-crowned, Virginia's, yellow-rumped, black-throated gray, Townsend's, MacGillivray's, Wilson's.

Mammals: Include black bear, mountain lion, lynx, raccoon, ringtail, marten, fisher, shorttail and longtail weasels, mink, badger, spotted and striped skunks; red, swift, and gray foxes; yellowbelly marmot, whitetail prairie dog. Ground squirrels: Richardson, thirteen-lined, Uinta, golden-mantled. Least, cliff, and Uinta chipmunks. Northern flying and red squirrels, pika, snowshoe hare, whitetail and blacktail jackrabbits, mountain and desert cottontails. Elk, mule deer, moose, pronghorn, bighorn sheep.

FEATURES

High Uintas Primitive Area: 162,586 roadless acres in the NW part of the Forest, plus 73,923 contiguous acres in the Wasatch-Cache National Forest on the N. This area is the highest part of the Forest. Ridges divide it into large scenic basins interspersed with high glacial moraines and glacial drifts. Ridges rise steeply from basin floors. Over half of the area is barren rock; most exposed rock is deep red. Many lakes and streams. Lower slopes are forested. Scattered meadows.

Snow and the May–June runoff limit high-country travel to about July 1–Sept. 10. In summer, afternoon rainstorms are common. Above 10,000 ft. temperature is rarely above 70°F. Average night temperature is 30–40°F, sometimes lower even in summer.

Motor vehicles are prohibited. Trails enter the area at many points on the perimeter. The Forest's map of the area is a good general guide, but for travel off main trails topographic maps are necessary; the Forest map is keyed to show which quads. Inquire at a Ranger District office about routes, destinations, trail conditions, and fire rules. Horse travel is possible on most trails.

The "Primitive Area" designation attracts many hikers. Some trails and campsites are heavily used. Those seeking isolation may find it more readily outside the designated Primitive Area.

The High Uintas are summer range for elk, mule deer, moose, possibly mountain sheep. Black bear are common. Fishing is excellent except in heavily fished waters.

Flaming Gorge National Recreation Area. The dam is near Dutch John. The reservoir extends N almost to Green River, WY. In UT, most of the reservoir is confined within the winding, vertical red-rock canyon walls of the Green River. Near the Wyoming border, the reservoir broadens. From here N the Forest land is a strip 1 to 2 mi. wide along each shore, with some inholdings. The WY environment is desert: low hills, shale badlands, desert shrubs.

Since the dam was completed in 1964, Flaming Gorge has become a major area for water-based recreation. On or near the lake shore are 34 campgrounds, several accessible only by boat. Although much commercial development has taken place, it's concentrated in a few places, chiefly near the dam, out of sight around the next bend. Most of the shoreline is undeveloped and far from any road.

High-water elevation is 6,040 ft. The main visitor season begins in May, peaks in July–Aug. We found some campgrounds closed for the season in late Aug. Although no Forest campgrounds are open in winter, lodgings are available nearby. Ice fishing is popular.

The lake is large, usually cold, subject to sudden strong winds.

Green River. Red Canyon was about 30 mi. long. 18 mi. is now above the dam, and the gorge contains the lower part of the reservoirs. Below the dam the canyon is little changed, except that the river flow is now controlled. This 12 mi. is said to have some of the best trout fishing in UT. Motors are not allowed. Boating is considered safe for amateurs, except for Red Creek Rapids at the lower end of the canyon. Most boating parties put in at Little Hole. Rafts can be rented, and guided tours are available. Hiking on a 7-mi. trail from Flaming Gorge Dam to the campground at Little Hole.

Below the rapids is BLM's Red Creek Boat Camp. Here the river leaves the Ashley National Forest and flows through Browns Park (see entry).

Sheep Creek Canyon Geological Area, 3,600 acres on SR 44 about 10 mi.

SW of Manila. On the S side of the Uinta Crest fault, the earth was once thrust up over 15,000 ft. On the N, strata were bent up, exposing millions of years of geological history. Sheep Creek originates in quartzite uplifts estimated to be 2 1/2 billion years old. In the area have been found fossils of ancient marine organisms, tracks of prehistoric reptiles, petrified wood. Picnic area; no camping. An interpretive program is planned.

Red Cloud Loop is a scenic drive, recommended for pickup trucks and 4-wheel-drive vehicles. On SR 44, 21 mi. N of Vernal, turn left; left again at mi. 23.4. At mi. 29.3, straight to begin Red Cloud Loop, which returns to Vernal, joining Maeser Highway at mi. 69.7. Side roads to several reservoirs and Forest trailheads.

INTERPRETATION

Visitor centers at Red Canyon, N of SR 44, W of Flaming Gorge Dam, and at the Dam. Both have exhibits, films, talks, literature, information. Red Canyon gives greater emphasis to natural history. Open Memorial Day–Labor Day.

Responding to our inquiry, Forest HQ reported no campfire programs, guided walks, or other naturalist activities.

ACTIVITIES

Camping: 50 campgrounds (including 4 in WY). 1,402 sites. Various seasons, May–Oct., but we found some closed in late Aug.

Hiking, backpacking: 780 mi. of trails. Hiking season begins May–June at lower elevations, July in High Uintas. Camp where you wish. Litter must be packed out, not buried.

Horse riding: All trails are open to horse travel. Horses have right-of-way over hikers. Commercial packers are located near Forest boundaries; ask at Ranger District office for list. Forage is limited, and horse grazing is restricted at some locations.

Hunting: Deer, elk, moose. State regulations.

Fishing: About half of the 500 lakes will support fish populations. 400 mi. of fishing streams. Rainbow, cutthroat, brown, brook, and lake trout; mountain whitefish. Excellent fishing in lightly traveled areas.

Boating: On Flaming Gorge Reservoir and the larger, more accessible lakes. Ramps and marinas on the reservoir; rentals. Boats use the reservoir all year, except when ice forms. Canoeing on some mountain lakes and in Red Canyon. Motors are prohibited in Red Canyon.

Rafting: Rafting is popular on the Green River below Flaming Gorge Dam, said to be generally safe even for the inexperienced, although the frigid water makes a spill hazardous. The only rapid is at the lower end of Red Canyon, 12 mi. below the dam. Several ramps make it possible to plan short or all-day trips, or to continue into Dinosaur National Monument in CO. Camping is possible at several points.

Swimming: Unsupervised. Water usually cold. Unsuitable when pool is low.

Ski touring: Not a major activity. Three trails, 4, 2 1/2, and 2 1/2 mi.; trailheads near SR 44.

Snowmobiling: Limited by terrain and snow conditions. Two designated trails, one groomed.

PUBLICATIONS
Forest map. $1.00.
High Uintas Primitive Area map. $1.00.
High Uintas folder with "temporary map."
Forest leaflet, small map.
Flaming Gorge folder with map.
Flaming Gorge booklet.
Travel Plans for each Ranger District showing rules for off-road vehicles.
Leaflets:
  Red Canyon Visitor Center
  Sheep Creek Canyon Geological Area
Information sheets:
  Welcome to the Ashley.
  The High Uintas.
  Backpacking information.
  List of outfitters and guides.
  Cross Country Skiing.
  Bird checklist.
  Animals of the Ashley National Forest.
  Checklist of vascular plants.
On rafting:
  Three Faces of the Green River. Folder, map.
  Green River Corridor Below Dam to Browns Park. Map and detailed
    information for rafting.
  Information for Running the Green River.

REFERENCE: Hall, Dave. *The Hiker's Guide to Utah.* Billings, MT: Falcon Press, 1982. Pp. 76–80, 93–100.

HEADQUARTERS: 1680 W Highway 40, Suite 1150, Vernal, UT 84078; (801) 789-1181.

RANGER DISTRICTS: Flaming Gorge R.D., P.O. Box 278, Manila, UT 84046; (801) 784-3445. Dutch John Unit, P.O. Box 157, Dutch John, UT 84023; (801) 885-3315. Roosevelt R.D., P.O. Box 338, Roosevelt, UT 84066; (801) 722-5018. Duchesne R.D., P.O. Box 1, Duchesne, UT 84021; (801) 738-2482. Vernal R.D., 650 N. Vernal Ave., Vernal, UT 84078; (801) 789-0323.

BEAR LAKE STATE RECREATION AREA
Utah State Division of Parks and Recreation
884 acres.

Marina (820 acres) on US 89, 1 1/2 mi. N of Garden City. Rendezvous
Beach (64 acres) on S shore, off SR 30, near Laketown. (MP #4.)

Bear Lake, about 21 mi. N–S, 7 mi. wide, is half in Idaho. An ID state park
with campground is on the N shore. The lake is at 5,924 ft. elevation. SR 30
and US 89 skirt the W shore, offering a view of the lake with a background
of mountains rising almost 2,000 ft. higher.

Except for these small bits of state land, the shoreline is privately owned.
Land speculation and unplanned development have caused clutter. Conversion of a natural lake to a storage reservoir has altered its ecology, promoting
proliferation of algae and weeds.

HEADQUARTERS: Box 99, Garden City, UT 84028; (801) 946-3208.

BEAR RIVER MIGRATORY BIRD REFUGE
U.S. Fish and Wildlife Service
65,030 acres.

15 mi. W of Brigham City. (MP #4.)

*Severe flooding occurred in 1983, and seasonal floods may close the access road
and tour route in future years. Call or write for current information.*

One of the great waterfowl refuges. The wetland area extends beyond the
boundaries, and there is usually good birding between Brigham City and the
entrance. The wetlands are the delta of Bear River where it drains into Great
Salt Lake. Another view of the wetlands is from SR 83, NW from Brigham
City. The Promontory Mountains lie to the W, the Wasatch Range to the E.
The refuge area is flat, with only about 15 ft. between its highest and lowest
points.

Annual precipitation is about 12 in., most of it received in winter and
spring, some as snow. Habitats include marsh, open water, and mudflats. A
number of impoundments have been created by dikes. Visitors drive a 12-mi.
tour route on dikes, giving excellent views of three of the five impoundments.
Along the route are numerous turnouts and several observation towers.

Spring and fall are the best birding seasons, but we have found much of interest in several summer visits. The tour route is closed Jan. to mid-Mar., actual dates depending on snow, weather, and road conditions. Inquire before coming.

Water law and recent U.S. Department of the Interior policies have subordinated the Refuge's water rights to irrigation interests. During the critical summer months, too little water reaches the Refuge. A dry year reduces both waterfowl reproduction for that year and the supply of food for fall migrants.

Plants: In open-water impoundments: widgeon grass, coontail, naiads, with sago pondweed dominant. Aquatic emergents include hardstem bulrush, cattail, phragmites, spike rush, cordgrass, bulrushes. On the alkali flats, salicornia, saltgrass, pickleweed. Dikes and islands have a variety of grasses and forbs, including stinging nettle, sweet clover, sunflowers, thistle, teasel, milkweed, pigweed, ragweed, mustard, wheat grasses, saltgrass, bromes, foxtail barley. A few Russian olive, tamarisk, willow, wild rose.

Birds: Checklist of 225 species. One of the few places where one can sample what early explorers described. Migrant waterfowl begin arriving in Aug. Soon the refuge has up to half a million, including up to 50,000 whistling swans, thousands of Canada and snow geese, northern pintail, green-winged teal, canvasback. Many remain until the water begins to freeze in early winter. Other seasonally abundant or common waterfowl include eared, western, and pied-billed grebes; American white pelican, mallard, gadwall, shoveler, redhead, ruddy duck, common merganser. Over 40 species of shorebirds use the refuge, 14 species nesting.

Canada goslings may be seen as early as May. In June, ducklings and young shorebirds are on view. Avocet are abundant; we have often seen recently hatched chicks in roadside ditches. 21 species of raptors, including bald eagle and peregrine falcon. Fall population of ring-necked pheasant often exceeds 1,000. Other nesting species include eastern and western kingbirds, horned lark, barn and cliff swallows, black-billed magpie, marsh wren, robin, yellow-rumped warbler, western meadowlark; yellow-headed, red-winged, and Brewer's blackbirds; lazuli bunting, savannah and vesper sparrows.

Mammals: Often seen: muskrat, striped skunk, longtail weasel, deer mouse, mountain cottontail. Present but seldom seen: mule deer, bobcat, badger, coyote, porcupine, red fox.

Reptiles and amphibians: Great Basin and red-sided garter snakes often seen. Present but seldom seen species include northern leopard and chorus frogs, northern side-blotched lizard.

Fishes: High population of carp in many wetlands, especially visible during spring spawning and, at low water, near water control outlets. On one of our summer visits, during a dry period, we saw a massive fish kill.

FEATURE

The 12-mi. tour route circles one-fourth of the refuge. Take it slowly. It's never the same on successive trips. In one impoundment, you may see great masses of waterfowl far out of binocular range. At the next, many will be so close no glass is needed. A car is a good blind. Choose a spot and settle for a while. Or sit quietly on one of the observation towers.

INTERPRETATION

Visitor center in the Refuge HQ area. Exhibits, films, literature. Open 9:00 A.M.–4:30 P.M. Mon.–Fri., except holidays, all year. Open weekends from mid-Mar.

Wayside exhibits along the tour route.

ACTIVITIES

Camping: It isn't publicized, but 7 campsites are available in the HQ area, most suitable for RV's. No reservations. Don't expect to find a vacancy during hunting season.

Hiking: On the dikes of the auto tour route, elsewhere as designated.

Hunting: Waterfowl and pheasant, subject to federal and state regulations. Hunting in specified areas only. Hunters must register. Boats may be used for hunting in season.

Fishing: Bank fishing permitted only in HQ area. Channel catfish, in the river, from boats.

Boating: The last half mile of Bear River is within the refuge; this is open to boating all year. Access is outside the refuge.

Mosquitoes and green flies may be present in summer. Repellents work against both.

Pets must be leashed or closely confined.

PUBLICATIONS

Refuge leaflet with map.
Bird checklist.
Seasonal abundance of birds on the Bear River Refuge.
Children's birdlist.
Common Plants of the Bear River Migratory Bird Refuge.
Public hunting leaflet with map.

HEADQUARTERS: P.O. Box 459, Brigham City, UT 84302; (801) 744-2201.

BONNEVILLE SALT FLATS
U.S. Bureau of Land Management
44,000 acres, 30,000 administered by BLM.

N of I-80 near the NV boundary. (MP #7.)

This natural area is a vast, bare plain. Part of the Great Salt Lake Desert, once under the waters of ancient Lake Bonneville. It is wet during winter and spring, hard salt in summer. Near I-80 is the International Speedway, where numerous world's land speed records have been set.

CEDAR MOUNTAINS
U.S. Bureau of Land Management
79,699 acres.

Extending 35 mi. S from I-80, 7 mi. W of Timpie, almost to Dugway. Access by dirt roads and jeep trails shown on MP #7.

Heavily eroded rolling hills. Slopes are not steep, rising from 4,500 ft. at the desert floor to 7,712-ft. Cedar Peak. A single ridgeline, many points above 6,800 ft. At lower elevations, sage, rabbitbrush, Mormon tea, blacksage, bluebunch wheatgrass, occasional juniper. Upper slopes and ridges chiefly bluebunch wheatgrass and juniper.

The N 7 mi. of the range is the less interesting, heavily impacted by mining, sheep grazing, and ORV's. This area is divided from the S portion by a mining road entering from the NW at Hastings Pass and climbing to 6,100 ft. This road probably provides the best access to the area, but strangers should inquire at the BLM office. We talked with men in this office who had hiked the crest S from the Hastings Pass road and judged the area interesting but not outstanding. While wildlife is not abundant, an estimated 200 wild horses roam the mountains. Drinking water must be carried in.

HEADQUARTERS: BLM, Salt Lake District Office, 2370 South 2300 West, Salt Lake City, UT 84119; (801) 524-5348.

DANIELS CANYON
U.S. Bureau of Land Management
5,920 acres.

Access through Dinosaur National Monument (entry in CO Zone 1). Pass the quarry. Continue to Josie Morris Cabin and road end. (MP #3.)

A rugged, scenic area for day hiking. We talked with local hikers who said this canyon offers one of their favorite outings. The landform is a large "V" sloping W. Deep, narrow, steep walls rising 1,600 ft. Scattered stands of pinyon-juniper, sagebrush. Perennial spring and stream. Excellent panoramic views of the Uintah Basin. Deer winter here and can usually be seen Apr.–May.

Hike 1 mi. beyond the Josie Morris Cabin. Here begins a seldom-used livestock trail on the right side of the canyon, suitable for foot or horse travel. 4 mi. to the top of Blue Mountain.

HEADQUARTERS: BLM, Vernal District Office, 170 South 5th St., Vernal, UT 84078; (801) 789-1362.

DEEP CREEK MOUNTAINS
See entry in Zone 2.

DESOLATION CANYON
See entry—Green River; Desolation Canyon—in Zone 2.

DIAMOND MOUNTAIN PLATEAU
Chiefly U.S. Bureau of Land Management
Roughly 190,000 acres.

Area between Browns Park (see entry) and Dinosaur National Monument, on the CO boundary. Principal access is a paved road E from 5th North in Vernal over Diamond Mountain to the Jones Hole National Fish Hatchery. An alternate route leaves SR 44 18 mi. N of Vernal. Or from Browns Park, over the Swinging Bridge (nothing heavier than a pickup) and by an unpaved road through Crouse Canyon; best for vehicles with high clearance. (MP #3.)

The scenic route from Vernal crosses sagebrush benchland at about 5,300 ft. elevation, climbs almost 3,000 ft. to the rim of Diamond Mountain Plateau, then descends sharply into Jones Hole, a deep gorge at the boundary of Dinosaur National Monument. To the N of the Plateau are several peaks over 8,000 ft. Crouse Reservoir is one of several fished for trout. The numerous ridges are cut by steep-walled draws. Sagebrush at lower elevations, then juniper, with aspen, fir, and ponderosa pine on high slopes.

Hoy Mountain, 8,870 ft., is near the CO border, E of Crouse Rese. Steep slopes, quartzite outcroppings. Pinyon-juniper with scattered areas of mountain-mahogany, ponderosa pine, fir, and aspen. Abundant wildlife.

Diamond Breaks, a roadless area, 3,900 acres in UT, 31,480 adjoining in CO, has been proposed for wilderness study. In CO it adjoins the Browns Park National Wildlife Refuge on the N, Dinosaur on the S.

ACTIVITIES

Camping: The most convenient campground is Steinaker Lake State Recreation Area on SR 44, 9 mi. N of Vernal. No campground, but ample opportunities for informal camping on BLM land along the way. Some land is privately owned; look for "No Trespassing" signs.

Hiking, backpacking: The only established trail begins at the hatchery, extends about 4 mi. to the Green River, within the National Monument. We were told it's a beautiful area with natural springs, petroglyphs, a good campsite about halfway. Opportunities for cross-country hiking said to be good.

Hunting: Deer, elk.

Fishing: Trout, in reservoirs and in the Jones Hole gorge.

REFERENCE: *Diamond Mountain & Jones Hole Mountain Fish Hatchery.* One of several tour leaflets available in Vernal. The Vernal Chamber of Commerce usually has them.

HEADQUARTERS: BLM, Vernal District Office, 170 South 5th East, Vernal, UT 84078; (801) 789-1362.

DINOSAUR NATIONAL MONUMENT

The Visitor Center and Dinosaur Quarry are in UT, N of US 40 at Jensen, but most of the acreage and Monument HQ are in CO. See entry in CO Zone 1.

FLAMING GORGE NATIONAL RECREATION AREA

See entry, Ashley National Forest.

FRANKLIN BASIN STATE FOREST

Utah State Division of State Lands and Forestry
13,500 acres.

US 89 crosses the SE corner about 20 mi. E of Logan. (MP #4.)

See the Utah Preface for comment on State Forests.

Surrounded by the Wasatch-Cache National Forest, but with several in-holdings on its boundaries. Multipurpose Map No. 4 shows an unpaved road running N across the site from US 89, paralleling the Logan River, and several jeep trails to mountain lakes. The Wasatch-Cache National Forest map doesn't mark State Forest boundaries, but it shows several trails linking with National Forest trails. Inquire locally.

Scenic area. Franklin Basin is a broad valley surrounded by high, rugged mountains with side canyons. Valley elevation is about 6,500 ft. Several peaks over 9,000 ft. Annual precipitation at high elevations is 40 in., most of it winter snow.

Streams flow from mountain slopes to the Logan River. Several 40- to 60-acre mountain lakes are in or just outside the site.

A proposed National Forest wilderness area is on the W. On the E, off US 89, is the Beaver Mountain ski area; the tops of the ski lifts are on state land.

As noted in the Utah Preface, recreation is not a management objective in State Forests, and no facilities are provided now. Snowmobiling use is heavy in winter. Picnicking and camping are increasing in warm months. Plans include sanitary facilities.

Plants: About 80% forested: spruce-fir, aspen, limber pine, Douglas-fir. Understory includes mountain-mahogany, common juniper. Alpine plant community above timberline, about 9,000 ft. Sagebrush on S-facing slopes. Mountain meadows along streams, with some riparian vegetation. We were told the area has "many, many kinds of wildflowers."

Birds: No checklist. Mentioned: red-tailed hawk, golden eagle, Steller's jay, blue and ruffed grouse.

Mammals: Mentioned as often or occasionally seen: mule deer, elk, moose, snowshoe hare, coyote, badger, marmot, beaver, chipmunk, ground squirrels, mountain lion. Black bear uncommon.

ACTIVITIES: No campground, marked trails, or other facilities. But visitors are free to camp, backpack, ride horses; state regulations govern hunting and fishing.

Sometimes closed to visitors in periods of high fire hazard, June–Oct. Posted when that occurs.

Mosquitoes in summer.

HEADQUARTERS: Bear River Area Office, Utah State Division of State Lands and Forestry, 55 East 100 North, Logan, UT 84321; (801) 752-8701.

GREAT SALT LAKE
State of Utah
1,700 sq. mi.

NW Utah. (MP #7, 8.)

Snowfall in the mountains was unusually heavy in the winter of 1982–83. Rain and an early spring thaw caused devastating floods. The level of Great Salt Lake rose alarmingly. Because the lake is shallow, an inch of rise moves the shoreline back by many feet.

Flooding breached the dikes in waterfowl refuges, salt water inundating what had been freshwater impoundments. High water closed the access road to the Bear River Migratory Bird Refuge and the causeway to Antelope Island.

As the winter of 1983–84 approached, the lake level was still high, so that even normal spring runoff would cause more flooding. But again winter snows were heavy, and the lake level rose higher. Sandbag dikes were needed to keep I-80 open.

The winter of 1984–85 began with record snowfalls.

It is too soon to determine the ecological consequences of these repeated floods or to predict when the lake level may recede.

The following entry was written before the floods.

Largest lake W of the Mississippi, the Great Salt Lake is a remnant of a far larger inland sea, the ancient Lake Bonneville. 75–80 mi. long, 30 mi. wide, it is shallow, average depth only 13 ft. Streams flow in, chiefly from the N, but the lake has no outlet. When evaporation exceeds inflow plus precipitation, the lake level drops and salinity increases. In a wet period, the level rises and salinity declines. Since 1847 the level has fluctuated between 4,211 ft. elevation and 4,192 ft. Until 1983 the trend appeared to be downward.

An estimated 2 million tons of minerals are carried into the lake each year; its total mineral content is about 5 billion tons. Only the Dead Sea is saltier. Salinity has been as high as 27%, eight times as salty as sea water.

Most forms of aquatic life cannot tolerate such saltiness, but certain algae, bacteria, and protozoa thrive. The lake produces brine flies and brine shrimp, the latter being its largest lifeform.

The streams flowing to the lake are no saltier than streams elsewhere, and they supply extensive freshwater marshes around the lake. The marshes attract and support large numbers of birds of many species. Three of the lake's eight islands are nesting grounds for pelicans and other migrants. They are off limits to visitors during the breeding season, Apr.–June, and difficult to reach at any time because of shallow water around them. Several mammal subspecies are thought to have evolved in the relative isolation of the islands.

Birds: 257 species recorded around the lake, 117 of them nesting. Of these, 112 species are associated almost exclusively with the lake's surrounding marshlands. About 30% of the ducks of the Pacific and Central Flyways use these marshes. Eight marsh areas around the lake are managed by Utah's Division of Wildlife Resources. Peak duck populations in these areas occur Aug.–Nov.; Sept. counts often exceed 500,000. The spring peak is Mar. through mid-Apr. Waterfowl include Canada and snow geese, pintail, green-winged teal, canvasback, mallard, gadwall, shoveler, redhead, ruddy duck, common merganser.

Counts of nongame bird species are even higher, phalaropes alone often exceeding 500,000 in midsummer. Also numerous: eared and western grebes, great egret, great blue heron, white-faced ibis, killdeer, dowitcher, American avocet, black-necked stilt, California and Franklin's gulls, Forster's and black terns; violet-green, tree, rough-winged, barn, and cliff swallows; black-billed magpie, marsh wren, red-winged and yellow-headed blackbirds, savannah and vesper sparrows.

GREAT SALT LAKE DESERT
U.S. Bureau of Land Management; and other agencies
4,000 sq. mi.

NW UT. Crossed by I-80. (MP #7.)
Many deserts have dunes, washes, and other topographic variety. Many have shrubs and, after spring rains, spectacular flowers. The Great Salt Lake Desert is almost featureless. Except for a few mountain ranges that rise abruptly, it's one of the flattest places on earth, and over much of it no plant or animal life can be seen. Like most of Utah W of the Wasatch Range, it was part of ancient Lake Bonneville. Unlike the Great Salt Lake, it has no inflowing streams. It is separated from the lake by a low divide. What you see is the dry lakebed. It was a formidable obstacle to E–W travel until construction of the railroad and, later, a highway.

One of the schemes proposed for flood abatement is large-scale pumping from the Great Salt Lake to this ancient lakebed.

GREAT SALT LAKE STATE PARK: ANTELOPE ISLAND
Utah State Division of Parks and Recreation
25,469 acres.

From I-15 N of Salt Lake City, exit left on SR 127 to Syracuse and continue on 6 1/2 mi. causeway to the island. (MP #7.)

In January 1984, the Park Manager wrote, "The Great Salt Lake has risen to an elevation of 4206.5 [ft.] at this time and is expected over the next couple of years to rise even higher. The park had to be closed due to this high water condition. The way it looks, the park will not be opened for quite some time, possibly three or four years. This will give us the time to develop a master plan that will fit the pristine conditions of the park."

The following entry reports preflood conditions.

Fifteen mi. long, 5 1/2 mi. wide, Antelope is the largest island in the Great Salt Lake. The island is a small mountain range rising from the lake, its highest point about 2,400 ft. above the water surface.

The Division of Parks and Recreation has had responsibility for the island only since 1981. Only the N tip, about 10% of the area, is now open to the public. A posted map shows this limit, and a chain link fence excludes visitors from the larger area. Neither the map nor a bulletin board explained why.

We visited the island on Labor Day. The information office was closed; so was the HQ. The marina was deserted, and we saw only one boat on the lake. A few families were picnicking, and about two dozen people were wading in the lake, only knee deep even when far from shore.

Even 10% of the island is enough for developments to be widely spaced. In addition to the marina, scattered picnic shelters, beach, and bathing pavilion, the park has a campground and a trail to a high overlook. It's an attractive area with splendid views of the Wasatch Mountains. It could accommodate many more people without congestion.

We looked again at the posted map and saw a tour route leading into the fenced-off area. The gate is open from 9 A.M. to 5 P.M. A sign at the gate says that vehicles must stay on the road; inside another sign tells visitors they must remain in their cars. The road was rough, and it penetrates a relatively short distance. We saw little of interest.

After several hours we found a ranger, who answered our many questions. The main part of the island is fenced off because it's still under study. A few archeological sites have been found, and presumably there are others; they don't want them vandalized. Old mine shafts are a hazard. So are the free-living bison, descendants of stock introduced in 1892. At times the fire hazard is extreme; a large section burned in 1981. Antelope, for which the island was named, have been absent since 1870; the possibility of reintroduction is under study.

The largest numbers of visitors come in early spring.

The exhibit on the causeway explained that salinity on the N side is 18%, while in Farmington Bay, on the S side, it's only 1.5%. Why is there no beach on the S side? The Bay is too polluted, we were told.

Plants: No botanical information is yet available. We saw few trees and were puzzled by the absence of sagebrush on the slopes along the tour route. This seems to be a result of frequent burns.

Birds: The causeway is a splendid birding area. Near the mainland we saw many gulls and shorebirds, notably a large number of black-necked stilt. Near the island we saw two large rafts of eared grebe, over 1,000 in each. The ranger said a local Audubon group has recorded over 250 species, chiefly along the causeway, but no list is yet available. The causeway has turnouts, and one can walk the beach.

HEADQUARTERS: 4528 West 1700 South, Syracuse, UT 84041; (801) 621-1217.

GREAT SALT LAKE STATE PARK: SALTAIR BEACH
Utah State Division of Parks and Recreation
1,524 acres.

Just off I-80, 16 mi. W of Salt Lake City. (MP #7.)

4 1/2 mi. of shoreline at the S end of the lake.
In the spring of 1984, the developed area was flooded. Indeed, I-80 was sand-bagged.

The acreage of the park varies. The shore and lakebed are so nearly flat that a small change in lake level causes the water's edge to advance or recede many feet. At times the water has been a mile from the highway.

Since the mid-nineteenth century, travelers have been fascinated by "the lake in which one cannot sink." Numerous resorts were built on the S shore, among them Saltair, beset by storms, fires, and receding lake waters until it closed in 1959. At its peak it had a great ornamented pavilion with a huge dance floor, roller-coaster, fun house, and other features attracting as many as 10,000 visitors a day. Several years after closing, it was destroyed by fire.

The state is now developing a resort patterned after the original, including the ornate pavilion, with swimming pool and amusement park rides.

Development is concentrated near the entrance. Beyond this a park road gives access to a great expanse of flat beach. Opportunities for beach hiking extend beyond the park limits, and we saw areas that may at times have interesting birding. (At the time of our visit, high winds were producing a sandstorm.)

Camping: Large open beach area; no formal sites.

PUBLICATIONS
Park leaflet.
Summer calendar of events.

HEADQUARTERS: P.O. Box 323, Magna, UT 84044; (801) 533-4080.

GREEN RIVER
See Ashley National Forest.

LAKETOWN CANYON
U.S. Bureau of Land Management
No acreage available.

Just S of Bear Lake. Unimproved road S from Laketown on SR 30. (MP #4.)

A BLM specialist recommended this as a pleasant, quiet area. (Another was less enthusiastic.) The canyon begins in the Wasatch-Cache National Forest and extends NE to Laketown. Near the top of the Canyon, Laketown Creek flows through a beautiful sylvan area that includes numerous beaver dams. The E wall of the canyon is steep, the W less so. The surrounding area has a number of jeep tracks, shown on Multipurpose Map No. 4 and the Wasatch-Cache National Forest map. The latter also shows a few foot trails, but it is unlikely that these are maintained.

HEADQUARTERS: BLM, Salt Lake District Office, 2370 South 2300 West, Salt Lake City, UT 84119; (801) 524-5348.

OURAY NATIONAL WILDLIFE REFUGE
U.S. Fish and Wildlife Service
11,483 acres.

Fom Vernal, 15 mi. SW on US 40, then 13 mi. S on SR 88, following signs. (MP #3.)

The refuge includes 12 mi. of the Green River and its wooded floodplain. This is desert country, annual precipitation about 7 in. Summer daytime temperatures may reach near 100°F, but evenings are cool.

Shallow ponds and marshes have been created by dikes, canals, and pumping from the river. The refuge attracts peak spring and fall migrant populations of about 75,000 waterfowl. Spring migration begins in early Mar., peaks in Apr. Fall arrivals begin in Aug., peak in Oct.

The Refuge wasn't doing much for visitors when we were there, a condition we attributed to the savage cuts made in Refuge budgets. We had seen their effects elsewhere—no maps, leaflets, exhibits or other visitor guidance. Signs along the road said "AREA CLOSED." The auto tour route was closed.

However, the Refuge manager writes that this situation has changed:

A new visitor contact station has been installed just west of the refuge headquarters area on the entrance road. This facility has a large colored map of the area, panels for display of current refuge information, and seasonal panels of informational material regarding the refuge. A leaflet dispenser is also located at this station. Immediately across the road is a new vault-pit type restroom for the public. Our auto tour route in Sheppard Bottom is open the year around, except for ten days during the Utah State deer season in mid-October, and interpretive signs and a visitor's tower are located on this tour route. This auto tour route is approximately 4 miles in length, exposing the visitor to farm fields, shallow marsh habitat, the river, and greasewood-sage habitat. We also have the Green River Overlook auto tour route on the bluffs along the west side of the river.

We followed the road along the banks of the river. This area is attractive, an avenue of green crossing the desert. On the left are clay bluffs, banded in shades of red and brown. At several turnouts we saw indications that people camp here.

Plants: Tall cottonwoods and dense brush line the river bottoms. On top of the clay bluffs are green needlegrass, Indian ricegrass, cactus, desert shrubs. Greasewood brush surrounds the marshes. If rainfall is adequate in spring, May and June offer a fine display of desert flowers.

Birds: 200 species recorded. Checklist available. Seasonally abundant or common waterfowl species include western and pied-billed grebes, Canada goose, mallard, gadwall, northern pintail; blue-winged, green-winged, and cinnamon teals; American wigeon, ring-necked duck, lesser scaup, common goldeneye, bufflehead, ruddy duck. Also great blue heron, snowy egret, black-crowned night-heron, white-faced ibis, American coot, killdeer, spotted sandpiper, willet, lesser yellowlegs, marbled godwit, American avocet, black-necked stilt, Wilson's and red-necked phalaropes. Many songbirds. Lewis' woodpecker often seen in cottonwood groves.

Mammals: Include whitetail prairie dog, blacktail and whitetail jackrabbits, cottontail, raccoon, skunk, coyote, porcupine, mule deer.

ACTIVITIES
Camping: Primitive camping permitted. No facilities.
Hiking: Except in posted areas.
Hunting: Ducks, pheasant, mule deer only, in designated areas.
Fishing: River. Catfish, carp.
Boating: No ramp, but one could launch a canoe or cartopper. Some people raft the Green River from Ouray to Sand Wash, but see entry, Green River.

PUBLICATIONS
   Refuge leaflet.
   Bird checklist.
   Refuge map.

HEADQUARTERS: 447 East Main, Suite 4, Vernal, UT 84078; (801) 789-0351.

PELICAN LAKE
U.S. Bureau of Land Management
About 840 water acres.

From Vernal, 15 mi. SW on US 40. S 7 mi. on SR 88. Turn right on road marked for Randlett. In about 2 mi., see sign on left with symbols for boat ramp and camping. About 4 mi. to lake. (MP #3.)

A shallow lake about 2 mi. long, 1 mi. wide, surrounded by gently rolling land, sagebrush and cottonwoods, most of it used for grazing. The recreation area has boat launching, latrines, informal camp sites, some with tables. Use seems to be chiefly by local fishermen.

The Ouray Refuge manager told us there's good birding here spring and fall. A pleasant, quiet overnight camp site not listed in campground directories.

A posted sign advises that swimming is inadvisable because of schistosomes, a parasite that causes intense itching.

PHIL PICO STATE FOREST
Utah State Division of State Lands and Forestry
4,300 acres.

From Manila (near WY border just W of Flaming Gorge area), 6 mi. W on SR 43, then left 5 mi. on unimproved road. (MP #3.) Must cross some private land. We suggest obtaining permission before entering.

See the Utah Preface for comment on State Forests.
Between the Ashley National Forest and the WY border. The Forest is

shown on Multipurpose Map No. 3. The Ashley National Forest map does not mark the State Forest, but does show its peaks, streams, and primitive roads.

Mountainous. Corson Peak is 9,500 ft. About 40% tree-covered. N- and E-facing slopes have good stands of Douglas-fir. Sagebrush on S- and W-facing slopes. Annual precipitation on the mountain is about 35 in., annual snowfall as much as 250 in.

The site attracts some hunters, few if any hikers.

ACTIVITIES

Backpacking: Jeep, game, and stock trails only. Intermittent streams.
Hunting: Grouse, rabbit, mule deer, elk, moose.

HEADQUARTERS: Division of State Lands and Forestry, Uintah Basin Area Office, 1325 West Highway 40, Vernal, UT 84078; (801) 789-2092.

ROCKPORT LAKE STATE PARK
Utah State Division of Parks and Recreation
1,030 acres; 550 water acres.

From I-80, 25 mi. E of Salt Lake City, S 7 mi. on US 189. (MP #3.)

The lake, a popular site for water-based activity, is not, in our terms, a natural area. The park ranger's response to our questionnaire persuaded us to include it. The response included a competent checklist of birds and mammals and many references to the nearby Wasatch-Cache and Uinta National Forest. The Park is an attractive base for exploring nearby natural areas.

Adjacent land is privately owned cattle range, used by hunters, with permission. Our informant wrote that she hikes and skis there but knows of no one else doing so.

Elevation at the lake is 6,000 ft. The park is surrounded by gently sloping hills, pinyon-juniper vegetation. The lake is 3 mi. long, 1/2 mi. wide. Fringe of trees and shrubs on part of the shoreline, and some marshy areas. A number of ducks were on the lake when we visited in late Aug.

Birds: 102 species recorded. Checklist available. Seasonally abundant or common species include Canada goose, mallard, pintail, loon, western grebe, great blue heron, killdeer, chukar, sage grouse. Checklist includes bald and golden eagles, red-tailed hawk, kestrel, great horned owl, whistling swan.

Mammals: Checklist available, including weasel, least chipmunk, marmot, porcupine, skunk, badger, beaver, mule deer.

INTERPRETATION
Exhibit.
Naturalist programs on request. Rangers have an interpretive slide program.

ACTIVITIES
Camping: One developed campground, 7 primitive. 300 sites.
Fishing: Rainbow, German brown, and cutthroat trout; mountain whitefish.
Boating: Ramp, marina. No hp limit. Rentals. Sailing is popular.
Swimming: Supervised, June–Oct.
Ski touring: Within the park and on frozen lake.
Snowmobiling: Unplowed roads.

June–Aug. is the busy season, when the main campground is often full.

PUBLICATION: *Rockport Wildlife.*

HEADQUARTERS: P.O. Box 457, Peoa, UT 84061; (801) 336-2241.

SAWTOOTH NATIONAL FOREST
U.S. Forest Service
71,183 acres in UT; 1,731,512 acres in ID.

No paved road enters the UT portion of the Forest. For Clear Creek Campground, turn W from I-84 on SR 42 for 26 mi. to Strevelle, ID. W 3 mi. on gravel road, then S 5 mi. Central and W areas of the UT portion by unpaved roads S from Yost, near the ID border. (MP #8.)

In the Raft River Mountains. The Raft River is outside the unit. Highest peak is 9,925 ft., several others over 8,000. Many springs and streams. The entire area is open to snowmobiles and other ORV's. Pinyon-juniper on most slopes. Ranger says people go there in the fall to gather pinyon pine nuts.

The one campground is not heavily used. Principal use of the area seems to be by hunters.

ACTIVITIES
Camping: One campground, 25 units. May–Oct.
Hiking: Forest map shows several trails, mostly following creeks. Also primitive roads.
Hunting: Deer, grouse.

Fishing: Trout. Beaver ponds and streams.

PUBLICATION: Forest map. $1.00.

HEADQUARTERS: Sawtooth National Forest, Burley R.D., 2621 S. Overland, Burley, ID 83318; (208) 678-0430.

STANSBURY MOUNTAINS
U.S. Forest Service; U.S. Bureau of Land Management
88,000 acres.

S of Great Salt Lake. Range begins at Rowley Junction on I-80, extends S to SR 199. Principal road access is South Willow Canyon, 5 mi. S of Grantsville. (MP #7.)

All but 15,000 acres is in the Grantsville Division of the Wasatch-Cache National Forest. Roadless except in South Willow Canyon, the site has been proposed for wilderness status. The 15,000 acres of BLM land is at the N and S ends of the range, plus a strip along the W foothills.

The mountains rise steeply from Skull Valley on the W, where the elevation is about 4,300 ft. Highest point is Deseret Peak, 11,031 ft. Vickory Mountain, in the S, is 10,305 ft., and 25 mi. of the ridge is over 8,000 ft. The high country is always snow-covered Dec.–May. Numerous springs and intermittent streams.

Terrain is generally rugged, with steep-walled canyons. Many rock outcrops. Lower slopes support sage and juniper. Conifers and conifer-riparian woodlands on the S slopes of the canyons above 6,500 ft.

An auto road in S. Willow Canyon ends in a parking area at 7,800 ft., from which a trail leads to the top of Deseret Peak, which offers a 360-degree vista.

The Forest Service recommended 43,800 acres as wilderness; BLM recommended 10,000 acres adjoining on the N.

ACTIVITIES
Camping: 6 campgrounds, 40 units, in S. Willow Canyon. May–Oct.

Hiking, backpacking: Hikers and backpackers enjoy the Stansburys in summer because it's cooler up there. While the campgrounds in S. Willow Canyon are sometimes full, the trails are uncrowded. Several unimproved roads and jeep tracks penetrate the area from the W, E, and S, usually connecting with trails. These roads and trails, known to local hikers and hunters, are not shown in sufficient detail by the Wasatch-Cache forest map. A newcomer to the area should have a topographic map.

REFERENCE: Hall, Dave. *The Hiker's Guide to Utah.* Billings, MT.: Falcon Press, 1982. Pp. 26–28.

HEADQUARTERS: Wasatch-Cache National Forest, Salt Lake R.D., 6944 S. 30th E, Salt Lake City, UT 84121; (801) 524-5042.

STARVATION LAKE STATE PARK
Utah State Division of Parks and Recreation
3,485 acres.

4 mi. off US 40, NW of Duchesne. (MP #3.)

An attractive man-made desert lake, about 3,445 acres. About 70 acres have been developed: boat ramp, beach, parking, campgrounds, etc. Parkland surrounds the lake, but 95% of visitor activity is water based. Some waterfowl visit the lake in migration; as many as 20 bald eagles visit the lake in migration.

We had planned to drive NW on SR 35 into the Ashley National Forest and spend the night at Wolf Creek Campground. We camped at Starvation Lake instead, and were glad we did. Next day we found SR 35 interesting but rough, slow going; we'd have camped late.

ACTIVITIES
Camping: 31 sites on a bluff overlooking the lake, attractive but exposed. 50 spaces near the shore.
Fishing: We were told it's only fair.
Swimming: Unsupervised.
Boating: Ramp. No posted hp limit.

HEADQUARTERS: Box 584, Duchesne, UT 84021; (801) 738-2326.

STEWART LAKE WATERFOWL MANAGEMENT AREA
Utah State Division of Wildlife Resources
635 acres.

From US 40, 10 mi. E of Vernal, turn S opposite entrance to Dinosaur National Monument. Where blacktop turns right, continue straight to entrance. (MP #3.)

If you visit Dinosaur, come in here for a short, quiet walk. The dirt road turns W, between the reservoir and the Green River, comes to a blacktop turning and parking area. Short trail from here to the Green River. The road ahead parallels a water channel, beyond which is a reed marsh. Cottonwoods and brush along the river.

Most of the land bordering the reservoir is private and fenced. We found no place within binocular range of the open water. Birding was moderately good in Aug., would doubtless be better in fall migration.

TIMPANOGOS CAVE NATIONAL MONUMENT
National Park Service
250 acres.

> From I-15 between Salt Lake City and Provo, Alpine exit; E 12 mi. on SR 92. (MP #7.)

Within the Uinta National Forest, on the Alpine Scenic Loop that circles the Mount Timpanogos Scenic Area, on the W side of the Wasatch Range. From the parking area, a strenuous 1 1/2-mi. hike, ascending 1,065 ft. along the S wall of American Fork Canyon to the cave entrance. Splendid views of the mountains, canyon, and Utah Valley. Allow 3 hours for the hike and cave tour.

Three caves are connected by man-made tunnels. Much of the interior is covered with sparkling white translucent crystals. Many of the stalactites, stalagmites, and other formations are "live," seeping water still forming dripstone.

The trail and caves are open as long as weather permits, usually May 1–Sept. 30. Visitors are admitted to the caves only in guided groups of 20. Tours leave at frequent intervals. Purchase tickets at the Visitor Center before hiking up the trail. From May 1–30 and Labor Day–Sept. 30 tickets are sold 8 A.M.–3:30 P.M. (in summer, the busy season, 8 A.M.–4:30 P.M.). Arrive early; on busy days a ticket purchased mid-morning may be for an afternoon tour, and all tours may be booked by early afternoon.

Wear walking shoes. Bring a coat or sweater; average cave temperature is 43°F. Outdoors, in visitor season, average daytime high temperatures range between 70° and 95°F. Sudden brief thunderstorms sometimes occur in summer and may cause temporary closing of the cave trail.

While the site is small, park naturalists have gathered much information on the flora and fauna of the canyon. A visit here is a good introduction to the natural history of the Wasatch Range.

Plants: Trees on the canyon floor include Engelmann and blue spruce, dogwood, narrow-leaf cottonwood. Shrubs, some growing to tree size, include bigleaf maple, hawthorn, alder, water birch. Utah juniper on the drier slopes. Scattered Douglas-fir on N and W exposures. The upper canyon walls are largely exposed rock, but orange, brown, and black lichens occur in patches, and small plants and shrubs grow from cracks and crevices.

Flowering plants include chokecherry, serviceberry, wild rose, snowberry, ninebark, Oregon grape, fairy bells, false hellebore, Solomon plume, coneflower, yarrow, thistle, aster, gentian, penstemon, buttercup, wild geranium, meadow rue, wild strawberry, clematis, lupine, violets.

Birds: Checklist available for the lower part of American Fork Canyon, at 5,000–7,500 ft. elevation. Of the 126 species listed, a surprising 104 are uncommon, occasional, or rare, only 22 even seasonally common or abundant. This suggests that the canyon is a restricted habitat. Abundant or common species include blue grouse, poor-will, common nighthawk, white-throated swift; black-chinned, broad-tailed, and rufous hummingbirds; ash-throated and olive-sided flycatchers, violet-green swallow, Steller's jay, black-capped and mountain chickadees, dipper, robin, Townsend's solitaire, golden-crowned kinglet, red-winged blackbird, western tanager, pine grosbeak, pine siskin, Oregon junco.

Mammals: Checklist available: mammals observed within the Monument or nearby in the Canyon. Include several shrews and bats, pika, snowshoe hare, whitetail jackrabbit, mountain cottontail, marmot, Uinta and golden-mantled ground squirrels; rock and red squirrels; northern flying squirrel, cliff and Colorado chipmunks, beaver, deer mouse, bushytail woodrat, vole, muskrat, Norway rat, porcupine, coyote, gray and red foxes, raccoon, black bear, ringtail, marten, short- and longtail weasels, mink, striped and spotted skunks, badger, mountain lion, bobcat, elk, mule deer, moose.

INTERPRETATION

Visitor Center has exhibits, 12-min. audiovisual program, literature.
Riverside nature trail. (Destroyed in 1983 flood; being rebuilt.)

PUBLICATIONS

Monument leaflet with map.
Along the Way to the Caves. Booklet, 28 pp., illustrated, $0.50.
Bird checklist.
Mammals checklist.
Vascular plants checklist.
Information pages:
    General information.

Data—information, cave and area.
Geology of American Fork Canyon.
Geological strata of American Fork Canyon.
Cave glossary.
Map of caves.
Local area map.
List of nearby areas to visit.
Legend of Timpanogos.
Bibliography.

REFERENCE: *Timpanogos Cave: Window into the Earth.* Globe, AZ: Southwest Parks and Monuments Association. 48 pp., illustrated, $4.95.

HEADQUARTERS: R.F.D. 3, Box 200, American Fork, UT 84003; (801) 756-5238.

UINTA NATIONAL FOREST
U.S. Forest Service
812,787 acres of Forest land; 889,208 acres within boundaries.

The largest block forms a giant U with Heber City at its center. The W side adjoins the Wasatch-Cache NF at the Salt Lake–Utah county line, extending S to Provo along the Wasatch Range. The base extends S to US 6/50, adjoining the Ashley NF S of Strawberry Reservoir. The E side of the U extends N, crossing the Duchesne Ridge, almost to the Provo River. Here it adjoins the Wasatch-Cache NF on the N, the Ashley NF on the NE. Access roads from SR 80, US 189, US 40, US 6/50.

A disjunct block is on the Wasatch Range E of I-15 between Payson and Nephi. Access by secondary roads. Another block is in the Sheeprock Mountains S of Vernon. Access by secondary roads from SR 36. (MP #3.)

The Forest was established in 1897 to conserve the Wasatch watershed, which had been damaged by misuse. Although timber is harvested, the Forest's primary product is water for the farms and cities at the foot of the Wasatch front.

Close to the metropolitan area, the accessible parts of the Forest are heavily used. Popular sites include American Fork Canyon; Mt. Timpanogos; Provo Canyon; the Right Fork of Hobble Creek, E of Springville; Diamond Fork; and Payson Lakes. Use is now 1.2 million visitor-days per year, increasing rapidly. Although the Forest is popular, it provides little information to visitors. No information about Forest flora and fauna is published, nor could we obtain it from office files. The Forest has few publications and virtually no interpretive program.

Land characteristics range from high mountain desert near Vernon to high peaks. Mountain valleys and meadows are broken by moderate to steep ridges. The steepest slopes are along the Wasatch Front.

The Uinta National Forest portion of the Wasatch Range is dominated by the huge mass of Mt. Timpanogos, 11,750 ft. high, its base covering 50 sq. mi. Numerous other peaks exceed 10,000 ft. In the block S of Payson, the highest is 11,877-ft. Mt. Nebo. Except for the few main routes over mountain passes, most access roads ascend canyons but do not cross the area, their upper sections closed by snow in winter.

In the Forest area E of Heber City, the Duchesne Ridge has peaks over 9,000 ft., but most of this region is less rugged, characterized by many basins, streams, small lakes, and rolling benchland.

Climate varies from place to place. Annual precipitation is about 15 in. at the base of the Wasatch Front, 60 in. or more on high slopes, most of this falling as snow.

Plants: The Forest has many life zones. The sagebrush-cliffrose association typifies areas up to about 6,500 ft. Next, up to 8,000 ft., is a mountain brush zone, with oakbrush, mountain-mahogany, and other species. The Canadian zone, from 8,000 to 9,500 ft., is characterized by aspen and white fir. Then, up to timberline, is the Hudsonian zone, with spruce and alpine fir. The arctic-alpine zone has primrose, alpine moss, tundra plants. About 60% of the area is forested. No plant list is available.

Birds: No checklist available. Species should be similar to those in Wasatch-Cache NF (see entry).

Mammals: No checklist available. HQ reports deer, elk, moose, bobcat often seen; black bear and mountain lion rarely.

FEATURES

Lone Peak Wilderness Area; 21,000 acres, plus 9,000 acres adjacent in Wasatch-Cache NF. On the Salt Lake-Utah county line. No map or description of the area is available. Principal trail access from American Fork Canyon.

Mount Timpanogos Scenic Area, 10,750 acres. The Alpine Scenic Highway, SR 80, leads N from US 189 in Provo Canyon. Mount Timpanogos Trail to Emerald Lake and snowfield. The highway continues, a 24-mi. loop around "Timpy."

In *Provo Canyon,* US 189 lies between two large sections of Forest and offers many scenic views, but most of the roadside land is privately owned. The road passes Bridal Veil Falls, a two-step cascade, and an aerial tramway.

Mount Nebo Recreation Area is 10 mi. from Nephi in the left fork of Salt Creek Canyon. The Mount Nebo Scenic Loop is a 32-mi. drive, Payson City to SR 132 E of Nephi. This route passes *Payson Lakes.*

ACTIVITIES

Camping: 40 campgrounds, 930 sites. Open season is May–Oct., shorter in high elevations.

Hiking, backpacking: 825 mi. of trails. No permits or special restrictions. Trails in scenic areas are heavily used.

Horse riding: Most trails are suitable for horse travel. Trailhead facilities at Granite Flat; special facilities at Blackhawk Campground. Some restrictions in wilderness area. Grazing near lakes and streams prohibited. No local outfitters.

Hunting: Deer, elk.

Fishing: Over 200 mi. of streams, plus small lakes and reservoirs. Rainbow, brown, cutthroat, and brook trout; Montana grayling.

Boating: On Currant Creek and Soldier Creek reservoirs. Ramps.

Ski touring: See Travel Plan for trails and information. Excellent opportunities.

Snowmobiling: In open valleys, on trails and roads closed by snow. See Travel Plan for map and information.

Some areas may be closed because of fire hazard July–Sept. Inquire.

PUBLICATIONS

Forest map. $1.00.
High Uintas Primitive Area folder and map.
Travel Plan: map and information.

REFERENCES

Hall, Dave. *The Hiker's Guide to Utah.* Billings, MT: Falcon Press, 1982. Pp. 58–66.
Paxman, Shirley and Monroe, and Gayle and Weldon Taylor. *Utah Valley Trails.* Salt Lake City: Wasatch, 1978.
Gates, Jon L., and Albert F. Regenthal. *Lakes of the High Uintas.* Salt Lake City: Utah State Department of Fish and Game, 1964.
Schimpf, Ann, and Mel Davis. *Cache Trails.* Salt Lake City: Wasatch, 1978.

HEADQUARTERS: 88 W 100 N, Provo, UT 84601; (801) 377-5780.

RANGER DISTRICTS: Heber R.D., 125 E 100 N, Heber City, UT 84032; (801) 654-0470. Pleasant Grove R.D., 390 N 100 E, Pleasant Grove, UT 84062; (801) 785-3563. Spanish Fork R.D., 44 W 400 N, Spanish Fork, UT 84660; (801) 798-3571.

UTAH LAKE STATE PARK
Utah State Division of Parks and Recreation
300 acres.

4 mi. W of Provo. (MP #7.)

Heavy flooding in the spring and summer of 1983 inundated and damaged the park. In early 1984 the park was still under 2 feet of water, and spring runoff was expected to raise lake levels above their 1983 peak. The park area is being diked. Plans to reopen depend on completion of the dike, pumping out the water, and repairing damage.

Utah Lake (surface area 150 sq. mi.) is the state's largest natural body of fresh water, receiving water from the Provo, Spanish Fork, and American Fork Rivers. Almost none of the shoreline is publicly owned.

The park is a popular center for water-based recreation.

ACTIVITIES
Camping: 60 sites.
Boating: Marina, 5 ramps. Lake is dangerous in high winds.
Fishing: Carp, catfish, bass, walleye pike, yellow perch.

HEADQUARTERS: 440 West Center, Provo, UT 84601; (801) 375-0733.

WASATCH-CACHE NATIONAL FOREST
U.S. Forest Service
1,302,523 acres of Forest land in UT; 2,026,088 UT acres within boundaries.

Many widely scattered blocks of land, large and small. (MP's #3, #4, #7.)

A. Along the Wellsville Mountains, N of Brigham City, between Honeyville and Wellsville. Access from SR 69 and US 89. No paved road within.

B. Along the Wasatch Mountains, from Brigham City S to the Salt Lake-Utah county line. This is a heavily used area. Principal access routes: SR 39 E from Ogden; Forest roads E from Farmington; Mill Creek Canyon E from Holladay; Big Cottonwood Canyon E from Cottonwood Heights.

C. Along the S Stansbury Mountains, W of Tooele. Access by S. Willow Canyon, about 5 mi. S of Grantsville.

D. One large and two smaller blocks along the N Wasatch Range, W of Bear Lake, extending S from the Idaho border. Principal access routes: US 89 NE from Logan, SR 101 E from Hyrum, SR 39 NE from Ogden.

E. By far the largest block, adjoining the N boundary of the Ashley National Forest, E of Kamas, extending to the WY boundary, with a small extension into WY. Crossed by SR 150, E and N from Kamas.

Some mountain routes are closed by snow between Oct. and May–June. Inquire.

Forest HQ reported 6 1/2 million visitor days in 1982, increasing 5% each year. This is more than any other National Forest. Popular destinations and campgrounds are crowded, in season, and some trails are busy. However, it's a vast area. One needn't follow the crowds. On foot or horseback, one can find quiet places.

Annual precipitation is about 35 in. at high elevations, mostly snow, which may exceed 100 in. Afternoon showers are common in summer and fall. Within the Forest are the headwaters of the Provo, Duchesne, Weber, Bear, and Logan Rivers.

A. The Wellsville Mountains block straddles the Cache-Box Elder county line. It extends along the ridge for 14 mi.; width is from 1 to 5 mi. Highest point is Box Elder Peak, 9,372 ft. Canyons cut into the mountain from both sides. A few short sections of primitive road penetrate but do not cross the area. Several trails lead to and along the ridge. No campground. Chief use is by day hikers and hunters.

B. The Wasatch Mountain section, next door to Salt Lake City and other cities, is one of the most heavily used National Forest areas. In the last half of the 19th century, many immigrants settled along canyon streams and in the Utah Valley. Timber cutting, overgrazing, and uncontrolled fires denuded mountain slopes, causing floods and polluting streams. The National Forest was established in 1906 to restore the watershed.

The highest country, with several peaks over 11,000 ft., is S of I-80, but many peaks exceeding 9,000 ft. are all along the ridge. Several stream canyons cut through the mountain mass, providing routes for transmountain roads. Forest campgrounds scattered along these routes are often full. The mountains are rugged, scenic, with many snow-fed tumbling streams. Snow falls on the mountains five months of the year. The Forest has several ski areas, and ski touring is popular. Many trails follow stream canyons and ridgelines.

C. See entry, Stansbury Mountains, Zone 1, combining Forest and BLM lands.

D. W of Bear Lake is a block of Forest land about 17 mi. wide, extending S for 26 mi. from the Idaho border along the N part of the Wasatch Range. US 89, the main route from the cities of the Utah Valley to Bear Lake, follows the Logan River diagonally across this block. The area is mountainous, with a number of peaks above 9,000 ft., but less rugged than the S Wasatch Range. Many popular campgrounds are along US 89. Others are along SR 101 E from Hyrum, which follows Blacksmith Fork Canyon across the S end of the block, and on a Forest Road following the Left Hand Fork of the canyon. An extensive network of trails can be reached from trailheads along US 89.

SR 39, E from Ogden, crosses the southernmost of these three blocks, a mountainous area about 14 mi. N–S, from 2 to 6 mi. W–E. The Causey Reservoir is at the SW corner. Many trails cross the area. The map shows numerous springs and streams. Campground at the N end on SR 39.

The middle block, N of SR 39, has similar terrain. The map shows several trails, springs, streams. No campground. A popular hunting area.

E. By far the largest block lies between the Ashley National Forest and the WY boundary, in the Uinta Mountains. SR 150 E from Kamas crosses the W portion of the block, providing easy access to a magnificently scenic region, with nearby peaks over 11,000 ft. and many mountain lakes. From Kamas to Mirror Lake, SR 150 follows the Provo River, then turns N along Bear River. Because it is accessible and attractive, the area is heavily used. The 440 campsites in the Kamas Ranger District are full most of the summer. (Although campgrounds are scheduled to open in May or June, snow sometimes delays openings.) Mirror Lake, a popular destination, is also a trailhead for the High Uintas Primitive Area. Highest point in the Wasatch-Cache National Forest is 13,442-ft. Gilbert Peak in the E part of the Uintas, about 3 mi. NE of 13,528-ft. Kings Peak, highest point in UT, in the Ashley NF.

Plants: About 60% of the area is forested, predominantly spruce-fir, lodgepole pine, aspen, oak-maple, and pinyon-juniper associations. 100 species of wildflowers recorded, including arrowleaf balsamroot, heartleaf arnica, wyethia, sego lily, wild onion, wild rose, wild strawberry, lupine, larkspur, Indian paintbrush, wild geranium, columbine, penstemon, elephant head.

Birds: 188 species recorded, including western and eared grebes. White pelican, great blue heron and black-crowned night-heron, snowy egret. Waterfowl include pintail, green-winged and cinnamon teals, mallard, gadwall, wood duck, redhead, ring-necked duck, Canada goose, common and red-breasted mergansers, ruddy duck. Raptors include goshawk; Cooper's, sharp-shinned, red-tailed, and ferruginous hawks; golden and bald eagles, prairie and peregrine falcons, northern harrier, American kestrel. Also ruffed, sage, and blue grouse; white-tailed ptarmigan, California quail, gray partridge, ring-necked pheasant. Owls: saw-whet, short-eared, long-eared, great horned, pygmy, screech, flammulated. Woodpeckers: downy, hairy, northern three-toed, Williamson's and yellow-bellied sapsuckers, northern flicker. Western, Hammond's, dusky, Traill's, gray, ash-throated, and olive-sided flycatchers. Also black-capped and mountain chickadees, plain titmouse, common bushtit, red-breasted and white-breasted nuthatches, brown creeper, dipper; canyon, rock, marsh, and house wrens; mountain bluebird, ruby-crowned and golden-crowned kinglets, cedar and bohemian waxwings. Warblers include yellow-rumped, black-throated blue, black-throated gray, yellow, Townsend's, Connecticut, MacGillivray's, orange-crowned, Tennessee, Wilson's.

Mammals: 68 species recorded, including black bear, ringtail, shorttail and longtail weasels, mink, badger, coyote, red and kit foxes, mountain lion, Canada lynx, bobcat; cliff, least, and Utah chipmunks; northern flying squirrel, Uinta and golden-mantled ground squirrels, rock and red squirrels, beaver, pica, snowshoe hare, blacktail and whitetail jackrabbits, pygmy rabbit, mountain cottontail, moose, elk, mule deer, pronghorn, mountain goat, bighorn sheep.

Reptiles and amphibians: Include collared, shorthorned, sagebrush, tree, and side-blotched lizards; rubber boa, racer, ring-necked snake, common kingsnake, western rattlesnake, tiger salamander, boreal chorus frog, leopard and spotted frogs.

FEATURES

In N–S sequence:

Logan Canyon on US 89 NE from Logan is one of the state's longest, about 30 mi. from mouth to a pass on the Bear River Range. About 20 Forest Service campgrounds and many trailheads are along the route. Informal turnouts are used by campers and fishermen. A number of unpaved Forest roads, some best suited to 4-wheel-drive vehicles, lead into the mountains. Parking areas are used in winter by snowmobilers. Sightseers enjoy the canyon, especially in spring and fall. US 89 is the principal route to Bear Lake and Yellowstone National Park. Needless to say, it is heavily impacted.

Blacksmith Fork Canyon, on SR 242 E from Hyrum, has high, steep walls, an attractive rushing stream. We saw one Forest Service campground along the road, a sign pointing to another, but all along the canyon were streamside turnouts used by campers and fishermen, some large enough for a dozen or more parties, others smaller. Even on Labor Day weekend we had a choice of sites. The road leads only to Hardware Ranch, so traffic drops almost to zero in late afternoon. Left Hand Fork, unpaved, turns N into the Forest, to campgrounds and trailheads.

Pine View Reservoir, E of Ogden on SR 39, about 6 mi. long, irregular in shape, is close to metropolitan areas and popular for water-based recreation. The shoreline is heavily developed. A Forest Service campground is commercially managed. A crowded area.

High Uintas Primitive Area, 73,923 acres adjoining 162,586 contiguous acres in the Ashley National Forest on the S. The highest portion of the

Forest. Roadless. Ridges divide it into large scenic basins interspersed with high glacial moraines and glacial drifts. Ridges rise steeply from the basin floors. Most exposed rock is deep red. Many lakes and streams. Forested on the lower slopes. Scattered meadows. Over half of the area is barren rock.

Snow and May–June runoff limit high-country travel to about July 1–Sept. 10. Afternoon rainstorms are common. Above 10,000 ft., temperature is rarely above 70°F. Average night temperature is 30–40°, sometimes lower even in summer.

Principal trailheads in the Wasatch-Cache portion are on or reached from SR 150. The Forest's Primitive Area map is a general guide, but for travel beyond main trails topographic maps are necessary; the Primitive Area map has a key. Inquire at the Kamas Ranger District office about routes, destinations, trail conditions, and fire rules. Some trails and campsites are heavily used. The "Primitive Area" designation attracts many hikers. Those seeking isolation may find it more readily elsewhere in the Forest. Horse travel is possible on most trails.

The High Uintas are summer range for elk, mule deer, moose, and possibly mountain sheep. Black bear are common. Fishing is excellent except in heavily fished waters.

Mirror Lake, elevation 10,200 ft., is not large but in a dramatic setting, Bald Mountain rising almost 2,000 ft. from its W shore. Easily reached, its 90-unit campground is almost always full. Trails lead to the mountaintop, to nearby lakes, and into the Primitive Area.

Beaver Creek Natural Arboretum is on SR 150 between Kamas and Mirror Lake.

Bountiful Peak Drive is a breathtaking 16-mi. mountain drive from Farmington to Bountiful. From Farmington it passes through a steep, narrow gorge, then climbs to about 9,000 ft., 5,000 ft. above the valley floor. In places the road is a narrow ledge.

Mill Creek Canyon, Big Cottonwood Canyon, and *Little Cottonwood Canyon* cut into the Wasatch Range S of I-80. All three are highly scenic. All three have Forest Service campgrounds and trailheads. The latter two have ski areas. This section of the Wasatch Range serves as a magnificent, popular regional park for the metropolitan area.

Lone Peak Wilderness, 8,922 acres in the Wasatch-Cache plus 21,166 acres in the Uinta NF. On the Salt Lake-Utah county line just S of Little Cottonwood Canyon. White Pine trailhead in Little Cottonwood is major all-year access.

INTERPRETATION

Information and literature at HQ and R.D. offices. Some exhibits.

Nature trails at several locations in Logan Canyon and on Mirror Lake Highway.

Forest HQ says there are no campfire talks or other naturalist programs.

ACTIVITIES

Camping. 76 campgrounds, 1,928 sites. Mid-June to Nov. 1. Popular campgrounds are often full.

Hiking, backpacking: 1,130 mi. of trails in all parts of the Forest. Those in the Wasatch Front (near the metropolitan area) and High Uintas Primitive Area are most heavily used. Hiking season usually begins in July in the high country.

Horse riding: Permitted except in Salt Lake City watershed, which includes Big and Little Cottonwood Canyons. About 900 mi. of trails. Forest HQ reports only one outfitter serves Forest travelers. For the High Uintas, other outfitters serve the Ashley NF; see entry.

Hunting: Deer, elk, mountain grouse, ducks, snowshoe hare.

Fishing: In streams and lakes throughout the Forest. Cutthroat, rainbow, brown, and eastern brook trout. Whitefish, arctic grayling.

Boating: Power boating chiefly on Pine View Reservoir, Mirror Lake, Trial Lake.

Swimming: Supervised only at Pine View Reservoir. Elsewhere at your risk; water in mountain lakes is generally cold.

Ski touring: Almost unlimited opportunities. One maintained trail in Big Cottonwood Canyon, one marked on Mirror Lake Highway.

Downhill skiing: 6 ski resorts. Two outfitters operate helicopters.

Snowmobiling: Many opportunities, including on roads closed to autos by snows. Groomed trail at Mirror Lake.

Areas are sometimes closed because of fire hazard; call (801) 486-6333 for information.

Ski areas are sometimes closed because of avalanche danger.

Dogs are prohibited in Salt Lake City watershed, which includes Big and Little Cottonwood Canyons.

PUBLICATIONS

Forest map. $1.00.
High Uintas Primitive Area map. $1.00.
High Uintas Primitive Area folder, small map.
Hikers trail map, Salt Lake Ranger District.
Ski touring route map, Alta and Brighton.
How to Know Wildflowers Near Your Camp.
Recreation site list with camping fees.

REFERENCES

Bottcher, Betty, and Mel Davis. *Wasatch Trails, Vol. 1.* Salt Lake City: Wasatch, 1973.

Geery, Daniel. *Wasatch Trails.* Vol. 2. Salt Lake City: Wasatch, 1976.

Davis, Mel. *High Uinta Trails.* Salt Lake City: Wasatch, 1974.

Gates, Jon L., and Regenthal, Albert F. *Lakes of the High Uintas.* Salt Lake City: Utah State Department of Fish and Game, 1964.

Hall, Dave. *The Hiker's Guide to Utah.* Billings, MT: Falcon Press, 1982. pp. 19–58, 67–76, 80–92.

Schimpf, Ann, and Mel Davis. *Cache Trails.* Salt Lake City: Wasatch, 1978.

Schimpf, Ann, and Scott Datwyler. *Cache Tours.* Salt Lake City: Wasatch, 1977.

HEADQUARTERS: 8226 Federal Building, 125 S. State, Salt Lake City, UT 84138; (801) 524-5030.

RANGER DISTRICTS: Salt Lake R.D., 6944 S. 30th E, Salt Lake City, UT 84121; (801) 524-5042. Kamas R.D., Kamas, UT 84036; (801) 783-4338. Evanston R.D., Federal Bldg, Evanston, WY 82930; (307) 789-3194. Mountain View R.D., Mountain View, WY 82939; (307)782-6555. Ogden R.D., P.O. Box 1433, Ogden, UT 84403; (801) 626-3431. Logan R.D., 21 W. Center, P.O. Box 488, Logan, UT 84321; (801) 753-2772.

WASATCH MOUNTAIN STATE PARK
Utah State Division of Parks and Recreation
22,000 acres.

From Heber City, W on SR 113 to Midway. NW 2 mi. on SR 224. (MP #7, 3.)

Utah's largest State Park, and its most developed. Developments include a 27-hole golf course, group and family campgrounds. But it's a large area, with thousands of undeveloped acres. Its W boundary is the Uinta National Forest. It adjoins the Uinta's Cascade Springs Scenic Area; the Forest's Cascade Scenic Drive links with Park roads. On the SE, Deer Creek Reservoir is nearby.

High elevation is 9,000 ft., lowest 5,600 ft. Annual precipitation here is about 12 in., much of it winter snow.

Plants: About 75% forested: Douglas-fir, white and subalpine fir, Engelmann and blue spruce, Gambel oak, quaking aspen, bigtooth maple. Understory includes fern, mountain lilac. Remaining 25% is grassland and sagebrush.

Flowering plants include sego lily, serviceberry, elderberry, chokecherry, Indian paintbrush, dandelion, columbine.

Birds: 56 species reported, improbably low for this area. No checklist. Mentioned: robin, red-winged and yellow-headed blackbirds, coot, killdeer, broad-tailed hummingbird, barn swallow, black-billed magpie, ruffed and spruce grouse, American goldfinch, mourning dove. Golden and bald eagles seen occasionally.

Mammals: No checklist. Mentioned as often or occasionally seen: Uinta ground squirrel, striped skunk, least chipmunk, porcupine, weasel, mule deer. Present but rarely seen: elk, mountain lion, beaver, raccoon, mountain cottontail, snowshoe hare, coyote, marmot.

INTERPRETATION

Visitor center. Literature.

Campfire talks: Saturday evenings in summer.

Nature trail, 1 1/2 mi., Upper Oak Hollow camp loop.

ACTIVITIES

Camping: 4 campgrounds, 147 sites. Apr. 1–Nov. 15. Reservations needed weekends and holidays, "strongly advised" on weekdays.

Backpacking: No marked, mapped, or maintained trails, but hiking opportunities within the Park and in the adjoining National Forest. Trailside camping is permitted, but backpacking does not seem to be a significant activity.

Hunting: Deer, elk, dove, grouse.

Fishing: Stream: brook, brown, and rainbow trout.

Ski touring: 6 mi. groomed. Unlimited backcountry.

Snowmobiling: On unplowed roads and into the National Forest.

HEADQUARTERS: P.O. Box 10, Midway, UT 84049; (801) 654-1791.

WILLARD BAY STATE RECREATION AREA
Utah State Division of Parks and Recreation
2,673 acres.

I-15 skirts the area at Willard, about 40 mi. N of Salt Lake City. (MP #4.)

While we received no official reports of flood damage here, this low-lying site was certainly inundated. Adjoining sites suffered substantial damage.

The park is a narrow strip between 9,900-acre Willard Bay and I-15. It's a heavily used site for water-based recreation.

In spring and fall especially, this area can be of interest to birders. The bay, formed by a dike closed in 1964, is just S of the impounds of Bear River Migratory Bird Refuge (see entry). The Harold S. Crane Waterfowl Management Area adjoins the site on the SW. A canoe or other shallow-draft boat would permit observing the marshes and mudflats bordering much of the bay.

Multipurpose Map No. 4 shows several secondary roads S of the area that penetrate marshes and salt flats.

ACTIVITIES
Camping: 66 sites. Apr.–Nov.
Fishing: Crappie, walleye, catfish.
Boating: 2 marinas. Ramps.

HEADQUARTERS: Box 319, Willard, UT 84340; (801) 734-9494.

ZONE 2

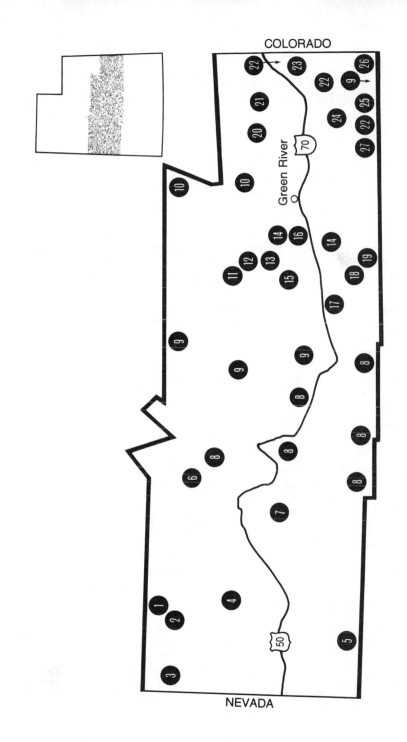

ZONE 2

Includes these counties (Multipurpose Maps Nos. 2, 3, 6, and 7):

Carbon	Juab	Sevier
Emery	Millard	
Grand	Sanpete	

The middle third of Utah is sparsely populated. Only 6% of the Utahns live here. Like Zone 1, this zone is divided N–S by the Wasatch Range. The W portion is within the Great Basin, but its basin-and-range topography is more rugged than the Great Salt Lake Desert to the N. Mountain crests are higher, trapping more moisture, and the slopes have more vegetation. The area has a few lakes and several rivers, although the rivers vanish in dry deserts.

Fish Springs National Wildlife Refuge is in the NW part of the zone, far from a paved road. From the E, one follows the Old Pony Express and Stage Route. Nearby is the Fish Springs Range. The Deep Creek Mountains are a bit farther W. Both are attractive, and visitors are few.

Most of the Fishlake National Forest and portions of the Manti-La Sal National Forest are in this zone. Both offer good opportunities for backcountry travel.

To the E of the Wasatch Range are the drainage basins of the Green and Colorado Rivers. This region is dry, dissected, with some spectacular scenery and exceptional features. I-70 crosses this region W–E. Both river canyons offer spectacular whitewater rafting.

Those who enjoy backroad driving might try the area S of Price. Points of interest include the Desert Lake Waterfowl Management Area, Cleveland-Lloyd Dinosaur Quarry, and Cedar Mountain Recreation Area. I-70 crosses an area of special interest called the San Rafael Swell. S of I-70, off SR 24, is Goblin Valley State Reserve, a unique and delightful natural playground.

Arches National Park is in the SE corner of the zone, just N of Moab. Many people, ourselves included, consider the Moab area—including the portion in Zone 3—among the most fascinating parts of Utah. From Moab one can make an almost limitless variety of side trips, by automobile, jeep, horse, boat, or on foot. Entrances to Canyonlands National Park are nearby, although most of the Park is in Zone 3.

REFERENCES

Birds of the Richfield BLM District. BLM, Richfield District Office, 150 East 900 North, Richfield, UT 84701.

Birds of the Moab BLM District. BLM, Moab District Office, 125 West Second South Main, Moab, UT 84532.

Barnes, F. A. *Canyon Country; Off-Road Vehicle Trails; Canyon Rims and Needles Areas.* Salt Lake City: Wasatch, 1978.

Barnes, F.A. *Canyon Country Hiking and Natural History.* Salt Lake City: Wasatch, 1977.

Barnes, F. A. *Canyon Country Camping.* Salt Lake City: Wasatch, 1978.

ARCHES NATIONAL PARK
National Park Service
73,234 acres.

5 mi. NW of Moab on US 163. (MP #2.)

In the red-rock country of SE UT, the Park has more natural stone arches, windows, spires, pinnacles than any other location. Water and wind have eroded the Entrada Sandstone into spectacular and bizarre shapes, grand and small.

Most visitors drive the 21-mi. paved tour route, along which are numerous viewpoints, parking areas, and short trails. The Park also has 11 mi. of fair-weather dirt roads and four principal hiking trails. The S boundary is on the Colorado River, but no Park road or trail touches the shoreline.

Elevations from 4,085 ft. to 5,653 ft. Annual precipitation is 7 to 10 in. Daytime summer temperatures as high as 110°F. Snow falls occasionally but seldom lasts more than a day.

The entire Park is scenic, viewed from any vantage point. Featured areas are the Windows, with 8 large arches and other formations; Delicate Arch, in a setting of cliffs and slickrock domes; Fiery Furnace, a maze of narrow passageways and high walls; Devil's Garden, where the paved road ends and trails lead to Landscape Arch, believed to be the world's longest, and other arches. A dirt road leads to Klondike Bluffs, but ask about road conditions before proceeding. Hikers can visit many formations that motorists see only from a distance, if at all.

Plants: Sparse pinyon-juniper community typical of the Great Basin Desert. Checklist of plants available. Except in especially dry years, many wildflowers in moist places, May–Aug. Flowering species include Mojave aster, sunflower, thistle, goldenrod, dandelion, wallflower, prince's plume, milkvetch, clovers, sego lily, false Solomon's-seal, death camas, blazing star, sand verbena, evening primrose, desert trumpet, columbine, wild rose, Indian paintbrush, scarlet monkeyflower, globemallow.

Birds: Checklist available, based on sightings but without indication of seasonality or abundance. Best birding is in spring. Some sightings were probably along the river. Raptors include Swainson's, red-tailed, ferruginous, sharp-shinned, and Cooper's hawks; northern harrier, goshawk, American kestrel, prairie and peregrine falcons, golden and bald eagles. Owls: screech, great horned, long-eared, flammulated, and burrowing. Also barn, cliff, bank, and violet-green swallows; rufous, broad-tailed, and black-chinned humming-birds; downy and hairy woodpeckers, common flicker, yellow-bellied sap-sucker, red-breasted nuthatch, brown creeper. Also Scott's and northern orioles, black-capped and mountain chickadees, blue-gray gnatcatcher, gold-en- and ruby-crowned kinglets; rose-breasted, black-headed, and blue gros-beaks; Cassin's, house, gray-crowned rosy, and black rosy finches; American and lesser goldfinches. Also scrub and pinyon jays, black-billed magpie, com-mon raven; warbling, solitary, and gray vireos.

Mammals: Checklist of 38 species available, most uncommon or rare. Abundant or common: western pipistrel, gray fox, whitetail antelope squirrel, Colorado chipmunk, Apache pocket mouse, Ord kangaroo rat; canyon, deer, and pinyon mice; desert woodrat, porcupine, blacktail jackrabbit, desert cot-tontail, mule deer.

Reptiles and amphibians: Include western spadefoot toad, leopard frog, bullfrog; collared, leopard, sagebrush, eastern fence, tree, and side-blotched lizards. Racer, spotted night snake, desert striped whipsnake; common, black-necked, and western garter snakes; western rattlesnake.

INTERPRETATION

Visitor center has exhibits, films, talks, literature. Open daily, 8 A.M.–4:30 P.M.

Nature trails at Devil's Garden and Delicate Arch.

Campfire programs in summer.

Guided walks, various locations, vary with seasons.

ACTIVITIES

Camping: One campground, 53 sites. All year, but no water in winter.

Hiking, backpacking: Trails are heavily used in season. Permit required for backcountry travel. Hikers are warned that they need a gallon of water per day. Flash flood hazard in washes.

About 18,000 acres in the Devil's Garden area was proposed for wilderness status. 8,420 acres of public land outside the Park on the NE has been proposed as a BLM wilderness study area. The area around Salt Wash and Lost Spring Canyon offers good hiking opportunity.

PUBLICATIONS

Leaflet with map.

Checklists: plants, birds, mammals, reptiles and amphibians.

Devil's Garden Trail Guide.

REFERENCES

Barnes, F. A. *Canyon Country Hiking and Natural History.* Salt Lake City: Wasatch, 1977. Pp. 59–68, 70.

Hall, Dave. *The Hiker's Guide to Utah.* Billings, MT: Falcon Press, 1982. Pp. 189–192.

Hoffman, John F. *Arches National Park.* San Diego, CA: Western Recreational Publications, no date.

The Guide to an Auto Tour of Arches National Park. Moab, UT: Canyonlands Natural History Association, no date.

HEADQUARTERS: 446 South Main, Moab, UT 84532; (801) 259-8161.

BOOK CLIFFS STATE FOREST
Utah State Lands and Forestry
100,000 acres within boundaries; 91,640 acres of state land.

From Thompson on I-70, N 20 mi. on unimproved road through Sego Canyon. (MP #2.) Must cross private land at S tip. We suggest obtaining permission before entry.

The road from Thompson passes the S tip of the Forest at the foot of the Roan Cliffs. The Roan Cliffs, together with the Book Cliffs adjoining on the E, form one of the nation's greatest escarpments, extending over 200 mi. A petroglyph site is 4 mi. N of Thompson.

Roads and jeep trails crossing the N sector are shown on Multipurpose Map No. 2. Most of the Forest is roadless, and consideration was given to declaring it a state wilderness. W boundary is the Uintah and Ouray Indian Reservation. Other adjoining lands are mostly public, administered by BLM.

Mountainous, rugged sandstone canyons, rising to the Winter Ridge plateau. Peaks of 9,035 and 9,050 ft. in the S sector. Several others over 8,000 ft. farther N. East Willow Creek is the principal perennial stream. Annual precipitation is 15–30 in. Snowfall up to 200 in. at high elevations.

As noted in the Utah Preface, Utah's State Forests are not managed for recreation. This Forest is extremely rugged. It has some use by hunters and hikers, but it's not popular, partly because access is difficult without a 4-wheel-drive vehicle.

Plants: About 40% forested. Areas of pinyon-juniper. Also Douglas-fir, aspen, spruce-fir, ponderosa pine, limber pine. Unconfirmed reports of bristlecone pine. Understory mostly grasses, forbs, common juniper. Drier slopes have sagebrush, other desert shrubs. Riparian vegetation in the bottoms. Many summer wildflowers.

Birds: No list available.
Mammals: No checklist. Mentioned: rabbit, beaver, coyote, mountain lion, black bear, mule deer, elk.

ACTIVITIES
Camping: Where you wish. No developed sites.
Hiking, backpacking: Some stock, game, and pack trails. Bring a topo map, water.
Horse riding: Good area for backcountry horse riding.
Hunting: Bear, deer, elk, grouse.

HEADQUARTERS: State Lands and Forestry, Southeastern Regional Office, P.O. Box 32, Moab, UT 84532; (801) 259-6316.

CEDAR MOUNTAIN RECREATION AREA
U.S. Bureau of Land Management
16,140 acres.

From Price on US 6 and 50, S 21 mi. on SR 10. E on SR 155 to Cleveland, then 20 mi. SE on dirt road. (MP #2.)

Cedar Mountain (not to be confused with "Cedar Mountains" in Zone 1) elevation is 7,665. The site is within a large area of public lands with many features of interest. Exceptional views. It was named for its abundance of juniper trees, commonly called "cedars." The site has picnic tables, grills, pit toilets.

Views to the S are of the Buckhorn Flats and the San Rafael Swell, an 80-mi.-long uplifted oval dome, 30 mi. wide, its E edge a huge saw-toothed sandstone ridge, the San Rafael Reef.

FEATURES
Staker Spring-Bob Hill Spring Trail, 7 mi., is well marked at the end, but a visitor can miss the midsection without a map (available at the Price BLM office). Through pinyon pine and juniper trees over moderate terrain. The spring water hasn't been tested.

Cedar Mountain Redwood is a form of petrified wood found about 3 mi. NW of the picnic site. Collection for personal use is permitted, no more than 250 lbs. in a year.

Fossil Ledge Nature Trail begins at the base of a metal railing at the picnic site.

Camping: No campground, but camp at any suitable place on BLM land.

NEARBY

Desert Lake Waterfowl Management Area (see entry).
Cleveland-Lloyd Dinosaur Quarry (see entry).
Sids Mountain (see entry).
Mexican Mountain (see entry).
Wedge Overlook (Point of Interest list, MP #2).
San Rafael Campground (BLM; campground list, MP #2).

PUBLICATION: *Cedar Mountain Recreation Area.*

HEADQUARTERS: BLM, Price Area Office, 900 North 7th East, Price, UT 84501; (801) 637-4584.

CLEAR LAKE WATERFOWL MANAGEMENT AREA
Utah State Division of Wildlife Resources
6,150 acres.

From Fillmore on US 91, just off I-15, W on County Road 100 about 18 mi. (MP #6.)

The floods that destroyed waterfowl marshes around the Great Salt Lake seem to have been beneficial here. We were told that hundreds of formerly dry acres have been added to the wetlands. Some waterfowl that formerly visited Great Salt Lake refuges are now finding their way here.

When we visited, Clear Lake had about 2,500 acres of marsh and open water surrounded by low, vegetated sandhills. The site is in the Sevier Desert, elevation about 4,600 ft. Annual precipitation here is less than 10 in. The ponds and marshes are supplied by brackish springs.

The area is about 8 mi. N–S, from 1/2 to 2 mi. W–E. The county road crosses the S end.

Waterfowl, in order of abundance: mallard, pintail, green-winged teal, cinnamon teal, wigeon, redhead, gadwall, shoveler, Canada goose.

Stop at Refuge HQ, on the left beyond the E entrance. Nonhunters should avoid during the waterfowl hunting season.

HEADQUARTERS: Division of Wildlife Resources, 1596 West North Temple, Salt Lake City, UT 84116; (801) 533-9333.

CLEVELAND-LLOYD DINOSAUR QUARRY
U.S. Bureau of Land Management
80 acres.

From Price, SR 10 S for 21 mi. E on SR 155 to Cleveland. Follow signs 15 mi. on unpaved road. (MP #2.)

Said to be the nation's largest known dinosaur graveyard. Digging began in 1931, but activity was sporadic until 1950. More than 10,000 bones have been removed, over 30 skeletons assembled in museums. An Allosaurus is displayed at the museum in Price.

The site has a small exhibit building, interpretive displays, and the quarry. Most of the surrounding land is public, managed by BLM.

We found the site closed on Tues.–Wed., a practice not mentioned in the then-current leaflet. A not-yet-published leaflet reads: "The Quarry is normally open weekends from Easter until Labor Day and some weekdays during the summer months." We suggest calling the BLM office before visiting.

NEARBY: Desert Lake Waterfowl Management Area, Cedar Mountain Recreation Area (see entries).

PUBLICATION: Leaflet with map.

HEADQUARTERS: BLM, Price Area Office, 900 North 7th East, Price, UT 84501; (801) 637-4584.

COLORADO RIVER: COLORADO BORDER TO MOAB
U.S. Bureau of Land Management
67.5 river mi.; about 90,000 acres of public land.

Upstream, river access is by unpaved roads, at Westwater, near the CO border, and from Cisco. Land access from unmapped jeep trails. Downstream, SR 128 follows the S bank from Dewey Bridge to Moab. (MP #2.)

Eastern rivers were once colonial highways, many towns and cities growing beside them. In the arid West, most farming depended on river water. But the Colorado river, cutting across Utah's SE corner, attracted neither towns nor farms. Flowing through deep, steep-walled canyons, the river and its water were generally inaccessible. The only significant settlement is at Moab, where a gentler terrain offered an easy river crossing.

The Westwater Ranger Station is 4 1/2 mi. from the CO border. Here, from Apr. through Oct., begins the raft trip through Westwater Canyon. This trip is for expert rafters; in the 17 mi. to the first take-out point, the river drops 125 ft. over 11 rapids, varying from I to V on the scale of V. Permits are required to run this section. The number issued is limited in order to preserve the canyon.

(The Colorado can be floated by canoe from the Loma boat launch near

Loma, CO, to the Westwater Ranger Station. No permit needed. See entry in CO Zone 2: Colorado River, Ruby Canyon.)

River flow is highly seasonal, reaching a peak in late May–early June. It declines through summer and autumn to about 15% of peak flow.

The river is tamer below Cisco Landing, much of it negotiable by canoe. At Moab, power boats, including sightseeing craft, use the river.

From Westwater to Cisco Landing, the canyon is surrounded by a largely roadless area of public land, including the canyon of Little Dolores River, Star and Marble Canyons, and Snyder Mesa. Best access seems to be from Dewey Bridge and from Gateway, CO, but inquire at the Moab BLM office.

Terrain is rugged: steep-walled canyons, sometimes meandering; tall buttes, undulating mesas, large boulders. Vegetation is mainly desert shrubs, pinyon-juniper, various grasses and forbs, greener riparian vegetation in canyon bottoms. Only rafters enjoy a full view of Westwater Canyon. The walls are dark metamorphic granite gneisses underlying layers of sandstone. Along the way are a few natural arches, one of them large, and numerous spires. Wildlife includes Canada goose, great blue heron, ducks, eagles in spring and fall migration, beaver, occasional deer.

The Dolores River meets the Colorado close to Dewey Bridge. Between the two rivers, near the CO border, an area of about 11,000 acres consists of open flats and rolling hills, bounded by shallow canyons. Vegetation here is low and sparse. The Dolores River offers a spectacular 31-mi. raft trip, including the most dangerous rapid in the area. The rafting season is short: mid-May to mid-June.

For motorists, the 30 mi. of SR 128 beside the river from Dewey Bridge to Moab is splendidly scenic, with views of colorful cliffs, towers, spires, pinnacles, and side canyons, as well as green riparian vegetation on the bottoms. At Dewey Bridge we ate lunch under a large cottonwood tree and could have parked for the night had we so wished.

ACTIVITIES

Camping: For rafters, campsites along the rivers. No established campground, but suitable sites at landings and along secondary roads.

Hiking, backpacking: "Interesting, not outstanding," we were advised. Pleasant day hikes, or scrambles, in canyons.

Boating: Below Dewey Bridge. See Moab entry.

Rafting: Permits limited in Westwater Canyon: 35 persons per day Sun.– Thurs., 75 persons Fri.–Sat. Permits are drawn 1 month in advance of competitive dates. Vacancies are filled on a first-come, first-served basis.

PUBLICATION: *Guide to Westwater, a Section of the Colorado River.* Leaflet with map.

HEADQUARTERS: BLM, Grand Resource Area Office, Sand Flat Road, P.O. Box M, Moab, UT 84532; (801) 259-8193.

CRACK CANYON; CHUTE CANYON; WILD HORSE BUTTE

U.S. Bureau of Land Management
About 75,000 acres.

N and W of Goblin Valley State Reserve (see entry). MP #2 shows unpaved roads surrounding the area, jeep trails penetrating it.

This area is a portion of the San Rafael Swell (see entry) and includes part of the San Rafael Reef. Crack Canyon, largest of several parallel N–S canyons, cuts through the Reef, its intermittent stream flowing into Wild Horse Creek (also intermittent). Wild Horse Butte is a prominent landmark near the base of the Reef, just outside the Goblin Valley reserve, rising about 800 ft. Highest point within the site is 6,808 ft.

The area has high visual interest, with canyons, cliffs, buttes, knolls, caves, arches, fins, folds, narrow twisting passageways. Tan, gray, orange, and yellow sandstone caps appear as petrified dunes. Other formats have layers of red, purple, yellow, brown, green, green-white. The colors are especially striking in Broken Rainbow Valley in the S end of the area. Many isolated pools of water provide an element of surprise and contrast.

Muddy Creek, on the SW boundary, is used for "technical tubing"—floating in innertubes through rapids, in the early spring. Later the creek bed is used for hiking and motorcycling.

Plants: Saltbush vegetation type is at lower elevations. Dominant species are shadscale, Castle Valley clover, mat saltbush, four-wing saltbush. Desert shrub association on gravelly benches and gently sloping sandy lowlands: Mormon tea, shadscale, rabbitbrush, snakeweed, blackbrush, fourwing saltbush, black sagebrush, wild buckwheat. Sandy soils also support wavyleaf oak, sand sagebrush, purple sage. Other common plants are curly grass, Indian ricegrass, sand dropseed, sandy muhly, blue grama, globemallow. Pinyon-juniper on foothills and mesas, other areas of relatively high elevation.

Birds: Diversity and populations are small. Raptors include golden eagle, prairie falcon, American kestrel; red-tailed, ferruginous, and rough-legged hawks.

Mammals: No record of observations. BLM's analysis notes the habitat is favorable for coyote, bobcat, cottontail, blacktail jackrabbit, woodrat, ringtail, badger, Ord kangaroo rat, gray fox, kit fox, whitetail antelope squirrel, chipmunk, rock squirrel, various bats and other rodents. Mule deer, desert bighorn, and pronghorn have been sighted on the Swell.

Reptiles and amphibians: BLM calls the area suitable for lizards: side-blotched, collared, leopard, short-horned, sagebrush, western fence, common tree. Also Great Basin gopher snake, striped whipsnake, western rattlesnake, Woodhouse's and Great Plains toads.

The area seems most suitable for day hiking, with Goblin Valley as a convenient base.

HEADQUARTERS: BLM, San Rafael Resource Area Office, 900 N 700 E, Price, UT 84501: (801) 637-4584.

DEAD HORSE POINT STATE PARK

The Park is in both Zones 2 and 3. Access is from Zone 2. Because of the close relationship to Canyonlands National Park, the entry is in Zone 3.

DEEP CREEK MOUNTAINS

U.S. Bureau of Land Management
About 150,000 acres.

On the Tooele-Juab county line near the NV border, between Callao and Goshute Indian Reservation. The Pleasant Valley road borders the site on the S, the Gandy road on the E, the Old Pony Express and Stage Trail on the NE; these are gravel roads. A few dirt roads or jeep trails penetrate E canyons. (MP #7.)

The Utah highway map shows a gravel road from Fish Springs to Callao, around the N end of the Fish Springs Range. Another gravel road to Callao comes W from US 50 and 6, just S of Jericho, through Sand Pass, which is the S end of the Fish Springs Range. This, known as the Weiss Highway, is regarded by some as the best available way to Callao.

Highest, most prominent and unique landmark in W Utah. Third highest range in the Great Basin. To the N and E is the Great Salt Lake Desert, to the S and W scattered mountain ranges typical of Great Basin topography. 30 mi. long. Ridgeline is 8,000 to 11,000 ft. elevation, with two peaks over 12,000 ft. The W side is a steep wall offering no practical access. Slopes on the E are more gradual. Alpine cirques with lush green meadows. Steep, rugged canyons serve as entry corridors for hikers. Jeep trails penetrate several of these canyons, but none ascends to the ridge.

This is the only range in the Great Salt Lake Desert with an abundance of water, supplied chiefly by snow melting on the upper slopes. Six perennial streams flow through the E canyons, disappearing into the desert below.

Because it is isolated, 140 air mi. from Salt Lake City, and much of the auto route is on unpaved roads, it has few visitors, only about 2,500 per year. The vast majority of the N area can be classified as "seldom seen." A BLM staff member praised its unique character: "wild, untouched . . . no trails, no trailheads, no campgrounds, no signs, no quota systems, and no garbage."

Plants: More than 600 plant species grow in this island ecosystem. Predominant vegetation is shrub juniper and several pine species. Quaking aspen in gently rolling valley pockets. At lower elevations: shadscale, big sagebrush, black sagebrush, greasewood, horsebrush, Indian ricegrass, bluebunch wheatgrass, squirreltail. Higher, on S and W slopes, montane forest with stands of spruce, white fir, Douglas-fir, limber pine, and aspen. A unique ecological community is a stand of bristlecone pine, some of the specimens nearly as large as those in California's Methuselah Grove. Tundra vegetation above timberline.

Flowering plants frequently found include sego lily, virgin's bower, buttercup, shepherd's purse, golden currant, spirea, lupine, white clover, blue flax, St. Johnswort, blazing star, evening primrose, phlox, scarlet gilia, mullein, Indian paintbrush, snakeweed, rushpink, balsamroot, wild buckwheat.

Birds: BLM list of 185 species shows abundance and habitat (general, montane, foothill, desert, lowland, farmlands, and wetlands). Common species include hawks: sharp-shinned, red-tailed, Swainson's, ferruginous, northern harrier, American kestrel. Turkey vulture, blue grouse, chukar, mourning dove, nighthawk, white-throated swift, Lewis' woodpecker, yellow-bellied sapsucker, western kingbird, Say's phoebe; willow, Hammond's, gray, and western flycatchers; horned lark; violet-green, rough-winged, and cliff swallows; Steller's and scrub jays, black-billed magpie, common raven, Clark's nutcracker, mountain chickadee, house wren, sage thrasher, American robin, mountain bluebird, water pipit, warbling vireo. Warblers: yellow, yellow-rumped, black-throated gray, Wilson's, and western yellowthroat. House sparrow, western meadowlark; yellow-headed, red-winged, and Brewer's blackbirds; house and rosy finches, gray-headed junco; chipping, Brewer's, and white-crowned sparrows. Nesting sites for golden eagle and prairie falcon.

Mammals: BLM lists as common: vagrant and water shrews, long-legged and small-footed myotis, big brown and western big-eared bats, blacktail jackrabbit, cottontail, Uinta and golden-mantled ground squirrels, rock squirrel; cliff, least, and Colorado chipmunks; valley pocket gopher, little and longtail pocket mice; canyon, harvest, pinyon and white-footed deer mice; desert woodrat, sagebrush vole, coyote, shorttail and longtail weasels, spotted skunk, bobcat, mule deer, pronghorn. Mountain lion present, uncommon.

Much of the area is winter range for mule deer, all year for pronghorn.

ACTIVITIES

Camping: No established campgrounds, but most of the surrounding area is public land, and many suitable sites are available.

Hiking, backpacking: People at the BLM office have hiked the site and can suggest routes and destinations. For anything more than a short canyon hike, bring a topo map.

Hunting: Major visitor activity. Deer, mountain lion, chukar.

Fishing: Rainbow and cutthroat trout.

PUBLICATIONS

Motor Vehicle Guide. Map, regulations.

An Inventory of the Wildlife of the Deep Creek Mountains Area, Utah Division of Wildlife Resources, 1977. Also available from BLM.

HEADQUARTERS: South half: BLM, House Range Resource Area Office, 500 North 15 East, Fillmore, UT 84631; (801) 743-6811. North half: BLM, Pony Express Resource Area Office, 2370 South 2300 West, Salt Lake City, UT 84119; (801) 524-5348.

DESERT LAKE WATERFOWL MANAGEMENT AREA
Utah State Division of Wildlife Resources
2,661 acres.

From Price on US 6, S 14 mi. on SR 10. Left on SR 155 and follow signs for Cleveland Lloyd Dinosaur Quarry. (MP #2.)

Our first reaction was "Not an entry." State land on both sides of the road was fenced, gates shut. Then the road passed close to a pond lively with waterfowl. Next came an unfenced area, where we walked to the top of a low bluff overlooking a large pond with many waterfowl in sight. Here we were greeted by the manager, who told us visitors are welcome. Most visitors are birders, not hunters. He is developing a tour route.

The environment is desert, gently rolling hills. The area has six ponds, including Desert Lake.

Plants: Aquatics include alkali and hardstem bulrushes, cattail, pondweed, cladophora, rumex. Scattered trees: cottonwood, Russian olive, willow. Shrubs include sagebrush, greasewood, shadscale, ephedra, yucca, wild rose, tamarisk, cactus.

Birds: Waterfowl population peaks at about 20,000 in the fall migration. We were too early for this event but saw white-faced ibis, American egret, great blue heron, shoveler, redhead, cinnamon and blue-winged teals, northern harrier. The manager reported nesting attempted by sandhill crane; unsuccessful this time. Occasional visitors: American white pelican, arctic loon, peregrine falcon.

Checklist available. Peak population, in fall migration, about 20,000. Listed as common: common loon; eared, western, and pied-billed grebes; great blue heron, snowy egret, black-crowned night-heron, American bittern, white-faced ibis, whistling swan, Canada and snow geese, mallard, gadwall, northern pintail, green-winged and cinnamon teals, American wigeon, shoveler, redhead, ring-necked duck, canvasback, lesser scaup, common goldeneye, bufflehead, ruddy duck, common and red-breasted mergansers. Also snowy plover, killdeer, common snipe, long-billed curlew; spotted, least, and western sandpipers; willet, greater and lesser yellowlegs, dowitcher, marbled godwit, American avocet, black-necked stilt, Wilson's and red-necked phalaropes. Red-tailed hawk, bald eagle, northern harrier, kestrel.

PUBLICATION: *Birds of Desert Lake.* Includes map and plant list.

HEADQUARTERS: 455 W Railroad Ave., Price, UT 84501; (801) 637-3310.

DESOLATION CANYON
See entry, Green River; Desolation Canyon, Zone 2.

DEVIL'S CANYON
U.S. Bureau of Land Management
9,610 acres.

Just S of I-70 for 7 mi., 45 mi. W of Green River. Bounded by unimproved roads and jeep trails. (MP #2.)

One of several BLM sites on the San Rafael Swell. This area is relatively small, about 10 mi. long, 4 mi. wide, surrounded by other public land. Noteworthy because of opportunity for canyon hiking close to I-70. Canyons deeply incised in undulating tableland. Devil's Canyon, roughly parallel to I-70, is the largest. Narrow, with sandstone walls 450 to 550 ft. deep, white-buff to dark red. The canyon drains to the SE. Above the canyon are rolling mesas, buff sandstone domes, low cliffs. The canyon is dry.

Dominant vegetation is pinyon-juniper with Mormon tea, shadscale, rabbitbrush, snakeweed, blackbrush, fourwing saltbush, black sagebrush, wild buckwheat.

Birds: Include golden eagle, prairie falcon, American kestrel; ferruginous, red-tailed, and rough-legged hawks; chukar, mourning dove.

Mammals: Include coyote, bobcat, cottontail, blacktail jackrabbit, woodrat, badger, Ord kangaroo rat, gray and kit foxes, whitetail antelope squirrel, chipmunk, rock squirrel. A small herd of wild horses frequents the area.

Most recreational use is camping along the Justensens Flat road and other unimproved roads bordering the site, ORV activity, and wild horse viewing.

These roads are best suited to high-clearance vehicles. ORV's can penetrate the E and W portions of Devil's Canyon for a mile or two. Backpacking is limited by lack of water and summer daytime temperatures above 100°F.

HEADQUARTERS: BLM, Price Area Office, 900 North 7th East, Price, UT 84501; (801) 637-4584.

DIAMOND CANYON; FLUME CANYON
U.S. Bureau of Land Management
150,000 acres.

> N of I-70 near CO border. About 10 mi. from the border an improved road runs N along Westwater Creek, the NE boundary of the site. Other access routes, some for 4-wheel drive, are further S. (MP #2.)

The Book Cliffs mark the SE boundary. The area is generally more than 1 mi. high, several ridges above 7,000 ft. Stepped benches and ledges are interspersed by many ridges and canyons. Portions of the site are marked by drill sites, pipelines, and other artifacts of oil and gas development, but much of it is in undisturbed natural condition. On the NW the site adjoins Book Cliffs State Forest (see entry).

Diamond Canyon is in the central portion of the site, joining Cottonwood Canyon at one of the access roads. Flume Canyon, branching off to the N, is in a roadless, undisturbed portion of the site. Perennial streams flow through Diamond Canyon and Cottonwood Wash.

Data from a nearby weather station suggests that annual precipitation here is 6 to 7 in., somewhat more at higher elevations, where much of it falls as snow.

This site doesn't merit high priority for someone making infrequent visits to Utah; the state has more splendid areas. However, it has wilderness qualities, year-round water, and isolation. One is unlikely to meet other visitors.

Plants: Vegetation ranges from desert shrub and pinyon-juniper to dense stands of ponderosa pine and Douglas-fir.

ACTIVITIES
Camping: No campgrounds. Suitable sites on access roads.
Hiking, backpacking: For more than a canyon day hike, advisable to visit the BLM office. Carry a topo map.
Horse riding: Consult BLM office for suitable routes.
Ski touring: Conditions vary from year to year.

HEADQUARTERS: BLM, Grand Resource Area Office, P.O. Box M, Sand Flat Road, Moab, UT 84532; (801) 259-8193.

FISHLAKE NATIONAL FOREST
U.S. Forest Service
1,525,668 acres within boundaries; 1,425,126 acres of Forest land.

Four large blocks of Forest land surrounding the town of Richfield. Two blocks on each side of US 89. I-70 crosses the two largest blocks. (MP's #6, 5.)

Central Utah. The Forest includes parts of the Wasatch, Awapa, Sevier, and Fishlake Plateaus, all of the Tushar Mountains and Canyon and Pavant Ranges, with some of the highest and most scenic mountains of the state.

A. The smallest block is about 27 mi. by 9 mi., just E of Oak City, W of I-15. It straddles the Canyon Range. From Oak City an improved road runs 4 mi. E to the Oak Creek campground. The block is crossed by several unimproved roads and jeep trails. 9,236-ft. Williams Peak is the highest point. Several other peaks over 8,000 ft.

B. Immediately to the S is the largest block, about 80 mi. long, 18 mi. wide, between I-15 and US 89. It includes the Pavant Range and Tushar Mountains. Several peaks over 10,000 ft., and the highest point of the Forest: 12,173-ft. Delano Peak. A few paved and unimproved roads cross this section. Several perennial streams, small reservoirs, campgrounds.

C. E of this section, S of Richfield, is a block about 26 mi. long, 12 mi. wide. It is not crossed by any paved or improved road. Highest point is 11,226-ft. Monroe Peak. Several small lakes, reservoirs, streams. One campground.

D. E of Richfield, crossed by I-70, is the fourth section, 34 mi. N–S, from 9 to 24 mi. W–E. Highest point is Mt. Marvine, 11,226 ft.; others over 10,000 ft. Fish Lake, 2,600 acres, is a popular recreation area. Several streams, small lakes, reservoirs. This section attracts the most visitors.

The Forest has many uses, and parts of it show marks of enterprise and abuse. Coal is mined in the canyon E of Salinas. Other mining has ranged from gold to gravel. Most of the Forest is subject to coal, oil, and gas leases, although a majority of the sites have not been exploited. More than 40,000 cattle and sheep graze. Special use permits have been issued for summer homes, resorts, power plants and transmission lines, broadcasting transmission towers, and other structures. Some of these uses conflict with recreation and wildlife management. Although campgrounds are often full on summer weekends, the largest visitor population is in deer-hunting season. Off-road vehicles, chiefly used by hunters, have caused extensive damage to vegetation on slopes. However, many of the conspicuous disturbances are localized, and one can still find places to enjoy nature. A 19,617-acre tract was considered suitable for wilderness designation.

Annual precipitation ranges from 8 to 10 in. at the Forest boundary to 40 in. at the highest elevations, much of this falling as snow. Over 700 mi. of perennial streams. 4,500 acres of lakes and reservoirs; more than half of this acreage is Fish Lake.

Plants: About 47% forested. Pinyon-juniper at middle elevations. Higher, aspen, Engelmann spruce, alpine fir, Douglas-fir, ponderosa pine, cottonwood.

A 1,200-acre Research Natural Area has been established in Block A, above, and a plant list compiled. The site lies between 6,400 ft. and 7,985 ft. elevation. 141 species identified here, including white fir, Rocky Mountain maple, bigtooth maple, Gambel oak. Also serviceberry, greenleaf manzanita, sagebrush, snowbrush ceanothus, mountain-mahogany, rabbitbrush, mountain snowberry.

Flowering species include yarrow, mountain dandelion, pussytoes, columbine, arrowleaf balsamroot, sego lily, Indian paintbrush, larkspur, daisy, wallflower, gilia.

Birds: Checklist of 112 species identified, plus others that probably or possibly occur. Those identified include arctic loon, western and eared grebes, white pelican, great blue heron, black-crowned night-heron, snowy egret, white-faced ibis, pintail; green-winged, blue-winged, and cinnamon teals; mallard, gadwall, lesser scaup, redhead, canvasback, Canada goose, American wigeon, common merganser, bufflehead, ruddy duck, shoveler. Raptors include turkey vulture, osprey; sharp-shinned, Cooper's, red-tailed, ferruginous, and Swainson's hawks; golden and bald eagles, northern harrier, kestrel, merlin, prairie and peregrine falcons. Also ruffed, sage, and blue grouse; chukar, Gambel's quail, turkey. Also killdeer, spotted sandpiper, long-billed curlew, American avocet, Wilson's phalarope, California and ring-billed gulls, Forster's tern. Owls: long-eared, great horned, screech, burrowing. Downy and hairy woodpeckers. Also western wood-pewee, Say's phoebe, western kingbird, western and willow flycatchers, horned lark; Steller's, pinyon, and gray jays; Clark's nutcracker, black-billed magpie, black-capped and mountain chickadees, brown creeper, dipper, sage thrasher, western and mountain bluebirds, robin, blue-gray gnatcatcher, ruby-crowned kinglet, loggerhead shrike. Warblers: yellow-rumped, yellow, Wilson's. Also house finch, gray-headed and Oregon juncos, red crossbill, black-headed grosbeak, rufoussided and green-tailed towhees, vesper and white-crowned sparrows.

Mammals: Checklist includes five species of shrews, 18 bat species, black bear, ringtail, raccoon, striped and spotted skunks, longtail weasel, badger, coyote, gray fox, mountain lion, bobcat, whitetail antelope squirrel; cliff, least, and Uinta chipmunks; Utah prairie dog, northern flying squirrel, yellowbelly marmot, golden-mantled and Townsend ground squirrels, chickaree, northern pocket gopher, kangaroo rats, Great Basin pocket mouse, beaver, voles, bushytail and desert woodrats, pinyon mouse, western jumping mouse, porcupine, pika, snowshoe hare, blacktail jackrabbit, mountain cottontail, elk, mule deer, pronghorn.

Reptiles and amphibians: Checklist includes tiger salamander, Great Basin spadefoot, western and Woodhouse's toads, leopard frog. Leopard, sagebrush, side-blotched, and short-horned lizards. Western whiptail, yellow-bellied racer, striped whipsnake, gopher snake, Great Basin rattlesnake.

FEATURES

Fishlake Mountain roadless area, 24,920 acres, is just NW of Fish Lake in Block D. Fishlake Hightop is a lava cap at 11,300 ft. elevation that forms a central plateau of about 5,000 acres. The plateau is rimmed by steep ledges. The landscape includes deep gorges, perennial streams, open meadows, and parks.

The area includes associations from upper Sonoran to high alpine: open sagebrush-grass and aspen at lower elevations, some stands of spruce above.

Most visitors come in the fall to hunt deer and elk; nonhunters do well to stay away then. At other times the area offers opportunities for quiet hiking, horse riding, and some fishing.

Delano Peak, 12,173 ft., is in the Tushar Mountains, in Block B. Day hike from the Mt. Holly Ski Area.

Chalk Creek Canyon: in the N portion of Block B, E of Fillmore. A scenic ravine with dense cottonwood, boxelder, maple. Four picnic areas.

Beaver Canyon, in the S portion of Block B, is the principal recreation area on the W side, many of the visitors coming from Nevada and California. River, small lakes and reservoirs, campgrounds.

Clear Creek Canyon is the route of I-70 W of US 89 from Sevier. A narrow cut between the Tushar and Pavant Ranges. 5 mi. W of Sevier, turn S for an unpaved scenic route, 24 mi. long, climbing to 10,000 ft., returning to US 89 at Marysvale. Steep, narrow road; advisable to inquire about road conditions. Between Marysvale and Sevier is Big Rock Candy Mountain, just outside the Forest boundary; brightly colored rock layers.

Fish Lake, in Block D, is about 6 mi. long. Campgrounds, resorts, boat ramps, fishing. Likely to be crowded in summer.

Sevier Plateau in Block C, is SE of Monroe. From Monroe a short road leads through Monroe Canyon to Monrovian Park, a picnic area. An unpaved road beyond the park climbs to the Plateau, at 10,000 ft. or more, with splendid views of the Tushar Range and the Sevier River valley. This road, shown on Multipurpose Map No. 6, is impassable when wet and may be difficult for cars at other times; inquire.

Pavant Range in Block B. From Salina on US 89, W about 8 mi. on US 50 (SR 26 on MP #6). Turn S on unpaved Forest road that climbs to and follows the ridge, at 8,000 to 10,000 ft., finally descending to Elsinore on US 89. A scenic mountain road, to be driven with care in dry weather. Inquire about road conditions.

INTERPRETATION: *Visitor center* at Fish Lake, June–Aug. Exhibits. No campfire talks or other naturalist programs.

ACTIVITIES
Camping: 19 campgrounds, 258 sites. Open May–Oct. Informal camping at any suitable site unless posted.

Hiking, backpacking: 897 mi. of trails, most shown on Forest map. Because of budget priorities, there is little trail maintenance. Hiking season is generally June–Oct.

Horse riding: No restrictions. Not much horsepacking. No local outfitters.

Hunting: Deer, elk. Comply with closed gate signs. Entering private inholdings is prohibited except on rights-of-way unless owner consents.

Fishing: Many miles of perennial streams; numerous small lakes, reservoirs. Lake, rainbow, cutthroat, brown, brook trout; kokanee, arctic grayling. Yellow perch is the only warmwater species.

Boating: On Fish Lake. Ramps, marinas, rentals.

Skiing: Ski area on Mt. Holly, E of Beaver, in S end of Block B. (MP #5.)

Ski touring: Good opportunities when snow is right. No maintained trails.

Snowmobiling: Snowmobile trailheads are marked on Multipurpose Maps No. 6 and No. 5. Miles of unplowed Forest roads. No maintained routes.

NEARBY
Little Sahara Recreation Area (see entry).
Yuba Lake State Recreation Area.
Lava Beds Volcanic Craters, W of Fillmore.
Paiute Lake State Beach.
Otter Creek Lake State Beach.

PUBLICATIONS
Forest map. $1.00.
Forest fact sheet.
Geology of the Fish Lake Area. Leaflet.
Checklists: plants (one area), birds, mammals, reptiles and amphibians.
Panoramaland Utah. Leaflet.
Travel Plan (showing areas restricted to motor vehicles), Loa and Richfield Ranger Districts.

REFERENCE: Hall, Dave. *The Hiker's Guide to Utah.* Billings, MT: Falcon Press, 1982. Pp. 112–116.

HEADQUARTERS: P.O. Box 628, 115 East 900 North, Richfield, UT 84701; (801) 896-4491.

RANGER DISTRICTS: Fillmore R.D., 390 South Main, P.O. Box 265, Fillmore, UT 84631; (801) 743-5721. Loa R.D., 150 South Main, P.O. Box 128, Loa, UT 84747; (801) 836-2811. Beaver R.D., 190 North 100 East, P.O. Box E, Beaver, UT 84713; (801) 438-2436. Richfield R.D., 55 South 100 East, P.O. Box 646; (801) 896-6429.

FISH SPRINGS NATIONAL WILDLIFE REFUGE
U.S. Fish and Wildlife Service
18,000 acres.

From Tooele, S on SR 36 to Faust Jct. Then W on Pony Express Rd., 66 mi. of graded unpaved road. (MP #7.)

Water rising from seven springs at the S end of the Great Salt Lake Desert made this a major stop on the Pony Express and Stage Trail. These and smaller springs supply about 10,000 acres of marsh, attracting large numbers of waterfowl and other migrants. The refuge, at about 4,300 ft. elevation, lies between the Fish Springs Range on the W and the Dugway and Thomas Ranges on the E.

The original marsh was largely degraded by land use practices. Now there are nine impoundments of 600 to 2,100 acres. On the dikes are 30 mi. of road.

Because of its isolated location, the Refuge doesn't receive large numbers of visitors, but some restrictions are needed. One can drive or walk over much of the Refuge. Check at HQ for restricted use areas.

Annual precipitation is about 8 in., much of it falling as snow in winter. July–Sept., hot and dry.

Plants: Marsh vegetation includes bulrush, wirerush, and aquatics. Saltgrass on extensive marsh meadows. On uplands: greasewood, Mormon tea, rabbitbrush.

Birds: 151 species recorded. Checklist available. Apr.–July best season for variety, Aug.–Nov. for abundance of waterfowl. In fall, Refuge receives more than 30,000 ducks, chiefly northern pintail, wigeon, green-winged teal, mallard, redhead. Also about 1,000 Canada geese. In winter, over 50 whistling swans and a few trumpeter swans.

Seasonally abundant or common species include eared grebe, snowy egret, black-crowned night-heron, gadwall, cinnamon teal, shoveler, redhead, mallard, ruddy duck, red-breasted merganser. Also killdeer, Virginia rail, sora, lesser yellowlegs, dowitcher, western sandpiper, American avocet, black-necked stilt, Wilson's and red-necked phalaropes, ring-billed gull, Forster's and black terns. Also northern flicker, downy woodpecker, horned lark, yellow-rumped warbler, Brewer's blackbird, brown-headed cowbird. Occasionals include bald and golden eagles, osprey, peregrine falcon.

Mammals: 32 species recorded. Often or occasionally seen: coyote, blacktail jackrabbit, desert cottontail, muskrat, antelope ground squirrel, kangaroo rat, various voles, mice, shrews. Present but seldom seen: badger, kit fox, spotted and striped skunks, weasel, mule deer.

Reptiles and amphibians: Include western rattlesnake, gopher snake, horned and collared lizards, bullfrog, leopard frog.

FEATURES

Visitor contact station at entrance has exhibit, literature.

An 11-mi. *auto tour route* is marked.

ACTIVITIES

Camping: Although camping is not permitted on the Refuge, most of the land crossed by Pony Express Rd. is public. Two mi. NW of Refuge HQ, BLM has a primitive campsite at the mouth of a canyon. About 27 mi. from Faust Junction, 39 mi. from the Refuge is BLM's Simpson Springs Campground, a watering stop on the famous trail. Water available Mar.–Oct.

Hiking: Anywhere, unless posted.

Hunting: Ducks, coots, mergansers, subject to special rules. Hunters must check in and out at HQ.

Horse riding: On dike roads, but check at Refuge HQ. No nearby livery.

Canoeing: Check at HQ. No motors. Ice in Jan.–Feb., low water Aug.– Sept.

Open: Sunrise–sunset.

Road approaching the refuge may be very rough and muddy for short periods Mar.–June. Call ahead for information on road conditions.

NEARBY: Fish Springs Range (see entry).

PUBLICATIONS

Leaflet with map.

Bird checklist.

HEADQUARTERS: P.O. Box 568, Dugway, UT 84022; (801) 522-5353.

FISH SPRINGS RANGE
U.S. Bureau of Land Management
68,900 acres.

From Tooele, S on SR 36 to Faust. Then W on Pony Express Rd., 66 mi. of graded unpaved road to Fish Springs National Wildlife Refuge. Through the Refuge to E side of the range. From the W, improved road from Callao. (MP #7.)

A N–S range in the Great Salt Lake Desert, about 20 mi. long, 4 to 6 mi. wide. Base elevation is about 5,000 ft. The range rises steeply to points on the ridge as high as 8,500 ft. Rugged terrain; deep, winding canyons. The mountain is roadless, no roads or jeep trails penetrating the canyons from the surrounding roads. Evidence of old mines mars the N end of the range; some recent exploration. Otherwise the range is in natural condition. Fine views from the ridge. No perennial stream or mapped spring; seasonal streams in canyons.

Plants: At lower elevations: sagebrush, ephedra, winterfat, rabbitbrush, shadscale. Pinyon-juniper community above. At highest elevations on the E side are very large junipers, some over 8-ft. base circumference.

Wildlife: No checklists. Great diversity of species, but no large populations. Joint studies by BLM and the Utah Division of Wildlife Resources suggest that chukar, blue and sage grouse, mourning dove, and ring-necked pheasant may be found where habitat is suitable. Active aerie sites for golden eagle have been noted, and both bald eagle and peregrine falcon are possibles. Probably 123 bird species may be found somewhere in the WSA, at some time of year.

Excellent range is available for mule deer and pronghorn. Coyote, kit fox, ringtail, bobcat, and mountain lion are also believed to be present, though not often seen.

ACTIVITIES

Camping: No campground. For camping from car, pickup, or 4-wheel drive, numerous suitable sites around the base.

Hiking, backpacking: No trails, but partially overgrown vehicle tracks may be used on the lower slopes. Bring water and topo map.

PUBLICATIONS
The Pony Express.
Pony Express Trail.

HEADQUARTERS: BLM, House Range Resource Area, P.O. Box 778, Fillmore, UT 84631; (801) 743-6811.

GOBLIN VALLEY STATE PARK
Utah State Division of Parks and Recreation
2,240 acres.

From Hanksville, NE 21 mi. on SR 24. Left 5 mi. on paved road, then left 7 mi. on gravel road to site. (MP #2.)

This is a very special place, unique and delightful. Bring children!

In the San Rafael Desert, near the base of the San Rafael Reef. The drive from Hanksville offers views of many large formations. ("It's a cat." "Looks more like an owl." "The map says it's Temple Mountain.") The Park is surrounded by buttes and mesas, the Reef to the N.

Goblin Valley has been carved by erosion in Entrada Sandstone. However, the principal visible layers are Curtis formation, creamy white above, terracotta below. The sandstone is soft, eroding quickly; the legs of our picnic table were 8 in. deep in sand washed from the nearby bluff. Approaching the site, the visitor sees sandstone columns, which have been eroded into many fanciful shapes, some about 2 ft. tall, some more than 12 ft. It takes little imagination to see them as goblins. They have also been called *mushrooms, hoodoos,* and *sand-babies.* Children need no prompting to see dwarfs, clowns, witches, demons. Neither do adults. We saw a castle with warriors on the ramparts.

Within the site is a great concentration of these delightful figures, many hundreds of them on the valley floor, seen first from above. The scale is just right for play. Children run among the figures, hiding behind them, inventing games.

If more people came, fences and "Keep Off" signs might follow. There are none now. Visitors are free to walk, climb, touch, sit, and play—as a social scientist would put it: "interact with the environment."

The campground is at the foot of a bluff about 150 ft. high, deeply eroded. At one point a narrow, winding passageway has been cut some distance into the bluff; one can hide in it. Three children from the next campsite scrambled to the top and leaped from crag to crag. On the valley floor near us were several rounded domes 15 to 25 ft. high. A family of four sat quietly on one of the domes for over an hour, watching the sunset.

Highest elevation in the Park is 5,200 ft., lowest 4,900 ft. Summer daytime temperatures hover around 100°F, often drop rapidly 30° or more after sunset. Below-freezing temperatures are common in winter. Annual precipitation is about 7 in., often in short, intense cloudbursts. Snow falls occasionally, doesn't last.

Goblin Valley is at the edge of Sinbad Country. For other sites of interest, see entry for San Rafael Swell. Most of the surrounding land is public. Multipurpose Map No. 2 shows the back roads between Goblin Valley and I-70, to the N, some fair-weather roads for cars, others best for pickups or 4-wheel drives.

Plants: High desert community includes rabbitbrush, sage, ricegrass, cheatgrass, wild buckwheat, shadscale, saltbrush, cacti, vetch, snakeweed, desert trumpet. Flowering species include soapweed yucca, sulphur flower, lupine, locoweed, prickly pear cactus, pale evening primrose, goldenweed, Mormon tea. Peak season for flowers: mid-May.

Birds: No checklist. Mentioned: western and mountain bluebirds, black-billed magpie, common raven, various warblers, finches, sparrows. Golden eagle in migration.

Mammals: Most species are nocturnal, seldom seen. Those present include bats, kangaroo rat, gophers, cottontail, jackrabbit, coyote, kit fox, badger, bobcat, porcupine, spotted skunk.

Reptiles and amphibians: Chuckwalla, whiptail, sagebrush and collared lizards, an occasional sidewinder and midget faded rattlesnake.

Invertebrates: We inquired. The reply: "Scorpions!"

INTERPRETATION: No formal program, but we found the Ranger on duty well informed about the area and its natural history. Interpretive talks on request when workload permits.

ACTIVITIES

Camping: 12 sites. Reservations advisable on major holidays.

Hiking: Curtis Bench Trail, 2 mi., moderately strenuous, to Observation Point. Carmel Canyon Trail, 1 1/2 mi., with spur trail to viewpoint. Longer hikes outside the Reserve; ask the Ranger. No trailside camping within the Reserve. Always carry plenty of water and bring a hat.

Flash floods are a desert hazard.

ADJACENT: Crack Canyon (see entry).

NEARBY: San Rafael Swell (see entry).

PUBLICATIONS

Information page: *Welcome to Goblin Valley State Reserve.*

Leaflets

Trail descriptions and map.

Roads, Trails, and Scenic Attractions in Sinbad Country.

HEADQUARTERS: P.O. Box 93, Green River, UT 84525; (801) 564-3633.

GREEN RIVER; DESOLATION CANYON

U.S. Bureau of Land Management

95 river mi. 342,160 acres.

For rafting, the major visitor use, principal access is Sand Wash Raft Ramp, 42 mi. S of US 40 near Myton, well marked at turnoff. At the S end, a county road follows the river N for a few mi. from Green River. Access to land areas by the Sand Wash road, Turtle Canyon road from SR 124, a few jeep trails; inquire at BLM office. (MP #2,3.)

Desolation Canyon is immense, up to 1 mi. deep, with many deep tributary canyons. The surrounding terrain is so rugged that this was among the last areas in the American West to be explored. Even today more people float through the canyon than explore the 535 sq. mi. of spectacularly scenic land around it on foot or horseback. Day hiking, backpacking, and horsepacking are increasing.

The area on both sides is roadless except for a jeep trail and a sometimes-passable dirt road. 341,160 acres, mostly on the W side, are public, managed by BLM. On the E is the Uintah and Ouray Indian Reservation. The Price River is the largest tributary. Many deep side canyons. The area extends to the sheer face of the Book Cliffs, above US 6 N of the town of Green River. Topography is complex, a highly dissected ridge and canyon system. Elevations from 4,200 to over 9,000 ft.

On the edge of the Tavaputs Plateau, the area has a rich diversity of features: rugged, irregular ridges; steep V-shaped side canyons; vertical rock walls, peaks, plateaus, pinnacles, arches, balanced rocks, buttresses, alcoves, caves, perennial streams and springs in most of the major canyons, waterfalls, pools, water pockets. Elevations range from 4,100 ft. to 9,600 ft. Some of the side canyons rise steeply: 3,000–5,000 ft. in 3 to 6 mi. Others are more gradual. Annual precipitation is 6–12 in.

One hiker access to this area is through Thompson Canyon; see *The Hiker's Guide to Utah,* pp. 127–131.

Sand Wash is at the head of Desolation Canyon. Although the 30 mi. from Ouray to Sand Wash can be rafted, that stretch is less interesting; most rafters put in here. Desolation Canyon, designated a National Historic Landmark, is one of the deepest and most splendid in the United States. Rafting is the most feasible way to see it.

A power company has proposed building a huge dam at the bottom of the gorge, flooding the canyon. Defenders hope to preserve the canyon by Wild and Scenic River protection and by declaring the best of the public land a wilderness area.

Rafting has become so popular that BLM has found it necessary to limit access, to preserve the natural qualities of the canyon. The trip takes 4 to 5 days at high water, longer when the current slows. About 50 sites are used for camping.

The river drops 536 ft. between Sand Wash and Green River, from 4,615 ft. at the old Sand Wash Ferry site to 4,079 ft. at the Green River spillway.

Plants: Three major plant associations along the river and tributaries. Tamarisk dominates on wet bottoms, with rubber rabbitbrush, common reed, saltgrass, alkali sacaton, pepperweed. Slightly drier is the tamarisk-greasewood complex, with cottonwood, Douglas and green rabbitbrush, cheatgrass, saltgrass, rush, sweetclover, pepperweed, seepweed, lambsquarter. The cottonwood-willow complex occurs beside rivers, with tamarisk, squawbush, boxelder, greasewood, rabbitbrush. Pinyon-juniper is the most extensive community on the land area, the sparse understory including Utah serviceberry, cliffrose, squawbush, curlleaf mountain-mahogany, birchleaf mountain mahogany, Mormon tea, snakeweed, black sagebrush.

Several other plant communities occur in the area, variations depending on soil, slope, drainage, and orientation, producing a diversity of wildlife habitats.

Birds: 93 species recorded, chiefly by summer observation in canyons. Included: great blue heron, snowy egret, black-crowned night-heron, white-faced ibis. Canada goose, mallard, cinnamon teal, common and red-breasted mergansers, turkey vulture; sharp-shinned, Cooper's, ferruginous, and red-tailed hawks; golden and bald eagles, prairie and peregrine falcons, American kestrel, merlin, osprey. Also sage, blue, and ruffed grouse; chukar, sandhill crane, American coot, killdeer, common snipe, spotted sandpiper, willet, long-billed dowitcher, American avocet, Wilson's phalarope, rock and mourning doves, long-eared and great horned owls, common nighthawk, poor-will, belted kingfisher, northern flicker, Lewis' and hairy woodpeckers, western kingbird, Say's phoebe, willow flycatcher; violet-green, bank, rough-winged, barn, and cliff swallows; scrub and pinyon jays, black-billed magpie, common raven, black-capped chickadee, bushtit, white-breasted nuthatch, dipper, house and canyon wrens, American robin, mountain bluebird, blue-gray gnatcatcher, loggerhead shrike, starling; Virginia's, yellow, and yellow-rumped warblers; western meadowlark; yellow-headed, red-winged and Brewer's blackbirds; northern oriole, brown-headed cowbird, blue grosbeak, lazuli bunting, house finch, American goldfinch, green-tailed and rufous-sided towhees; lark, black-throated, chipping, Brewer's, white-crowned, and song sparrows.

Mammals: No checklist available. Reported: mule deer, bighorn sheep, coyote, gray fox, bobcat, ringtail, mountain lion, black bear, cottontail.

ACTIVITIES

Camping: Suitable river campsites are heavily used by rafters and 4-wheel-drive visitors. All are required to carry out all trash, ashes, and human waste. Upland camping on jeep trails.

Hiking, backpacking: Extensive opportunities. Inquire at BLM office for attractive routes. Bring topo map, water.

Fishing: Brown and rainbow trout in side streams. Channel cat, bullhead, carp. Several threatened species occur in the river. A section is within an Indian reservation, and fishing here requires a tribal permit.

Rafting: Limited to one 25-person party per day. Dates are filled by a mid-Mar. drawing, often well into the following year. Any open dates or cancellations are filled on a first-come, first-served basis. BLM will supply a list of outfitters.

PUBLICATION: *Running the Green River from Sand Wash to Green River, Utah.*

REFERENCES

Evans, Laura, and Buzz Belknap. *Green River Wilderness: Desolation River Guide.* Boulder City, NV: Westwater Books, 1974.

Mutschler, Felix E. *Desolation and Gray Canyons.* Denver: Powell Society, 1969.

Zwinger, Ann. *Run, River, Run.* New York: Harper & Row, 1981.

HEADQUARTERS: BLM, Price Area Office, 900 North 7th East, Price, UT 84501; (801) 637-4584.

LA SAL MOUNTAIN STATE FOREST
Utah State Division of State Lands and Forestry
28,000 acres.

From SR 128, 16 mi. NE of Moab, SE 21 mi. on Castle Valley road. The
first 10 mi. are part of the La Sal Mountain Scenic Loop (see Moab Area
entry). (MP #2.)

As noted in the Utah Preface, Utah State Forests are managed primarily for
revenue generation, rather than for recreation or wildlife.

The La Sal Mountains are the second highest range in the state, several
peaks over 12,000 ft. The Forest is in two blocks, 11,000 and 17,000 acres, 3
mi. apart, both near the Colorado border, surrounded by the Manti-La Sal
National Forest (see entry). Forest land occupies the E slopes of Mt. Waas,
Mt. Tomasaki, and Mt. Peale. Highest point: 11,200 ft., lowest 7,800 ft. Landforms change dramatically from W to E, from alpine to mid-slopes, steep
cliffs, and semidesert floor.

Annual precipitation ranges from 20 in. at lower elevations to 50 in. on the
upper slopes, which receive 100 to 300 in. of winter snow. Although maps
show only intermittent streams, the regional office says there is stream fishing,
indicating that some streams are perennial.

Plants: About 70% of the site is forested: aspen, Gambel oak, ponderosa
pine, Engelmann spruce, subalpine fir, Douglas-fir. At lower elevations: juniper, sagebrush slopes, grassy meadows. Many wildflowers.

Birds: No checklist. Forester says many species present: eagles, hawks,
owls, grouse, turkey, songbirds.

Mammals: Mentioned: ground squirrels, cottontail, snowshoe hare, jackrabbit, badger, coyote, beaver, mule deer, elk. Mountain lion, bobcat, black
bear present, seldom seen.

FEATURE: *Don's Lake,* 80 acres in the Beaver Creek drainage, near the W
border of the Forest, is a popular fishing spot, the only place in the Forest
said to be overused. (Lake not shown on MP #2 or on the Manti-La Sal
National Forest map.)

ACTIVITIES

Camping: No developed campground. Numerous suitable sites for primitive camping.

Hiking, backpacking: No trail system, but hiking on jeep, stock, and game
trails. Bring topo map, water.

Hunting: Grouse, rabbit, turkey, bear, deer, elk.

Fishing: Rainbow trout; lake and stream.

Swimming: Don's Lake; unsupervised. Cold water, fed by snowmelt.

HEADQUARTERS: State Lands and Forestry, Southeastern Regional Office, P.O. Box 32, Moab, UT 84532; (801) 259-6316.

LITTLE SAHARA RECREATION AREA
U.S. Bureau of Land Management
60,000 acres.

From I-15 at Santaquin, 38 mi. W and S on US 6 and 50 to Jericho Junction, then 4 mi. W. (MP #6, 7.)

Utah's most extensive sand dune area. Two-thirds of the area has been assigned to ORV activity: hill climbing, dune buggy races, drag racing, etc. About a third is covered with very large, free-moving sand dunes. Visitor use is heavy.

A portion of the site has been set aside as the Rockwell Natural Area, from which vehicles are excluded. The area includes dunes, juniper-covered hills, and sagebrush flats. It is said to be the only place in the world where the giant fourwing saltbush is known to grow naturally. Unlike the other, smaller fourwing saltbushes, the giant species grows 10–12 ft. tall, and may spread out to cover an area with a radius of 6 to 8 ft.

Camping: Three campgrounds; 175 sites. Water available.

PUBLICATION: *Little Sahara Recreation Area.*

HEADQUARTERS: BLM, House Range Resource Area, P.O. Box 778, Fillmore, UT 84631; (801) 743-6811.

MANTI-LA SAL NATIONAL FOREST; MANTI DIVISION
U.S. Forest Service
730,239 acres; 794,172 acres within boundaries.

Within the area enclosed by US 89, US 6, SR 10, and I-70. Crossed by Forest roads entering from both W and E. (MP #2; N tip in MP #3; W edge in MP #6.)

The La Sal Division of this Forest is more than 100 mi. distant (see entry in Zone 3).

The Manti Division is on a rugged, rambling strip of the Wasatch Plateau, about 72 mi. N–S, 14 to 27 mi. W–E. Land form is a block uplift with some folding on the W escarpment. The Sanpete Valley on the W, along US 89, is agricultural, depending for its water on streams from the Plateau. The steeper escarpment on the E side overlooks Castle Valley. Deep canyons cut into the plateau, the widest and longest of them on the E side. Elevations from 6,500 ft. to 11,300 ft.

Before the National Forest was established, about half a million cattle and sheep grazed on the slopes. Overgrazing and forest fires eliminated much of the water-retaining vegetation, causing damaging floods and droughts during the growing season in the valleys. Grazing permits have been reduced and cattle excluded from some areas to permit recovery.

Annual precipitation ranges from 8 in. at low elevations to 36 in. on the upper slopes, where annual snowfall is about 8 ft. The area has two wet seasons: Dec. through Mar. and mid-July to mid-Sept. Runoff is sufficient to maintain more than 200 mi. of streams and many small lakes and reservoirs.

The recreation season begins about Easter on the desert floor, mostly BLM land. As soon as they can, visitors move into the Forest and up to the Plateau. Hiking season in the high country begins about June 15.

Skyline Drive, running the length of the Division, is one of the most scenic routes in Utah, with spectacular views on both sides.

Most Forest visitors are from nearby communities, although this is changing, partly because of crowding in the Wasatch-Cache National Forest to the N. Hiking and backpacking are minor activities but increasing. A high proportion of residents of the surrounding area own 4-wheel-drive vehicles, and 4-wheel-drive use is heavy, especially in vacation periods and hunting season. The Travel Plan map shows areas closed to ORV's because of watershed damage. Some reservoirs have been fenced to keep 4-wheel-drive vehicles away from the water's edge. Snowmobiling is also popular.

Plants: About 46% forest, 38% brushland, 16% grassland. Above 9,000 ft., down to 7,500 ft. on N exposed slopes: spruce-fir association. On most sites the dominant species, Engelmann spruce and alpine fir, are very dense. Understory includes sticky currant, wild gooseberry, huckleberry, elderberry.

A large area between 8,000 and 9,500 ft. on upper benchlands, slumps, pediment bottoms, and morainal deposits is dominated by quaking aspen. Dense understory includes cow parsnip, Engelmann aster, wild rye. One grove of giant aspens.

Douglas-fir/white fir forests occur on N and E slopes between 7,500 and 8,500 ft. This association includes limber pine and bristlecone pine. Understory includes sticky currant, wild gooseberry, snowberry, creeping barberry, mountain-lover, spike fescue.

Ponderosa pine occurs at mid-elevations in canyons and on benchlands along the E escarpment. Other species in this association include Gambel oak, snowberry, serviceberry, common juniper, manzanita, sagebrush. Also at mid-elevations are areas of Gambel oak, serviceberry, curlleaf mountain-mahogany, big sagebrush, snowberry, chokecherry, wild currant.

The lowest slopes are chiefly pinyon-juniper woodland. In the bottoms are desert shrubs, including saltbush, greasewood, winterfat, others.

The Forest has a 55-page list of plant species occurring on the Plateau. Only Latin species names are given, and the list does not distinguish between abundant species and the extremely rare.

Birds: Checklist of 199 species available. Seasonally common or abundant species include eared and pied-billed grebes, snowy egret, black-crowned night-heron, Canada goose, mallard, gadwall, northern pintail, green-winged and cinnamon teals, American wigeon, northern shoveler, redhead, canvasback, lesser scaup, ruddy duck, common merganser. Also turkey vulture, goshawk; Cooper's, red-tailed, and rough-legged hawks; golden eagle, northern harrier, prairie falcon, American kestrel; blue, ruffed, and sage grouse, California quail, chukar, ring-necked pheasant, American coot, killdeer, black-bellied plover, common snipe; spotted, least, and western sandpipers; lesser yellowlegs, long-billed dowitcher, marbled godwit, American avocet, black-necked stilt, Wilson's and red-necked phalaropes, Franklin's gull, Forster's and black terns. Also great horned and long-eared owls, common nighthawk, poor-will. Hummingbirds: black-chinned, broad-tailed, rufous, and calliope. Northern flicker, yellow-bellied sapsucker, hairy and downy woodpeckers, western kingbird; ash-throated, willow, dusky, and western flycatchers; Say's phoebe, horned lark; violet-green, tree, bank, rough-winged, barn, and cliff swallows; Steller's, scrub, and pinyon jays; black-billed magpie, common raven, Clark's nutcracker. Also black-capped and mountain chickadees, bushtit; white-breasted, red-breasted, and pygmy nuthatches; brown creeper, dipper; house, rock, canyon, and Bewick's wrens; sage thrasher, American robin, hermit and Swainson's thrushes, Townsend's solitaire, bluegray gnatcatcher, ruby-crowned kinglet, water pipit, loggerhead shrike, European starling, warbling vireo. Warblers: orange-crowned, Virginia's, yellowrumped, yellow, MacGillivray's, yellow-breasted chat, Wilson's. Also house sparrow, western meadowlark; yellow-headed, red-winged, and Brewer's blackbirds; northern oriole, brown-headed cowbird, western tanager; blackheaded, blue, and evening grosbeaks; lazuli bunting, green-tailed and rufoussided towhees. Sparrows: vesper, lark, chipping, Brewer's, white-crowned, song. Dark-eyed and gray-headed juncos; Cassin's, house, and rosy finches; pine siskin, American goldfinch.

Mammals: Checklist of 79 species. Common species include: vagrant, masked, dusky, and northern water shrews; little brown, long-eared, longlegged, and California myotis; silver-haired, big brown, western big-eared, pallid, and Mexican free-tailed bats; western pipistrel, pika, whitetail and blacktail jackrabbits, mountain and desert cottontails, whitetail prairie dog; red and rock squirrels; golden-mantled and Uinta ground squirrels, whitetail antelope squirrel, yellowbelly marmot, least and Uinta chipmunks, northern pocket and valley gophers, Ord kangaroo rat, Great Basin pocket mouse, beaver. Mice: western harvest, canyon, deer, brush, pinyon, house. Desert and bushytail woodrats, muskrat. Voles: meadow, mountain, Richardson's, longtail, sagebrush; black and Norway rats; western jumping mouse, porcupine, coyote, gray fox, black bear, ringtail, longtail weasel, badger, striped and spotted skunks, mountain lion, mule deer, elk.

Reptiles and amphibians: Great Basin spadefoot toad, Woodhouse's toad, chorus and leopard frogs. Lizards: collared, leopard, eastern fence, desert spiny, sagebrush, tree, side-blotched, short-horned, western whiptail. Rubber boa, striped whipsnake, racer, gopher snake, western terrestrial garter snake, night snake, midget faded rattlesnake.

FEATURES

Skyline Drive, a scenic mountain road, begins at Tucker on US 6, 50, extending S along the top of the Plateau to the road crossing the Forest between Mayfield and Ferron. The route continues S to Exit 72 on I-70; the final section is single-lane with turnouts. Skyline Drive is narrow, winding, unpaved. Snow closes the route. It should be avoided in wet weather. The central section was closed by landslides in 1983, was scheduled for reopening in 1985.

Great Basin Experimental Range, 4,600 acres, is in Ephraim Canyon just E of Ephraim, UT, reached by the Ephraim-Orangeville road, passing Joes Valley Reservoir and Skyline Drive. A scenic route with fine viewpoints. Ephraim Canyon was chosen as a site to study the effects of watershed damage. A pamphlet for a self-guided auto tour is available at Forest or Experiment Station HQ in Ephraim.

Joes Valley Reservoir, 1,170 acres, is set in the Joes Valley graben, a 1,500-ft. displacement. Pinyon-juniper association, just below the ponderosa pine zone. Marina, boat ramp, 46-site campground.

Grove of the Aspen Giants Scenic Area is in 12 Mile Canyon, 13 mi. E of Mayfield, 1/4 mi. N of the Ferron-Mayfield road. When the site was designated in 1951, there were 20 giant aspens. Since then the largest of them have fallen and others show rot. The site is maintained for scientific reasons.

ACTIVITIES

Camping: 15 campgrounds, 136 sites. Generally June–Oct., some open in May, high-altitude campgrounds in July.

Hiking, backpacking: As noted, this use of the Forest has been minor, but is increasing. The Division has available brief descriptions of 10 trails, 4 to 16 mi. long, with a small map showing their locations. There has been little trail maintenance. No potable water.

Horse riding: Suitable roads and trails, but this is a minor activity. No local outfitters.

Hunting: Deer, elk. One of the principal activities.

Fishing: 222 mi. of fishable streams. Five lakes with over 100 acres, many smaller ponds and reservoirs. Mostly rainbow trout; also brown and cutthroat.

Boating: Joes Valley Reservoir, Ferron Reservoir. Ramps, marinas, rentals. Ramp on Electric Lake. No hp limit.

Ski touring: Usual season Nov. 25–Mar. 15. No maintained trails. (The Snowland Ski Area has been abandoned.)

Snowmobiling: Same season. Some areas closed; see Travel Plan.

ADJACENT

Millsite Lake State Beach is on a 435-acre reservoir W of Ferron. The reservoir extends into the Forest. Fishing, boating; ramp. Primitive camping. The site is barren. No water.

Palisade Lake State Recreation Area is on a small reservoir 6 mi. S and 1 mi. E of Manti, at the mouth of Six Mile Canyon. 27 campsites and overflow. All year. P.O. Box H, Manti, UT 84642; (801) 835-9151.

Scofield Lake State Recreation Area. From US 6, 50 N of Price, W 13 mi. on SR 96. (MP #3.) A 312-acre park on a 2,800-acre reservoir at the end of Fish Creek. Open all year. 40 campsites. Hunting, fishing, swimming, boating (no hp limit), ramp, rentals. Lake freezes in winter. Nature trail; naturalist talks. P.O. Box 75, Scofield Route, Helper, UT 84526; (801) 448-9449.

PUBLICATIONS

Forest map. $1.00. (1962 map, not current.)

Wildlife species checklists.

Auto tour pamphlet, Great Basin Experimental Range.

Descriptions of hiking trails.

Travel plan; map showing areas closed to ORV's.

REFERENCE: Hall, Dave. *The Hiker's Guide to Utah.* Billings, MT: Falcon Press, 1982. Pp. 117–122.

HEADQUARTERS: U.S. Forest Service, 599 West Price River Dr., Price, UT 84501; (801) 637-2817.

RANGER DISTRICTS: Price R.D., 10 N. Carbon Ave., Price, UT 84501; (801) 637-2817. Ferron R.D., 50 S. Main St., Ferron, UT 84523; (801) 384-2372. Sanpete R.D., 150 S. Main St., Ephraim, UT 84627; (801) 283-4151.

MEXICAN MOUNTAIN

U.S. Bureau of Land Management

104,000 acres.

From I-70, 30 mi. W of Green River, N 19 mi. up Cottonwood Draw. This is a 2-wheel-drive road in dry weather. Here a primitive dead-end road extends SE through the heart of the area. (MP #2.)

On the San Rafael Swell, N of I-70. The Sids Mountain area lies to the W (see entry). The San Rafael River crosses this area, S of and roughly parallel to the primitive road, cutting down through the San Rafael Reef near the intersection of I-70 and SR 24. A narrow, deep section of the steep, meandering gorge of the San Rafael River, near the center of the area, is called the Black Box. It offers interesting and challenging hiking and tubing when water flows are low.

Mexican Mountain is in the E part of the area, near the Reef. At 6,393 ft., it rises little more than a thousand feet above the Mexican Bend of the San Rafael River.

Petroglyphs and pictographs are found in the area.

About three-fifths of the area consists of natural, scenic red-rock canyons, white Navajo sandstone buttes, and petrified dunes. The area is under wilderness study. It is one of several attractive natural areas on the Swell where hiking and backpacking can be enjoyed in solitude.

Plants: Vegetation is a mix of grasses, desert shrubs, pinyon-juniper woodlands, and riparian trees and shrubs.

HEADQUARTERS: BLM, Price Area Office, 900 N 700 E, P.O. Drawer AB, Price, UT 84501; (801) 637-4584.

MOAB AREA

On US 163 at the Colorado River. (MP #2.)

Moab, population about 5,000, is between Arches and Canyonlands National Parks, near the Manti-La Sal National Forest. Most of the surrounding land is public. One could spend a season or a lifetime exploring this spectacular region by car, jeep, horse, boat, or on foot.

FEATURES

Dead Horse Point State Park. See entry.

Colorado River in Canyonlands. Commercial boat tours from Moab travel downstream, a flatwater area, into Canyonlands National Park, below Dead Horse Point State Park and Island in the Sky. Points of interest include Indian ruins, pictographs, fossil beds, a petrified forest.

Colorado River: Colorado border to Moab. See entry. River outfitters are located in Moab.

La Sal Mountain Scenic Loop Drive. 70 mi. on paved and improved roads along the Colorado River, through Castle Valley. You may recognize Castle Rock, featured in TV commercials with an automobile on its top. Route continues into Manti-La Sal National Forest, returns to Moab by Spanish Valley. Possible side trips to mountain lakes, backpacking trips of several days. Forested mountain slopes; scenic canyons.

Fisher Towers. From SR 128, along the Colorado River, about 23 mi. NE of Moab, a short unpaved road leads to the parking and picnic area. A cluster of dark red spires. Highest is 900 ft. A 2.2-mi. foot trail circles the towers. The leaflet lists 21 motion pictures made here.

Petroglyph Drive. Called "Scenic Drive" on MP #2. From US 163, 2 mi. W of the river bridge at Moab, turn S on SR 279. Paved road follows the N bank of the Colorado River for about 14 mi. to a large potash mine. From there an unpaved road W to White Rim Drive and Canyonlands National Park.

Behind the Rocks, a fascinating, lightly visited area just SW of Moab. Access from US 163 about 2 mi. S of Moab on Pritchett Canyon road. Also from US 163 about 39 mi. S of Moab. (See MP #1, road to Wind Whistle campground, Needles Overlook, etc.) From the N, in dry weather, a car can reach Hurrah Pass; from the S to Canyon Rims Recreation Area. 4-wheel drive is needed between these points. Splendid vistas, interesting geological formations, including prominent red-rock fins; fine hiking in such areas as Harts Draw, below Wind Whistle campground. BLM staff members were enthusiastic about this area. See them in Moab before planning a trip.

Mill Creek, 9,780 acres of roadless BLM land 3 mi. ESE of Moab. Includes the drainages of the South and North Forks of Mill Creek. Canyons up to 400 ft. deep; toplands flat to rolling. Exposed sandstone fins and ridges in the NW. Mill Creek is perennial, with some opportunity for swimming. Vegetation ranges from riparian communities in the canyon bottoms to scattered pinyon-juniper above. In the E a few stands of ponderosa pine. Several petroglyph panels on the North Fork. A pleasant area for quiet hiking, backpacking.

Negro Bill Canyon, about 3 mi. E of Moab, extends from the Colorado River about 11 mi. E. Steep-walled, over 400 ft. deep for much of its length. Several small side canyons. The stream is perennial, with limited opportunities for swimming. Riparian vegetation, often dense, includes rushes, cattails, cottonwood trees, tamarisk, willow, Indian ricegrass, single-leaf ash, blackbrush. The Moab Slickrock Bike Trail is above the canyon and has two overlooks near the trailhead. The Bike Trail leaflet has a map showing the canyon.

Multipurpose Map No. 2 shows many unpaved roads around Moab, leading to and through quiet scenic areas with camping and hiking opportunities. When dry and well maintained, such roads may be suitable for ordinary cars. Inquire locally before driving. Several tour companies in Moab offer backcountry trips in 4-wheel-drive vehicles. Such vehicles can also be rented.

ACTIVITIES

Camping: In the National Parks and National Forest. Also BLM's Wind Whistle and Hatch Point in the Canyon Rims Recreation Area. Many possible sites for informal camping along secondary roads.

Hiking, backpacking: Many possibilities. See the References, and consult BLM office.

Horse riding: Outfitters in Moab offer trail rides.

Boating: Excursion boats and rentals available at Moab. Sightseeing in the canyon of the Colorado River.

Rafting: See entry, Colorado River.

PUBLICATIONS

Fisher Towers, BLM leaflet.

Moab Activities Guide. Tourist leaflet distributed locally.

A Scenic Tour of the Colorado River, Castle Valley, and Manti-La Sal National Forest. Leaflet with map. Grand County Travel Council, Moab, UT 84532.

Moab Slickrock Bike Trail. BLM leaflet with map.

REFERENCES

Barnes, F. A. *Canyon Country Hiking and Natural History.* Salt Lake City: Wasatch, 1977.

Barnes, F. A. *Canyon Country Off-Road Vehicle Trails, Canyon Rims and Needles Areas.* Salt Lake City: Wasatch, 1978.

Hall, Dave. *The Hiker's Guide to Utah.* Billings, MT: Falcon Press, 1982. Pp. 192–197.

HEADQUARTERS: BLM, Moab District Office, 82 East Dogwood, P.O. Box 970, Moab, UT 84532; (801) 259-6111.

SAN RAFAEL SWELL

Mostly U.S. Bureau of Land Management
About 40 mi. long, 20 mi. wide.

Crossed by I-70. Traveling W, from about 17 mi. W of Green River. (MP #2.)

The Swell is a great oval-shaped uplift, elevated 2,500 to 3,000 ft. above the desert floor. Erosion has cut the perimeter into a saw-toothed ridge, the San Rafael Reef, steepest on the E side. This made the interior area, known as "Sinbad Country," almost inaccessible until the Interstate was built.

The flat interior, Sinbad Country, is natural pasture bordered by sandstone castles. The colorful sandstone layers of the Swell have been carved into many

bizarre and fascinating shapes. We have several entries for this scenic area:
Cedar Mountain Recreation Area
Cleveland-Lloyd Dinosaur Quarry
Crack Canyon
Devil's Canyon
Goblin Valley State Park
Muddy Creek
Sids Mountain
The San Rafael River has cut a deep, spectacular canyon across the N end of the Swell. It is at the N edge of the Sids Mountain site. The Wedge Overlook (see MP #2) is a fine viewpoint.

PUBLICATIONS

The San Rafael Swell. Illustrated leaflet. Castle Country, P.O. Box 1037, Price, UT 84501.

Roads, Trails, and Scenic Attractions in Sinbad Country. Goblin Valley State Reserve.

SIDS MOUNTAIN

U.S. Bureau of Land Management
93,000 acres.

From I-70, 30 mi. W of Green River, N up Cottonwood Draw, a fair-weather road. County roads on the N, W, and SW boundaries, BLM-maintained roads in the N, W, and S portions. (MP #2.)

On the San Rafael Swell, between the Wedge overlook and I-70. Until recently there have been few visitors, but the site's popularity is growing. During the spring runoff, visitors come to float the San Rafael River through Little Grand Canyon, using rubber rafts, inner tubes, canoes, and kayaks. In midsummer, hikers and backpackers travel the canyon bottoms. At times the San Rafael Campground and Buckhorn Canyon have heavy use by ORV enthusiasts; on a recent Easter weekend, BLM reported over 1,000 campers in Buckhorn Canyon. However, other areas of the site are quiet. Wilderness status for the area has been proposed. Such status would exclude motor vehicles.

The area includes Sids Mountain, colorful badlands and mesas, deep canyons, parklands, and interesting rock formations. BLM specialists rated it highly for scenic qualities and botanical, archeological, and geological features. Most of the area is cut by an intricate canyon system. Canyons are up to 1,500 ft. deep, twisting and winding, with massive sandstone walls and many tributary canyons. Colors are red, buff, orange, brown, yellow, and gray. Elevations range from 5,100 ft. in canyon bottoms to 6,800 ft.

The San Rafael River flows E near the N boundary, through Little Grand Canyon. Other large canyons in the system are Bullock Draw, McCarty, Coal Wash, Salt Wash, Saddle Horse, Eagle, Cane Wash, and Virgin Springs. The San Rafael River and the lower Salt Wash are the principal perennial streams. Portions of other canyons have intermittent flow from springs and seeps. Some springs flow all year. Stream water is untested and may be unsafe, especially when the streams receive runoff from agricultural land upstream.

Scattered through the area are sandstone monoliths, spires, arches, and other formations shaped by erosion. Many hanging gardens.

Annual precipitation is 8 to 12 in. Snowfall about 15 in. Temperatures range from winter low of 5° to summer high around 100°.

Plants: Pinyon-juniper woodland predominates on foothills and mesas. In drier benches and sloping sandy lowlands, Mormon tea, shadscale, rabbit-brush, snakeweed, blackbrush, fourwing saltbush, black sagebrush, wild buckwheat. Along the river, tamarisk, cottonwood, black greasewood, rabbit-brush, snakeweed, alkali sacaton.

Wildlife: Limited water and vegetation produce sparse wildlife populations. Cliffs provide habitat for raptors, including golden eagle, prairie falcon, American kestrel; red-tailed, ferruginous, and rough-legged hawks. The river attracts some waterfowl and shorebirds. Mule deer are present. Desert bighorn sheep were reintroduced, but we heard of no recent sightings. Reported: coyote, bobcat, cottontail, blacktail jackrabbit, woodrat, badger, Ord kangaroo rat, gray fox, whitetail antelope squirrel.

ACTIVITIES

Camping: BLM's San Rafael Campground is on the Cottonwood Draw road, just outside the unit. "It's not much," we were told. Camp in any suitable place.

Hiking, backpacking: Carry water and a topo map.

REFERENCE: Hall, Dave. *The Hiker's Guide to Utah.* Billings, MT: Falcon Press, 1982. P. 122.

HEADQUARTERS: BLM, Price Area Office, 900 North 7th East, Price, UT 84501; (801) 637-4584.

SWASEY MOUNTAIN
U.S. Bureau of Land Management
83,320 acres.

From 12 mi. W of Delta on US 6 and 50, 24 mi. W on unnumbered road, then 8 mi. NW to Dome Canyon Pass and N on road to Swasey Peak. Check road conditions. (MP #6.)

This scenic hiking-backpacking area now has less than 200 visitors per year.

In the N House Range. 50 mi.-long block fault formation, typical of Great Basin. W slopes are steep, some on the E side more gradual. Several large canyons on the E; narrow, twisting canyons higher up. High peaks: Swasey, 9,669 ft., Tatow Knob, 8,416 ft. Several caves are known to local spelunkers.

The Antelope Springs Trilobite Beds on Swasey Mountain, shown on Multipurpose Map No. 6, are one of the most outstanding fields in the United States for gathering fossils of the Cambrian geologic era. Forty different species of trilobites have been found in this area, including Agnostus, one of the earliest forms of differentiated life.

Annual precipitation: 12 to 20 in. Extreme temperature range, from −14 to 105°F. Six springs, quality untested. No perennial streams.

Plants: At mid-elevations, pinyon-juniper woodland. On S and W slopes, montane forest with Douglas-fir, white fir, limber pine, some bristlecone pine. Most drainages have ponderosa pine, chokecherry, aspen, heavy mountain shrub.

Wildlife: No species lists, but BLM records 104 species of birds, 50 mammals, 15 reptiles and amphibians. Winter deer range. Mentioned: pronghorn, wild horse, mountain lion, eagles, chukar.

ACTIVITIES: *Hiking, backpacking:* Day hiking to Swasey Peak. Backpacking from there on pack trail to Tatow Knob, Robbers Roost Canyon. Bring topo map.

REFERENCE: Hall, Dave. *The Hiker's Guide to Utah.* Billings, MT: Falcon Press, 1982. Pp. 103–107.

HEADQUARTERS: BLM, House Range Resource Area, P.O. Box 778, Fillmore, UT 84631; (801) 743-6811.

WAH WAH MOUNTAINS
U.S. Bureau of Land Management
97,200 acres.

From I-15 at Beaver, 62 mi. W on SR 21. Here SR 21 crosses the Wah Wah Range. The entry is for the area to the N. (MP #6.)

The upper elevations are one of the most remote and undisturbed areas in Utah, receiving few visitors. The area is roadless, 42,140 acres of the high ground considered suitable for wilderness study.

This portion of the Wah Wah Range is about 20 mi. long, 7–9 mi. wide at the S end, narrowing to about 3 mi. wide at the N. Steep, rugged cliffs on the W side. Slopes on the E are slightly less steep but still rugged. The S half has a well-defined ridge above 7,000 ft. elevation, about 2,000 ft. higher than the valleys on either side. In the N a pass separates Crystal Peak from the main ridge. Fine views from the ridge.

Highest elevation is 8,990 ft. Crystal Peak, 7,106 ft., a large white rock made of volcanic tuff, is a prominent landmark.

Annual precipitation ranges from 6 in. to about 20 in. The area has no perennial streams and no known reliable spring.

Plants: Typical desert vegetation below. At mid-elevations, dense stands of juniper. Higher, stands of ponderosa pine, Douglas-fir, white fir, Engelmann spruce. Also bristlecone pine, some specimens thought to be 4,000 years old.

Wildlife: No checklist. BLM records show 100 bird species, 50 mammals, 15 reptiles and amphibians. None abundant. Mentioned: eagles, hawks, deer, pronghorn, mountain lion.

REFERENCE: A hike in the Wah Wah range S of SR 21 is described in Hall, Dave. *A Hiker's Guide to Utah.* Billings, MT: Falcon Press, 1982. Pp. 109–112.

HEADQUARTERS: BLM, Richfield District Office, 150 East 900 North, Richfield, UT 84701; (801) 896-8221.

WESTWATER CANYON
See entry, Colorado River: Colorado border to Moab.

ZONE 3

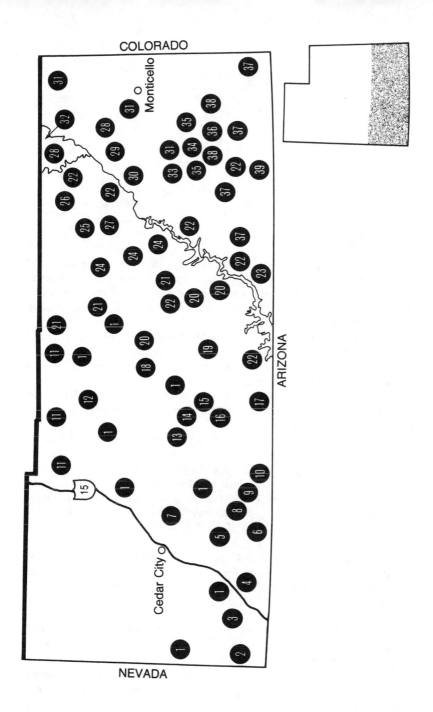

ZONE 3

Includes these counties (Multipurpose Maps Nos. 1, 2, 5, and 6):

Beaver	Kane	Washington
Garfield	Piute	Wayne
Iron	San Juan	

This zone is canyon country. There's nothing like it anywhere. Four National Parks, three National Monuments, a huge National Recreation Area, and three National Forests, plus a scattering of state-owned sites. Almost all the remaining land is public domain, managed by the U.S. Bureau of Land Management, with many features rivaling those of the National Parks.

Almost the entire zone is spectacular. Most roads are scenic routes. Traffic on most of them is light. Only 5% of Utah's population lives here. The National Parks are well attended in season, but few other places are ever crowded. It's easy to find solitude.

Many visitors combine Zion and Bryce National Parks and Cedar Breaks National Monument in their tours. Zion draws the most visitors, and the average stay is longer than at the other two sites. Most visits to Bryce and Cedar Breaks are for less than a day. Zion also offers more opportunities for backcountry travel.

Most visitors to Capitol Reef National Park cross its N sector on SR 24, a good paved road. Only a few visit the S end of the Park. Canyonlands, largest of the Utah National Parks, has no paved roads and only primitive facilities. Those who come by car can enjoy some magnificent views of the Colorado River canyon, but most of the Park is accessible only with 4-wheel drive or on foot.

Most visitors come to the Glen Canyon National Recreation Area to enjoy boating, fishing, and other water recreation. Few know that this NRA has more land acres than all Utah's National Parks and National Monuments combined, including some splendid hiking country. By far the best-known route is through the Escalante Canyon.

Most of the high country in the Zone is in the National Forests, the Dixie in the W, Manti-La Sal in the E. Both have extensive roadless areas and fine backpacking opportunities.

In this desert country, canyons attract the most hikers. The mesas above are hot and dry. The canyons are usually cooler, with more vegetation. Many have seeps and springs, and some have flowing streams. It's an adventurous undertaking. The canyon bottoms have no maintained trails. Hikers must scramble over rocks, wade, sometimes even swim. Narrows must be hiked with caution because of flash floods. Once one is committed to a hike of several days, there may be no way out until the end. Search and rescue operations are slow and difficult. Despite all these problems—or perhaps because of them—hikers come from far away to travel the Dark Canyon, Paria Canyon, North Fork of the Virgin River, Grand Gulch, Parunuweep Canyon, and other routes. These are the best-known routes, so popular that travel permits are sometimes rationed. No one need be disappointed: the zone has many lovely canyons which have as few as a dozen visitors per year.

The Colorado and Green Rivers join in Canyonlands National Park. Float trips are possible on both as well as on the San Juan River.

REFERENCES

Barnes, F. A. *Canyon Country Camping.* Salt Lake City: Wasatch, 1977.
Barnes, F. A. *Canyon Country Hiking and Natural History.* Salt Lake City: Wasatch, 1977.
Geerling, Paul F. *Down the Grand Staircase.* Boulder City, NV: Westwater Books, 1981.

BEAVER DAM WASH

U.S. Bureau of Land Management
95,000 acres.

SW corner of UT. SR 56 runs NW from St. George, turns SW at Shivwits and crosses the Beaver Dam Mountains. (MP #5.)

Highest point in the Beaver Dam Mountains is 7,746 ft. Most of the ridge is below 6,000 ft. SR 56 crosses the summit at 4,600 ft. The steep W slope is an environment unique in UT (though not in states to the W and S), with Joshua trees, Utah agave, cottontop cactus, and barrel cactus, all at the N edge of their range. The Joshua Tree Natural Landmark is E of SR 56, about 2 mi. N of the AZ border.

Beaver Dam Wash is W of the Mountains. Near the highway at the border, the Wash is the lowest point in UT: 2,100 ft.

The slope provides habitat for the endangered desert tortoise. Population here may once have been 1,000–2,000. It is now estimated at 200–300 and declining, partly because of collectors, partly because the perennial grasses are vanishing. Since the tortoises spend much of the daytime underground, they are not often seen.

Plants: The lower fringe of Joshua trees begins at about 2,000 ft. along the S slope of the Beaver Dam Mountains, where the ridges drop into the low desert scrub environment of Beaver Dam Wash. Joshua trees intermix with pinyon-juniper at about 5,500 ft., above which pinyon-juniper dominates.

Vegetation along the SW slope is typical of the Mohave Desert association: Spanish bayonet, blackbrush, creosotebush, Mormon tea, cholla, goldenhead, wolfberry, burrobrush, bursage, filaree, dwarf milkvetch; desert almond and honey mesquite in the larger washes.

Birds: Species typical of the Mohave Desert community. The cactus wren and Scott's oriole are here near the N edge of their ranges. Nesting species include red-tailed hawk, great horned owl, roadrunner, poor-will, black-chinned and broad-tailed hummingbirds, ladder-backed woodpecker, western kingbird, ash-throated flycatcher, Bewick's wren, mockingbird, crissal thrasher, blue-gray gnatcatcher, loggerhead shrike, rufous-sided towhee, black-chinned and black-throated sparrows.

Mammals: Mountain lion, coyote, bobcat, and ringtail "are still considered part of the fauna." Bighorn sheep not reported since the 1940s.

Collecting tortoises is illegal.
Cars must stay on roads.

PUBLICATION: Leaflet.

HEADQUARTERS: BLM, Cedar City District, 1579 North Main, Cedar City, UT 84720; (801) 586-2401.

BRYCE CANYON NATIONAL PARK
National Park Service
35,240 acres.

From US 89, 17 mi. E on SR 12. (MP #5.)

Begin looking before you get here. SR 12 passes through Red Canyon, in the Dixie National Forest. On either side are colorful formations like those in the Park, not on so grand a scale but impressive when seen from below rather than above. Frequent turnouts; campground; nature trail; marked hiking trail.

Your first stop in the Park should be the visitor center. If you're towing a trailer, leave it here or at the campground just ahead; it won't fit in overlook parking areas.

This is a hiker's park. From parking space to an overlook is a short walk. Once there, it's tempting to stroll along the rim. The trails below the rim look inviting. Many people join ranger-led hikes. The more adventurous can shoulder packs and spend a night or two below the rim.

Bryce Canyon isn't a canyon but numbers of great amphitheaters cut into the E edge of the Paunsaugunt Plateau. Erosion has carved the pink and white limestone down to badlands a thousand feet below.

Elevation at the visitor center is 7,915 ft. Highest point in the Park is 9,105 ft. at Rainbow Point. The valley is at about 6,600 ft.

Indians, the first white visitors (in the 19th century), and many since have sought to describe the formations: "sentinels on the walls of castles, monks and priests in their robes, cathedrals and congregations . . ." ". . . walls and windows, minarets, gables, pagodas and pedestals, temples, and even 'platoons of Turkish soldiers in pantaloons.' " ". . . rampantly Gothic . . . world of monsters and grotesque beasts which fill the capitals, grin from gargoyles and corbels, and look across the parapets . . ." ". . . lions couchant, gargoyles, dragons, idols and heathen gods, limboes and purgatories and torture chambers, nave and architrave, pagoda and pantheon and mosque." A pioneer cattleman, Ebenezer Bryce, after whom the park is named, summed up: "It's a hell of a place to lose a cow."

The colors are dramatic and ever changing, predominantly red, pink, and cream, but with shades of yellow, orange, green, violet, and purple appearing in early morning and late afternoon light. Winter snow accents the display.

From the visitor center the main Park road runs S for 17 mi. to Rainbow Point, back from the rim. Spurs lead to parking areas at Sunset Point, Inspiration Point, Bryce Point, and Paria View. A spur to Fairyland View is near the Park entrance, before the visitor center.

SR 12 crosses the N end of the Park and turns S. About 4 mi. beyond the Park boundary is the small town of Tropic. From Tropic, a dirt road runs W on the valley floor about 3 mi. to the Park and the Navajo Loop Trail leading to the rim.

Some parking areas are trailheads. Trails below the rim and down into the badlands offer opportunities for both day hiking and backpacking.

The Park is open all year, although cars may need snow tires or even chains in winter. Spring and fall temperatures are pleasant; in summer, the average maximum temperature is only 80°F, and nights are cool. In Dec.–Feb. the average minimum is 10–11°F, with days in the 30s and 40s. Annual precipitation is 18–22 in., annual snowfall about 120 in. Roads to all major viewpoints near the visitor center are kept open in winter.

Plants: Several plant communities: big sagebrush on the valley floor, pinyon-juniper below the rim up to about 6,900 ft. elevation. A ponderosa forest surrounds the visitor center and campground, including greenleaf manzanita, Rocky Mountain juniper, and antelope bitterbrush. As the land rises southward toward Rainbow Point, composition changes to spruce-fir. Small stands of bristlecone pine.

Wildflower displays include sego lily, star lily, ceanothus, antelope bitterbrush, arrowleaf balsamroot, yarrow, bush cinquefoil, wax currant, yellow evening primrose, wild iris, Indian paintbrush, penstemon, wallflower, twin-pod, Oregon grape, wild rose, blue columbine, Arizona thistle, scarlet gilia, aster, clematis, blue flax, rabbitbrush, goldenrod, gumweed, senecio. Peak blooming season: May–July.

Birds: 172 species recorded. Checklist available gives habitat, seasonality, rarity. Seasonally common species include common nighthawk, white-throated swift; black-chinned, broad-tailed, and rufous hummingbirds; northern flicker, western wood-pewee, horned lark, violet-green swallow, Steller's jay, common raven, mountain chickadee; white-breasted, red-breasted, and pygmy nuthatches; robin, Brewer's blackbird, vesper and chipping sparrows. Best birding season: May–July.

Mammals: Checklist of 48 species available gives habitat, seasonality, rarity. Common species include long-legged and small-footed myotis, big brown bat, striped skunk, badger, gray fox, mountain lion, bobcat, yellowbelly marmot; golden-mantled ground squirrel; red and rock squirrels; Colorado chipmunk, northern pocket gopher, beaver, deer mouse, Utah whitetail prairie dog, coyote, mule deer.

Reptiles and amphibians: 15 species recorded. Checklist available gives habitat, rarity. Common species include tiger salamander; northern sagebrush, side-blotched, tree, and mountain short-horned lizards; striped whipsnake, Great Basin rattlesnake, Rocky Mountain toad, Great Basin spadefoot, leopard frog.

FEATURES

Fairyland Point is the first overlook, 1 mi. off the main road, just inside the Park boundary. Fairyland-Tower Bridge loop trail, 8 mi., strenuous. Rim Trail, 5.5 mi. one way, begins here; easier going.

Sunrise Point is 1 mi. from the visitor center. Trail to Queen's Garden, 1.5 mi. round trip, is the least strenuous route below the rim. Other trails to Tower Bridge and along the rim.

Sunset Point is trailhead for the 1.5 mi. Navajo Loop, moderately strenuous. It can be combined with a visit to Queen's Garden.

Inspiration Point is near the beginning of a spur road to *Bryce Point* and *Paria View.* Several trails from Bryce Point, including the 22-mi. Under-the-Rim Trail to Rainbow Point.

Rainbow Point, at the end of the road, highest point in the Park, offers a sweeping view of the entire area.

INTERPRETATION

Visitor center has exhibits, slide program, literature, information. Open daily, 8 A.M.–5 P.M. Dec.–Mar., 8 A.M.–8 P.M. June–Sept.; hours adjusted to needs.

Campfire programs: One or two per night, June–Sept.

Guided hikes: Several each day, June–Sept. Announced at visitor center.

Naturalists: At least one all year, 4 or 5 May–Sept.

The concessioner may offer tram tours.

ACTIVITIES

Camping: 2 campgrounds; 230 sites. North Campground open all year, weather permitting. If campgrounds are full, sites can be found in the adjoining National Forest or commercial campgrounds.

Hiking, backpacking: About 60 mi. of trails. Longest is 22 mi., with campsites along the way. Shorter trails interconnect. Permit required for overnight trips. Overuse is not yet a problem; permits are not rationed. Trails below the rim may be closed by snow in winter.

Horse riding: Limited to guided 2- or 3-hour trips offered by the concessioner.

PUBLICATIONS

Leaflet with map.

Information pages:

Descriptions of hiking trails.

Hiking trail map.

Descriptions of backpacking trails; map.

Backcountry trail information.

Weather.

Species checklists.

The Geology of Bryce Canyon. $1.99.

Living Color—Wildflower Communities of Bryce Canyon and Cedar Breaks. $1.95.

REFERENCES

Hall, Dave. *The Hiker's Guide to Utah.* Billings, MT: Falcon Press, 1982. Pp. 144–148.

Bezy, John. *Bryce Canyon: The Story Behind the Scenery.* Las Vegas, NV: KC Publications, 1980.

Yandell, Michael, ed. *National Parkways—Zion and Bryce Canyon.* Casper, WY: World-Wide Research and Publishing, 1972.

Stroud, Tully. *The Bryce Canyon Auto and Hiking Guide.* Bryce Canyon, UT: Bryce Canyon Natural History Association, 1983.

HEADQUARTERS: Bryce Canyon, UT 84717; (801) 834-5322.

BUTLER WASH

U.S. Bureau of Land Management

30,000 acres.

The Needles District of Canyonlands National Park is on the N and E; Manti-La Sal National Forest on the S; Dark Canyon Primitive Area on the SW. High-clearance access only, from the National Forest or SW from SR 211. (MP #1.)

An isolated area, far from a paved road. Most visitors who come this way go to the Dark Canyon Primitive Area (see entry) or take the foot trail N into The Needles District, passing several natural arches.

The land adjoining The Needles is similarly rugged and colorful, with banded sandstone spires and pinnacles, canyons dropping 800 ft. in 1 1/2 mi. The W and N portion of the area has open parks and wide, flat drainages separated by buttes up to 750 ft. high. Vegetation is sparse, pinyon-juniper in higher areas, sage and grasses in the parks and wash bottoms. Streams are intermittent; no springs are mapped.

Hiking opportunities include several forks of Salt Creek, or following Butler Wash and side canyons among the buttes. Cliff dwelling ruins are nearby.

HEADQUARTERS: BLM, Moab District Office, 125 West Second South Main, Moab, UT 84532; (801) 259-6111.

CANAAN MOUNTAIN
U.S. Bureau of Land Management
62,710 acres in UT, 6,482 acres in AZ.

Between Zion National Park and the AZ border. Trail access S from Rockville or E from Colorado City-Hilldale and SR 59 just N of the border. (MP #5.)

A large irregular plateau capped by massive exposures of Navajo sandstone, the slickrock surface extremely rough and broken. Canyons penetrating the plateau are generally deep and narrow, with dense vegetation. On top of the plateau: ponderosa forest, a small pond, evidence of historic cable logging operation, splendid views into Zion NP and S to the Grand Canyon. Large natural arch in Water Canyon. The Vermillion Cliffs are the effective SW boundary of the area, roughly parallel to SR 59, rising to about 6,500 ft. Highest elevation of Canaan Mountain, in the central portion, is about 7,400 ft. The site is roadless.

Backpacking: A BLM staff member called this one of the better areas for backpacking. Another called it an "incredible area." The two developed trailheads are Eagle Crag, out of Rockville, and Water Canyon, just N of the AZ border. The N–S hike takes about 2 days. Hiking season is usually Mar.–Nov., depending on snow.

HEADQUARTERS: BLM, Cedar City District, 1579 North Main, Cedar City, UT 84720; (801) 586-2401.

CANYONLANDS NATIONAL PARK
National Park Service
337,559 acres.

> Automobile access to two areas: (A) Island in the Sky. From Moab, 13 mi. NW on US 163; 26 mi. SW and S on SR 313. (MP #2.) (B) The Needles. From Monticello, 15 mi. N on US 163; 36 mi. W and NW on SR 211. (MP #3.) 4-wheel-drive access to two principal areas: White Rim, below Island in the Sky, and The Maze, in the SW sector. The Maze itself is restricted to foot travel. Other jeep roads penetrate the Park. Check road conditions and bring a good map.

A primitive National Park. The two principal entrance roads are unpaved and often rough. Most of the area is accessible only on foot or by 4-wheel-drive vehicle. Don't expect fancy visitor centers, restaurants, campgrounds with hot showers. It's wild, colorful, magnificent, glorious.

The Park is about 39 mi. N–S, 12 to 24 mi. W–E. The Colorado River enters on the NE, the Green River on the NW, both in great twisting canyons, converging. The V-shaped area between them is Island in the Sky. They meet somewhat below the midpoint of the Park, and the Colorado then flows SW. The Needles is SE of the confluence, The Maze on the W.

From the 6,000-ft. elevation at Island in the Sky, the land drops in two giant steps: 1,000 ft. to White Rim, a wide bench with foot and jeep trails, then another 1,000 ft. to the Colorado River. Highest point is 6,987 ft. at Cedar Mesa in the extreme SE. (Utah has more than one "Cedar Mesa.") Lowest is 3,720 ft., where the river leaves the Park. Rivers cut the canyons through layers of red, orange, brown, tan, yellow, and white sandstone and limestone. Weathering has carved the rock into spires, needles, castles, arches, fins, buttes. At the crests are balancing rocks and shapes suggesting human and animal figures.

At Island in the Sky, average temperatures range between 19°F in winter to 90°F in summer; The Needles District can be a few degrees colder in winter, warmer in summer. Annual precipitation is 8–9 inches; July–Oct. is the wettest season. Annual snowfall is less than 2 ft. Fall and spring are probably the best seasons, but the Park can be enjoyed at any time.

A visit should begin at Dead Horse Point State Park (see entry, Zone 2), which serves as a visitor center, with exhibits, films, literature, naturalists. The views from here are unexcelled, and the State Park has a good campground.

Plants: No plant checklist available; no response to our questionnaire. Sparse desert vegetation, much the same as in Arches National Park (Zone 2) and Natural Bridges National Monument (Zone 3), both of which have plant lists.

Birds: Checklist available, based on limited observation; visitors are asked to report sightings. Seasonally common: snowy egret, mallard, green-winged and cinnamon teals, ruddy duck, red-breasted merganser; sharp-shinned, Cooper's, red-tailed, and Swainson's hawks; golden eagle, northern harrier, American kestrel, killdeer, black-bellied plover, common snipe, spotted sandpiper, greater and lesser yellowlegs, least sandpiper, long-billed dowitcher, American avocet, Wilson's phalarope, Franklin's gull, mourning dove, great horned and long-eared owls, common nighthawk, poor-will, white-throated swift; black-chinned, broad-tailed, and rufous hummingbirds; belted kingfisher, northern flicker, yellow-bellied sapsucker, hairy woodpecker, horned lark, western kingbird, ash-throated and western flycatchers, Say's phoebe, violet-green swallow; Steller's, scrub, and pinyon jays; black-billed magpie, common raven, American crow, Clark's nutcracker, black-capped and mountain chickadees, plain titmouse, bushtit; white-breasted, red-breasted, and pygmy nuthatches; house, canyon, and rock wrens; sage thrasher, robin, western and mountain bluebirds, Townsend's solitaire, blue-gray gnatcatcher, ruby-crowned kinglet, water pipit, loggerhead shrike. Warblers: orange-crowned, Virginia's, yellow, yellow-rumped, black-throated gray, Wilson's. Western meadowlark; yellow-headed, red-winged, and Brewer's blackbirds; northern oriole, brown-headed cowbird, western tanager, black-headed and evening grosbeaks; Cassin's, house, and gray-crowned rosy finches; pine siskin, American and lesser goldfinches, green-tailed and rufous-sided towhees. Sparrows: vesper, lark, chipping, Brewer's, white-crowned, song. Dark-eyed and gray-headed juncos.

Mammals: Checklist available. Bats: Yuma, hairy-winged, and small-footed myotis; western pipistrel, Townsend's and Allen's big-eared, pallid. Blacktail jackrabbit, desert and Nuttall's cottontails, Colorado chipmunk, rock squirrel, whitetail antelope squirrel, valley pocket gopher, Apache and Great Basin pocket mice. Other mice: western harvest, canyon, deer, brush, pinyon. Northern grasshopper mouse, Ord's kangaroo rat; white-throated, Mexican, desert, and bushy-tailed woodrats; beaver, porcupine, gray fox, coyote, badger, bobcat, mule deer, pronghorn, bighorn sheep. Checklist includes other species presumed present.

Reptiles and amphibians: Checklist available. Tiger salamander; red spotted, western spadefoot, and Woodhouse's toads; leopard frog, bullfrog. Lizards: collared, leopard, short-horned, sagebrush, desert spiny, eastern fence, tree, side-blotched, western whiptail. Racer, desert striped whipsnake, gopher snake; common, black-necked, and western garter snakes; midget faded rattlesnake.

FEATURES

Island in the Sky is a Y-shaped area 2,000 ft. above the Green and Colorado Rivers. A small Ranger Station is near the entrance. Just beyond is The Neck, a narrow strip that is the only vehicle access to the mesa. The road extends 13 mi. to Grand View Point. Along the way are many short trails and viewpoints overlooking the two river canyons. At the junction of the Y, a dead-end road leads about 5 mi. NW to Upheaval Dome. Near the junction is a small primitive campground at the Green River Overlook.

White Rim is a wide bench about 1,000 ft. below Island in the Sky, 1,000 ft. above the two rivers. The 4-wheel-drive trail can be driven in a day, but most visitors prefer to camp for at least one night. The route is rough, steep in places, with some stretches of soft sand. Some visitors hike. Access is from the end of SR 279, the scenic drive along the Colorado River from near Moab, or from Island in the Sky via the Shafer Trail.

Shafer Trail descends from Island in the Sky, about 1 mi. beyond the Ranger Station, to White Rim, connecting with SR 279. At times a standard auto can descend—or climb—this route, but only experienced mountain drivers should attempt it, and only after checking road conditions. When wet, it can be hazardous even for a 4-wheel-drive vehicle.

The Needles District, named for the many spires in the area, is E of the Colorado River canyon. This is the second area visitors can enter by car, through 30 mi. of scenic canyon country. Beyond Elephant Hill, a 40% grade, travel is on foot or by 4-wheel-drive vehicle.

The Maze is W of the rivers. Park literature warns, "Travel to the Maze Overlook, Horseshoe Canyon, and the Land of the Standing Rocks can provide a severe test for even the best four-wheel-drive vehicle." Most of this area is roadless, accessible only on foot.

Horseshoe Canyon includes a disjunct part of the Park. See separate entry in Zone 3.

ADJACENT

Newspaper Rock State Historical Monument. SR 211, from US 163 to The Needles area, passes through Indian Creek Canyon, scenic, green with riparian vegetation, many petroglyphs and pictographs. The best are on Newspaper Rock, 11 mi. from US 163, a smooth face protected by an overhang. The 10-acre site has a nature trail with plant identification guide and a small campground.

Orange Cliffs district of Glen Canyon National Recreation Area (see entry) is on the W boundary. This area is roadless except for jeep trails. Most other adjacent land is public domain, administered by the Bureau of Land Management. Nearby, on the S, are the Dark Canyon Primitive Area and wilderness areas of the Manti-La Sal National Forest (see entries).

ACTIVITIES

Camping: 12 sites at Green River Overlook, Island in the Sky; 27 at Squaw Flat, The Needles. Both primitive. No water. These are the only campgrounds accessible by car. Numerous backcountry sites.

Hiking, backpacking. Spring and autumn are the best seasons. Check with Ranger for best routes and destinations. Carry ample water, compass, topo map.

Horse riding: Outfitters in Green River offer horse pack trips.

Boating: Outfitters in Moab offer power boat and canoe rentals, tours, and pickup service in the river canyons.

Pets are not allowed on trails.

PUBLICATIONS

Park leaflet with map.

Island in the Sky. Folder with map.

Guide to the White Rim Trail. Folder with map.

The Needles District. Information page, map.

The Maze District. Map.

Upheaval Dome. Folder.

Checklists: Birds, mammals, reptiles and amphibians.

Information pages:

Outfitters and tour operators: vehicle, horse, boat.

Vehicle rental agencies.

REFERENCES

Barnes, F. A. *Canyon Country Hiking and Natural History.* Salt Lake City: Wasatch, 1977. Pp. 48, 122–125, 130–133.

Hall, Dave. *The Hiker's Guide to Utah.* Billings, MT: Falcon Press, 1982. Pp. 168–171.

Barnes, F. A. *Canyon Country Exploring.* Salt Lake City: Wasatch, 1979.

Barnes, F. A. *Canyon Country Geology for the Layman and Rockhound.* Salt Lake City: Wasatch, 1979.

Belknap, Bill and Buzz. *Canyonlands River Guide.* Boulder City, NV: Westwater Books, 1980.

Barnes, F. A. *Canyon Country Off-Road Vehicle Trails; Canyon Rims & Needles Areas.* Salt Lake City: Wasatch, 1978.

Huser, Verne. *Canyon Country Paddles.* Salt Lake City: Wasatch, 1977.

Mutschler, F. E. *River Runners Guide to the Canyons of the Green and the Colorado.* Denver: Powell Society, 1977.

Rigby, J. Keith, W. Kenneth Hamlin, Ray Matheny, and Stanley L. Welsh, *Guidebook to the Colorado River.* Part 3: *Moab to Hite through Canyonlands National Park.* Boulder, NV: Westwater Books, 1982.

HEADQUARTERS: 446 S. Main St., Moab, UT 84532; (801) 259-7164.

CAPITOL REEF NATIONAL PARK
National Park Service
222,753 acres; 241,904 acres within boundaries.

From Hanksville on SR 95, W 39 mi. on SR 24. (MP #1,#2.)

The Park is about 70 mi. long, mostly less than 5 mi. wide, about 12 mi. wide at the N end where SR 24 crosses. The reef, Waterpocket Fold, is a 100-mi.-long uplifted cliff, named "waterpocket" for the many shallow depressions that hold rainwater for long periods. The crest of the fold rises about 2,000 ft. above the desert floor. Streams have carved gorges through the fold, sometimes less than 50 ft. apart.

The multicolored sandstone layers have been eroded into pinnacles, buttes, castles, canyons, arches, and other shapes. The banded colors are exceptionally bright and varied. The term *capitol* refers to rounded domes of light-colored sandstone that suggest capitol buildings. Capitol Dome and many other impressive formations are near SR 24.

The Waterpocket Fold was almost inaccessible until SR 24 was completed in 1962, although 37,000 acres had been proclaimed a National Monument in 1937. Several additions were made, and the enlarged area became a National Park in 1971. By 1981 annual visitation was about 400,000, and the limited visitor facilities were overtaxed. A 1982 Environmental Impact Statement reviewed the problems and considered alternatives ranging from no action to parkwide development.

Most facilities are in the Headquarters District, where SR 24 crosses the Park. South and North Districts have few visitor facilities, and access is by dirt roads. Only 2% of visitors drive to the South District, 1% to the North District. The average duration of visits is just under one day.

Elevation at the visitor center is 5,418 ft. Summer daytime temperatures here are in the 80s and 90s; nights are generally cool. Spring and autumn temperatures are mild. In winter, average daytime highs are 40 to 56°F, lows from 18 to 29°F. Annual precipitation is about 7 in. Summer storms may cause flash floods. Snowfall is generally light.

Plants: The Fremont Valley, route of SR 24, is green with riparian vegetation. Elsewhere desert conditions prevail. Yet over 600 plant species have been identified in or near the Park. Checklist shows all known species in Capitol Reef. A list of commonly observed plants is also available, classified by flower type and color. Flowering begins in late Feb. or early Mar. with thin-leaf alder, silver-leafed buffaloberry, pussywillow. Next come purple and white locoweed along roadsides, with buffaloberry in mid-Mar., squawbush and hopsage following. Many more blooms appear in late Mar. and early Apr., including river willows, dandelion, barrel cactus. The last half of Apr. sees mulberry, dogwood, yellow pea, sunflower, orange mallow, and evening primrose in bloom.

May flowers include trefoil clover, wild rose, black locust, tamarisk, flea-bane, yellow clover, serviceberry, mountain-mahogany, prince's plume, Mormon tea, prickly pear, scarlet gilia, rimrock daisy. Summer blooms include virgin's bower, buckwheatbrush, rabbitbrush, snakeweed, desert trumpet, Indian paintbrush, aster.

Birds: Checklist available. Year-round residents include American kestrel, chukar, northern flicker, horned lark, scrub and pinyon jays, common raven, canyon and rock wrens, American robin, song sparrow. Seasonally common species include mourning dove, common nighthawk, white-throated swift, black-chinned hummingbird, western kingbird, ash-throated flycatcher, Say's phoebe, violet-green swallow, blue-gray gnatcatcher, ruby-crowned kinglet, yellow-rumped and Wilson's warblers, red-winged blackbird, northern oriole, black-headed grosbeak, lazuli bunting, green-tailed towhee; black-throated, chipping, and white-crowned sparrows; dark-eyed junco.

Mammals: Checklist available. Species identified within or very near the Park include gray shrews, long-legged and small-footed myotis, western pipistrel, western big-eared and pallid bats, black bear, ringtail, shorttail weasel, mink, badger, spotted and striped skunks, coyote, red fox, mountain lion, bobcat, yellowbelly marmot, rock squirrel, golden-mantled ground squirrel, whitetail antelope squirrel, Colorado chipmunk, valley pocket gopher, Ord's kangaroo rat, beaver. Mice: western harvest, canyon, deer, northern grass-hopper. Desert woodrat, muskrat, porcupine, blacktail jackrabbit, desert cottontail, mule deer. Visitors are asked to report sightings.

Reptiles and amphibians: Checklists available. Include lizards: collared, leopard, desert spiny, northern plateau, sagebrush, side-blotched, tree, short-horned, chuckwalla, desert night lizard, Great Basin whiptail lizard. Striped whipsnake, Great Basin gopher snake, California kingsnake, wandering garter snake, western rattlesnake. Also tiger salamander, Rocky Mountain toad, canyon treefrog, leopard frog.

FEATURES

Headquarters District: The visitor center and principal campground are on SR 24. No food, gasoline, or lodgings are available within the Park. SR 24 is a fine scenic drive with many viewpoints. Entering from the E, it follows the Fremont River through a green valley where settlers planted many fruit trees. An unpaved but well-kept scenic drive extends about 10 mi. to the S. W of the visitor center, SR 24 passes through an area of impressive, colorful formations known as Torrey Breaks, which extends some distance beyond the Park boundary.

Cathedral Valley is in the North District. This scenic area is accessible only by high-clearance vehicles.

South District. To reach the S half of the Park, one must drive S from SR 24 on a road outside the Park, paralleling its E boundary, reentering at the midpoint. Cedar Mesa Campground, with 5 sites, is 24 mi. S of this entrance (no water). This district is favored by backpackers and backcountry day hikers.

ACTIVITIES

Camping: The main campground in the central area has 53 sites. Car camping is permitted only here and at the primitive campground in the South District. Because these sites are often full, the visitor center has a list of National Forest campgrounds and private facilities 20 to 50 mi. away.

Hiking, backpacking: Many day hiking opportunities on maintained trails in and near the HQ area. Consult a Ranger at the visitor center about backpacking permits, routes, and destinations in Cathedral Valley and the South District.

PUBLICATIONS

Leaflet with map.
Information pages
> *A Geologic Tour.*
> *Climate.*
> *Brief History.*
> *Lower Muley Twist Canyon.*
> *Upper Muley Twist Canyon.*
> *Some Common Plants of Capitol Reef.*
> *Seasonal Plant Blooming.*
> Checklists: birds, mammals, reptiles and amphibians, fishes, plants, cacti.
> *Access at Capitol Reef National Park* (facilities for visitors with impairments).
> *Story of Fruita and the Orchards.*
> Rock climbing policy and information.
> *Backpacking and hiking.*
> *Capitol Reef Trails* (central area).
Publications List from Capitol Reef Natural History Association.
The Hickman Natural Bridge Trail. Pamphlet. $0.25.
This Ancient Rock: A Guide to the Scenic Drive. $1.00.

REFERENCES

Hall, Dave. *The Hiker's Guide to Utah.* Billings, MT: Falcon Press, 1982. Pp. 154–157.

Olson, Virgil J., with David Muench. *Capitol Reef, the Story Behind the Scenery.* Las Vegas, NV: KC Publications, 1972.

Roylance, Ward J. *Seeing Capitol Reef National Park: A Guide to the Roads and Trails.* Salt Lake City: Wasatch, 1979.

HEADQUARTERS: National Park Service, Torrey, UT 84775; (801) 425-3871.

CEDAR BREAKS NATIONAL MONUMENT
National Park Service
6,155 acres.

From Cedar City, 18 mi. E on SR 14, then N on SR 143.

The Monument is about 4 mi. N–S, less than 3 mi. W–E. The 5-mi. Rim Drive winds along the E side at about 10,400 ft. elevation. Near the drive is the rim, overlooking a gigantic amphitheater, walls dropping over 2,000 ft. to the valley below. The erosion that cut this deep canyon in the Markagunt Plateau shaped canyons, ramparts, ledges, knife-sharp ridges, and bizarre sculptured shapes. Colors are white and shades of red and yellow, glowing in early morning and late afternoon sunlight.

The plateau is green, with forest and meadows, streams and lakes. Annual precipitation here is over 30 in., snowfall almost 260 in. From the rim one looks down on much drier badlands. ("Breaks" was a settlers' term for badlands. Settlers called the trees "cedars"; botanists call them "junipers.") The Monument is surrounded by the Dixie National Forest.

Along Rim Drive are overlooks. The longest trail within the Monument is 4 mi., with no trail from the rim to the bottom. Most visitors will find a half-day here sufficient, but it's a memorable half-day, not to be missed.

Plants: The plateau has fine stands of ponderosa pine, Douglas-fir, subalpine fir, and Engelmann spruce. Aspen and mountain maple provide brilliant fall colors. Small stands of bristlecone pine grow along the rim, one specimen more than 1,600 years old. Also found in the Monument: Colorado blue spruce, limber pine, white fir, juniper, lanceleaf cottonwood, willow.

The wildflower display begins as snow melts and peaks during July and early Aug. Flowering species include: red elderberry, gooseberry currant, Utah bush honeysuckle, Whipple and scarlet penstemons, yellow monkeyflower, Indian paintbrush, elephant head, butter-and-eggs, Parry primrose, western shootingstar, gentians, phlox, scarlet gilia, phacelia, geraniums, yellow evening primrose, lupines, locoweed, western wallflower, heartleaf arnica, blue daisy, mountain sunflower, goldenrods, coneflower, western yarrow, cinquefoils, serviceberry, desert globemallow, saxifrage, blue flax, pussytoes, asters, mariposa lily, wild iris, orchids, eriogonum, columbine, anemone, larkspur.

Birds: Checklist of 89 species available. Common species include golden eagle, Swainson's hawk, American kestrel, blue grouse, white-throated swift, broad-tailed and rufous hummingbirds, common flicker, hairy woodpecker, olive-sided flycatcher, horned lark, violet-green swallow, gray jay, common raven, Clark's nutcracker, mountain chickadee, brown creeper, dipper, canyon and rock wrens, robin, hermit and Swainson's thrushes, mountain bluebird, golden-crowned and ruby-crowned kinglets, water pipit; orange-crowned, MacGillivray's, and yellow-rumped warblers; western tanager, pine grosbeak, Cassin's finch, red crossbill, green-tailed towhee; vesper, fox, and white-crowned sparrows; Oregon and gray-headed juncos.

Mammals: Checklist available. Includes dusky and northern water shrews; little brown, big brown, and western big-eared bats; black bear, longtail weasel, striped and spotted skunks, badger, red and gray foxes, coyote, mountain lion, bobcat, yellowbelly marmot, golden-mantled and red squirrels, Colorado chipmunk, northern and valley pocket gophers, Great Basin pocket mouse; pinyon, western harvest, canyon, house, and deer mice; Norway rat, longtail and mountain voles, bushytail woodrat, porcupine, pika, whitetail jackrabbit, mule deer, elk.

FEATURES

Rim Drive, 5 mi. through forest and wildflower fields. Four major overlooks.

Wasatch Ramparts Trail: 2 mi. along the rim from Point Supreme. Stand of bristlecone pine on Spectra Point.

Alpine Pond Trail: Short walk to a pond between Rim Drive and the canyon rim. Wildflowers surround.

Bristlecone Pine Trail: Short walk from the Chessman Ridge overlook.

INTERPRETATION

Visitor center has exhibits, films, talks, literature. Open 8 A.M.–6 P.M. daily, June 1–Sept. 30, longer if weather permits.

Nature trail, 4 mi., at Alpine Pond.

Campfire programs every evening in season.

Guided hikes twice daily in season.

ACTIVITIES

Camping: 30 sites. June 15–Sept. 5.

Ski touring: Entire park open.

Snowmobiling: Limited to 6 mi. of unplowed roads.

Travel season extends from early June to late Oct., depending on weather. Check road conditions before planning a visit at other times.

Visitors on skis or snowmobiles may enter the Monument in winter, subject to park rules.

No gasoline or other services are available.

PUBLICATIONS

Leaflet with map.

Alpine Pond. $0.25.

Buchanan, Hayle. *Living Color—Wildflower Communities of Bryce Canyon and Cedar Breaks.* Bryce Canyon, UT: Bryce Canyon Natural History Association. $2.25.

Gilchrist, Beth. *Views of Cedar Breaks.* Springdale, UT: Zion Natural History Association. $1.50.

Plant and animal checklists.

HEADQUARTERS: Box 749, Cedar City, UT 84720; (801) 586-9451.

CORAL PINK SAND DUNES
Utah State Division of Parks and Recreation
3,730 acres.

From Kanab, 13 mi. NW on US 89, then 11 mi. S on paved road. (MP #5.)

Wind-swept basin with about 2,000 acres of dunes of fine coral-pink sand washed and blown from nearby formations. Dunes have scattered vegetation and some large trees. Many wildflowers. Area has been used as a film location.

ORV's are allowed on the dunes but must avoid vegetation.

Average daytime summer temperature: 95°F, nights 55°. Winter temperatures range from 55° by day to below zero at night.

ADJACENT: Moquith Mountains (see entry).

Camping: 22 sites. All year, but water is cut off late Oct.–Easter. Reservations are accepted.

PUBLICATION: Information page.

HEADQUARTERS: P.O. Box 95, Kanab, UT 84741; (801) 874-2408.

DARK CANYON PRIMITIVE AREA
U.S. Bureau of Land Management
49,900 acres.

The Primitive Area is an irregularly shaped block about 16 mi. square, a NW–SE strip excluded from roadless status because of established jeep tracks. Most hiking trails begin in Manti-La Sal National Forest, La Sal Division (see entry), where the upper portion of Dark Canyon and Woodenshoe Canyon are a proposed 50,000-acre wilderness. Most trailheads are inaccessible before June 1 in most years. BLM says route should be checked before spring or fall hike. (MP #1.)

A huge, impressive, wilderness canyon system, isolated, with minor signs of human activity. Except for a few places, foot travel is not difficult. Although some people have used horses in the upper canyon, most is negotiable only on foot.

Dark Canyon has many tributaries, including Black Steer Canyon, Youngs Canyon, Bowdie Canyon, Gypsum Canyon, Lost Canyon, Lean-to Canyon, and Fable Valley. On the N, the Primitive Area adjoins the 105,980-acre Maze wilderness area of Canyonlands National Park. On the W and NW is a wilderness area of Glen Canyon National Recreation Area. More BLM-administered land, Lower Horse Flats, is on the S.

Amateur geologists will find great diversity: the mixed hues of the Cutler Formation above; the stream flowing down stair-step sandstones, shales, and gray limestones, with steep benches and slopes. Small oil seeps occur in the fossil-bearing layer. Still lower are cherty limestones, shales, and sandstones. Most visitors will just enjoy the splendid scenery, and photographers will wish for more film.

The upper reaches of the main canyon are wide, with many large open clearings. In the Primitive Area, the canyon walls become higher and higher, up to 1,400 ft. Water is scarce in the upper Dark Canyon and Woodenshoe Canyon. The *Hikers' Guide to Utah* (Hall, 1982) identifies springs that may flow in dry weather but cautions hikers to carry an ample supply. Water becomes more abundant in the Primitive Area, and about 2 mi. below Black Steer Canyon the stream becomes perennial, with clear, flowing water and deep plunge pools. Water should be treated before drinking.

In all such canyons, flash floods are a serious hazard. Warm-weather storms come quickly, and runoff is rapid. Hikers should camp well above high-water marks.

Plants: Generally the area is sage or blackbrush ecosystem. Ponderosa pine and Douglas-fir are common in the upper canyon, giving way to pinyon-juniper and cottonwood in the Primitive Area.

Birds: No checklist available. Hikers' guide mentions common raven, chickadee, golden eagle, dipper, northern flicker, pinyon jay, red-tailed hawk, black-billed magpie, grouse, white-crowned sparrow.

Mammals: Mentioned are black bear, bobcat, mountain lion, coyote, ring-tail, beaver, fox, cottontail, mule deer, bighorn sheep.

Backpacking: Not the place for a short day hike. Access routes are so long that only trips of several days should be considered. Permits are required, obtainable from either HQ office. An undeveloped trail, lying mostly in the canyon bottom, connects Sundance and Lake Powell.

Although most trails are easy, the hikers' guide describes two difficult places, where hikers must climb high over talus; not recommended for people who fear heights or for small children. It also warns that rescue operations here are slow. If a hiker broke a leg, it might be two days before rescuers arrived, and the victim would have to be carried out by hand.

Check trail conditions before entering. Carry topo map, water.

PUBLICATION: Hikers' guide with maps.

REFERENCES
Hall, Dave. *A Hiker's Guide to Utah.* Billings, MT: Falcon Press, 1982. Pp. 171–174.
Barnes, F. A. *Canyon Country Hiking and Natural History.* Salt Lake City: Wasatch, 1977. Pp. 141–143.

HEADQUARTERS: BLM, San Juan Resource Area, Box 7, Monticello, UT 84535; (801) 587-2201. Manti-La Sal National Forest, Monticello Ranger District, 185 N. 100 E., Monticello, UT 84535; (801) 587-2114.

DEAD HORSE POINT STATE PARK
Utah State Division of Parks and Recreation
7,000 acres.

From US 163 NW of Moab, take SR 313 W and S for 16 mi. Where road continues into Canyonlands National Park, turn left, keeping on paved road, 8 mi. (MP #2.)

Many visitors think the State Park has the best of it. The road into the National Park's Island in the Sky is rough, and visitor facilities are minimal. The State Park has a fine visitor center and campground, and the views of the Colorado River 2,000 ft. below couldn't be better.

The Point is a high desert promontory. Its narrow neck made it a natural corral; legend has it that a group of mustangs died here. The overlooks give visitors spectacular views of the canyon, mesas, pinnacles, and buttes, the distinctive layers representing 150 million years of geological history.

The highest point is about 6,000 ft. elevation. Annual precipitation is little more than 8 in., most of this winter snow. Daily summer temperatures often exceed 90°F, dropping as low as 40° at night. Spring and autumn weather is excellent, and the peak visitor months are May, June, and Sept. The Park is open all year.

Hiking opportunities within the Park are limited to the trail along the rim. The Shafer Trail can be seen below the Point, but access is from the National Park.

Include the National Park in your visit, by all means, but the State Park offers great views, a fine interpretive program, and comfortable camping.

Plants: About 40% of the site is pinyon-juniper woodland, understory including cliffrose, alderleaf mountain-mahogany, blackbrush, rabbitbrush, big sagebrush. Flowering species include prince's plume, globemallow, prickly pear cactus, locoweed, primrose, sego lily, Indian paintbrush, sand verbena, Utah penstemon, lupine, fleabane daisy, longleaf phlox, larkspur, aster.

Birds: Checklist of 48 species. Includes bald and golden eagles, red-tailed and sharp-shinned hawks, northern harrier, American kestrel, common barn-owl; great horned, long-eared, and burrowing owls; poor-will, white-throated swift, broad-tailed hummingbird; gray, ash-throated, and willow flycatchers; Say's phoebe, horned lark, violet-green swallow, pinyon and scrub jays, black-billed magpie, common raven, common bushtit, canyon wren. Also robin, blue-gray gnatcatcher, loggerhead shrike, gray vireo. Warblers: black-throated gray, yellow, yellow-breasted chat. House finch, rufous-sided towhee; vesper, lark, black-throated, and chipping sparrows; Brewer's blackbird, northern flicker.

Mammals: Checklist of 38 species. Bats: western big-eared, Brazilian free-tailed, spotted, silver-haired, hoary, big brown, western pipistrel, mouse-eared, pallid. Mice: deer, canyon, brush, pinyon. Apache pocket mouse, bushytail and desert woodrats, Ord kangaroo rat, valley pocket gopher, beaver, porcupine. Also mountain lion, bobcat, red and gray foxes, ringtail, coyote, longtail weasel, spotted and striped skunks, badger, bighorn sheep, mule deer.

View of desert bighorn sheep rutting ground, in winter.

Reptiles and amphibians: Lizards: collared, leopard, short-horned, sagebrush, spiny, eastern fence, tree, side-blotched, western whiptail. Racer, spotted night snake, milk snake, common and striped whipsnakes, gopher snake; common, black-necked, and western garter snakes; midget faded rattlesnake.

Other fauna: Fairy and tadpole shrimp appear in potholes where rainwater collects after summer thunderstorms.

INTERPRETATION

Visitor center has exhibits, films, talks, literature. Open 8 A.M.–7 P.M. May–Sept., 9 A.M.–5 P.M. Oct.–Apr.

Nature trail at visitor center.

Campfire programs, guided hikes Apr.–Oct.

ACTIVITIES

Camping: 21 sites. Apr. 1–Oct. 31. Half of the sites are assigned by mail reservation; reservations needed on busy weekends. Winter camping available nearby.

Hiking: 6 3/4 mi. of trails within the Park.

Ski touring, Dec.–Feb. when there is enough snow, not every year.

PUBLICATIONS
    Leaflet with map.
    Nature trail guide. $0.25.
    Flora, fauna checklists.

HEADQUARTERS: Box 609, Moab, UT 84532; (801) 259-6511.

DIRTY DEVIL

U.S. Bureau of Land Management
61,000 acres.

Between Hanksville and Glen Canyon National Recreation Area. Access from unpaved roads off SR 95, notably: road to Beaver Wash, about 11 mi. S of Hanksville; Poison Spring Canyon road, about 17 mi. S of Hanksville. (MP #1, 2.)

This irregularly shaped roadless area is about 20 mi. long, 10 mi. wide. Within it are more than 100 mi. of hiking routes. Perennial stream; riparian vegetation in canyons; many good campsites, some under rock overhangs. But as yet it has only about 125 visitors per year.

The Fremont and Muddy Rivers join at Hanksville to form the Dirty Devil, which flows SE and S into the Glen Canyon NRA. The area has high, narrow ridges and mesas, cut deeply and abruptly by narrow, sheer-walled, meandering canyons, chiefly on the E side of Dirty Devil. Ridges and mesas are mostly at 5,200–5,400 ft. elevation, canyon bottoms 600 to 1,000 ft. lower. Moderate slopes on benches; vertical canyon walls. Canyon walls show rich color variety, shades of white, beige, yellow, brown, red. Many slickrock outcrops eroded into interesting shapes. Some petrified wood deposits. Petroglyphs and pictographs.

Semidesert vegetation: sand sage, Nuttall saltbush, Indian ricegrass, rabbitbrush, greasewood, snakeweed, blackbrush, pinyon-juniper. Moisture in the canyons attracts wildlife, including mule deer (uncommon). Beaver colony reportedly in lower end of Beaver Canyon.

The Dirty Devil Canyon can't be seen from SR 95, but nonhikers can drive to two overlooks and a ford. The overlook at Burr Point is shown on Multipurpose Map No. 1. Both Burr Point and Angels Point overlooks are shown on BLM's brochure on the Henry Mountains. Both the BLM map and Multipurpose Map No. 1 show the Poison Spring Canyon Road, which crosses the Dirty Devil at a shallow ford, becoming the North Hatch Canyon road into Glen Canyon NRA. Inquire at the BLM office in Hanksville before trying it.

ACTIVITIES

Backpacking: Several access routes; advisable to consult BLM office. No maintained trails.

The Dirty Devil is also used for horse-packing and rafting.

Flash floods are a summer hazard.
Stream water isn't potable.

PUBLICATION: *The Henry Mountains and Surrounding Deserts,* with map.

HEADQUARTERS: Manager, BLM, Henry Mountains Resource Area, Box 99, Hanksville, UT 84734; (801) 542-3461.

DIXIE NATIONAL FOREST

U.S. Forest Service
1,883,745 acres; 1,967,188 acres within boundaries.

Four large blocks in SW Utah. (A) Pine Valley Ranger District. Between the NV border and I-15, S of SR 56. Crossed by SR 18. (B) Cedar City Ranger District. Between Cedar City on I-15 and Panguitch on US 89. Crossed by SR 14. Surrounds Cedar Breaks National Monument. (C) Powell Ranger District. E of US 89. Bryce Canyon National Park is at the SE corner. Crossed by SR 12. (D) Teasdale and Escalante Ranger Districts. N of Escalante. Bryce Canyon National Park is at the SW corner, Capitol Reef National Park at the NE. (MP #5)

Scenic, richly diverse mountain country, between the Escalante Desert and Capitol Reef. Three spectacular National Parks and a National Monument are within this region, but only signs tell where they begin and end. The whole countryside is dramatic and splendid.

The Dixie's lowest elevation is 3,500 ft., the highest 11,307 ft., from desert to high alpine meadows. The Forest is predominantly a series of high plateaus, from 8,000 ft. to 10,000 ft. elevation, the major exception being the Pine Valley Mountain Range in Block B. Between the plateaus and mountains are deep canyons with colorful rock formations. The Forest is known for its red cliffs and bright fall colors.

Annual precipitation ranges from 12 in. at low elevations to more than 30 in. on high slopes. About two-thirds of the 30 in. falls as snow, much of the rest in summer rainstorms. Snow can be expected Oct.–Apr. Accumulations to 12 ft. up high, with snowpacks remaining until early June. After the snow has gone, daytime temperatures in the high country will reach 80°F, 15 to 20 degrees higher below 8,000 ft. Summer nighttime temperatures can drop to freezing or below at high elevations.

The forest is better supplied with moisture than most of southern UT. The high country is dotted with ponds, lakes, and reservoirs, and many perennial streams rush down the slopes. Availability of water supports productive plant communities and wildlife.

A few areas have become popular recreation sites, many of the visitors coming from nearby. Of the 22 campgrounds, a few may be crowded on fine-weather weekends or at the beginning of hunting season. But most of the Forest is lightly used, especially the backcountry. It isn't difficult to find a quiet place to camp. Thus far there has been little need for trailhead facilities.

Plants: About one-third of the area is classed as productive timber land. Species include ponderosa pine, Douglas-fir, white fir, Engelmann spruce, subalpine fir, whitebark limber pine, aspen. Bristlecone pine occurs at high elevations. About 45% of the area is classed as unproductive forest; much of this is pinyon-juniper.

For list of flowering plants, see entry for Cedar Breaks National Monument. The Monument is within the Cedar City Ranger District.

Birds: Checklist of 210 species does not distinguish between common and rare species or indicate seasonality. (The checklist for Cedar Breaks National Monument does indicate rarity; see entry.) However, the great diversity of habitats suggests that even more species could be logged. Among those listed: common loon, American white pelican, great blue heron, American bittern, black-crowned night-heron, white-faced ibis, northern pintail; green-winged, cinnamon, and blue-winged teals; mallard, gadwall, lesser scaup, redhead, canvasback, bufflehead, common and Barrow's goldeneyes, American wigeon, common and red-breasted mergansers, ruddy duck, shoveler, Canada goose, whistling swan. Golden and bald eagles, northern harrier, goshawk; Cooper's, sharp-shinned, red-tailed, rough-legged, ferruginous, and Swainson's hawks; osprey, merlin, prairie and peregrine falcons.

Also sage and blue grouse, chukar, Gambel's quail, wild turkey, American coot, sora, Virginia rail, killdeer, spotted sandpiper, common snipe, long-billed curlew, willet, American avocet, black-necked stilt, California and ring-billed gulls, roadrunner, yellow-billed cuckoo. Hummingbirds: black-chinned, broad-tailed, rufous, calliope. Woodpeckers: Lewis', downy, hairy, northern three-toed, ladder-backed; common flicker, Williamson's and yellow-bellied sapsuckers. Gray, ash-throated, western, Hammond's, dusky, Traill's, and olive-sided flycatchers; western wood-pewee, Say's phoebe, western kingbird. Warblers: yellow-rumped, Grace's, yellow, Townsend's, Mac-Gillivray's, orange-crowned, Virginia's, Wilson's, black-throated gray, yellow-breasted chat, common yellowthroat.

Mammals: Checklist includes masked, dusky, vagrant, and northern water shrews; 17 species of bats, black bear, ringtail, striped and spotted skunks, shorttail and longtail weasels, badger, coyote, red and gray foxes, bobcat, mountain lion. Also cliff, least, Colorado, and Uinta chipmunks; Utah prairie dog, northern flying squirrel, yellowbelly marmot, rock and red squirrels, whitetail antelope squirrel, golden-mantled and Townsend ground squirrels. Western jumping mouse, porcupine, pika, snowshoe hare, blacktail and whitetail jackrabbits, desert and mountain cottontails, pygmy rabbit, elk, mule deer, pronghorn.

Reptiles and amphibians: Lizards: western collared, mountain short-horned, desert long-horned, Great Basin sagebrush, yellow-backed spiny, Great Basin fence, Colorado tree, northern side-blotched, Upper Colorado Basin. Western red-tailed skink, Great Basin and northern whiptails. Rocky Mountain rubber boa, western yellow-bellied racer, regal ring-necked snake, desert night snake, California kingsnake, Utah mountain kingsnake, red racer, desert striped whipsnake, Great Basin gopher snake, western long-nosed snake, Utah black-headed snake, wandering garter snake, Sonora lyre snake, Great Basin rattlesnake.

FEATURES

A. *Pine Valley Ranger District.*

Pine Valley, Bull Valley, and Harmony Mountains rise sharply to elevations over 8,000 ft. Volcanic activity has modified many landscapes, leaving cinder cones, basalt mesas, and undulating benches. Pine Valley is cooled by air flowing down from peaks and mountain meadows.

The Pine Valley Mountains, in the SE portion of the R.D., include some of the most rugged mountains in southern UT. Highest point is Signal Peak, 10,365 ft. Slope on the W side is steep, cut by numerous short canyons. E slope is more gradual. Over 150 mi. of trails provide routes to high mountain meadows and the mountaintop. Fine viewpoints. The entire Pine Valley Mountain area, proposed for wilderness status, is closed to all motor vehicles.

Pine Valley Recreation Area is on the W side of the wilderness. From St. George, SR 18 N to Central, then E into the Forest along the Santa Clara River. Campground.

Honeycomb Rocks Campground is on Upper Enterprise Reservoir, in the NW sector. Fishing, boating, ramp.

The R.D. has many streams and springs.

B. *Cedar City Ranger District*

Markagunt Plateau is the dominant feature, an extensive plateau even higher than the Pine Valley Mountains. Brian Head is 11,307 ft., over 7,000 ft. higher than parts of the Pine Valley R.D. less than 50 mi. away. Several peaks in the central and N sectors of the R.D. are over 10,000 ft. On the S and W edges, the Plateau drops off dramatically to the valleys in spectacular canyons, amphitheaters, cliffs, and pinnacles. Cedar Breaks National Monument is part of this W side formation. Numerous springs and streams.

Winter sports are popular on the Plateau. Parking areas on SR 14, maintained for cross-country skiers and snowmobilers, are often full. Fall colors attract many visitors.

Cedar Canyon is the route of SR 14 from Cedar City to the National Monument. We thought this drive almost as spectacular as the Monument itself.

Ashdown Gorge is a proposed wilderness area, adjoining Cedar Breaks National Monument on the W, NW, and SW, a continuation of the outstanding steep canyons and sheer cliffs seen within the Monument.

Panguitch Lake is a popular recreation area on the road from the Monument to Panguitch. Camping, fishing, boating, swimming. Resorts.

Navajo Lake, SE of the Monument, is also a popular resort, with camping, fishing, boating, swimming, and commercial facilities.

Brian Head is a commercial ski area, N of the Monument.

We were told there isn't much backpacking in this R.D. Too many roads. Most are dirt roads, many requiring 4-wheel drive. Rangers can suggest some attractive areas.

C. *Panguitch (Powell) Ranger District*

Includes all of the *Paunsaugunt Plateau* and the S part of the *Sevier Plateau.* The Paunsaugunt, with elevations from 6,900 to 9,600 ft., consists of flat-topped mesas and buttes, broad ridgetops, and moderately entrenched streams. The slow, meandering East Fork of the Sevier River drains the Plateau to the N. The Paunsaugunt rim and breaks are extremely rugged, with numerous cliffs, pinnacles, intricately dissected canyons. The E rim forms part of Bryce Canyon National Park. On the W are the Sunset Cliffs.

The Sevier Plateau in the N part of the R.D. ranges from 6,900 to 10,360 ft. elevation. The plateau top is a gently rolling tableland cut by steep canyons.

Highest point in the R.D. is Mt. Dutton, in the N, at 11,041 ft.

Red Canyon is on the W side, on SR 12, which crosses the R.D. from US 89 N of Hillsdale. Pink limestone amphitheaters. Formations much like those of Bryce Canyon, though not as extensive. Areas N and S of the Canyon have been proposed for wilderness status. Campground in the Canyon, often full in summer as it serves as a bedroom for Bryce Canyon.

Tropic Reservoir, on the Sevier River, elevation 7,500 ft., is near Bryce Canyon National Park, although the nearest road link is 7 mi. away. Campground, fishing, boating swimming—but it's a small water body.

D. *Escalante and Teasdale Ranger Districts*

These R.D.'s attract backcountry visitors because of *Aquarius Plateau,* almost 700,000 acres, sometimes called the grandest of UT's many high plateaus, certainly the most unusual. The Plateau has as its summit Boulder Top, a relatively flat volcanic tableland of more than 50,000 acres, most of it higher than 10,000 ft. Bluebell Knoll, the highest point, is 11,322 ft., Lookout Peak, 3 mi. to the W, is 11,124 ft. The Plateau is unusual because of its large number of lakes and ponds and its fine stands of spruce and fir, unexpected at this elevation. Most of Boulder Top is closed to motor vehicles, as is the Deer Creek-Criss Lake area adjoining on the SW.

Table Cliff Plateau is at the S end of the Escalante R.D. The Plateau reaches an elevation of 10,577 ft. on the Barney Top. Here a volcanic cap overlies sedimentary formations. The Plateau is surrounded by brightly colored white and pink cliffs. Powell Point, at the S end of the Plateau, was used by John Wesley Powell as an observation post for mapping.

Forest Road 569 runs S from Teasdale, passing E of Boulder Top, joining SR 12 at Boulder. The Grover-Boulder segment is being paved, providing a better link between Bryce Canyon and Capitol Reef National Parks. Several Forest campgrounds are on this route.

Hells Backbone is a scenic fair-weather road that crosses a knife-edge ridge, sharp drops on both sides. Forest Road 153 starts at Escalante and makes a loop to the N and E, ending at Boulder. The drop on the S side is into the Box and Death Hollow drainages, canyons proposed for wilderness status, and the beginning of a hiking route to the Escalante Canyon (see entry, Escalante River).

ACTIVITIES

Camping: 17 campgrounds, 601 sites. Seasons begin May or June, end Sept. or Oct.

Hunting: Deer, elk, pronghorn.

Fishing: Many streams and lakes.

PUBLICATIONS

Forest maps, 2 sections. $2.00 each.

Off-Road Vehicle Travel Plan. Maps.

Recreation folder; Cedar City and Pine Valley Ranger Districts. Includes campground list, outline maps.

Species checklists.

Information for Trail and Backcountry Use.

HEADQUARTERS: 82 North 100 East, Cedar City, UT 84720; (801) 586-2421.

RANGER DISTRICTS: Pine Valley R.D., Federal Bldg., St. George, UT 84770; (801) 673-3431. Cedar City R.D., 82 North 100 East, Cedar City, UT 84720; (801) 586-4462. Powell R.D., 57 N. Main St., Panguitch, UT 84759; (801) 676-8815. Escalante R.D., Escalante, UT 84726; (801) 826-4312. Teasdale R.D., Teasdale, UT 84773; (801) 425-3435.

ESCALANTE RIVER
U.S. Bureau of Land Management; National Park Service
About 600,000 acres.

The upper end of the area is crossed by SR 12, E of Escalante, and the Burr Trail E from Boulder. Hole-in-the-Rock Road ("Trail" on some maps), a county-maintained graveled road, 62 mi. long, from near Escalante SE to Lake Powell, is the W boundary. (MP #1, 5.)

We met people who love this area with eloquence. One described it thus:

> One of the finest backpacking areas *in the world*. Highly scenic and well-watered. Escalante River was the last major river to be discovered in the contiguous U.S. (by John Wesley Powell on his second trip). The canyon and tributary canyons are reminiscent of Glen Canyon, now under Lake Powell. The canyon country is characterized by esthetic Navajo sandstone ("slickrock," "water-bearing sandstone"). Classic "ribbon of green" in white and red rock landscape. Escalante River heads on the Aquarius Plateau and drains to the Colorado River in Glen Canyon . . . .

Another wrote,

> From the headwaters of the Escalante high on Boulder Mountain, one can gaze over the expanse of sand, rock, and plateaus of one of the largest unbroken wilderness areas left in the United States. The core of this great wilderness is the Escalante River, which has carved this land, shaped its history, and whose heartbeat gives it life . . . .
> At normal level, the river's depth is ankle high in its upper reaches and mid-calf in its lower. The water is spring-fed and clear. The banks are uniformly sandy, shaded with cottonwood, willow, and tamarisk. Numerous sandbanks form excellent campsites. As a hiking trail, the river itself is unsurpassed, and its easy grade, lack of obstructions, and scenic magnificence have made it increasingly popular.
> . . . At periods of flash flooding (which occurs principally in the summer) and at times of high spring runoff, the canyon floor becomes an entirely different kind of world. The river bed becomes the home of a raging, muddy torrent that may carry whole trees and tons of sand and be capable of rolling large boulders along its bottom like marbles. . . .

This 100-mi.-long canyon attracts hikers and backpackers from everywhere, up to 50,000 of them a year. Such heavy use prompted cooperative backcountry planning by the two agencies principally involved: the National Park Service, for 250,000 acres in Glen Canyon National Recreation Area, and the Bureau of Land Management, for 350,000 acres. Adjoining areas in the Dixie National Forest may eventually be included.

The area extends NW from Lake Powell to the Death Hollow area of Dixie National Forest. The W boundary is Hole-in-the-Rock Road, near the base of the Straight Cliffs (see entry, Kaiparowits Plateau). The E boundary is at the base of Waterpocket Fold, partly within the Glen Canyon NRA, further N near the boundary of Capitol Reef National Park. Except for SR 12 crossing in the N, the area is largely roadless.

The Escalante Canyon cuts NW–SE through the area, bisecting it. Steep-walled and tortuous, it has many side canyons, labyrinthine, many of them narrow and deep. Most of the river is slow and shallow, with deeper water near the lower end. Flash floods make the river dangerous. Canyon hikers must cross the river many times, wading in narrow places, so canvas shoes are in order.

Hiking the canyon from SR 12 to Hurricane Wash is a 10-day trip. Many shorter hikes are possible, entering the canyon from the N or from any of several points along Hole-in-the-Rock Road. Three areas—Harris Wash, Coyote Gulch, and Hurricane Wash—have become too popular. One planning objective is to divert visitors to areas now lightly used.

Flora and fauna: See entry, Glen Canyon National Recreation Area.

FEATURES

Hole-in-the-Rock Road was the route of Mormon pioneers in 1879. The obstacles were so great they could move less than 2 mi. per day. Now the route can be driven in half a morning. The following are special points along the road:

The Box-Phipps-Death Hollow is E and N of the town of Escalante, N of SR 12, the upper portion of the Escalante River. Easy access from SR 12, Hells Backbone Road, in the National Forest, and other points. 34,288 acres have been designated an Outstanding Natural Area. Deep, winding canyons, some with 1,000-ft. walls, cliffs, benches, some open flats. Abundant vegetation in some canyons. Elevations along the canyon rims about 5,500 ft.; many buttes and mesas over 6,500 ft. Perennial streams; some trout fishing. BLM gave this region its highest rating for scenic qualities. Hiking opportunities range from easy to challenging. The area includes archeological sites with pictographs, petroglyphs, cave dwellings. Also see:

Calf Creek Recreation Area, on SR 12. The 2 3/4 mi. trail to Lower Falls, 126 ft. high, follows the clear stream, passes archeological sites, ponds, marshes. Trail guide. Campground. Upper Falls, 86 ft. high, is 5 1/2 mi. upstream, a difficult 1-mi. hike over slickrock from SR 12.

Escalante Natural Bridge is a 2-mi. hike from the SR 12 bridge over the Escalante River.

Death Hollow, a deep, narrow gorge, can be seen by hiking 7 mi. from the bridge. Part of it is in the National Forest. Some hikers try the 30-mi. trip through the Hollow from Hells Backbone, at the N boundary of the area, to SR 12. The first 11 mi. are dry. Thereafter, the hike requires some swimming and strenuous rock scrambling.

SR 12, Calf Creek to Boulder, is scenic, breathtaking, to be driven with caution.

Steep Creek is a 22,391-acre roadless area E of Boulder, N of the Burr Trail. The Circle Cliffs are the E boundary. Good hiking in deep, winding canyons with riparian vegetation. Rockhounding for petrified wood. Primitive campground on Deer Creek. Access from campground area and where Burr Trail crosses the Gulch.

North Escalante Canyons: A roadless area of 141,743 acres S of SR 12. Hole-in-the-Rock Road is the W boundary. The main canyon of the Escalante is within the area. Deep side canyons. Abundant riparian vegetation. Steep cliffs, benches, open flats. Three popular hiking routes from SR 12: Deer Creek, the Gulch, and Escalante River. Includes archeological sites, Wolverine Petrified Wood Area, North Escalante Canyons, and the Gulch Outstanding Natural Areas.

Lower Escalante Canyons. The following mileages are along Hole-in-the-Rock Road from Escalante:

13 mi. *Harris Wash.* A popular access to Escalante Canyon. The canyon hike from SR 12 is about 37 mi., moderately strenuous.

17 mi. *Devils Garden* is a small area with bizarre rock formations, some standing like statues.

28 mi. *The Scorpion* is a 46,000-acre roadless area between Devils Garden and Hurricane Wash, extending from Hole-in-the-Rock Road into the Glen Canyon NRA, with additional acreage in the NRA. Access across Scorpion Flat through Scorpion Gulch or, farther N, down Twentyfive Mile Wash. Much of the area is a basin between the cliffs of Allen Dump on the N and those of Early Weed Bench on the S. The side canyons of Twentyfive Mile Wash and of the Dry Fork of Coyote Gulch are winding and exceptionally narrow. A scenic area with many features of interest, less heavily impacted than Harris Wash and Hurricane Wash.

38 mi. *Hurricane Wash* is another popular access route. 5.3 mi. to Coyote Gulch, a spectacular gorge with natural arches and bridges. 7.9 mi. through the Gulch to the Escalante. From Harris Wash to Hurricane Wash via the Escalante is an 8-day, 66-mi. hike, moderately strenuous.

At this point an unimproved dirt road climbs partway up the Straight Cliffs, returning 13 mi. to the S. Fine views, but the road probably requires 4-wheel drive.

Lake Powell has inundated most of Escalante Canyon below Coyote Gulch. At high water it floods the lower end of Coyote Gulch.

ACTIVITIES

Camping: At Calf Creek campground and Deer Creek primitive campground. Many suitable informal sites.

Hiking, backpacking: Some of Utah's best, from easy day hikes to the 10-day trek from SR 12 to Coyote Gulch. Spring and fall are best. Deer flies are often troublesome in summer. BLM warns that search and rescue operations are slow and difficult in canyon country. Treat water. Carry extra rations, first aid supplies. Tell BLM where you're going.

Horse riding: Consult BLM. Some trails are unsuitable.

Fishing: Trout, in Deer Creek, Calf Creek, other streams N of SR 12. S of SR 12 the water becomes too warm.

ADJACENT: Dixie National Forest (see entry).

PUBLICATIONS
  From BLM:
    Hiking the Escalante River. Map, for orientation only. Travel requires topo maps.
    Hole in the Rock. Pamphlet.
    Calf Creek Falls trail guide, leaflet.
    Cooperative Management Area map; for orientation only.
  From Glen Canyon NRA:
    Hiking the Escalante River Canyon Country. Information, map.

HEADQUARTERS: BLM, Cedar City District, 1579 N. Main, Cedar City, UT 84720; (801) 586-2401. Glen Canyon National Recreation Area, P.O. Box 1507, Page, AZ 86040; (602) 645-8883. BLM and National Park Service have adjacent information offices in Escalante. BLM's telephone: (801) 826-4291.

ESCALANTE PETRIFIED FOREST STATE RESERVE
Utah State Division of Parks and Recreation
2,900 acres.

From Escalante, 1 mi. W on SR 12; 1/2 mi. N.

This attractive park is a convenient base for exploring nearby scenic areas. On 30-acre Wide Hollow reservoir. Largely surrounded by public lands. Petrified wood deposits on nearby hills. About 50% forested with pinyon-juniper; sagebrush and rabbitbrush understory. Two nature trails. Seldom crowded.

Camping: 22 sites. All year.

PUBLICATIONS
  Leaflet.
  Trail map.

HEADQUARTERS: Box 350, Escalante, UT 84726; (801) 586-4497.

FIDDLER BUTTE
U.S. Bureau of Land Management
100,000 acres.

W of Glen Canyon National Recreation Area. Bounded on W by SR 276 and SR 95. Access by Poison Springs Wash road; 4-wheel drive recommended. (MP #1.)

A rugged area, difficult to reach without 4-wheel drive. A jeep trail goes down South Hatch Canyon, up North Hatch Canyon, over Gunsight Butte, and into the Waterhole area of the National Recreation Area. Much of the area is roadless.

The N–S canyon of the Dirty Devil River divides the area. (See entry, Dirty Devil.) The W half, between the state roads and Dirty Devil Canyon, is mostly high desert and slickrock formations. The Cedar Point sand dunes are in the N portion of this half. Stair, Butler, and Marinus Canyons in the S portion offer interesting hiking.

Fiddler Butte, in the E half, is 6,027 ft. Highest point, 6,805 ft., is S of Fiddler Butte on a large mesa covered with pinyon-juniper trees, called The Block. Much of the E half is sparsely vegetated benchlands.

Opportunities for rockhounding. Occasional pictographs.

HEADQUARTERS: BLM, Henry Mountain Resource Area, Box 99, Hanksville, UT 84734; (801) 542-3461.

FISH AND OWL CANYONS
U.S. Bureau of Land Management
52,000 acres.

From SR 261, 9 mi. S of SR 95, turn E 5 mi. on dirt road. Check road conditions. (MP #1.)

If there are too many backpackers for your taste in the Grand Gulch Primitive Area, try this one, not far away.

Fish and Owl Creeks have cut canyons about 500 ft. deep in flat to gently rolling Cedar Mesa. The canyons run generally SE, converging several miles before they enter Comb Wash. Narrow in places, the canyons are attractive to backpackers because of their isolation, scenic beauty, and cool pools of water.

Nevill's Arch is a prominent feature in Owl Canyon, high on a fin.

Access to Owl Canyon from the road end. Canyon hiking requires some rock scrambling and detouring large pour-offs. Plateau vegetation is pinyon-juniper mixed with sagebrush-desert shrub. Cottonwood and pine stands on benches in the upper forks. Riparian vegetation in moist canyon bottoms. Sage and cactus flats in the lower ends. Canyon flowers observed include vetches, penstemon, cliffrose, various composites.

Wildlife is scarce. Bobcat and ringtail tracks seen in the canyon.

Streams are often dry from the convergence upstream a mile or two. Other sections may be dry in hot summer. Pools remain, as well as several springs; water untested.

ACTIVITIES

Camping: From car, suitable sites on access road.

Hiking, backpacking: BLM advises allowing 3 to 4 days to see the canyons. One route is down Owl Creek, up Fish Creek. Hiking conditions vary from easy to difficult. Lower Fish Creek is easy going for 5 mi.; the main fork, running due N to SR 95 is often blocked by pour-offs and talus. Bring topo maps, water.

PUBLICATION: Hiking map. Most useful if discussed at BLM office, used in conjunction with topo.

REFERENCES

Hall, Dave. *The Hiker's Guide to Utah.* Billings, MT: Falcon Press, 1982. Pp. 181–183.

Barnes, F. A. *Canyon Country Hiking and Natural History.* Salt Lake City: Wasatch, 1977. Pp. 163–164.

HEADQUARTERS: BLM, San Juan Resource Area Office, 480 South First St. West, Monticello, UT 84535; (801) 587-2201.

FISHLAKE NATIONAL FOREST

See entry in Zone 2.

GLEN CANYON NATIONAL RECREATION AREA

National Park Service

1,157,463 acres, of which 1,061,738 acres in UT. (MP #1.)

Glen Canyon Dam is in AZ, near Page on US 89. In UT, SR 95 crosses the upper end of the impoundment, Lake Powell. From SR 95, SR 276 goes S to Bullfrog Basin Marina, SR 263 to Halls Crossing Marina on the opposite shore. Jeep trails to a few other points on the shore or to foot trailheads.

Lake Powell attracts the visitors, but the NRA includes more land area than all of Utah's National Parks and Monuments combined. Much of it is road-less, and it adjoins other public lands.

Glen Canyon Dam, built between 1956 and 1964 across the Colorado River, has backed up a pool, Lake Powell, 186 mi. long, in a narrow, twisting canyon. With many even narrower side canyons, it has a shoreline of about 2,000 mi., depending on the height of the pool. Conservationists, valuing Glen Canyon, fought unsuccessfully to block the project. They were dismayed when the pool first reached maximum height 17 years later, flooding the lower portions of Coyote Gulch and Escalante Canyon; they thought they had been assured this wouldn't happen. They argued that federal law prohibited flooding any part of a National Monument, but the lake waters extend under Rainbow Bridge.

The lake quickly became a popular boating and fishing area. On weekends processions of cars with boat trailers can be seen on nearby desert highways. But as yet there are only 4 marinas on the lake and less than a dozen places where a car can be driven to the lakeshore. Speedboats and water skiers don't venture far from their marinas. Most of the lake is quiet, much of the shore wilderness. Almost all of the surrounding land is public, including wilderness areas of Capitol Reef National Park, Canyonlands National Park, Dark Canyon Primitive Area, Grand Gulch Primitive Area, and various roadless areas administered by BLM. Camping from boats is permitted, and one can hike or backpack into many roadless areas from the shore.

In addition to flooding Glen Canyon, the dam also backed up a pool on the San Juan River. The National Recreation Area includes the N shore of the San Juan all the way to the Goosenecks State Reserve; the S shore is the Navajo Indian Reservation.

Glen Canyon was carved by the Colorado River in sedimentary rock, much of it brick-red Navajo sandstone. It is a region of canyons, large and small, many of them deep and steep-walled, separated by narrow ridges or broader mesas. Most of the land area is between 4,500 and 5,500 ft. elevation, with occasional mesas over 6,000 ft. Highest point is 7,451 ft.

Average maximum temperatures are in the 90s in summer, 45–55°F in winter. Average winter lows are 25–35°F. Annual precipitation is about 10 in. Most winters see some snow but no significant accumulation.

Plants: Five principal associations: (1) *Streamside.* Prominent species are sandbar willow, tamarisk, arrowweed, common reed, saltgrass; may include Gambel oak, hackberry, Fremont cottonwood, cheatgrass, cattail. (2) *Terrace.* Old floodplains now above flood level. Prominent species are greasewood, rabbitbrush, sand sagebrush, dropseed grass, Indian ricegrass; may include arrowweed, shadscale, hackberry, blackbrush, snakeweed. (3) *Hillside association:* chiefly widely spaced low shrubs. Prominent species: snakeweed, shadscale, hackberry, blackbrush; may include Indian ricegrass, pricklypear, hedgehog cactus, serviceberry, silver buffaloberry, cliffrose. Also sego and mariposa lilies, eriogonum, prickly poppy, prince's plume, gaillardia, lupine, locoweed, euphorbia, globemallow, blazing star, evening primrose, gilia, penstemon, Indian paintbrush, golden aster. (4) *Hanging gardens,* where moisture seeps from canyon walls. Species include maidenhair fern, columbines, red monkeyflower, cardinal flower, false Solomon's-seal, evening prim-rose. (5) *Plateau.* Pinyon-juniper association includes bitterbrush, cliffrose, galleta, blue grama, Indian ricegrass.

Birds: Checklist of 65 waterfowl or shorebirds, 127 land species, plus 58 species known to occur in immediately adjacent areas. Seasonally common species include western, eared, and pied-billed grebes; American white peli-can, great blue heron, snowy egret, Canada goose, mallard, green-winged and cinnamon teals, shoveler, ring-necked duck, common goldeneye, turkey vul-ture, red-tailed and Swainson's hawks, northern harrier, prairie falcon, American kestrel, American coot, American avocet, black-necked stilt, kill-deer, long-billed curlew; spotted, least, and Wilson's sandpipers; California, ring-billed, Franklin's, and Bonaparte's gulls; mourning and rock doves, black-throated gray and MacGillivray's warblers, house sparrow, red-winged blackbird, Cassin's finch; vesper, sage, and chipping sparrows; gray-headed junco, great horned and long-eared owls; black-chinned, broad-tailed, and rufous hummingbirds; downy woodpecker, western and Cassin's kingbirds, Say's phoebe, dusky flycatcher, western wood-pewee, horned lark, violet-green and cliff swallows, American crow, mountain chickadee, pygmy nut-hatch, mockingbird.

Fall migration of many species begins in late June or July. Canyons and shoreline of Lake Powell are fall and winter habitat. Sandbars and beaches are resting places for migrants.

Mammals: Checklist available; does not indicate whether common or rare, but does indicate habitats. Includes 5 species of shrews, 13 of bats. Pika, whitetail and blacktail jackrabbits, mountain and desert cottontails. Squirrels: Abert, red, rock. Spotted, antelope, and golden-mantled ground squirrels. Whitetail prairie dog; least, Uinta, Colorado, and cliff chipmunks; northern and valley pocket gophers. 5 species of pocket mice, Ord kangaroo rat, beaver, 10 species of mice, 5 species of wood rats, muskrat, heather and Mexican voles, porcupine. Also coyote, red and gray foxes, black bear, ringtail, longtail and shorttail weasels, badger, striped and spotted skunks, river otter, bobcat, mountain lion, mule deer, pronghorn, elk.

Lizards: Checklist includes chuckwalla, collared, leopard, lesser earless, side-blotched, eastern fence, desert spiny, western whiptail, plateau striped whiptail, desert horned.

Snakes: Checklist includes striped whipsnake, western patch-nosed, go-pher, common kingsnake, western diamondback rattlesnake, western rattle-snake.

FEATURES

Wahweap is the principal recreation area, with marina, campground, lodge, other facilities. Reached by a short scenic drive from the dam.

Warm Creek-Smokey Mountain road is a scenic route from Big Water (formerly Glen Canyon City). Moonscape scenery.

Rainbow Bridge National Monument is 45 mi. uplake from the dam. The huge red and yellow natural sandstone arch is the largest yet discovered. Getting there by land is difficult. The bridge now spans a flooded canyon, and boat access is easy. Floating marina at Dangling Rope Canyon has Ranger Station, restrooms, boat fuel, camp supplies, emergency communications. Courtesy dock a short hike from the Bridge.

Hole-in-the-Rock, 60 mi. uplake from the dam, is a slot in the canyon wall through which Mormon pioneers lowered wagons to the river for ferrying. The Hole-in-the-Rock Road, a county-maintained graveled road, extends 61 mi. to Escalante, between the Straight Cliffs of the Kaiparowits Plateau and Escalante Canyon, one of UT's best known and most visited backcountry areas. (See entry, Escalante River.)

Hurricane Wash is a route from Hole-in-the-Rock Road into Coyote Gulch, an area with several natural arches. Trailhead is 20 mi. from the lake shore. The trail down Coyote Gulch connects with the Escalante Canyon Trail.

Escalante River enters Lake Powell about 63 mi. from the dam. About 3 mi. up this river, on the left, is the mouth of Davis Gulch, with several natural arches nearby. About 9 mi. upstream, how far depending on the lake level, is the beginning of the hike up Escalante Canyon.

Bullfrog is 96 mi. up-lake, on the N side, at the end of SR 276. Campground, marina, store, service station, lodge, Ranger Station.

Halls Crossing, across the lake at the end of SR 263, also has campground, marina, store, lodge.

Hite is at the head of the lake, 156 mi. from the dam, at the end of Cataract Canyon. SR 95 crosses here. Primitive campground, store, boat-fuel service. Boats can travel 30 mi. up Cataract Canyon. Hite is the takeout point for float trips down the canyon.

Dark Canyon ends in Cataract Canyon. (See entry, Dark Canyon Primitive Area.) The only boat-hiker contact in Cataract Canyon is here, about 1 1/2 mi. from the river channel.

San Juan River (see entry) is backed up 71 mi. from its confluence with the Colorado. No facilities available. Raft trips from upstream on the San Juan often take out at Clay Hills Crossing.

Orange Cliffs district extends about 30 mi. N from Cataract Canyon along the entire W boundary of Canyonlands National Park. Many 4-wheel-drive routes and hiking possibilities.

ACTIVITIES

Camping: 4 campgrounds with 156 spaces; 1 primitive campground with no marked sites. No reservations. Informal camping is permitted except in or adjacent to developed areas. Camping from boats is permitted, but campers are warned that some sites have natural hazards.

Hiking, backpacking: The site map shows several hiking trails, but handout information is available only for the most popular: those in the Escalante Canyon area. Many opportunities for day hikes, up canyons from the lake-shore or from unpaved roads. For longer hikes, consult Ranger.

Fishing: Rainbow and brown trout, largemouth bass, black crappie, channel catfish, walleye, bluegill, striped bass.

Boating: Houseboating is one of the best ways to enjoy the remote areas of the lake. Rentals at major marinas. Other craft can also be rented. While narrow, the lake is often windy and rough. Sailing is best in the three large bays, canoeing in side canyons.

Swimming: Favorable water temperatures June–Sept. Beach at Wahweap, unsupervised.

PUBLICATIONS
Folder with map.
Checklists: Plants, birds, mammals, lizards, snakes, fishes.
Information pages
Geology.
Climate.
Hiking the Escalante River Canyon Country.

REFERENCES
Barnes, F. A. *Canyon Country Hiking and Natural History.* Salt Lake City: Wasatch, 1977. Pp. 141–142, 168–169.
Hall, Dave. *The Hiker's Guide to Utah.* Billings, MT: Falcon Press, 1982. Pp. 159–168.
Glen Canyon-Lake Powell: The Story Behind the Scenery. Las Vegas, NV: KC Publications, no date.

HEADQUARTERS: P.O. Box 1507, Page, AZ 86040; (602) 645-2471.

GRAND GULCH PRIMITIVE AREA
U.S. Bureau of Land Management
35,000 acres.

From SR 261, 4 mi. S of SR 95, turn W to BLM's Kane Gulch Ranger Station. About 1 1/2 mi. to Primitive Area Boundary. S end of Gulch best entered from raft on San Juan River (see entry), or via Collins Canyon. (MP #1.)

Grand Gulch is the main drainage of Grand Gulch Plateau, an area of 1,000 sq. mi. The main gulch, about 50 mi. long, is the center of a complex of tributary canyons, including Kane Gulch, Bullet Canyon, Collins Canyon,

Coyote Wash, Pine Canyon, and Dripping Canyon. The Primitive Area is roadless, closed to vehicles, protected as a wilderness.

The upper part of the Gulch is 400–600 ft. deep; the lower, over 700 ft. Much of the Plateau is slickrock, from which water runs quickly, so that even a light rain may produce a flash flood in the Gulch. Annual precipitation is only 10 in., but much of it comes in sudden downpours. Then the Gulch is swept by torrents 20–30 ft. deep, hurling logs and other debris. Flooding happens most often in July–Aug. Summer temperatures up to 110°F. Snow and ice make winter travel difficult and dangerous. Spring and fall are the best seasons for canyon hiking.

The Gulch ranks high in scenic value: towering, colorful sandstone walls, petrified sand dunes, wide canyon bottoms with sagebrush, grasses, cottonwood, willow, between erosion-sculptured ramparts topped by fanciful figures. The Gulch has several natural arches, Indian pictographs, a few ruins of Anasazi dwellings.

Water is scarce, especially in dry periods. The hikers' map marks springs, but these are often intermittent, and most of the pools that gather after rain are temporary. Hikers should inquire about current conditions, carry water, and use water purification measures. Hikers traveling down the canyon sometimes arrange to be picked up by raft at the river.

Plants: No checklist available. The Anasazi tribe depended on native plants: Indian ricegrass, fourwing saltbush, blackbrush, Mormon tea, wild turnip, sunflower, prickly pear, broadleaf yucca, pinyon pine, juniper.

Birds: No checklist. BLM leaflet mentions wrens, blackbirds, chickadees, finches, flycatchers, vireos, warblers, swallows, owls, hawks, eagles. Visitors are asked to report sightings so a list can be compiled.

No motorized vehicles are allowed in the Primitive Area.

ACTIVITIES

Backpacking: Permit required. Obtain at Kane Gulch Ranger Station or San Juan Resource Area Office in Monticello. Trash must be packed out, not buried or burned. No camping within 100 ft. of a water source.

Horseriding: Horse travel is possible in the upper canyon, not the lower. Contact the San Juan Resource Area in Monticello for reservations.

PUBLICATION: Folder with map.

REFERENCES

Hall, Dave. *The Hiker's Guide to Utah.* Billings, MT: Falcon Press, 1982. Pp. 178–181.

Barnes, F. A. *Canyon Country Hiking and Natural History.* Salt Lake City: Wasatch, 1977. Pp. 164–166.

Zwinger, Ann. *Wind in the Rock.* New York: Harper & Row. (Explores side canyons and trails.) $2.25.

HEADQUARTERS: BLM, San Juan Resource Area, Box 7, Monticello, UT 84535; (801) 587-2201.

HENRY MOUNTAINS
U.S. Bureau of Land Management
About 500,000 acres.

On SR 276 and 24; S of the Wayne County-Garfield County line. The three principal peaks are W of the highway; two others, known as the "Little Rockies," on the E side. Several fair-weather roads and jeep tracks cross the area. (MP #1.)

A rugged, dry, sparsely settled region of the Colorado Plateau. Explorers avoided the region until the late 1800s, and the Henry Mountains are said to be the last in the Lower 48 to be named and mapped. They are not a range with a recognizable ridgeline, but a group of separate peaks on a NW–SE line about 32 mi. long, rising abruptly from the desert floor at about 5,000 ft. elevation. Largest and highest, at the N end, is 11,615-ft. Mt. Ellen. Bull Mountain, 9,187 ft., is joined to Mt. Ellen by Wickiup Ridge. Mt. Pennell, 11,371 ft., is about 11 mi. to the S, 10,723-ft. Mt. Hillers 10 mi. SE of Pennell. E of SR 276, near the boundary of Glen Canyon National Recreation Area, are two lower mountains: Mt. Holmes, 7,930 ft., and Mt. Ellsworth, 8,235 ft., together known as the Little Rockies.

Multipurpose Map No. 1 shows a network of unpaved roads in the area W of SR 276. One from the N ascends Mt. Ellen; a lower route circles the peak. However, these roads enclose several large roadless areas, including one of 160,000 acres around Mt. Pennell.

The region is scenic and diverse, with good timber at higher elevations, numerous springs, flowing water, seasonal wildflower display, a free-roaming buffalo herd, considerable wildlife. Yet it has only about 6,500 visitors per year, an estimated half of them hunters.

Plants: Desert shrubs, sagebrush, and juniper at lower elevations, pinyon-juniper dominating at mid-elevations, with mountain-mahogany, shrub oak, aspen. Higher, Douglas-fir, ponderosa pine. Mt. Ellen and Mt. Hillers have stands of bristlecone pine.

Birds: No checklist. Mentioned: chukar, quail, dove, band-tailed pigeon, turkey, blue grouse, Clark's nutcracker, raven, American kestrel, chickadee, Steller's jay, pinyon jay, towhee, horned lark. Occasional waterfowl fall and spring.

Mammals: No checklist. Mentioned: cottontail, jackrabbit, mountain lion, mule deer. Free-roaming bison herd since 1941 transplant. Desert bighorn in Little Rockies.

FEATURES
Mt. Ellen: A series of high peaks and ridges separated by large basins and creek drainages. The most accessible of the Henry Mountains peaks; a 3-mi.

trail leads to the summit from Bull Creek Pass. Summer range for the buffalo herd, often seen grazing at 11,000 ft. Vegetation ranges from open meadow to thick forest. BLM has two campgrounds on the mountain: McMillan Springs and Lonesome Beaver. A 156,000-acre roadless area includes most of the mountain and extensive desert mesas and badlands to the N and NW.

Mt. Pennell: Second highest of the Henrys. A high dome 6 to 8 mi. in diameter rising from desert badlands. Many ridges, canyons, creeks. As on Mt. Ellen, vegetation is in four life zones: upper Sonoran, transition, Canadian, and Hudsonian. Part of the mountain is summer range for the buffalo herd. Easy access from unpaved road on E side. Along the road are undeveloped campsites. Hiking and backpacking opportunities are rated above average: routes to the summit and in such side canyons as Scratch, Dark, Swap, and Bullfrog.

Mt. Hillers: Steepest and most rugged of the Henrys, rising 5,000 ft. above the surrounding plateau. A high central peak surrounded by slightly lower peaks at the ends of long, radiating ridges, separated from the summit by low saddles. Vegetation is dense even at the summit. The most difficult of the Henrys to ascend, although an energetic hiker can reach the summit in 3 to 4 hours. BLM's Starr Springs Campground is on the S side. Pink Cliffs, an interesting formation, is nearby.

Little Rockies: Designated a National Natural Landmark because of interesting geology. The Henrys are composed of igneous material that intruded as magma into sedimentary layers later removed by erosion. A 66,000-acre roadless area includes Mt. Holmes and Mt. Ellsworth, surrounded by mesas and narrow plateaus cut by deep, narrow, meandering canyons. The E side of the area has massive slickrock formations. Easy access to this area from SR 276. Good opportunities for camping, day hiking, backpacking, with hiking routes continuing down to Lake Powell. But BLM reports only 125 visitors per year.

Sand Dunes: A small photogenic area SW of the junction of SR 276 and SR 95.

ACTIVITIES

Camping: BLM has several primitive and undeveloped campgrounds, none on the paved roads. Many suitable sites for informal camping.

Hiking, backpacking: Good opportunities for day hiking and backpacking. Trails are not marked or maintained, and meeting other hikers is unlikely. Check route, destination, and water sources with BLM. Carry compass, topo map, water.

Some backcountry roads may be suitable for ordinary cars in dry weather, but check road conditions before venturing far.

PUBLICATIONS

The Henry Mountains and Surrounding Deserts. Folder with map.
Across Public Lands on U-95. Leaflet with map.

REFERENCE: Hall, Dave. *The Hiker's Guide to Utah.* Billings, MT: Falcon
Press, 1982. Pp. 157–159.

HEADQUARTERS: BLM, Henry Mountain Resource Area, Box 99, Hanksville, UT 84734; (801) 542-3461.

HOLE-IN-THE-ROCK ROAD (OR "TRAIL")
See entry, Escalante River.

HORSESHOE CANYON
U.S. Bureau of Land Management; National Park Service
BLM: 144,840 acres; NPS: 5,120 acres.

Difficult access. From Hanksville, 21 mi. NE on SR 24, then about 24 mi.
S and E on unpaved road, which continues to the Maze in Canyonlands
National Park. From Green River, about 12 mi. S to the beginning of the
BLM site, which borders the Antelope Valley road. From Hans Flats in
Glen Canyon National Recreation Area (see MP #1) a dirt road with sharp
switchbacks drops down to the canyon bottom; for 4-wheel-drive vehicles.
For other routes into the canyon, consult BLM or a Park Ranger. (MP
#2.)

Several slickrock canyons converge in this deep gorge, which ends in the
Labyrinth Canyon of the Green River. The canyons are separated by sparsely
vegetated tables. Colorful, sheer sandstone walls 300 to 500 ft. high. Although
it was cut by water, the canyon now has only an intermittent stream.

The central portion of Horseshoe Canyon was added to Canyonlands National Park, some miles away, because of its many rock paintings and petroglyphs. The paintings, made with red dyes, show human and animal figures,
some life-size or larger. Visiting the paintings requires a 2-mi. hike beyond
the end of the road from Hans Flats. Adjacent lands are managed by BLM.

Between Horseshoe Canyon and the main portion of the National Park, N
of Hans Flats, is the Orange Cliffs section of Glen Canyon National Recreation Area (see entry). This section and Horseshoe Canyon are under wilderness study.

Plants: Desert shrub is dominant, particularly Mormon tea, shadscale,
rabbitbrush, snakeweed, blackbrush, fourwing saltbush, black sagebrush, and
wild buckwheat.

Wildlife: Habitat is available for sparse populations of coyote, bobcat,
cottontail, blacktail jackrabbit, woodrat, ringtail, badger, Ord kangaroo rat,

gray, red, and kit foxes, whitetail antelope squirrel, chipmunk, rock squirrel, raccoon, weasel, striped skunk, mice, and voles. Some mule deer frequent the canyon and river bottoms, and pronghorn have been seen. Beaver are found in the bordering Green River, and have used Barrier Creek and its cottonwood vegetation.

Bird life is sparse. Among the more common raptors are the golden eagle, prairie falcon, American kestrel, and red-tailed, ferruginous, and rough-legged hawks.

Side-blotched, collared, leopard, shorthorned, sagebrush, western fence, and common tree lizards are among the more common lizards, while Great Basin gopher snakes, striped whipsnakes, and western rattlesnakes are the most common snakes.

Camping: No developed campground. Camping in the canyon at road's end, and at other suitable places on BLM land.

HEADQUARTERS: Canyonlands National Park, 446 S. Main St., Moab, UT 84532; (801) 259-7164. BLM, San Rafael Resource Area Office, 900 N 700 E, Price, UT 84501; (801) 637-4584.

JOHNS CANYON; SLICKHORN CANYON
U.S. Bureau of Land Management
60,710 acres.

(1) To lower end of Johns Canyon: dirt road along the N rim of the San Juan River, from Goosenecks State Reserve (see entry), off SR 261. To upper end, by dirt road off SR 261. Not shown on MP #1; see hiker's map. (2) Access to Slickhorn Canyon, also off SR 261, is more difficult, requires hikers' map.

On Cedar Mesa W of SR 261. Between Grand Gulch Primitive Area on the N and a narrow strip of the Glen Canyon National Recreation Area along the San Juan River. Flat to rolling mesa cut by two large canyon systems. Slickhorn and Johns Canyons are deep, meandering, trending SW. Sagebrush and rabbitbrush common in canyon bottoms, with cottonwood, tamarisk, willow in moist areas. A 48,600-acre portion of this area was judged suitable for wilderness study.

Johns Canyon is narrow and confined in the N, broadening to more than a mile wide in the S. Four springs are shown on the hikers' map. Archeological sites.

Slickhorn is a canyon of many shapes and colors. Sandstone walls from 300 ft. in the N to 800 ft. near the San Juan River. Good water is scarce in summer and fall. Hikers' map shows seasonal springs, only two dependable springs, one of them in tributary Trail Canyon.

ACTIVITIES

Camping: Informal, along access roads.

Hiking, backpacking: Johns Canyon is relatively easy hiking. Allow 2 days from N to S, more if you explore side canyons. Hiking in Slickhorn Canyon is rugged. One must work around boulders, pour-offs, talus. Allow 4 days to hike the entire canyon. Advisable to discuss the route and hikers' map at BLM office. Bring topo map, water. Don't hike alone.

Some hikers arrange to be met by boat at the river.

PUBLICATION: Hikers' map; use in conjunction with topo.

REFERENCES

Barnes, F. A. *Canyon Country Hiking and Natural History.* Salt Lake City: Wasatch, 1977. Pp. 166–167.

Zwinger, Ann. *Wind in the Rock.* New York: Harper & Row. (Explores side canyons and trails.)

HEADQUARTERS: BLM, Moab District Office, 125 West Second South Main, Moab, UT 84532; (801) 259-6111. BLM, San Juan Resource Area, 480 South First Street West, Monticello, UT 84535; (801) 587-2201.

KAIPAROWITS PLATEAU
U.S. Bureau of Land Management
About 250,000 acres.

Principal access is Smoky Mountain Road, which runs from near Escalante S to Glen Canyon City. On MP #5, this road runs E; entering MP #1, it turns N on Smoky Mountain ("Smokey" on the map). Returning to MP #5, it continues N past the legend "Upper Valley Oil Field." The map shows other access by roads not well maintained.

This vast, uninhabited plateau, a maze of steep-walled canyons, has remained largely undeveloped except for cattle grazing, an oil field, and the relics of coal exploration. That almost changed when a gigantic coal-mining and electricity-generating complex was announced in 1964, a project including a new city. The environmental impacts would have affected nearby National Parks, National Monuments, and wilderness areas. Public opposition was so intense that the sponsors withdrew. About 150,000 acres bordering Glen Canyon National Recreation Area are still roadless and in natural condition. The Plateau is a rough triangle, with Lake Powell at its base. The E boundary is the escarpment of the Straight Cliffs. At the foot of the Cliffs is the Hole-in-the-Rock Road (see entries for Glen Canyon NRA and Escalante River). The Straight Cliffs rise about 1,000 ft. to the top of Fiftymile Mountain, offering fine views to the E. The Fiftymile Mountain area contains two natural arches, fossils, dinosaur tracks, and numerous archeological sites, including pictographs, petroglyphs, camp sites, cliff dwellings, and rock shelters.

Vegetation is sparse. We have no information on plant species, but the plateau species of Glen Canyon National Recreation Area are indicative. Wildlife species are also similar. The study mentioned under Reference includes observations along the Colorado River area that is now Lake Powell.

If you live in Utah and have ample time to explore, you might wish to become acquainted with the Plateau. It's vast, largely pristine, seen by few. "However," a BLM advisor wrote, "it is surrounded by big-league scenery and great backpacking areas such as the Escalante River, Paria-Hackberry, Boulder Mountain, Lake Powell, and Glen Canyon. Thus it is a lesser area sitting in the midst of superlatives. . . . It is dry and thus not very amenable to extended overnight trips."

The exception is Fiftymile Mountain. Not named on the Multipurpose Maps, this is the SE portion of the Plateau, where the legend "Kaiparowits Plateau" appears on Multipurpose Map No. 1. A green island rising from the arid canyon landscape, Fiftymile is the largest plateau or mesa still roadless in SW Utah. S end of the mountain is in the Glen Canyon National Recreation Area. The area has a small but discriminating following among backpackers and horse packers.

REFERENCE: Atwood, N. Duane, Clyde L. Pritchett, Richard D. Porter, and Benjamin W. Wood. "Terrestrial Vertebrate Fauna of the Kaiparowits Basin." *Great Basin Naturalist,* vol. 40, no. 4, December 1980.

HEADQUARTERS: BLM, Cedar City District, P.O. Box 724, 1579 North Main, Cedar City, UT 84720; (801) 586-2401.

KODACHROME BASIN STATE RESERVE
Utah State Division of Parks and Recreation
2,240 acres.

From Bryce Canyon junction, E 22 mi. on SR 12. (MP #5.)

So named because of the rich colors of its spectacular rock formations. Among the many formations are about 40 monolithic spires, or "chimneys," jutting up from the valley floor or protruding from sandstone rocks. The spires, different in composition and color from the rocks on which they rest, are from a few feet up to 130 ft. tall. They are said to be unique in the world. A recently discovered natural arch is about 90 ft. high.

Elevations 5,000–6,000 ft. Moderate semidesert climate. Annual precipitation about 12 in., average snowfall 2–3 ft.

The Reserve is an attractive base for exploring nearby areas.

Plants: Pinyon-juniper association. Plants typical of the upper Sonoran life zone include yucca, prickly pear, sagebrush, snakeweed, evening primrose, beeplant.

Birds: 30 species recorded. Partial list includes golden eagle, raven, pinyon jay, mourning dove, robin, loggerhead shrike, mountain and western bluebirds, blue grosbeak, lazuli bunting.

Mammals: 20 species recorded. Partial list includes mule deer, mountain lion, coyote, spotted skunk, gray fox, bobcat, kit fox, kangaroo rat, antelope ground squirrel.

INTERPRETATION
Slide show and *guided walks* on request, not scheduled.
Exhibit at campground.

ACTIVITIES
Camping: 24 sites. All year.
Hiking: 3-mi. loop trail to Panorama Point. Trail to newly discovered arch. Dirt-road trail 1 1/2 mi. to Chimney Rock, a sand pipe.

NEARBY
Paria-Hackberry. See entry.
Grosvenor Arch. 10 mi. on Cottonwood Canyon road.
Bryce Canyon National Park. SR 12 NW to Tropic. 3 mi. W of Tropic, on the canyon floor, is a trail up to the rim near the Park lodge.

PUBLICATIONS
Park brochure.
Nature trail guide.

HEADQUARTERS: P.O. Box 238, Cannonville, UT 84718; (801) 679-8562.

LA VERKIN CREEK
See entry, Zion National Park.

MANTI-LA SAL NATIONAL FOREST; LA SAL DIVISION

U.S. Forest Service
535,184 acres; 543,789 acres within boundaries. (27,105 acres in CO.)

Two areas near the CO border. (A) The Moab Ranger District, E of Moab and US 163. Access to N via Castle Valley Road, from the W via Spanish Valley Road (see entry, Moab Area, in Zone 2). To the S portion from SR 46, E of La Sal. (MP #2.) (B) The Monticello Ranger District, W of Monticello. Access from Monticello and Blanding on US 163. (MP #1.)

A. *The Moab Ranger District,* 174,658 acres, is in the La Sal Mountains, second highest range in Utah. Waas, Tomasaki, Peale, and three other peaks are over 12,000 ft. The mountain mass, more than 15 mi. long, 6 mi. wide, rises more than 6,000 ft. above the valley floor. The slopes are broad and gradual below, becoming much steeper above 10,000 ft. elevation.

Annual precipitation ranges from 8 in. at low elevations to 36 in. on the upper slopes, where winter snowfall totals about 8 ft. This R.D. has a few small ponds and reservoirs, no notable streams.

Visitor use of this R.D. is low but increasing gradually. The principal activity is hunting. The La Sal Mountains Scenic Loop, which passes through the R.D., is advertised by the Grand County Travel Council, and more tourists make the circuit each year. Spur roads off the loop lead to points of interest. Snowmobiling is popular. Hiking and backpacking are minor activities, despite attractive opportunities.

This R.D. surrounds the La Sal Mountain State Forest (see entry).

B. *The Monticello Ranger District,* 369,131 acres, attracts somewhat more visitors, chiefly near its E boundary. The E half is a ponderosa pine-covered mesa surrounding the Abajo Mountains. The highest point, Abajo Peak, is 11,360 ft. elevation. The W half is a jumble of ridges, mountains, canyons, and mesas, the highest point 9,200 ft. Except for hunting, most public use is along the access roads from Monticello and Blanding.

Snowfall is variable. One year there may be large snowdrifts in Monticello, at the mountain base, with mountain snowbanks still present in July. The next winter may have so little snow that mountain roads remain open.

The Monticello R.D. and a large part of the Moab R.D. are in San Juan county, one of the largest counties in the United States with a population of only 12,500, more than half of them Navajo Indians. About 90% of the land is federally owned. Terrain is generally rugged and wild. Cattle ranching was the principal activity until overgrazing reduced carrying capacity.

Both R.D.'s offer excellent opportunities for quiet backcountry enjoyment.

Plants: The lower slopes and mesa tops are mostly pinyon-juniper woodland, from below 6,000 ft. in canyon bottoms to about 8,500 ft. on some S slopes. Mountain brush—chiefly Gambel oak, serviceberry, and birchleaf mahogany—occupies much of the area between 7,000 and 9,000 ft. Ponderosa pine occurs on mesa tops, ridges, and benchlands between 7,000 and 8,500 ft., with oakbrush, snowberry, and manzanita dominant in the understory. Aspen typifies the Canadian life zone, between 8,000 and 9,000 ft., with a great variety of understory species. Douglas-fir and white fir appear on steep N and E slopes above 7,500 ft., subalpine fir and Engelmann spruce becoming dominant up to 10,000 ft., sticky currant and wild gooseberry common in the understory.

Some 530 species and varieties of plants occur in the zone. No checklist of flowering species is available.

Birds: Checklist of 207 species available. Seasonally common or abundant species include eared grebe, snowy egret, black-crowned night-heron, Canada goose, mallard, gadwall, northern pintail, green-winged and cinnamon teals, American wigeon, northern shoveler, redhead, canvasback, lesser scaup, ruddy duck, common merganser. Also turkey vulture, goshawk; Cooper's, red-tailed, and rough-legged hawks; golden eagle, northern harrier, prairie falcon, American kestrel; blue, ruffed, and sage grouse, California quail, chukar, ring-necked pheasant, American coot, killdeer, black-bellied plover, common snipe; spotted, least, and western sandpipers; lesser yellowlegs, long-billed dowitcher, marbled godwit, American avocet, black-necked stilt, Wilson's and northern phalaropes, Franklin's gull, Forster's and black terns. Also great horned and long-eared owls, common nighthawk, poor-will. Hummingbirds: black-chinned, broad-tailed, rufous, and calliope. Northern flicker, yellow-bellied sapsucker, hairy and downy woodpeckers, western kingbird; ash-throated, willow, dusky, and western flycatchers; Say's phoebe, horned lark; violet-green, tree, bank, rough-winged, barn, and cliff swallows; Steller's, scrub, and pinyon jays; black-billed magpie, common raven, Clark's nutcracker. Also black-capped and mountain chickadees, bushtit; white-breasted, red-breasted, and pygmy nuthatches; brown creeper, dipper; house, rock, canyon, and Bewick's wrens; sage thrasher, American robin, hermit and Swainson's thrushes, Townsend's solitaire, blue-gray gnatcatcher, ruby-crowned kinglet, water pipit, loggerhead shrike, European starling, warbling vireo. Warblers: orange-crowned, Virginia's, yellow-rumped, yellow, MacGillivray's, yellow-breasted chat, Wilson's. Also house sparrow, western meadowlark; yellow-headed, red-winged, and Brewer's blackbirds; Bullock's oriole, brown-headed cowbird, western tanager, black-headed and blue grosbeaks, lazuli bunting, green-tailed and rufous-sided towhees. Sparrows: vesper, lark, chipping, Brewer's, white-crowned, song. Dark-eyed and gray-headed juncos, evening grosbeak; Cassin's, house, and rosy finches; pine siskin, American goldfinch.

Mammals: Checklist of 82 species. Common species include: vagrant, dusky, and northern water shrews; little brown, long-eared, long-legged, and California myotis; silver-haired, big brown, western big-eared, pallid, and Mexican free-tailed bats; western pipistrel, pika, blacktail jackrabbit, mountain and desert cottontails, Zuni and white-tailed prairie dogs; red and rock squirrels, golden-mantled ground squirrel, whitetail antelope squirrel, yellow-belly marmot; least, Colorado, and Uinta chipmunks; northern and valley pocket gophers, Ord kangaroo rat, Apache pocket mouse, beaver. Mice: western harvest, canyon, deer, brush, pinyon, house. Desert and bushytail woodrats, muskrat. Voles: meadow, mountain, Richardson's, longtail, sagebrush; black and Norway rats; western jumping mouse, porcupine, coyote, gray fox, black bear, ringtail, longtail weasel, badger, striped and spotted skunks, mountain lion, mule deer, elk.

Reptiles and amphibians: Great Basin spadefoot, red spotted, and Woodhouse's toads; chorus and leopard frogs. Lizards: collared, leopard, eastern fence, desert spiny, sagebrush, tree, side-blotched, short-horned, western whiptail. Striped whipsnake, racer, gopher snake, western terrestrial garter snake, night snake, midget faded rattlesnake.

FEATURES

In Monticello Ranger District:

Dark Canyon-Woodenshoe Canyon: 60,000 acres. On the W side of the R.D. A wishbone-shaped area including the main canyons and side canyons below the mesa shoulder. Deep sandstone canyons, vertical walls from a few hundred to several thousand feet. Three natural arches in Dark Canyon. Remote, roadless, proposed for wilderness status. Road access from SR 95 to Kilgalia Guard Station, then jeep trail. (MP #1.) Inquire about road conditions. Adjoins the Dark Canyon Primitive Area (see entry); some backpackers enter by trail from there.

Arch, Butts, and Texas Canyons, 11,500 acres, near the SW corner of the R.D., join together near the boundary. Access by dirt road from SR 95 just W of the bridge over Comb Wash, 16 mi. W of Blanding. (*The Hiker's Guide to Utah,* pp. 183–187.) Access and part of Arch Canyon on BLM land. Sandstone sheer canyon walls, benches, some gentle slopes. Arch Canyon is about 13 mi. long, ascends from 5,000 ft. to 8,000 ft. Stream with deep pools. Sagebrush, yucca, pinyon, juniper, cacti, wildflowers; ponderosa pine at the upper end.

Hammond and Notch Canyons, 20,000 acres. Roadless. Access from Kilgalia Guard Station. Benches, vertical canyon walls, many rock spires.

Ruin Canyon, 9,000 acres, at the NW corner of the R.D., adjoining BLM land. So named for cliff dwellings on the BLM side. Benches, slopes, canyon walls. Scattered stands of ponderosa pine, Douglas-fir, aspen. Jeep trail access.

ACTIVITIES

Camping: In Moab R.D.: 4 campgrounds, 36 sites. June–Oct. In Monticello R.D.: 4 campgrounds, 58 sites. June–Oct. Many suitable places for informal camping throughout the area.

Hiking, backpacking: Moab R.D. has descriptions of 7 trails, 3 to 14 1/2 mi., which can be linked in a 25-mi. chain; small map. Monticello R.D. describes 9 trails, 3 to 19 mi., with small map. Some trails are in poor condition and trail maintenance budgets are uncertain. Backpackers should consult R.D. Office, carry topo map, compass, water.

Horse riding: No special rules or facilities. No local outfitters.

Hunting: Deer, elk. Deer herd, once large, is now small.

Fishing: Limited. A few small reservoirs.

Skiing: Some helicopter skiing in Moab R.D. Usual season: Nov. 1–Mar. 15. Blue Mountain Ski Area in Monticello R.D. Usual season: Nov. 15–Mar. 1.

Ski touring: No special areas. Seasons same as for skiing.

Snowmobiling: Popular. No special trails.

PUBLICATIONS

Forest map. $1.00. (1962 edition; not current.)
La Sal Division map. $1.00. (1965 edition, about 1 in. = 2 mi.)
Forest trails descriptions, small maps.
Wildlife species checklists.
Archeology leaflet, Monticello R.D.
Travel Plan, map showing areas closed to off-road vehicles.

REFERENCES

Barnes, F. A. *Canyon Country Hiking and Natural History.* Salt Lake City: Wasatch, 1977. Pp. 77–78, 82–86, 138–141.
Hall, Dave. *The Hiker's Guide to Utah.* Billings, MT: Falcon Press, 1982. Pp. 183–187.

HEADQUARTERS: 599 S. Price River Dr., Price, UT 84501; (801) 637-2817.

RANGER DISTRICTS: Moab R.D., 446 S. Main, Moab, UT 84532; (801) 259-7155. Monticello R.D., 185 N. First East, Monticello, UT 84535; (801) 587-2114.

MONUMENT VALLEY TRIBAL PARK
Navajo Indian Reservation
29,816 acres.

Crossed by US 163 in UT and AZ. (MP #1.)

Everyone has seen it, in films, TV commercials, photographs: widely spaced maroon spires, towers, castles, buttes, pinnacles rising a thousand feet above the flat desert floor.

Goulding's Trading Post and the turn off US 163 to the visitor center are in UT, but the visitor center, campground, and most of the Park are in Arizona.

The formations can be seen from the highway, at some distance. A 17-mi. dirt tour route begins at the visitor center and passes among some of the more impressive monuments. The route is open during daylight hours. Guided tours are available.

Camping: 100 sites.

PUBLICATION: Information folder with map.

HEADQUARTERS: Box 93, Monument Valley, UT 84536; (801) 727-3287.

MOQUITH MOUNTAIN
U.S. Bureau of Land Management
14,830 acres.

W of Kanab on the AZ border. Adjoins Coral Pink Sand Dunes State Reserve on the W. Cottonwood Canyon is E boundary. (MP #5.)

Sand dunes in the W and N. Moquith Mountain extends less than 4 mi. N from the AZ border, on the W side of the area. Highest point is 7,028 ft. The Vermillion Cliffs, large red and orange cliffs, lie on both E and W sides of Moquith Mountain. Deep canyons in the E portion of the area.

Perennial water in some of the canyons. Seeps, springs, and hanging gardens in several canyons and alcoves. Upper Water Canyon is pristine; no grazing has occurred. Ephemeral ponds collect in the sand dune area after rain.

Indian pictographs in the South Fork area, in the N portion of the site.

Plants: Most of the mountain slopes are covered with thick stands of ponderosa pine, pinyon, juniper, and Gambel oak. The deep canyons have some cottonwood and boxelder. Stands of Douglas-fir on S canyon walls. Ponderosa pine grows on sand dunes.

HEADQUARTERS: BLM, Cedar City District, 1579 North Main, Cedar City, UT 84720; (801) 586-2401.

NATURAL BRIDGES NATIONAL MONUMENT
National Park Service
7,780 acres.

40 mi. W of Blanding on SR 95.

The Monument is near the intersection of SR 261, where the Trail of the Ancients (see entry) turns S. The central features are three arches stream-carved in sandstone. The largest is 210 ft. high, with a span of 204 ft.; the smallest is 106 ft. high, with a span of 180 ft. Beyond the visitor center is an 8-mi. auto tour loop with numerous viewpoints. From this loop trails lead down to other viewpoints, into White Canyon, and along the stream bed.

The Monument serves as an interpretive center for surrounding canyon-lands. Only limited data is available on the flora and fauna of this vast area, including most of the sites named in our entry for Trail of the Ancients. The Monument's visitor center and publications explain the geological history. Monument Rangers have gathered weather data daily since 1965. Checklists of plants, birds, and mammals are available.

The Monument is open all year. Spring and early summer are the best season for wildflower displays, mid-Sept. to mid-Nov. for ideal climate. Summer days can be too warm for pleasant hiking. Winter snows add drama to the scenery, but most trails are closed in winter because of snow, ice, and mud.

Annual precipitation is 12.5 in. May–June are the driest months, July–Aug. the wettest, although Oct., Nov., and Dec. also have above-average precipitation. Annual snowfall is about 50 in., two-thirds of it in Dec.–Feb.

Recorded temperatures range from −11° to 104°F, but these are the extremes. The average maximum in the hottest month, July, is 91°, with humidity below 20%. Daytime winter temperatures are usually above 40°, average minimums near 20°.

Plants: Extensive checklist available. Vegetation is sparse but varied. On the plateau, pinyon-juniper dominates. Douglas-fir, oak, and maple occur along the cliffs. Below the plateau, desert shrubs predominate except in the moister canyon bottoms, where cottonwood and willow grow.

Flowering species include snowberry, common yarrow, pussytoes, aster, Utah thistle, fleabane, sunflower, goldenrod, prince's plume, phacelia, lupines, clovers, false Solomon's-seal, blazing star, globemallow, four-o'clock, primrose, scarlet gilia, phlox, eriogonum, columbine, larkspur, clematis, wild rose, Indian paintbrush, penstemon.

Birds: A checklist, "Birds of the Canyon Country," was sent to us after we had completed our fieldwork. We were surprised by its length and diversity, and by the designation of so many species as "common." It applies to a more extensive area than the Monument, with more diverse habitats. The checklist includes species observed in the Monument and its vicinity. Seasonally common: eared, western, and pied-billed grebes; white pelican, American bittern. White-faced ibis, whistling swan, Canada goose, mallard, gadwall, pintail, green-winged and cinnamon teals, American wigeon, northern shoveler, redhead, canvasback, lesser scaup, common and red-breasted mergansers, turkey vulture, goshawk; sharp-shinned, Cooper's, red-tailed, Swainson's, rough-legged, and ferruginous hawks; golden eagle, northern harrier, prairie falcon, merlin, American kestrel, Gambel's quail, chukar, wild turkey. Also Virginia rail, sora, American coot, killdeer, common snipe, spotted sandpiper, greater and lesser yellowlegs, least sandpiper, long-billed dowitcher, western sandpiper, marbled godwit, American avocet, black-necked stilt, Wilson's and northern phalaropes; California, ring-billed, and Franklin's gulls; Forster's and black terns, mourning dove. Owls: screech, great horned, long-eared, short-eared. Common nighthawk, poor-will, white-throated swift. Hummingbirds: black-chinned, broad-tailed, rufous, and calliope. Northern flicker, yellow-bellied sapsucker, hairy woodpecker; dusky, ash-throated, willow, gray, and western flycatchers; horned lark, eastern and western kingbirds. Swallows: violet-green, tree, bank, rough-winged, barn, and cliff. Steller's, scrub, and pinyon jays; black-billed magpie, common raven, American crow, Clark's nutcracker. Also black-capped and mountain chickadees, plain titmouse, bushtit; white-breasted, red-breasted, and pygmy nuthatches; brown creeper, dipper; house, canyon, and rock wrens; sage thrasher, robin, hermit and Swainson's thrushes, western and mountain bluebirds, Townsend's solitaire, blue-gray gnatcatcher, ruby-crowned kinglet, water pipit, bohemian waxwing, loggerhead shrike, European starling, warbling vireo. Warblers: yellow-breasted chat, orange-crowned, Virginia's, yellow, yellow-rumped, black-throated gray, Grace's, MacGillivray's, common yellowthroat.

Also western meadowlark; yellow-headed, red-winged, and Brewer's blackbirds; northern oriole, brown-headed cowbird, western tanager; black-headed, blue, and evening grosbeaks; lazuli bunting. Finches: Cassin's, house, gray-crowned rosy, pine siskin, American and lesser goldfinches, green-tailed and rufous-sided towhees. Sparrows: savannah, vesper, lark, dark-eyed, chipping, Brewer's, white-crowned, Lincoln's song; dark-eyed and gray-headed juncos.

Mammals: Checklist available. Common or abundant species include California myotis, little brown, pallid, and silver-haired bats; mule deer, coyote, desert and Mexican woodrats; brush, canyon, deer, and pinyon mice; western harvest mouse, northern grasshopper mouse, Apache pocket mouse, blacktail jackrabbit, desert and mountain cottontails, Merriam shrew, Colorado and least chipmunks, rock squirrel. Uncommon here: mountain lion; gray, red, and kit foxes; valley pocket gopher, bushytail and whitethroat woodrats, Ord kangaroo rat, raccoon, ringtail, desert shrew, whitetail antelope squirrel, badger, longtail weasel, spotted and striped skunks.

INTERPRETATION

Visitor center has historical and geological exhibits, slide show. Open daily 8 A.M.–6 P.M. May to Labor Day, 8 A.M.–4:30 P.M. rest of the year. *Campfire programs,* June–Sept.

ACTIVITIES

Camping: Primitive. 13 sites. No other camping in the Monument. Drinking water at visitor center only. Nearest sites with hookups are private campgrounds at Blanding, Mexican Hat, Monticello, 38 to 64 mi. distant. Several public campgrounds without hookups within the same radius. Many suitable, informal sites on nearby public land.

Hiking: 10 trails, one-way travel times 1/2 hr. to 1 1/2 hrs. Trailheads on loop road. No trailside or backcountry camping in the Monument.

PUBLICATIONS

Leaflet with map.
Trail map and information.
Information pages:
Geology of the area.
Weather information.
Fees, interpretive activities, general.
Plant checklist.
Bird checklist.
Mammal checklist.
Alternative campgrounds.
Photovoltaics. Leaflet.
Bridge to the Future. Solar energy pamphlet.

REFERENCES

Hall, Dave. *The Hiker's Guide to Utah.* Billings, MT: Falcon Press, 1982. Pp. 174–178.
Barnes, F. A. *Canyon Country Hiking and Natural History.* Salt Lake City: Wasatch, 1977. Pp. 143–147.
Welsh, Stanley L., and Glen Moore. *Plants of Natural Bridges National Monument.* Provo, UT: Brigham Young University Press, no date.

HEADQUARTERS: 446 S. Main St., Moab, UT 84532; (801) 259-7164.

PARIA RIVER

The headwaters of the Paria River are in the pink cliffs formations of Bryce Canyon National Park and the Table Cliffs Plateau in the Dixie National

Forest. The river flows to the Colorado River at Lees Ferry in the Glen Canyon National Recreation Area. This area has some of the nation's outstanding scenic geology in extensive natural areas.

Following are entries for two sections of the river: BLM's Paria-Hackberry unit and Paria Canyon Primitive Area. See also Kodachrome Basin State Reserve.

PARIA CANYON PRIMITIVE AREA
U.S. Bureau of Land Management
27,515 acres.

> From Kanab, 43 mi. E on US 89. Beyond the Paria River crossing, look for sign; S 3 mi. on an unpaved road to the White House entrance. An alternative hiking route begins in Buckskin Gulch. From US 89 about 38 mi. E of Kanab, S on House Rock Valley Road; access points at 4 and 8 mi. S of US 89. (MP #5.)

One of the classical backpacking treks, a 4- to 6-day 35-mi. journey through a rugged, spectacular canyon, ending at Lee's Ferry, AZ, below Glen Canyon Dam. It was designated a Primitive Area in 1969 to preserve its wilderness qualities. The Arizona Wilderness Act, if adopted, will establish a 110,000-acre Paria Canyon-Vermillion Cliffs Wilderness Area.

The hike is considered moderately strenuous. There are no major obstacles for the first 23 mi. At a boulder slide, most hikers detour. About 2,000 hikers per year make the trip. Mar.–June and Sept.–Oct. are the popular seasons. Summers are hot, and the water is cold in winter. Spring hiking is in ankle-deep water with several waist-deep crossings. The upper river is dry in summer, with shallow water below. However, flash floods are frequent from July through Sept., and hiking may be impossible then.

The Narrows begins 4.2 mi. from the White House ruins. For the next 5 mi. there is no possible escape from a flash flood. The hiker must get a weather forecast before setting out, and at 3.9 mi. must decide whether to camp or continue to the next possible campsite at 9.0 mi. Hiking upstream from Lee's Ferry is prohibited because the hiker's weather information would be outdated when he or she approached The Narrows.

The Buckskin Gulch route is about 10 mi. longer and much more difficult. Under the best conditions, the gorge can be traversed in 12 hours of hard going. The 12-mi.-long canyon is highly dangerous in flash floods. Swift, turbulent water can reach depths of 20 ft., and there are few places where one can climb. At The Dive, the canyon narrows to as little as 3 ft., and average width beyond is less than 15 ft. Near the confluence with the Paria, a rock jam with 30-ft. drop requires use of ropes.

Drinking water is available at the entrance station. The first reliable water source in the canyon is 11 mi. downstream; no water is available in the last 11 mi. All water should be treated.

Plants: Vegetation is typical of the semidesert region. Pinyon-juniper with occasional ponderosa pine dominate the canyon rims. Areas of relatively heavy clay soils support sparse stands of sand dropseed, shadscale brush, prickly pear. Looser sandy soils support fair stands of Indian ricegrass with buckwheat, rabbitbrush, fourwing saltbush. Riparian species include cottonwood, willow, boxelder.

Wildlife: No inventory has been made. Observed bird species include eagles, raven, hawks, dove, killdeer, white-throated swift, cliff swallow. Mammals mentioned include raccoon, fox, beaver, bobcat, mule deer.

FEATURES

Wrather Arch, a 200-ft. natural formation, is 2 mi. up a side canyon.

ACTIVITIES

Backpacking: Permit required. Can be obtained at the Kanab office during regular office hours or by telephone, no more than 24 hrs. before departure. During the high season (late Mar. through Oct.) permits may be obtained from a Ranger at the Canyon entrance Thurs. through Mon., 8 A.M.–11 P.M.; however, funding for this service is not assured.

PUBLICATION: *Hikers Guide to Paria.* Folder with map.

HEADQUARTERS: BLM, Cedar City District, 1579 North Main, Cedar City, UT 84720; (801) 586-2401. Kanab Area Office, 320 North First East, Kanab, UT 84741; (801) 644-2672.

PARIA-HACKBERRY
U.S. Bureau of Land Management
150,080 acres.

SE of Bryce Canyon. S of Cannonville and Henrieville, extending to US 89. E boundary is the Cottonwood Wash road from Cannonville past Kodachrome Basin State Reserve SE and S past Grosvenor Arch. (MP #5.)

Outstandingly scenic, the backdrop for many western films. The area has long had a devoted following of backpackers and backcountry guides. Attractive features throughout the area and numerous access routes tend to disperse visitors, so they seldom meet. While a few thousand people visit the Old Paria Townsite movie set area yearly, backpackers number only a few hundred.

This Wilderness Study Area includes 22 mi. of the river. Extremely varied and rugged terrain. Central features are the deeply entrenched canyon of the Paria River and Hackberry Canyon, converging in the S sector. Each has numerous side canyons that can be hiked. On the E is The Cockscomb, technically the East Kaibab Monocline, a high N–S ridge about 150 mi. long, colorful, with a jagged crest. The road from Kodachrome Basin follows Cottonwood Wash, a fair-weather road, at the base of the ridge.

Visitors to the National Parks of SW Utah soon hear about the "ascending staircase," the colorful layers of geological history exposed by the cliff-and-terrace physiography from the Grand Canyon northward. Conspicuous in this region are the Vermillion Cliffs, White Cliffs, and Pink Cliffs. At Bull Valley Gorge and Deer Creek Canyon, the Paria River is the easternmost extension of the White Cliffs. Height of these white or yellow cliffs varies from 600 to 1,200 ft. The cliffline is interrupted by eight major canyons. Side canyons also have vertical walls. The major canyons are as much as 6 1/2 mi. long, with walls over 700 ft. high for much of their length.

The Vermillion Cliffs are also part of the area's visual features. Here the landscape includes the cliffs, benches, moderately entrenched canyons, and badlands beneath the cliffs.

The diverse topography offers a display of cliffs, nobs, domes, aprons, monoclines, anticlines, mesas, and natural arches in shades of white, red, blue, gray, and purple, contrasting with the strips of brilliant green riparian vegetation along the streams.

Paria, Hackberry, and Cottonwood Canyons all contain perennial streams. Water quality is poor, not recommended for human consumption. The Paria transports much sediment. The area has two dozen undeveloped springs.

Plants: Pinyon-juniper woodland predominates, with some ponderosa pine in suitable habitats. Smaller areas of other associations: sagebrush, bunchgrass, Mormon tea.

Wildlife: No inventory has been made. Known to be in the area: mule deer, cottontail, a few mountain lion in winter.

Wilderness designation would outlaw ORV's. At present there is no ban, but activity is limited. ORV's have driven the canyon, infrequently; tracks wash away with the next high water.

ACTIVITIES

Hiking, backpacking: Easy access. Hundreds of miles of possible routes. During the summer, hikers are advised to consult BLM's Paria Ranger.

Horse riding: Opportunities are good but more limited than for foot travel. Consult.

REFERENCE: Hall, Dave. *The Hiker's Guide to Utah.* Billings, MT: Falcon Press, 1982. Pp. 148–154.

HEADQUARTERS: BLM, Cedar City District, 1579 North Main, Cedar City, UT 84720; (801) 586-2401.

PARKER MOUNTAIN STATE FOREST
Utah Division of State Lands and Forestry
94,000 acres.

W of Capitol Reef National Park. From intersection of SR 24 and SR 72
at Loa, about 11 mi. W to Piute-Wayne county line on summit. 12 mi. S on
unimproved road. (MP #6 for access route; MP #5 for site.)

Most of the Forest is on the Awapa Plateau, which slopes to the E. Most of
the plateau is above 8,000 ft.; highest point is 9,995 ft. The plateau ends
abruptly on the W, steep cliffs dropping 3,000 ft. to Grass Valley and Otter
Creek reservoirs. Splendid views on W escarpment.

Sagebrush slopes and open rangeland to the E, with stands of aspen toward
the W. Only 25% of the area is forested. Annual precipitation is 15–20 in.,
snowfall about 100 in.

Several unimproved roads on the E side. Access for two-wheel-drive vehicles in good weather. Hiking opportunities on jeep, stock, and game trails.

Plants: Primarily sagebrush with stands of aspen on E side. Some areas of
spruce-fir, Douglas-fir, limber pine, and pinyon-juniper.

Birds: Sage grouse, forest grouse.

Mammals: Cottontail, jackrabbit, snowshoe hare, pronghorn, mule deer,
coyote, elk.

ACTIVITIES
Camping: No developed campground. Numerous unimproved sites.
Hunting: Deer, pronghorn, sage grouse.

HEADQUARTERS: Division of State Lands and Forestry, Southwestern Regional Office, 130 North Main St., Richfield, UT 84701; (801) 896-6494.

PARUNUWEAP CANYON
U.S. Bureau of Land Management; National Park Service
47,696 acres of BLM land; also crosses Zion National Park.

From Mt. Carmel Junction on US 89 to Springdale at S entrance of Zion
National Park. Access from US 89 crosses private land. (MP #5.)

This was described to us as "a very special place," but we were asked to
emphasize the difficulties, beginning with the need to cross private land at the

beginning and end of the hike. Alternative routes are possible, but only with advice from a Zion National Park or BLM staff member or someone else who has been there.

This hike is considered more difficult than the trip through the Zion Narrows on the North Fork of the Virgin River. Flash flooding is a hazard, especially in the narrows. ("Last week the water was 35 feet deep.") *Parunuweap* means "roaring water." Among the obstacles is 30-ft. Labyrinth Falls inside Zion NP; the way around it is a high, narrow ledge. Search and rescue operations here would be slow and difficult.

The Canyon is on the East Fork of the Virgin River. About 8 mi. of the route is on BLM-managed land, about 8 mi. across the S end of Zion National Park. The BLM portion lies in a large basin nearly encircled by the White Cliffs, which extend E from Zion NP. The roadless area includes 31 mi. of major tributary canyons.

The canyons are serpentine and narrow. The narrowest section along the East Fork is called The Barracks. Heavy riparian vegetation, including wild grapes and many wildflowers. Numerous springs. BLM and the National Park Service give the area their highest scenic rating.

At low water it is said to be a 2- to 3-day hike to Springdale. At high water one may have to wait for the water to go down. Carry an air mattress to float gear across pools.

Trail guides issued by Zion National Park make no mention of Parunuweap, suggesting that there is no good public access below that section of the canyon.

HEADQUARTERS: BLM, Cedar City District, 1579 North Main, Cedar City, UT 84720; (801) 586-2401.

RAINBOW BRIDGE NATIONAL MONUMENT
National Park Service
160 acres.

Difficult land access. By boat on Lake Powell.
Largest of the world's known natural bridges: 270 ft. span, 290 ft. high. The surrounding Rainbow Plateau is so rugged that few people, Indian or white, had seen it before the filling of Lake Powell provided a water route.

A few hardy souls make it each year, 24 mi. on foot or horseback by the trail from Navajo Mountain Trading Post, 13 mi. on foot from abandoned Rainbow Lodge. Most come by commercial cruise boat or private craft from one of the lake's marinas to the floating marina near the great arch. See entry, Glen Canyon National Recreation Area.

HEADQUARTERS: Glen Canyon National Recreation Area, Box 1507, Page, AZ 86040; (602) 645-2471.

RED CLIFFS RECREATION SITE
U.S. Bureau of Land Management

About 12 mi. NE of St. George, off I-15. (MP #5.)

At the base of the Red Cliffs, within the desert climatic zone. A 1/2-mi. nature trail emphasizes desert plants.

We include this site because of its strategic location, near the Kolob section of Zion National Park, the Dixie National Forest, and other sites for which we have entries; see the zone map.

Camping: 13 sites. All year.

PUBLICATIONS
Red Cliffs Recreation Site.
Red Cliffs Recreation Site: Desert Trail.

HEADQUARTERS: BLM, Cedar City District, 1579 North Main Street, Cedar City, UT 84720; (801) 586-2401.

SAN JUAN RIVER: BLUFF TO CLAY HILLS CROSSING
Most adjacent land is public domain.

Sand Island, near Bluff on US 163, is a BLM campground and launch site. From here, float trip to Mexican Hat is 1 to 2 days. The river then enters the Goosenecks and flows through a canyon to Clay Hills Crossing, at the head of the Glen Canyon impoundment. Mexican Hat to Clay Hills Crossing is 2-plus days. (MP #1.)

From Sand Island to 18 mi. below Mexican Hat, the N bank is mostly public land, and the S bank is Navajo Indian Reservation. From that point to Clay Hills Crossing, both sides of the river are in the Glen Canyon National Recreation Area.

Mostly flatwater. One Class III rapid. Float trips can be arranged with outfitters at Mexican Hat or Bluff. Float traffic is not heavy, except for May and June. The season here is longer than on Utah whitewater streams.

From the river one can hike up Johns Canyon or Slickhorn Canyon, or into the Grand Gulch Primitive Area (see entries). Some hikers come down the canyons and, by arrangement, are met by rafts.

The river is navigable by power boats from Lake Powell. See entry, Glen Canyon National Recreation Area.

REFERENCE: Zwinger, Ann. *Wind in the Rock.* New York: Harper & Row. (Explores side canyons and trails.)

HEADQUARTERS: BLM, Moab District Office, 125 West Second South Main, Moab, UT 84532; (801) 259-6111.

SNOW CANYON STATE PARK; RED MOUNTAIN
Utah State Division of Parks and Recreation; U.S. Bureau of Land Management
6,200 acres; 20,260 acres.

9 mi. N of St. George. (MP #5.)

Most of this picturesque 3-mi.-long canyon is in Snow Canyon State Park. Carved in red Navajo sandstone, portions covered by black lava from cones near the canyon head. Red sand dunes, pictographs. Elevations from 2,600 ft. at the canyon floor to 3,500 ft. atop the volcanic cinder cones. The canyon has been used as a film set.

Among the sandstone domes are desert tanks, natural pools formed by rain runoff. Lava caves are 3/4 mi. from the road. Johnson's Arch is reached by a 3/4-mi. trail. Panorama Point overlook drive is off SR 18.

At the head of the canyon are two cinder cones marking the most recent Utah volcanoes. The cones are similar to Sunset Crater in Arizona. One has been damaged by quarrying.

Red Mountain is a large mass of red sandstone rising abruptly to 1,400 ft. above terrain to the S. The rise on the N side is more moderate. The top is a large plateau with buttes, spires, perennial ponds, shallow canyons. Snow Canyon is partially within the BLM-managed area, and the plateau overlooks the canyon.

Hiking routes to the roadless plateau include an old jeep road from Upper Sand Cave Reservoir to the N; the road is not signed and is easily missed. From Ivins, on the S, there is an old stock trail, used when sheep were moved to the plateau for the summer.

Our BLM contact called it "just a nice backcountry area," good for early spring and late fall hiking because of the moderate climate.

Camping: At Snow Canyon SP. 27 sites, all year.

NEARBY: Gunlock State Recreation Area. 240-acre lake. Camping, all year, no designated spaces; boating, fishing.

PUBLICATION: State Park leaflet with map.

HEADQUARTERS: Snow Canyon SP, Box 140, Santa Clara, UT 84765; (801) 628-2255. BLM, Cedar City District, 1579 North Main, Cedar City, UT 84720; (801) 586-2401.

TRAIL OF THE ANCIENTS
Most adjacent land is public domain.
107 highway miles.

A highway loop. From Blanding, 32 mi. W on SR 95 to SR 261. S 32 mi. on SR 261 to US 163. Then 43 mi. on SR 163 back to Blanding. (MP #1.)

A splendidly scenic route with many points of interest along the way. A good road, lightly traveled, paved except for the switchbacks down the escarpment beyond the Moki Dugway Overlook on SR 261. We saw no open service station on SR 95 or 261.

The loop is in the center of the Colorado Plateau. Elevations at road level between 5,000 and 6,500 ft. up to Moki Dugway, near the end of 261, where the road drops 1,100 ft. down an almost vertical escarpment.

Climate, flora, fauna: Information is fragmentary or lacking for most of the following sites. Chief exception is Natural Bridges National Monument (see entry), which has good data. One can assume these data are applicable throughout the plateau.

1. SR 95, Blanding to SR 261. The road crosses an area that is largely wilderness. Many small canyons on either side, some close to the road with easy foot access. Rising above the road are buttes, cliffs, spires. Sandstone colors range from flower-pot red through reddish-brown and tan to light cream, with touches of green. A few dirt roads and jeep trails on both sides, some suitable for ordinary cars in dry weather, most offering opportunities for easy backcountry hiking. Several overlooks.

We preferred this section to Monument Valley. The scale is less grand, but sight lines are shorter. We felt more involved with the landscape.

FEATURES
Comb Ridge, 14 mi. W of Blanding. A narrow N–S uplift about 25 mi. long, sloping on the E, almost vertical on the W. The road was cut through it.

Arch Canyon Road, at Mile Marker 108, is a graded gravel road through a small valley with sagebrush, cottonwoods. Several places where people have camped. In the canyon, the road becomes a jeep track extending 7 mi. to a roadless area in the Manti-La Sal National Forest (see entry). Riparian vegetation in the canyon bottom, scattered pinyon-juniper on talus slopes, ponderosa pine near the National Forest boundary.

Mule Canyon Indian Ruins are just beyond Mile Marker 102. Tower, kiva, access to a canyon.

Dark Canyon Primitive Area (see entry), *Woodenshoe Canyon,* and other roadless areas of the Manti-La Sal National Forest (see entry) can be reached by jeep road to Kigalia Guard Station. Off the entrance road to Natural Bridges National Monument, N of SR 95 2 mi. W of the SR 261 intersection.

Natural Bridges National Monument (see entry).

2. *SR 261, from SR 95 S to US 163.* A good road across Cedar Mesa, paved to the Moki Dugway Overlook. The canyons on either side are attractive to backpackers, partly because of their isolation.

FEATURES

Grand Gulch Primitive Area (see entry). BLM's Kane Gulch Ranger Station, portal to the Primitive Area, is 6 mi. S of SR 95.

Fish and Owl Canyons (see entry).

Johns Canyon; Slickhorn Canyon (see entry).

Moki Dugway Overlook. One of the most breathtaking views anywhere, overlooking the San Juan River and Monument Valley. Mile after mile of striking rock formations: castles, chimneys, spires, buttes, in bright red, purple, brown, tan, gray, green. From here the road descends 1,100 ft. in 3 mi. on ledges cut into the vertical escarpment. Many switchbacks. In places the road isn't wide enough for two cars. Check brakes before descending. Not recommended in wet weather. We took a 23-ft. motor home down and up without difficulty; a car towing a 23-ft. travel trailer might have problems.

Muley Point Overlook turnoff is just beyond Moki Dugway. 5 mi. of unpaved road to the rim of Cedar Mesa. Another spectacular view, looking down into the San Juan canyon. Popular geologists refer to Utah's "Grand Staircase," on which Gooseneck State Reserve is the first step, Muley Point the next higher, then Canyon Rims, Dead Horse Point, and Grand View point, followed by the summit of the Henry Mountains (see entry).

Valley of the Gods, an unpaved 17-mi. scenic route on the E side of SR 261 near the foot of the escarpment. This area has been called a scaled-down Monument Valley, a fantastic red landscape few people see. The road ends at US 163 5 mi. from its intersection with SR 261. Cars with low clearance may have problems.

Goosenecks State Reserve is a 10-acre state park, 4 mi. off SR 261 from a turn 1 mi. from Mexican Hat. At the edge of the canyon with a fine view of the goosenecks—meanders cut deep into the rock. Camping is permitted; facilities include latrines and a few tables, no water. Exhibit. From the access road, a dirt road follows the canyon rim, soon entering the Glen Canyon National Recreation Area and coming eventually to the mouth of Johns Canyon.

Annual precipitation about 6 1/2 in. July to Oct. are the wettest months. Temperature range: −4°F to 109°.

The Goosenecks area has some information on fauna and flora that may also be applicable to neighboring areas.

Plants: Vegetation is scanty, blackbrush dominant, with Indian ricegrass, Mormon tea, fourwing saltbush, pricklypear, Russian thistle, common yucca, sand sage, mustard. Roadside flowers observed include snakeweed, goldenrod, Indian paintbrush, globemallow, locoweed, penstemon, evening primrose, chicory, scarlet gilia, purple vetch, lupine, sunflowers, aster, yucca, beeplant.

Birds: Not abundant. Mentioned are golden and bald eagles, red-tailed hawk, prairie falcon, nighthawk, common raven, horned lark, mountain bluebird, white-throated swift, swallows.

Mammals: Also limited by arid conditions. Common: jackrabbit, cottontail, skunk, whitetail antelope squirrel, kangaroo rat, other desert rodents. Present, seldom seen: bobcat, coyote, badger, gray fox.

3. US 163, from SR 261 to Blanding. Engineers seek the easiest route for roads. This one traverses miles of gently rolling desert shrub, while more varied terrain is on either side, often close.

FEATURES

Sand Island, about 15 mi. E of 261, is a launch site on the San Juan River (see entry). Primitive BLM campground.

SR 262 is 26 mi. from SR 261. It enters the Navajo Indian Reservation en route to Hovenweep National Monument, site of prehistoric Anasazi ruins.

ACTIVITIES

Camping: Primitive campgrounds at Goosenecks and Sand Island. Many opportunities for roadside camping, especially on side roads.

Hiking, backpacking: Several UT outdoorsmen said this canyon country is their favorite for backpacking. Hiking season is generally Apr. to late fall, but winter hiking is feasible. BLM office can suggest routes. Bring topo map, water.

PUBLICATIONS

Across Public Lands on U-95. Folder with map.

Leaflet on local geology.

Trail of the Ancients. Folder with map. San Juan County Development Board. Box 490, Monticello, UT 84535.

REFERENCE: Hikes in Arch Canyon, Mule Canyon, Dark Canyon, Natural Bridges National Monument, Grand Gulch, and Fish and Owl Canyons are described in Hall, Dave. *The Hiker's Guide to Utah.* Billings, MT: Falcon Press, 1982.

HEADQUARTERS: BLM, Moab District Office, 125 West Second South Main, Moab, UT 84532; (801) 259-6111.

ZION NATIONAL PARK
National Park Service
147,035 acres.

From I-15, 6 mi. N of Washington, SR 9 crosses the Park to US 89. (MP #5 labels this route SR 15—an error.) (MP #5.)

At Bryce National Park and Cedar Breaks National Monument, visitors look down from the rims. At Zion, the main road and most visitor facilities are on the canyon floor. The North Fork of the Virgin River enters the Park near its NE corner and exits near the midpoint of the S boundary. Here SR 9 enters the river's canyon, following it upstream. A little over a mile inside the Park, SR 9 turns E and follows Pine and Clear Creeks to the E entrance. The canyon road continues along the North Fork for another 6 mi., to the Temple of Sinawava.

Enter from the E, if you can. Our cassette-recorded notes began, "We're overwhelmed!" The E entrance is at 5,700 ft. elevation. In the next 3 mi. the road descends about 600 ft., twisting and turning, following the course of Clear Creek through Navajo sandstone slickrock formations. Then comes a mile-long tunnel, providing a dramatic transition into the canyons of Zion, a magnificent, sweeping vista. Few cars pass the overlooks above and below the Great Arch without stopping. Six switchbacks descend the wall of Pine Creek Canyon, each turn offering a different view.

Two other roads enter the Park. From SR 9 at Virgin, a paved and graveled road runs N, cutting across a neck of the Park en route to Kolob Reservoir and Cedar City; a short spur ends at Lava Point, where there is a lookout and an isolated primitive campground. At the Kolob Canyon exit on I-15, a paved road enters the spectacular Kolob Canyons area in the far NW portion of the Park. The higher portion of the road to Kolob Reservoir is often closed by snow in winter.

The Park's central area is roadless, accessible only on foot or horseback.

The situation in Zion Canyon is similar to that in Yosemite Valley. Each is a small part of a large park. Because of roads and facilities, the Canyon, like the Valley, may be overcrowded in summer while there are few people elsewhere. Some of the same remedies have been considered: removing Zion Lodge and nearby buildings, providing shuttle buses. Come in spring or fall if you can; the weather is at its best, and you'll miss the summer heat, near 100°F each day.

The canyon floor is about 4,000 ft. elevation at the S entrance, 4,400 where the road ends. Above it tower massive formations eroded in multicolored sandstone, shale, and limestone: the East Temple (7,110 ft.), the West Temple

(7,810 ft.), Altar of Sacrifice (7,410 ft.), Three Patriarchs, the Great White Throne, Angels Landing.

In early morning and late afternoon the canyon floor is shadowed, while the walls above are brightly lit: the highest formations white and red, lower strata in changing tones of yellow, brown, blue, purple, and pink. Photographers find this light challenging. It may be midafternoon before the sun reaches a desired subject in the canyon. The contrast between brilliant colors above, shadows below, produces many dramatic pictures.

The sculptured shapes are as diverse and bizarre as those at Bryce and Cedar Breaks, but they seem to be on a grander scale, perhaps because one is looking up rather than down. At Bryce and Cedar Breaks, one is a spectator. Here in the canyon, one feels like a participant. Indeed, one *must* participate: the automobile is convenient transportation on the canyon floor, but it's not for sightseeing because the scenery is above its roof. Park the car and walk or hike. Many pleasant trails begin on the canyon floor, for short strolls or all-day outings.

The Park is open all year. Annual precipitation is about 15 in. Snow falls occasionally in winter but usually lasts only a day or two on the canyon floor. Snow and ice close most high-country trails Nov.–Feb. The average minimum winter temperature on the canyon floor is about 30°F. Daytime summer temperatures range from 72 to 103°, nights from 45 to 73°.

Plants: Zion seems greener than other canyon parks because the visitor is down below, where moisture gathers. Trees of the canyon bottoms include cottonwood, boxelder, velvet ash, willow. Maple, aspen, and Gambel oak provide bright fall colors. Tules and rushes grow in some creeks. Moist cliff faces may become hanging gardens in spring and summer, luxuriant with maidenhair fern, cardinal flower, monkeyflower, columbine, and shooting star.

N-facing slopes are favorable for stands of ponderosa pine and Douglas-fir. Drier slopes have the pinyon-juniper association, with yucca and cacti.

Wildflowers of Zion include four o'clock, larkspur, clematis, buttercup, meadow rue, prince's plume, wallflower, cliffrose, lupine, wild geranium, blazing star, evening primrose, phlox, scarlet gilia, sacred datura, penstemon, Indian paintbrush, daisies, sunflower, wild marigold, golden aster, rush pink.

Birds: 271 species recorded in Park or within 3 mi. of boundary. Checklist includes habitat, seasonality, rarity. Seasonally common species include mallard, green-winged teal, turkey vulture, red-tailed hawk, American kestrel, mourning dove, great horned owl, poor-will, white-throated swift; black-chinned, broad-tailed, and rufous hummingbirds; northern flicker, hairy woodpecker, western kingbird; ash-throated, dusky, western, and olive-sided flycatchers; Say's phoebe, western wood-pewee, violet-green swallow, scrub jay, common raven, black-capped and mountain chickadees, common bushtit, dipper; Bewick's, canyon, and rock wrens; American robin, hermit thrush, mountain bluebird, blue-gray gnatcatcher, ruby-crowned kinglet, starling, solitary and warbling vireos; yellow-rumped, Grace's, and black-throated gray warblers; yellow-breasted chat, red-winged blackbird, northern oriole, western tanager, black-headed grosbeak, house finch, pine siskin, green-tailed and rufous-sided towhees; black-throated, chipping, and white-crowned sparrows; dark-eyed junco. Best birding season: late Apr.–early June.

Mammals: Checklist of 72 species. Common or "fairly common": small-footed myotis; silver-haired, big brown, pallid, and Mexican free-tailed bats; western pipistrel, blacktail jackrabbit; least, cliff, and Uinta chipmunks; whitetail antelope squirrel, rock and red squirrels, valley and northern pocket gopher, Merriam kangaroo rat, beaver; canyon, brush, pinyon, and deer mice; desert woodrat, porcupine, coyote, gray fox, ringtail, mountain lion, mule deer. Bighorn sheep reintroduced in SE section.

Reptiles and amphibians: Checklist of 33 species. Common or "fairly common": red-spotted, southwestern, and Woodhouse's toads; canyon treefrog. Lizards: desert spiny, eastern fence, sagebrush, side-blotched. Western and plateau whiptails, western garter snake, striped whipsnake, gopher snake.

FEATURES

A few of the short, easy, popular trails in or near the canyon:

Gateway to the Narrows. At the Temple of Sinawava, the road ends because the canyon isn't wide enough for it. The trail, which follows the river for a mile, is the most popular in the Park. Paved, shady, attractive, hanging gardens on moist canyon walls. At The Narrows the canyon becomes a vertical slot about 50 ft. wide, walls 2,000 ft. high. Hiking beyond this point may require a permit. See "The Narrows" below.

Canyon Overlook Trail begins at the E end of the tunnel on SR 9, on the road to the E entrance. 1/2 mi. following rock ledges to a point above the Great Arch, overlooking Pine Creek Canyon and lower Zion Canyon.

Emerald Pools Trail crosses the Virgin River by footbridge across from Zion Lodge. Upper and lower pool, with falls between. About 1 mi.

Watchman Trail is one of the best birding routes. 1.2 mi., the first half is fairly steep, the second gradual, through pygmy forest. From near the Watchman Campground.

The rim of Zion Canyon can be reached only by trail.

East Rim Trail is 3.6 mi. long, average round-trip time about 6 hrs. This trail is popular, and portions of it have been paved.

West Rim Trail is 13.3 mi., a 2-day backpacking trip into Zion's backcountry.

For those who would like more solitude:

The Kolob Canyons area in the far NW sector of the Park has been lightly visited. Driving on fair-weather roads, one could see Zion's backcountry without hiking and with little traffic. One loop route is 108 mi. from the S entrance, an alternate 127 mi. The dirt roads reach elevations of 9,000 ft. This area has some fine day hikes and backpacking trails.

The Kolob Canyons Contact Station opened in 1984, and the signs on the Interstate were changed. Roads in the Kolob area are being improved, and Park officials expect the present visitation of 40,000 per year to leap to 400,000. Few of them will venture far from the paved or graveled road.

Ask at the Zion Canyon Visitor Center about road conditions, and get a copy of the *Kolob Tour Guide.* Be sure your car is in good condition. Carry water.

The Narrows is one of Zion's best-known backcountry trips, but it is not to be undertaken casually. The canyon of the Virgin River is here a deep, narrow slot. There is no trail. One wades, crosses slippery rocks; some places may require swimming, so it is inadvisable to make the trip in cold weather. Flash floods are a hazard; rangers close the route when a storm is expected, but weather is unpredictable. When we last visited, the trail was closed because of a rock slide.

Access to the Narrows is from outside the Park. Three routes:

1. From the E entrance, E 2 1/2 mi. on SR 9; N 18 mi. on a gravel road to the *North Fork of the Virgin River;* cross the stream; left 1/2 mi. to Chamberlain's Ranch. From here it's a strenuous 12-mi. hike.

2. The Narrows can also be reached by hiking down *Orderville Canyon.* The gravel road just mentioned crosses Orderville Canyon (also called Orderville Gulch) about 6 mi. N of SR 9. From the road, the hiker must cross private land, having asked permission, to the public land administered by BLM. From here to the Park boundary is 7.8 mi., followed by 9.2 mi. within the Park. Orderville Canyon joins the North Fork of the Virgin River in Zion Narrows. The canyon is deep, narrow, serpentine, moderately vegetated with oakbrush, ponderosa pine, Douglas-fir, and white fir. Perennial stream. Canyon terrain is rough, with boulders and deadfalls, making the use of a rope desirable. It received BLM's highest scenic rating.

3. The *Deep Creek* route requires driving W on SR 14 from US 89. 1.9 mi. beyond the Zion Canyon Overlook, turn left on Webster Flat Road for 6.4 mi. to Deep Creek. This deeply entrenched canyon winds its way S, joining the North Fork of the Virgin River inside the Park. Flowing stream; thick vegetation. This route to and through The Narrows is usually a 3-day trip.

All three routes are through BLM-managed areas with wilderness qualities. Though all three begin outside the Park, hikers must have permits, obtained at the Zion Canyon or Kolob Canyon visitor center. No one should attempt the journey without discussing route and conditions with Park Rangers.

La Verkin Creek is the principal drainage in the Kolob section. With several tributaries, it provides some of Zion's best backcountry experience. Elevations below 5,000 ft. allow hiking earlier in spring, later in fall, than on the plateau, yet it's reasonably cool in summer. Several connecting trails offer opportunities for both day hiking and backpacking. The canyon continues S beyond the Park boundaries through public land administered by BLM, Cedar City District. It can be hiked for about 10 mi. to SR 17 at Toquerville.

Part of the S end is private land, and BLM should be consulted about access. The combination of a narrow canyon, perennial stream, and green vegetation attracts about 1,000 hikers per year. The area has been recommended for wilderness status.

INTERPRETATION

Zion Canyon Visitor Center has information, slide program, exhibits, publications. Open daily, 9 A.M.–5 P.M. in winter; 8 A.M.–9 P.M. in summer; 8 A.M.–7 P.M. spring and fall.

Kolob Canyon Contact Station has information, publications. Open daily, 8 A.M.–5 P.M., later in summer.

Evening programs daily mid-Mar. to Nov. See posted schedules. *Guided walks* and other naturalist activities are announced in weekly bulletins available at the visitor centers. These also give the topics of the evening programs.

Nature trails at Weeping Rock, Gateway to the Narrows, Canyon Overlook.

Zion Nature Center is for students ages 6–12. Registration daily Tues.–Sat. 8:30–9:00 A.M. and 1:00–1:30 P.M. for morning and afternoon classes.

ACTIVITIES

Camping: 2 campgrounds, 373 sites, in the Canyon. One is kept open all year. A 5-space primitive campground at Lava Point in the Kolob Terrace sector.

Hiking, backpacking: About 65 mi. of maintained trails, about 80 unmaintained, many miles of unmarked backcountry routes. Permit required for overnight use. Snow and ice limit high backcountry travel to June–Oct.; season varies from year to year. The Coalpits Wash area is excellent for off-season hiking.

Horse riding: About 60 mi. of trails open to horse travel. Concessioner offers guided day trips.

Ski touring: Very limited; little snow. Best near Lava Point.

Snowmobiling: Limited to unplowed road to Kolob Terrace. No travel off road.

Pets must be leashed or confined; not allowed on trails or in buildings.

PUBLICATIONS

Leaflet with map.
Information pages:
Making the Most of Your Time in Zion.
The Naming of Zion Canyon.
Zion Tunnel.
Indians of Zion and Vicinity.
The Geologic Story of the Zion National Park Area.
You Asked About the Geology.
Kolob Tour Guide, with map.

Plant checklist.

Bird, mammal, reptile and amphibian checklists.

The Zion Narrows Trip

Zion Narrows Permit Bulletin.

Camping in Zion National Park.

Backcountry Camping.

Backpacking Areas in Zion.

Naturalist Choice Walks and Talks.

Visitor center and guided walk programs; weekly.

Zion Nature Center.

Accommodations and Services, Springdale, Utah. (Just outside the S entrance.)

Zion Photography Hints.

Picture-Taking in Grand Canyon, Bryce Canyon, Zion National Park, and Glen Canyon National Recreation Area. Folder.

Publications of the Zion Natural History Association. Springdale, UT 84767:

Birds of Zion National Park and Vicinity. $0.75.

Cacti of Zion National Park. $0.50.

Reptiles and Amphibians of Zion National Park. $0.75.

Canyon Overlook Trail Guide. $0.25.

Guide to the Trails, Zion National Park. $0.50.

Jackson, Victor L. *Discover Zion.* $3.95. (Translations into French, Spanish, German, and Japanese.)

Nelson, Ruth E. A. *Plants of Zion National Park: Wildflowers, Trees, Shrubs, and Ferns.* $6.95.

Hagood, Allen. *This Is Zion.* 1980, $1.75.

Topographic Map of Zion National Park (includes Zion Canyon and Kolob sections. 1979, $2.00.

REFERENCES

Hall, Dave. *The Hiker's Guide to Utah.* Billings, MT: Falcon Press, 1982. Pp. 134–138.

National Parkways—Zion and Bryce Canyon. Casper, WY: Worldwide Research and Publishing Co., 1983.

Zion: The Story Behind the Scenery. Las Vegas, NV: KC Publications, 1980.

HEADQUARTERS: Springdale, UT 84767; (801) 772-3256.

INDEX

THE PERRYS, long residents of the Washington, D.C., area, moved to Winter Haven, Florida, soon after work on these guides began. Their desks overlook a lake well populated with great blue herons, anhingas, egrets, ospreys, gallinules, and wood ducks, plus occasional alligators and otters.

Jane, an economist, came to Washington as a congressman's secretary and thereafter held senior posts in several executive agencies and presidential commissions. John, an industrial management consultant, was for ten years assistant director of the National Zoo.

Married in 1944, they have hiked, backpacked, camped, canoed, and cruised together in all fifty states. They have written more than a dozen books and produced more than two dozen educational filmstrips, chiefly on natural history and ecology.

Both have been involved in conservation action, at home and abroad. Since 1966 John has been a member of the Survival Service Commission and the International Union for the Conservation of Nature (IUCN), with many trips—with Jane—to South America, Europe, Africa, and Asia. In Florida they are active participants in the Sierra Club and The Nature Conservancy.